CHRISTMAS:
ITS ORIGIN AND ASSOCIATIONS

BRINGING IN THE YULE LOG.

William Hamilton Gibson

CHRISTMAS:
ITS ORIGIN AND ASSOCIATIONS

Together with Its Historical Events
and Festive Celebrations During
Nineteen Centuries

DEPICTING, BY PEN AND PENCIL,
MEMORABLE CELEBRATIONS,
STATELY MEETINGS OF EARLY KINGS,
REMARKABLE EVENTS, ROMANTIC EPISODES, BRAVE DEEDS,
PICTURESQUE CUSTOMS, TIME-HONOURED SPORTS,
ROYAL CHRISTMASES, CORONATIONS AND ROYAL MARRIAGES,
CHIVALRIC FEATS, COURT BANQUETINGS AND REVELLINGS,
CHRISTMAS AT THE COLLEGES AND THE INNS OF COURT,
POPULAR FESTIVITIES, AND CHRISTMAS-KEEPING
IN DIFFERENT PARTS OF THE WORLD,
DERIVED FROM THE MOST AUTHENTIC
SOURCES, AND ARRANGED
CHRONOLOGICALLY.

At home, at sea, in many distant lands,
This Kingly Feast without a rival stands!

BIBLIOBAZAAR

CHRISTMAS:

ITS ORIGIN AND ASSOCIATIONS

PREFACE.

In the third quarter of the nineteenth century, it fell to my lot to write an article on Christmas, its customs and festivities. And, although I sought in vain for a chronological account of the festival, I discovered many interesting details of its observances dispersed in the works of various authors; and, while I found that some of its greater celebrations marked important epochs in our national history, I saw, also, that the successive celebrations of Christmas during nineteen centuries were important links in the chain of historical Christian evidences. I became enamoured of the subject, for, in addition to historical interest, there is the charm of its legendary lore, its picturesque customs, and popular games. It seemed to me that the origin and hallowed associations of Christmas, its ancient customs and festivities, and the important part it has played in history combine to make it a most fascinating subject. I resolved, therefore, to collect materials for a larger work on *Christmas*.

Henceforth, I became a snapper-up of everything relating to Christmastide, utilised every opportunity of searching libraries, bookstalls, and catalogues of books in different parts of the country, and, subsequently, as a Reader of the British Museum Library, had access to that vast storehouse of literary and historical treasures.

Soon after commencing the work, I realised that I had entered a very spacious field of research, and that, having to deal with the accumulated materials of nineteen centuries, a large amount of labour would be involved, and some years must elapse before, even if circumstances proved favourable, I could hope to see the end of my task. Still, I went on with the work, for I felt that a complete account of Christmas, ancient and modern, at home and abroad, would prove generally acceptable, for while the historical events and legendary lore would interest students and antiquaries, the holiday sports and popular celebrations would be no less attractive to general readers.

The love of story-telling seems to be ingrained in human nature. Travellers tell of vari-coloured races sitting round their watch fires reciting deeds of the past; and letters from colonists show how, even amidst forest-clearing, they have beguiled their evening hours by telling or reading stories as they sat in the glow of their camp fires. And in old England there is the same love of tales and stories. One of the chief delights of Christmastide is to sit in the united family circle and hear, tell, or read about the quaint habits and picturesque customs of Christmas in the olden time; and one of the purposes of *CHRISTMAS* is to furnish the retailer of Christmas wares with suitable things for re-filling his pack.

From the vast store of materials collected it is not possible to do more than make a selection. How far I have succeeded in setting forth the subject in a way suited to the diversity of tastes among readers I must leave to their judgment and indulgence; but I have this satisfaction, that the gems of literature it contains are very rich indeed; and I acknowledge my great indebtedness to numerous writers of different periods whose references to Christmas and its time-honoured customs are quoted.

I have to acknowledge the courtesy of Mr. Henry Jewitt, Mr. E. Wiseman, Messrs. Harper, and Messrs. Cassell & Co., in allowing their illustrations to appear in this work.

My aim is neither critical nor apologetic, but historical and pictorial: it is not to say what might or ought to have been, but to set forth from extant records what has actually taken place: to give an account of the origin and hallowed associations of Christmas, and to depict, by pen and pencil, the important historical events and interesting festivities of Christmastide during nineteen centuries. With materials collected from different parts of the world, and from writings both ancient and modern, I have endeavoured to give in the present work a chronological account of the celebrations and observances of Christmas from the birth of Christ to the end of the nineteenth century; but, in a few instances, the subject-matter has been allowed to take precedence of the chronological arrangement. Here will be found accounts of primitive celebrations of the Nativity, ecclesiastical decisions fixing the date of Christmas, the connection of Christmas with the festivals of the ancients,

Christmas in times of persecution, early celebrations in Britain, stately Christmas meetings of the Saxon, Danish, and Norman kings of England; Christmas during the wars of the Roses, Royal Christmases under the Tudors, the Stuarts and the Kings and Queens of Modern England; Christmas at the Colleges and the Inns of Court; Entertainments of the nobility and gentry, and popular festivities; accounts of Christmas celebrations in different parts of Europe, in America and Canada, in the sultry lands of Africa and the ice-bound Arctic coasts, in India and China, at the Antipodes, in Australia and New Zealand, and in the Islands of the Pacific; in short, throughout the civilised world.

In looking at the celebrations of Christmas, at different periods and in different places, I have observed that, whatever views men hold respecting Christ, they all agree that His Advent is to be hailed with joy, and the nearer the forms of festivity have approximated to the teaching of Him who is celebrated the more real has been the joy of those who have taken part in the celebrations.

The descriptions of the festivities and customs of different periods are given, as far as possible, on the authority of contemporary authors, or writers who have special knowledge of those periods, and the most reliable authorities have been consulted for facts and dates, great care being taken to make the work as accurate and trustworthy as possible. I sincerely wish that all who read it may find as much pleasure in its perusal as I have had in its compilation.

WILLIAM FRANCIS DAWSON.

CONTENTS

While shepherds watched their flocks by night,
    All seated on the ground;
The angel of the Lord came down,
    And glory shone around.

Carol.

THE HERALD ANGELS.

Lo! God hath ope'd the glist'ring gates of heaven,
    And thence are streaming beams of glorious light:
All earth is bath'd in the effulgence giv'n
    To dissipate the darkness of the night.
The eastern shepherds, 'biding in the fields,
    O'erlook the flocks till now their constant care,
And light divine to mortal sense reveals
    A seraph bright descending in the air.

Hark! strains seraphic fall upon the ear,
    From shining ones around th' eternal gates:
Glad that man's load of guilt may disappear,
    Infinite strength on finite weakness waits.

Why are the trembling shepherds sore afraid?
    Why shrink they at the grand, the heavenly sight?
"Fear not" (the angel says), nor be dismay'd,
    And o'er them sheds a ray of God-sent light.
O matchless mercy! All-embracing love!
    The angel speaks and, gladly, men record:—
"I bring you joyful tidings from above:
    This day is born a Saviour, Christ the Lord!"

Hark! "Peace on earth, and God's good-will to men!"
    The angels sing, and heaven resounds with praise—
That fallen man may live with God again,
    Through Christ, who deigns the sons of men to raise.

W. E. D

CHAPTER I.

THE ORIGIN AND ASSOCIATIONS
OF CHRISTMAS.

THE FIRST CHRISTMAS: THE ADVENT OF CHRIST.

Behold, a virgin shall conceive,
And bear a Son,
And shall call His name Immanuel.

(*Isaiah* vii. 14.)

Now the birth of Jesus Christ was on this wise: When His mother Mary had been betrothed to Joseph, before they came together she was found with child of the Holy Ghost. And Joseph her husband, being a righteous man, and not willing to make her a public example, was minded to put her away privily. But when he thought on these things, behold, an angel of the Lord appeared unto him in a dream, saying, Joseph, thou son of David, fear not to take unto thee Mary thy wife: for that which is conceived in her is of the Holy Ghost. And she shall bring forth a Son; and thou shalt call His name Jesus; for it is He that shall save His people from their sins. Now all this is come to pass, that it might be fulfilled which was spoken by the Lord through the prophet, saying,

> Behold, the virgin shall be with child and shall bring forth
> a Son,
> And they shall call His name Immanuel;

which is, being interpreted, God with us. And Joseph arose from his sleep, and did as the angel of the Lord commanded him, and took unto him his wife; and knew her not till she had brought forth a Son; and he called His name Jesus.

(*Matthew* i. 18-25.)

"There went out a decree from Cæsar Augustus that all the world should be taxed. And Joseph went to be taxed with Mary his espoused wife, being great with child."

(*Luke* ii. 1-5.)

And there were shepherds in the same country abiding in the field, and keeping watch by night over their flock. And an angel of the Lord stood by them, and the glory of the Lord shone round about them: and they were sore afraid. And the angel said unto them, Be not afraid; for behold, I bring you good tidings of great joy which shall be to all the people: for there is born to you this day in the city of David a Saviour, which is Christ the Lord. And this is the sign unto you; Ye shall find a babe wrapped in swaddling clothes, and lying in a manger. And suddenly there was with the angel a multitude of the heavenly host praising God, and saying,

> Glory to God in the highest,
> And on earth peace among men in whom He is well
> pleased.

And it came to pass, when the angels went away from them into heaven, the shepherds said one to another, Let us now go even unto Bethlehem, and see this thing that is come to pass, which the Lord hath made known unto us. And they came with haste, and found both Mary and Joseph, and the Babe lying in the manger. And when they saw it, they made known concerning the saying which was spoken to them about this child. And all that heard it wondered at the things which were spoken unto them by the shepherds. But Mary kept all these sayings, pondering them in her heart. And the shepherds returned, glorifying and praising God for all the things that they had heard and seen, even as it was spoken unto them.

(*Luke* ii. 8-20.)

THE PLACE OF THE NATIVITY.

The evangelist Matthew tells us that "Jesus was born in Bethlehem of Judæa in the days of Herod the king;" and Justin Martyr, who was born at Shechem and lived less than a century after the time of Christ, places the scene of the Nativity in a cave. Over this cave has risen the Church and Convent of the Nativity, and there is a stone slab with a star cut in it to mark the spot where the Saviour was born. Dean Farrar, who has been at the place, says: "It is impossible to stand in the little Chapel of the Nativity, and to look without emotion on the silver star let into the white marble, encircled by its sixteen ever-burning lamps, and surrounded by the inscription, '*Hic de Virgine Maria Jesus Christus natus est.*'"

To visit such a scene is to have the thoughts carried back to the greatest event in the world's history, for it has been truly said that the birth of Christ was the world's second birthday.

> Now, death is life! and grief is turn'd to joy!
>> Since glory shone on that auspicious morn,
> When God incarnate came, not to destroy,
>> But man to save and manhood's state adorn!

W. F. D.

THE NATIVITY BY SANDRO BOTTICELLI.
Centre Portion of Picture in National Gallery

THE WORD "CHRISTMAS": ITS ORTHOGRAPHY AND MEANING.

"Christmas" (pronounced Kris'mas) signifies "Christ's Mass," meaning the festival of the Nativity of Christ, and the word has been variously spelt at different periods. The following are obsolete forms of it found in old English writings: Crystmasse, Cristmes, Cristmas, Crestenmes, Crestenmas, Cristemes, Cristynmes, Crismas, Kyrsomas, Xtemas, Cristesmesse, Cristemasse, Crystenmas, Crystynmas, Chrystmas, Chrystemes, Chrystemasse, Chrystymesse, Cristenmas, Christenmas, Christmass, Christmes. Christmas has also been called *Noël* or *Nowel*. As to the derivation of the word *Noël*, some say it is a contraction of the French *nouvelles* (tidings), *les bonnes nouvelles*, that is "The good news of the Gospel"; others take it as an abbreviation of the Gascon or Provençal *nadaü, nadal,* which means the same as the Latin *natalis*, that is, *dies natalis*, "the birthday." In "The Franklin's Tale," Chaucer alludes to "Nowel" as a festive cry at Christmastide: "And 'Nowel' crieth every lusty man." Some say *Noël* is a corruption of *Yule, Jule,* or *Ule,* meaning "The festival of the sun." The name *Yule* is still applied to the festival in Scotland, and some other places. Christmas is represented in Welsh by *Nadolig,* which signifies "the natal, or birth"; in French by *Noël;* and in Italian by *Il Natale,* which, together with its cognate term in Spanish, is simply a contraction of *dies natalis,* "the birthday."

> CHRISTMAS:blest Feast of the Nativity!
> H eaven made thy lowly shrine
> R esplendent with the gift of the eternal Deity
> I n whom we live and move, whose large benignity
> S pared not His Son divine:
> T hat well-beloved Son by God was given,
> Mankind to save with His redeeming blood;
> A nd Jesus freely left the bliss of Heaven,
> S uffering death, to achieve our lasting good.—W. F. D.

VIRGIN AND CHILD (*Relievo*)

CHAPTER II.

THE EARLIER CELEBRATIONS OF THE FESTIVAL.

GROUP FROM THE ANGELS' SERENADE, THEODORE MINTROP

The Angels' Song has been called the first Christmas Carol, and the shepherds who heard this heavenly song of peace and goodwill, and went "with haste" to the birthplace at Bethlehem, where they "found Mary, and Joseph, and the Babe lying in a manger," certainly took part in the first celebration of the Nativity. And the Wise Men, who came afterwards with presents from the East, being led to Bethlehem by the appearance of the miraculous star, may also be regarded as taking part in the first celebration of the Nativity, for the name Epiphany (now used to commemorate the manifestation of the Saviour) did not come into use till long afterwards, and when it was first adopted among the Oriental Churches it was designed to commemorate both the birth and baptism of Jesus, which two events the Eastern Churches believed to have occurred on January 6th. Whether the shepherds commemorated the Feast of the Nativity annually does not appear from the records of the Evangelists; but it is by no means improbable that to the end of their lives they would annually celebrate the most wonderful event which they had witnessed.

ADORATION OF THE MAGI (RELIEVO.) FROM PULPIT OF PISA-NICOLA:PISANO

Within thirty years after the death of our Lord, there were churches in Jerusalem, Cæsarea, Rome, and the Syrian Antioch. In reference to the latter, Bishop Ken beautifully says:—

"Fair Antioch the rich, the great,
Of learning the imperial seat,
    You readily inclined,
    To light which on you shined;
It soon shot up to a meridian flame,
You first baptized it with a Christian name."

Clement, one of the Apostolic Fathers and third Bishop of Rome, who flourished in the first century, says: "Brethren, keep diligently feast-days, and truly in the first place the day of Christ's birth." And according to another of the early Bishops of Rome, it was ordained early in the second century, "that in the holy night of the Nativity of our Lord and Saviour, they do celebrate public church services and in them solemnly sing the Angels' Hymn, because also the same night He was declared unto the shepherds by an angel, as the truth itself doth witness."

But, before proceeding further with the historical narrative, it will be well now to make more particular reference to the fixing of the date of the festival.

FIXING THE DATE OF CHRISTMAS.

Whether the 25th of December, which is now observed as Christmas Day, correctly fixes the period of the year when Christ was born is still doubtful, although it is a question upon which there has been much controversy. From Clement of Alexandria it appears, that when the first efforts were made to fix the season of the Advent, there were advocates for the 20th of May, and for the 20th or 21st of April. It is also found that some communities of Christians celebrated the festival on the 1st or 6th of January; others on the 29th of March, the time of the Jewish Passover: while others observed it on the 29th of September, or Feast of Tabernacles. The Oriental Christians generally were of opinion that both the birth and baptism of Christ took place on the 6th of January. Julius I., Bishop of Rome (A.D. 337-352), contended that the 25th of December was the date of Christ's birth, a view to which the majority of the Eastern Church ultimately came round, while the Church of the West adopted from their brethren in the East the view that the baptism was on the 6th of January. It is, at any rate, certain that after St. Chrysostom Christmas was observed on the 25th of December in East and West alike, except in the Armenian Church, which still remains faithful to January 6th. St. Chrysostom, who died in the beginning of the fifth century, informs us, in one of his Epistles, that Julius, on the solicitation of St. Cyril of Jerusalem, caused strict inquiries to be made on the subject, and thereafter, following what seemed to be the best authenticated tradition, settled authoritatively the 25th of December as the anniversary of Christ's birth, the *Festorum omnium metropolis*, as it is styled by Chrysostom. It may be observed, however, that some have represented this fixing of the day to have been accomplished by St. Telesphorus, who was Bishop of Rome A.D. 127-139, but the authority for the assertion is very doubtful. There is good ground for maintaining that Easter and its accessory celebrations mark with tolerable accuracy the anniversaries of the Passion and Resurrection of our Lord, because we know that the events themselves took place at the period of the Jewish Passover; but no such precision of date can be adduced as regards Christmas. Dr. Geikie[1] says: "The *season* at which Christ was born is inferred from the fact that He was six months younger than John, respecting the date of whose birth we have the help of knowing the time of the annunciation during his father's ministrations in Jerusalem. Still, the whole subject is very uncertain. Ewald appears to fix the date of the birth as five years earlier than our era. Petavius and Usher fix it as on the 25th of December, five years before our era; Bengel, on the 25th of December, four years before our era; Anger and Winer, four years before our era, in the spring; Scaliger, three years before our era, in October; St. Jerome, three years before our era, on December 25th; Eusebius, two years before our era, on January 6th; and Ideler, seven years before our era, in December." Milton, following the immemorial tradition of the Church, says that—

    "It was the winter wild."

But there are still many who think that the 25th of December does not correspond with the actual date of the birth of Christ, and regard the incident of the flocks and shepherds in the open field, recorded by St. Luke, as indicative of spring rather than winter. This incident, it is thought, could not have taken place in the inclement month of December, and it has been conjectured, with some probability, that the 25th of December was chosen in order to substitute the purified joy of a Christian festival for the license of the *Bacchanalia* and *Saturnalia* which were kept at that season. It is most probable that the Advent took place between December, 749, of Rome, and February, 750.

Dionysius Exiguus, surnamed the Little, a Romish monk of the sixth century, a Scythian by birth, and who died A.D. 556, fixed the birth of Christ in the year of Rome 753, but the best authorities are now agreed that 753 was not the year in which the Saviour of mankind was born. The Nativity is now placed, not as might have been expected, in A.D. 1, but in B.C. 5 or 4. The mode of reckoning by the "year of our Lord" was first introduced by Dionysius, in his "Cyclus Paschalis," a treatise on the computation of Easter, in the first half of the sixth century. Up to that time the received computation of events through the western portion of Christendom had been from the supposed foundation of Rome (B.C. 754), and events were marked accordingly as happening in this or that year, *Anno Urbis Conditæ*, or by the initial letters A.U.C. In the East some historians continued to reckon from the era of Seleucidæ, which dated from the accession of Seleucus Nicator to the monarchy of Syria, in B.C. 312. The new computation was received by Christendom in the sixth century, and adopted without adequate inquiry, till the sixteenth century. A more careful examination of the data presented by the Gospel history, and, in particular, by the fact that "Jesus was born in Bethlehem of Judæa" before the death of Herod, showed that Dionysius had made a mistake of four years, or perhaps more, in his calculations. The death of Herod took place in the year of Rome A.U.C. 750, just before the Passover. This year coincided with what in our common chronology would be B.C. 4—so that we have to recognise the fact that our own reckoning is erroneous, and to fix B.C. 5 or 4 as the date of the Nativity.

Now, out of the consideration of the time at which the Christmas festival is fixed, naturally arises another question, viz.:—

THE CONNECTION OF CHRISTMAS WITH ANCIENT FESTIVALS.

Sir Isaac Newton[2] says the Feast of the Nativity, and most of the other ecclesiastical anniversaries, were originally fixed at cardinal points of the year, without any reference to the dates of the incidents which they commemorated, dates which, by lapse of time, it was impossible to ascertain. Thus the Annunciation of the Virgin Mary was placed on the 25th of March, or about the time of the vernal equinox; the Feast of St. Michael on the 29th of September, or near the autumnal equinox; and the Birth of Christ at the time of the winter solstice. Christmas was thus fixed at the time of the year when the most celebrated festivals of the ancients were held in honour of the return of the sun which at the winter solstice begins gradually to regain power and to ascend apparently in the horizon. Previously to this (says William Sandys, F.S.A.),[3] the year was drawing to a close, and the world was typically considered to be in the same state. The promised restoration of light and commencement of a new era were therefore hailed with rejoicings and thanksgivings. The Saxon and other northern nations kept a festival at this time of the year in honour of Thor, in which they mingled feasting, drinking, and dancing with sacrifices and religious rites. It was called Yule, or Jule, a term of which the derivation has caused dispute amongst antiquaries; some considering it to mean a festival, and others stating that Iol, or Iul (spelt in various ways), is a primitive word, conveying the idea of Revolution or Wheel, and applicable therefore to the return of the sun. The *Bacchanalia* and *Saturnalia* of the Romans had apparently the same object as the Yuletide, or feast of the Northern nations, and were probably adopted from some more ancient nations, as the Greeks, Mexicans, Persians, Chinese, &c., had all something similar. In the course of them, as is well known, masters and slaves were supposed to be on an equality; indeed, the former waited on the latter.[4] Presents were mutually given and received, as Christmas presents in these days. Towards the end of the feast, when the sun was on its return, and the world was considered to be renovated, a king or ruler was chosen, with considerable power granted to him during his ephemeral reign, whence may have sprung some of the Twelfth-Night revels, mingled with those in honour of the Manifestation and Adoration of the Magi. And, in all probability, some other Christmas customs are adopted from the festivals of the ancients, as decking with evergreens and mistletoe (relics of Druidism) and the wassail bowl. It is not surprising, therefore, that Bacchanalian illustrations have been found among the decorations in the early Christian Churches. The illustration on the following page is from a mosaic in the Church of St. Constantine, Rome, A.D. 320.

GRAPE GATHERING AND THE VINTAGE.
MOSAIC IN THE CHURCH OF ST. CONSTANTINE, ROME, A.D. 320.

Dr. Cassel, of Germany, an erudite Jewish convert who is little known in this country has endeavoured to show that

FROM AN IVORY (PART OF BOOK COVER) GERMAN NINTH CENTURY, BRITISH MUSEUM.

the festival of Christmas has a Judæan origin. He considers that its customs are significantly in accordance with those of the Jewish festival of the Dedication of the Temple. This feast was held in the winter time, on the 25th of Cisleu (December 20th), having been founded by Judas Maccabæus in honour of the cleansing of the Temple in B.C. 164, six years and a half after its profanation by Antiochus Epiphanes. In connection with Dr. Cassel's theory it may be remarked that the German word *Weihnachten* (from *weihen*, "to consecrate, inaugurate," and *nacht*, "night") leads directly to the meaning, "Night of the Dedication."

ANCIENT ROMAN ILLUSTRATIONS.

In proceeding with our historical survey, then, we must recollect that in the festivities of Christmastide there is a mingling of the Divine with the human elements of society—the establishment and development of a Christian festival on pagan soil and in the midst of superstitious surroundings. Unless this be borne in mind it is impossible to understand some customs connected with the celebration of Christmas. For while the festival commemorates the Nativity of Christ, it also illustrates the ancient practices of the various peoples who have taken part in the commemoration, and not inappropriately so, as the event commemorated is also linked to the past. "Christmas" (says Dean Stanley) "brings before us the relations of the Christian religion to the religions which went before; for the birth at Bethlehem was itself a link with the past. The coming of Jesus Christ was not unheralded or unforeseen. Even in the heathen world there had been anticipations of an event of a character not unlike this. In Plato's Dialogue bright ideals had been drawn of the just man; in Virgil's Eclogues there had been a vision of a new and peaceful order of things. But it was in the Jewish nation that these anticipations were most distinct. That wonderful people in all its history had looked, not backward, but forward. The appearance of Jesus Christ was not merely the accomplishment of certain predictions; it was the fulfilment of this wide and deep expectation of a whole people, and that people the most remarkable in the ancient world." Thus Dean Stanley links Christianity with the older religions of the world, as other writers have connected the festival of Christmas with the festivals of paganism and Judaism. The first Christians were exposed to the dissolute habits and idolatrous practices of heathenism, as well as the superstitious ceremonials of Judaism, and it is in these influences that we must seek the true origin of many of the usages and institutions of Christianity. The old hall of Roman justice and exchange—an edifice expressive of the popular life of Greece and Rome—was not deemed too secular to be used as the first Christian place of worship: pagan statues were preserved as objects of adoration, being changed but in name; names describing the functions of Church officers were copied from the civil vocabulary of the time; the ceremonies of Christian worship were accommodated as far as possible to those of the heathen, that new converts might not be much startled at the change, and at the Christmas festival Christians indulged in revels closely resembling those of the *Saturnalia*.

ANCIENT ROMAN ILLUSTRATIONS.

It is known that the Feast of the Nativity was observed as early as the first century, and that it was kept by the primitive Christians even in dark days of persecution. "They wandered in deserts, and in mountains, and in dens and caves of the earth" (Heb. xi. 38). Yet they were faithful to Christ, and the Catacombs of Rome contain evidence that they celebrated the Nativity.

The opening up of these Catacombs has brought to light many most interesting relics of primitive Christianity. In these Christian cemeteries and places of worship there are signs not only of the deep emotion and hope with which they buried their dead, but also of their simple forms of worship and the festive joy with which they commemorated the Nativity of Christ. On the rock-hewn tombs these primitive Christians wrote the thoughts that were most consoling to themselves, or painted on the walls the figures which gave them the most pleasure. The subjects of these paintings are for the most part taken from the Bible, and the one which illustrates the earliest and most universal of these pictures, and exhibits their Christmas joy, is "The Adoration of the Magi." Another of these emblems of joyous festivity which is frequently seen, is a vine, with its branches and purple clusters spreading in every direction, reminding us that in Eastern countries the vintage is the great holiday of the year. In the Jewish Church there was no festival so joyous as the Feast of Tabernacles, when they gathered the fruit of the vineyard, and in some of the earlier celebrations of the Nativity these festivities were closely copied. And as all down the ages pagan elements have mingled in the festivities of Christmas, so in the Catacombs they are not absent. There is Orpheus playing on his harp to the beasts; Bacchus as the god of the vintage; Psyche, the butterfly of the soul; the Jordan as the god of the rivers. The classical and the Christian, the Hebrew and the Hellenic elements had not yet parted; and the unearthing of these pictures after the lapse of centuries affords another interesting clue to the origin of some of the customs of Christmastide. It is astonishing how many of the Catacomb decorations are taken from heathen sources and copied from heathen paintings; yet we need not wonder when we reflect that the vine was used by the early Christians as an emblem of gladness, and it was scarcely possible for them to celebrate the

Feast of the Nativity—a festival of glad tidings—without some sort of *Bacchanalia.* Thus it appears that even

ANCIENT AGAPE.

(*From Withrow's "Catacombs of Rome,"* which states that the inscriptions, according to Dr. Maitland, should be expanded thus IRENE DA CALDA[M AQVAM —"Peace, give hot water,' and AGAPE MISCE MI [VINVM CVM AQVA —"Love, mix me wine with water," the allusion being to the ancient custom of tempering wine with water, hot or cold)

beneath the palaces and temples of pagan Rome the birth of Christ was celebrated, this early undermining of paganism by Christianity being, as it were, the germ of the final victory, and the secret praise, which came like muffled music from the Catacombs in honour of the Nativity, the prelude to the triumph-song in which they shall unite who receive from Christ the unwithering crown.

But they who would wear the crown must first bear the cross, and these early Christians had to pass through dreadful days of persecution. Some of them were made food for the torches of the atrocious Nero, others were thrown into the Imperial fish-ponds to fatten lampreys for the Bacchanalian banquets, and many were mangled to death by savage beasts, or still more savage men, to make sport for thousands of pitiless sightseers, while not a single thumb was turned to make the sign of mercy. But perhaps the most gigantic and horrible of all Christmas atrocities were those perpetrated by the tyrant Diocletian, who became Emperor A.D. 284. The early years of his reign were characterised by some sort of religious toleration, but when his persecutions began many endured martyrdom, and the storm of his fury burst on the Christians in the year 303. A multitude of Christians of all ages had assembled to commemorate the Nativity in the temple at Nicomedia, in Bithynia, when the tyrant Emperor had the town surrounded by soldiers and set on fire, and about twenty thousand persons perished. The persecutions were carried on throughout the Roman Empire, and the death-roll included some British martyrs, Britain being at that time a Roman province. St. Alban, who was put to death at Verulam in Diocletian's reign, is said to have been the first Christian martyr in Britain. On the retirement of Diocletian, satiated with slaughter and wearied with wickedness, Galerius continued the persecutions for a while. But the time of deliverance was at hand, for the martyrs had made more converts in their deaths than in their lives. It was vainly hoped that Christianity would be destroyed, but in the succeeding reign of Constantine it became the religion of the empire. Not one of the martyrs had died in vain or passed through death unrecorded.

> "There is a record traced on high,
> That shall endure eternally;
> The angel standing by God's throne
> Treasures there each word and groan;
> And not the martyr's speech alone,
> But every word is there depicted,
>   With every circumstance of pain
> The crimson stream, the gash inflicted—
>   And not a drop is shed in vain."

CELEBRATIONS UNDER CONSTANTINE THE GREAT.

With the accession of Constantine (born at York, February 27, 274, son of the sub-Emperor Constantius by a British mother, the "fair Helena of York," and who, on the death of his father at York in 306, was in Britain proclaimed Emperor of the Roman Empire) brighter days came to the Christians, for his first act was one of favour to them. He had been present at the promulgation of Diocletian's edict of the last and fiercest of the persecutions against the Christians, in 303, at Nicomedia, soon after which the imperial palace was struck by lightning, and the conjunction of the events seems to have deeply impressed him. No sooner had he ascended the throne than his good feeling towards the Christians took the active form of an edict of toleration, and subsequently he accepted Christianity, and his example was followed by the greater part of his family. And now the Christians, who had formerly hidden away in the darkness of the Catacombs and encouraged one another with "Alleluias," which served as a sort of invitatory or mutual call to each other to praise the Lord, might come forth into the Imperial sunshine and hold their services in basilicas or public halls, the roofs of which (Jerome tells us) "re-echoed with their cries of Alleluia," while Ambrose says the sound of their psalms as they sang in celebration of the Nativity "was like the surging of the sea in great waves of sound." And the Catacombs contain confirmatory evidence of the joy with which relatives of the Emperor participated in Christian festivities. In the tomb of Constantia, the sister of the Emperor Constantine, the only decorations are children gathering the vintage, plucking the grapes, carrying baskets of grapes on their heads, dancing on the grapes to press out the wine. This primitive conception of the Founder of Christianity shows the faith of these early Christians to have been of a joyous and festive character, and the Graduals for Christmas Eve and Christmas morning, the beautiful Kyrie Eleisons (which in later times passed into carols), and the other festival music which has come down to us through that wonderful compilation of Christian song, *Gregory's Antiphonary*, show that Christmas stood out prominently in the celebrations of the now established Church, for the Emperor Constantine had transferred the seat of government to Constantinople, and Christianity was formally recognised as the established religion.

EPISCOPAL REFERENCES TO CHRISTMAS AND CAUTIONS AGAINST EXCESSES.

Cyprian, the intrepid Bishop of Carthage, whose stormy episcopate closed with the crown of martyrdom in the latter half of the third century, began his treatise on the Nativity thus: "The much wished-for and long expected Nativity of Christ is come, the famous solemnity is come"—expressions which indicate the desire with which the Church looked forward to the festival, and the fame which its celebrations had acquired in the popular mind. And in later times, after the fulness of festivity at Christmas had resulted in some excesses, Bishop Gregory Nazianzen (who died in 389), fearing the spiritual thanksgiving was in danger of being subordinated to the temporal rejoicing, cautioned all Christians "against feasting to excess, dancing, and crowning the doors (practices derived from the heathens); urging the celebration of the festival after an heavenly and not an earthly manner."

In the Council, generally called *Concilium Africanum*, held A.D. 408, "stage-plays and spectacles are forbidden on the Lord's-day, Christmas-day, and other solemn Christian festivalls." Theodosius the younger, in his laws *de Spectaculis*, in 425, forbade shows or games on the Nativity, and some other feasts. And in the Council of Auxerre, in Burgundy, in 578, disguisings are again forbidden, and at another Council, in 614, it was found necessary to repeat the prohibitory canons in stronger terms, declaring it to be unlawful to make any indecent plays upon the Kalends of January, according to the profane practices of the pagans. But it is also recorded that the more devout Christians in these early times celebrated the festival without indulging in the forbidden excesses.

1   Notes to "Life of Christ."
2   "Commentary on the Prophecies of Daniel."
3   Introduction to "Christmas Carols," 1833.
4   The Emperor Nero himself is known to have presided at the *Saturnalia*, having been made by lot the *Rex bibendi*, or Master of the Revels. Indeed it was at one of these festivals that he instigated the murder of the young Prince Britannicus, the last male descendant of the family of the Claudii, who had been expelled from his rights by violence and crime; and the atrocious act was committed amid the revels over which Nero was presiding as master.

CHAPTER III.

EARLY CHRISTMAS CELEBRATIONS IN BRITAIN.

EARLY CELEBRATIONS IN BRITAIN.

It is recorded that there were "saints in Cæsar's household," and we have also the best authority for saying there were converts among Roman soldiers. Cornelius, a Roman centurion, "was a just man and one that feared God," and other Roman converts are referred to in Scripture as having been found among the officers of the Roman Empire. And although it is not known who first preached the Gospel in Britain, it seems almost certain that Christianity entered with the Roman invasion in A.D. 43. As in Palestine some of the earlier converts served Christ secretly "for fear of the Jews," so, in all probability, did they in Britain for fear of the Romans. We know that some confessed Christ and closed their earthly career with the crown of martyrdom. It is also certain that very early in the Christian era Christmas was celebrated in Britain, mingling in its festivities some of the winter-festival customs of the ancient Britons and the Roman invaders, for traces of those celebrations are still seen in some of the Christmas customs of modern times. Moreover, it is known that Christians were tolerated in Britain by some of the Roman governors before the days of Constantine. It was in the time of the fourth Roman Emperor, Claudius, that part of Britain was first really conquered. Claudius himself came over in the year 43, and his generals afterwards went on with the war, conquering one after another of the British chiefs, Caradoc, whom the Romans called Caractacus, holding out the longest and the most bravely. This intrepid King of the Silurians, who lived in South Wales and the neighbouring parts, withstood the Romans for several years, but was at last defeated at a great battle, supposed to have taken place in Shropshire, where there is a hill still called Caer Caradoc. Caradoc and his family were taken prisoners and led before the Emperor at Rome, when he made a remarkable speech which has been preserved for us by Tacitus. When he saw the splendid city of Rome, he wondered that an Emperor who lived in such splendour should have meddled with his humble home in Britain; and in his address before the Emperor Claudius, who received him seated on his throne with the Empress Agrippina by his side, Caradoc said: "My fate this day appears as sad for me as it is glorious for thee. I had horses, soldiers, arms, and treasures; is it surprising that I should regret the loss of them? If it is thy will to command the universe, is it a reason we should voluntarily accept slavery? Had I yielded sooner, thy fortune and my glory would have been less, and oblivion would soon have followed my execution. If thou sparest my life, I shall be an eternal monument of thy clemency." Although the Romans had very often killed their captives, to the honour of Claudius be it said that he treated Caradoc kindly, gave him his liberty, and, according to some historians, allowed him to reign in part of Britain as a prince subject to Rome. It is surprising that an emperor who had shown such clemency could afterwards become one of Rome's sanguinary tyrants; but Claudius was a man of weak intellect.

There were several of the Roman Emperors and Governors who befriended the Christians, took part in their Christmas festivities, and professed faith in Christ. The Venerable Bede says: "In the reign of Marcus Aurelius Antonius, and his partner in the Empire, Lucius Verus, when Eleutherius was Bishop of Rome, Lucius, a British king, sent a letter to his prelate, desiring his directions to make him a Christian. The holy bishop immediately complied with this pious request; and thus the Britons, being brought over to Christianity, continued without warping or disturbance till the reign of the Emperor Diocletian." And Selden says: "Howsoever, by injury of time, the memory of this great and illustrious Prince King Lucy hath been embezzled and smuggled; this, upon the credit of the ancient writers, appears plainly, that the pitiful fopperies of the Pagans, and the worship of their idol devils, did begin to flag, and within a short time would have given place to the worship of the true God." As this "illustrious Prince King Lucy"—Lucius Verus—flourished in the latter part of the second century, and is credited with the erection of our first Christian Church on the site of St. Martin's, at Canterbury, it seems clear that even in those early days Christianity was making progress in Britain. From the time of Julius Agricola, who was Roman Commander from 78 to 84, Britain had been a Roman province, and although the Romans never conquered the whole of the island, yet during their occupation of what they called their province (the whole of Britain, excepting that portion north of the Firths of Forth and Clyde), they encouraged the Christmas festivities and did much to civilise the people whom they had conquered and whom they governed for more than three hundred years. They built towns in different parts of the country and constructed good roads from one town to another, for they were excellent builders and road-makers. Some of the Roman emperors visited Britain and others were chosen by the soldiers of Britain; and in the reigns of Constantine the Great and other tolerant emperors the Britains lived like Romans, adopted Roman manners and customs, and some of them learned to speak the Latin language. Christian churches were built and bishoprics founded; a hierarchy was established, and at the Council of Arles, in 314, three British bishops took part—those of York, London, and Camulodunum (which is now Colchester or Malden, authorities are divided, but Freeman says Colchester). The canons framed at Arles on this occasion became the law of the British Church, and in this more favourable period for Christians the Christmas festival was kept with great rejoicing. But this settled state of affairs was subsequently disturbed by the departure of the Romans and the several invasions of the Anglo-Saxons and the Danes which preceded the Norman Conquest.

CHRISTMAS AGAIN IN TROUBLOUS TIMES: THE DEPARTURE OF THE
ROMANS AND THE INVASION OF THE ANGLO-SAXONS.

The outgoing of the Romans and the incoming of the
Angles, the Saxons, and the Jutes disastrously affected the festival
of Christmas, for the invaders were heathens, and Christianity
was swept westward before them. They had lived in a part of the
Continent which had not been reached by Christianity nor classic
culture, and they worshipped the false gods of Woden and Thunder,
and were addicted to various heathenish practices, some of which
now mingled with the festivities of Christmastide. Still, as these
Angles came to stay and have given their name to our country, it
may be well to note that they came over to Britain from the one
country which is known to have borne the name of Angeln or
the Engle-land, and which is now called Sleswick, a district in the
middle of that peninsula which parts the Baltic from the North Sea
or German Ocean. The Romans having become weakened through
their conflicts with Germany and other nations, at the beginning
of the fifth century, the Emperor Honorius recalled the Roman
legions from Britain, and this made it much easier for the Angles
and Saxons (who had previously tried to get in) to come and remain
in this country. Thus our Teuton forefathers came and conquered
much the greater part of Britain, the Picts and Scots remaining
in the north and the Welsh in the west of the island. It was their
custom to kill or make slaves of all the people they could, and
so completely did they conquer that part of Britain in which they
settled that they kept their own language and manners and their
own heathenish religion, and destroyed or desecrated Christian

churches which had been set up. Hence Christian missionaries were required to convert our ancestral worshippers of Woden and Thunder, and a difficult business it was to Christianise such pagans, for they stuck to their false gods with the same tenacity that the northern nations did.

In his poem of "King Olaf's Christmas" Longfellow refers to the worship of Thor and Odin alongside with the worship of Christ in the northern nations:—

"At Drontheim, Olaf the King
Heard the bells of Yule-tide ring,
    As he sat in his banquet-hall.
Drinking the nut-brown ale,
With his bearded Berserks hale
    And tall.

* * * * *

O'er his drinking horn, the sign
He made of the Cross divine
    As he drank, and muttered his prayers;
But the Berserks evermore
Made the sign of the Hammer of Thor
    Over theirs."

In England, too, Christ and Thor were worshipped side by side for at least 150 years after the introduction of Christianity, for while some of the English accepted Christ as their true friend and Saviour, He was not accepted by all the people. Indeed, the struggle against Him is still going on, but we anticipate the time when He shall be victorious all along the line.

The Christmas festival was duly observed by the missionaries who came to the South of England from Rome, headed by Augustine, and in the northern parts of the country the Christian festivities were revived by the Celtic missionaries from Iona, under Aidan, the famous Columbian monk. At least half of England was covered by the Columbian monks, whose great foundation upon the rocky island of Iona, in the Hebrides, was the source of Christianity to Scotland. The ritual of the Celtic differed from that of the Romish missionaries, and caused confusion, till at the Synod of Whitby (664) the Northumbrian Kingdom adopted the Roman usages, and England obtained ecclesiastical unity as a branch of the Church of Rome. Thus unity in the Church preceded by several centuries unity in the State.

QUEEN BERTHA.

In connection with Augustine's mission to England, a memorable story (recorded in Green's "History of the English People") tells how, when but a young Roman deacon, Gregory had noted the white bodies, the fair faces, the golden hair of some youths who stood bound in the market-place of Rome. "From what country do these slaves come?" he asked the traders who brought them. "They are English, Angles!" the slave-dealers answered. The deacon's pity veiled itself in poetic humour. "Not Angles, but Angels," he said, "with faces so angel-like! From what country come they?" "They come," said the merchants, "from Deira." "De ira!" was the untranslatable reply; "aye, plucked from God's ire, and called to Christ's mercy! And what is the name of their king?" "Ælla," they told him, and Gregory seized on the words as of good omen. "Alleluia shall be sung in Ælla's land!" he cried, and passed on, musing how the angel-faces should be brought to sing it. Only three or four years had gone by when the deacon had become Bishop of Rome, and the marriage of Bertha, daughter of the Frankish king, Charibert of Paris, with Æthelberht, King of Kent, gave him the opening he sought; for Bertha, like her Frankish kinsfolk, was a Christian.

And so, after negotiations with the rulers of Gaul, Gregory sent Augustine, at the head of a band of monks, to preach the gospel to the English people. The missionaries landed in 597, on the very spot where Hengest had landed more than a century before, in the Isle of Thanet; and the king received them sitting in the open air on the chalk-down above Minster, where the eye nowadays catches, miles away over the marshes, the dim tower of Canterbury. Rowbotham, in his "History of Music," says that wherever Gregory sent missionaries he also sent copies of the Gregorian song as he had arranged it in his "Antiphonary." And he bade them go singing among the people. And Augustine entered Kent bearing a silver cross and a banner with the image of Christ painted on it, while a long train of choristers walked behind him chanting the *Kyrie Eleison*. In this way they came to the court of Æthelberht, who assigned them Canterbury as an abode; and they entered Canterbury with similar pomp, and as they passed through the gates they sang this petition: "Lord, we beseech Thee to keep Thy wrath away from this city and from Thy holy Church, Alleluia!"

As papal Rome preserved many relics of heathen Rome, so, in like manner, Pope Gregory, in sending Augustine over to convert the Anglo-Saxons, directed him to accommodate the ceremonies of the Christian worship as much as possible to those of the heathen, that the people might not be much startled at the change; and, in particular, he advised him to allow converts to kill and eat at the Christmas festival a great number of oxen to the glory of God, as they had formerly done to the honour of the devil. The clergy, therefore, endeavoured to connect the remnants of Pagan idolatry with Christianity, and also allowed some of the practices of our British ancestors to mingle in the festivities of Christmastide. The religion of the Druids, the priests of the ancient Britons, is supposed to have been somewhat similar to that of the Brahmins of India, the Magi of Persia, and the Chaldeans of Syria. They worshipped in groves, regarded the oak and mistletoe as objects of veneration, and offered sacrifices. Before Christianity came to Britain December was called "Aerra Geola," because the sun then "turns his glorious course." And under different names, such as Woden (another form of Odin), Thor, Thunder, Saturn, &c., the pagans held their festivals of rejoicing at the winter solstice; and so many of the ancient customs connected with these festivals were modified and made subservient to Christianity.

Some of the English even tried to serve Christ and the older gods together, like the Roman Emperor, Alexander Severus, whose chapel contained Orpheus side by side with Abraham and Christ. "Rœdwald of East Anglia resolved to serve Christ and the older gods together, and a pagan and a Christian altar fronted one another in the same royal temple."[5] Kent, however, seems to have been evangelised rapidly, for it is recorded that on Christmas Day, 597, no less than ten thousand persons were baptized.

Before his death Augustine was able to see almost the whole of Kent and Essex nominally Christian.

Christmas was now celebrated as the principal festival of the year, for our Anglo-Saxon forefathers delighted in the festivities of the Halig-Monath (holy month), as they called the month of December, in allusion to Christmas Day. At the great festival of Christmas the meetings of the Witenagemot were held, as well as at

Easter and Whitsuntide, wherever the Court happened to be. And at these times the Anglo-Saxon, and afterwards the Danish, Kings of England lived in state, wore their crowns, and were surrounded by all the great men of their kingdoms (together with strangers of rank) who were sumptuously entertained, and the most important affairs of state were brought under consideration. There was also an outflow of generous hospitality towards the poor, who had a hard time of it during the rest of the year, and who required the Christmas gifts to provide them with such creature comforts as would help them through the inclement season of the year.

Readers of Saxon history will remember that chieftains in the festive hall are alluded to in the comparison made by one of King Edwin's chiefs, in discussing the welcome to be given to the Christian missionary Paulinus: "The present life of man, O King, seems to me, in comparison of that time which is unknown to us, like to the swift flight of a sparrow through the hall where you sit at your meal in winter, with your chiefs and attendants, warmed by a fire made in the middle of the hall, while storms of rain or snow prevail without."

AN ANCIENT FIREPLACE.

The "hall" was the principal part of a gentleman's house in Saxon times—the place of entertainment and hospitality—and at Christmastide the doors were never shut against any who appeared to be worthy of welcome. And with such modes of travelling as were in vogue in those days one can readily understand that, not only at Christmas, but also at other seasons, the rule of hospitality to strangers was a necessity.

To this period belong the princely pageants and the magnificent

Christmas Entertainments of King Arthur

and the Knights of his Round Table. We know that some people are inclined to discredit the accounts which have come down to us of this famous British King and Christian hero, but for our own part we are inclined to trust the old chroniclers, at all events so far as to believe that they give us true pictures of the manners and customs of the times of which they write; and in this prosaic age it may surely be permitted to us at Christmastide to linger over the doings of those romantic days,

> "When every morning brought a noble chance,
> And every chance brought out a noble knight."[6] 0

TRAVELLING IN THE OLDEN TIME WITH A "CHRISTMAS FOOL"
ON THE FRONT SEAT.

Sir John Froissart tells us of the princely pageants which King Arthur held at Windsor in the sixth century, and of the sumptuous Christmas banquetings at his Round Table—the very Round Table (so we are to believe, on the authority of Dr. Milner)[7] which has been preserved in the old chapel, now termed the county hall, at Winchester. It consists of stout oak plank, perforated with many bullets, supposed to have been shot by Cromwell's soldiers. It is painted with a figure to represent King Arthur, and with the names of his twenty-four knights as they are stated in the romances of the old chroniclers. This famous Prince, who instituted the military order of the Knights of the Round Table, is also credited with the reintroduction of Christianity at York after the Saxon invaders had destroyed the first churches built there. He was unwearying in his warfare against enemies of the religion of Christ. His first great enterprise was the siege of a Saxon army at York, and, having afterwards won brilliant victories in Somersetshire and other parts of southern England, he again marched northward and penetrated Scotland to attack the Picts and Scots, who had long harassed the border. On returning from Scotland, Arthur rested his wearied army at York and kept Christmas with great bountifulness. Geoffrey of Monmouth says he was a prince of "unparalleled courage and generosity," and his Christmas at York was kept with the greatest joy and festivity. Then was the round table filled with jocund guests, and the minstrels, gleemen, harpers, pipe-players, jugglers, and dancers were as happy round about their log-fires as if they had shone in the blaze of a thousand gas-lights.

THE WILD BOAR HUNT: KILLING THE BOAR.

King Arthur and his Knights also indulged in out-door amusements, as hunting, hawking, running, leaping, wrestling, jousts, and tourneys. "So," says Sir Thomas Malory,[8] "passed forth all the winter with all manner of hunting and hawking, and jousts and tourneys were many between many great lords. And ever, in all manner of places, Sir Lavaine got great worship, that he was nobly renowned among many of the knights of the Round Table. Thus it passed on until Christmas, and every day there were jousts made for a diamond, that whosoever joust best should have a diamond. But Sir Launcelot would not joust, but if it were a great joust cried; but Sir Lavaine jousted there all the Christmas passing well, and most was praised; for there were few that did so well as he; wherefore all manner of knights deemed that Sir Lavaine should be made a Knight of the Round Table, at the next high feast of Pentecost."

THE ANGLO-SAXON EXCESSES

are referred to by some of the old chroniclers, intemperance being a very prevalent vice at the Christmas festival. Ale and mead were their favourite drinks; wines were used as occasional luxuries. "When all were satisfied with dinner," says an old chronicler, "and their tables were removed, they continued drinking till the evening." And another tells how drinking and gaming went on through the greater part of the night. Chaucer's one solitary reference to Christmastide is an allegorical representation of the jovial feasting which was the characteristic feature of this great festival held in "the colde frosty season of December."

> "Janus sits by the fire with double beard,
> And drinketh of his bugle horn the wine:
> Before him stands the brawn of tuskéd swine,
> And 'Nowel' cryeth every lusty man."[9]

The Saxons were strongly attached to field sports, and as the "brawn of the tuskéd swine" was the first Christmas dish, it was provided by the pleasant preliminary pastime of hunting the wild boar; and the incidents of the chase afforded interesting table talk when the boar's head was brought in ceremoniously to the Christmas festival.

Prominent among the Anglo-Saxon amusements of Christmastide, Strutt mentions their propensity for gaming with dice, as derived from their ancestors, for Tacitus assures us that the ancient Germans would not only hazard all their wealth, but even stake their liberty, upon the turn of the dice: "and he who loses submits to servitude, though younger and stronger than his antagonist, and patiently permits himself to be bound and sold in the market; and this madness they dignify by the name of honour." Chess and backgammon were also favourite games with the Anglo-Saxons, and a large portion of the night was appropriated to the pursuit of these sedentary amusements, especially at the Christmas season of the year, when the early darkness stopped out-door games.

> "When they had dined, as I can you say,
> Lords and ladies went to play;
> Some to tables, and some to chess,
> With other games more and less."[10]

Our Saxon forefathers were very superstitious. They had many pretenders to witchcraft. They believed in the powers of philtres and spells, and invocated spirits; and they relished a blood-curdling ghost story at Christmas quite as much as their twentieth-century descendants. They confided in prognostics, and believed in the influence of particular times and seasons; and at Christmastide they derived peculiar pleasure from their belief in the immunity of the season from malign influences—a belief which descended to Elizabethan days, and is referred to by Shakespeare, in "Hamlet":—

> "Some say that ever 'gainst that season comes,
> Wherein our Saviour's birth is celebrated,
> The bird of dawning singeth all night long:
> And then, they say, no spirit dares stir abroad;
> The nights are wholesome; then no planets strike,
> No fairy takes, nor witch hath power to charm,

We cannot pass over this period without mentioning a great Christmas in the history of our Teutonic kinsmen on the Continent, for the Saxons of England and those of Germany have the same Teutonic origin. We refer to

THE CROWNING OF CHARLEMAGNE EMPEROR OF THE ROMANS ON CHRISTMAS DAY.

The coronation took place at Rome, on Christmas Day, in the year 800. Freeman[11] says that when Charles was King of the Franks and Lombards and Patrician of the Romans, he was on very friendly terms with the mighty Offa, King of the Angles that dwelt in Mercia. Charles and Offa not only exchanged letters and gifts, but each gave the subjects of the other various rights in his dominions, and they made a league together, "for that they two were the mightiest of all the kings that dwelt in the Western lands." As conqueror of the old Saxons in Germany, Charles may be regarded as the first King of all Germany, and he was the first man of any Teutonic nation who was called Roman Emperor. He was crowned with the diadem of the Cæsars, by Pope Leo, in the name of Charles Augustus, Emperor of the Romans. And it was held for a thousand years after, down to the year 1806, that the King of the Franks, or, as he was afterwards called, the King of Germany, had a right to be crowned by the Pope of Rome, and to be called Emperor of the Romans. In the year 1806, however, the Emperor Francis the Second, who was also King of Hungary and Archduke of Austria, resigned the Roman Empire and the Kingdom of Germany. Since that time no Emperor of the Romans has been chosen; but a new German Emperor has been created, and the event may be regarded as one of Christmastide, for the victorious soldiers who brought it about spent their Christmas in the French capital, and during the festival arranged for the re-establishment of the German Empire. So it happens, that while referring to the crowning of the first German Emperor of the Roman Empire, on Christmas Day, 800, we are able to record that more than a thousand years afterwards the unification of the German Empire and the creation of its first Emperor also occurred at Christmastide, under the influence of the German triumphs over the French in the war of 1870. The imposing event was resolved upon by the German Princes on December 18, 1870, the preliminaries were completed during the Christmas festival, and on January 18, 1871, in the Galerie des Glaces of the château of Versailles, William, King of Prussia, was crowned and proclaimed first Emperor of the new German Empire.

Now, going back again over a millennium, we come to

CHRISTMAS IN THE TIME OF ALFRED THE GREAT.

During the reign of Alfred the Great a law was passed with relation to holidays, by virtue of which the twelve days after the Nativity of our Saviour were set apart for the celebration of the Christmas festival. Some writers are of opinion that, but for Alfred's strict observance of the "full twelve holy days," he would not have been defeated by the Danes in the year 878. It was just after Twelfth-night that the Danish host came suddenly—"bestole," as the old Chronicle says—to Chippenham. Then "they rode through the West Saxons' land, and there sat down, and mickle of the folk over sea they drove, and of others the most deal they rode over; all but the King Alfred; he with a little band hardly fared after the woods and on the moor-fastnesses." But whether or not Alfred's preparations for the battle just referred to were hindered by his enjoyment of the festivities of Christmastide with his subjects, it is quite certain that the King won the hearts of his people by the great interest he took in their welfare. This good king—whose intimacy with his people we delight to associate with the homely incident of the burning of a cottager's cakes—kept the Christmas festival quite as heartily as any of the early English kings, but not so boisterously as some of them. Of the many beautiful stories told about him, one might very well belong to Christmastide. It is said that, wishing to know what the Danes were about, and how strong they were, King Alfred one day set out from Athelney in the disguise of a Christmas minstrel, and went into the Danish camp, and stayed there several days, amusing the Danes with his playing, till he had seen all he wanted, and then went back without any one finding him out.

Now, passing on to

CHRISTMAS UNDER THE DANISH KINGS OF ENGLAND,

we find that in 961 King Edgar celebrated the Christmas festival with great splendour at York; and in 1013 Ethelred kept his Christmas with the brave citizens of London who had defended the capital during a siege and stoutly resisted Swegen, the tyrant king of the Danes. Sir Walter Scott, in his beautiful poem of "Marmion," thus pictures the "savage Dane" keeping the great winter festival:—

> "Even, heathen yet, the savage Dane
> At Iol more deep the mead did drain;
> High on the beach his galleys drew,
> And feasted all his pirate crew;
> Then in his low and pine-built hall,
> Where shields and axes deck'd the wall,
> They gorged upon the half-dress'd steer;
> Caroused in seas of sable beer;
> While round, in brutal jest, were thrown
> The half-gnaw'd rib, and marrow bone:
> Or listen'd all, in grim delight.
> While Scalds yell'd out the joys of fight.
> Then forth, in frenzy, would they hie,
> While wildly-loose their red locks fly,

And dancing round the blazing pile,
They make such barbarous mirth the while,
As best might to the mind recall
The boisterous joys of Odin's hall."

When the citizens of London saw that Swegen had succeeded all over England except their own city, they thought it was no use holding out any longer, and they too, submitted and gave hostages. And so Swegen was the first Dane who was king, or (as Florence calls him) "Tyrant over all England;" and Ethelred, sometimes called the "Unready," King of the West Saxons, who had struggled unsuccessfully against the Danes, fled with his wife and children to his brother-in-law's court in Normandy. On the death of Swegen, the Danes of his fleet chose his son Cnut to be King, but the English invited Ethelred to return from Normandy and renew the struggle with the Danes. He did so, and the Anglo-Saxon Chronicle says: "He held his kingdom with great toil and great difficulty the while that his life lasted." After his death and that of his son Edmund, Cnut was finally elected and crowned. Freeman,[12] in recording the event, says that: "At the Christmas of 1016-1017, Cnut was a third time chosen king over all England, and one of the first things that he did was to send to Normandy for the widowed Lady Emma, though she was many years older than he was. She came over; she married the new king; and was again Lady of the English. She bore Cnut two children, Harthacnut and Gunhild. Her three children by Ethelred were left in Normandy. She seems not to have cared at all for them or for the memory of Ethelred; her whole love passed to her new husband and her new children. Thus it came about that the children of Ethelred were brought up in Normandy, and had the feelings of Normans rather than Englishmen, a thing which again greatly helped the Norman Conquest."

Cnut's first acts of government in England were a series of murders; but he afterwards became a wise and temperate king. He even identified himself with the patriotism which had withstood the stranger. He joined heartily in the festivities of Christmastide, and atoned for his father's ravages by costly gifts to the religious houses. And his love for monks broke out in the song which he composed as he listened to their chant at Ely: "Merrily sang the monks in Ely when Cnut King rowed by" across the vast fen-waters that surrounded their Abbey. "Row, boatmen, near the land, and hear we these monks sing."[13]

> "'All hail!' the monks at Christmas sang;
> The merry monks who kept with cheer
> The gladdest day of all the year."[14]

It is said that Cnut, who is also called Canute, "marked one of his royal Christmases by a piece of sudden retributive justice: bored beyond all endurance by the Saxon Edric's iteration of the traitorous services he had rendered him, the King exclaimed to Edric, Earl of Northumberland: 'Then let him receive his deserts, that he may not betray us as he betrayed Ethelred and Edmund!' upon which the ready Norwegian disposed of all fear on that score by cutting down the boaster with his axe, and throwing his body into the Thames."[15]

In the year 1035, King Cnut died at Shaftesbury, and was buried in Winchester Cathedral. His sons, Harold and Harthacnut, did not possess the capacity for good government, otherwise the reign of the Danes might have continued. As it was, their reigns, though short, were troublesome. Harold died at Oxford in 1040, and was buried at Westminster (being the first king who was buried there); Harthacnut died at Lambeth at a wedding-feast in 1042, and was buried beside his father in Winchester Cathedral. And thus ended the reigns of the Danish kings of England.

Now we come to

THE REIGN OF EDWARD THE CONFESSOR

who, we are told, was heartily chosen by all the people, for the two very good reasons, that he was an Englishman by birth, and the only man of either the English or the Danish royal families who was at hand. He was the son of Ethelred and Emma, and at the Christmas festival of his coronation there was great rejoicing. As his early training had been at the court of his uncle, Richard the Good, in Normandy, he had learnt to prefer Norman-French customs and life to those of the English. During his reign, therefore, he brought over many strangers and appointed them to high ecclesiastical and other offices, and Norman influence and refinement of manners gradually increased at the English court, and this, of course, led to the more stately celebration of the Christmas festival. The King himself, being of a pious and meditative disposition, naturally took more interest in the religious than the temporal rejoicings, and the administration of state affairs was left almost entirely to members of the house of Godwin during the principal part of his reign. Many disturbances occurred during Edward's reign in different parts of the country, especially on the Welsh border. At the Christmas meeting of the King and his Wise Men, at Gloucester, in 1053, it was ordered that Rhys, the brother of Gruffydd, the South Welsh king, be put to death for his great plunder and mischief. The same year, the great Earl Godwine, while dining with the king at Winchester at the Easter feast, suddenly fell in a fit, died four days after, and was buried in the old cathedral. A few years later (1065), the Northumbrians complained that Earl Tostig, Harold's brother, had caused Gospatric, one of the chief Thanes, to be treacherously murdered when he came to the King's court the Christmas before. King Edward kept his last Christmas (1065), and had the meeting of his Wise Men in London instead of Gloucester as usual. His great object was to finish his new church at Westminster, and to have it hallowed before he died. He lived just long enough to have this done. On Innocent's Day the new Minster was consecrated, but the King was too ill to be there, so the Lady Edith stood in his stead. And on January 5, 1066, King Edward, the son of Ethelred, died. On the morning of the day following his death, the body of the Confessor was laid in the tomb, in his new church; and on the same day—

HAROLD WAS CROWNED KING

in his stead. Thus three very important events—the consecration of Westminster Abbey, the death of Edward the Confessor, and the crowning of Harold—all occurred during the same Christmas festival.

In the terrible year 1066 England had three kings. The reign of Harold, the son of Godwine, who succeeded Edward the Confessor, terminated at the battle of Senlac, or Hastings, and on the following by Archbishop Ealdred. He had not at that time conquered all the land, and it was a long while before he really possessed the whole of it. Still, he was the king, chosen, crowned, and anointed, and no one ever was able to drive him out of the land, and the crown of England has ever since been held by his descendants.

5   Green's "History of the English People."
6   Tennyson.
7   "History of Winchester."
8   "History of King Arthur and His Noble Knights."
9   "The Franklin's Tale."
10   "Romance of Ipomydon."
11   "Old English History."
12   "Short History of the Norman Conquest."
13   "History of the English People."
14   J. G. Whittier.
15   "Chambers's Journal," Dec. 28, 1867.

CHAPTER IV.

CHRISTMAS, FROM THE NORMAN CONQUEST TO MAGNA CHARTA.

(1066 to 1215.)

A KING AT DINNER.

Now we come to the

CHRISTMAS CELEBRATIONS UNDER THE NORMANS.

Lord Macaulay says "the polite luxury of the Normans presented a striking contrast to the coarse voracity and drunkenness of their Saxon and Danish neighbours." And certainly the above example of a royal dinner scene (from a manuscript of the fourteenth century) gives an idea of stately ceremony which is not found in any manuscripts previous to the coming over of the Normans. They "loved to display their magnificence, not in huge piles of food and hogsheads of strong drink, but in large and stately edifices, rich armour, gallant horses, choice falcons, well-ordered tournaments, banquets delicate rather than abundant, and wines remarkable rather for their exquisite flavour than for their intoxicating power." Quite so. But even the Normans were not all temperate. And, while it is quite true that the refined manners and chivalrous spirit of the Normans exercised a powerful influence on the Anglo-Saxons, it is equally true that the conquerors on mingling with the English people adopted many of the ancient customs to which they tenaciously clung, and these included the customs of Christmastide.

The Norman kings and nobles displayed their taste for magnificence in the most remarkable manner at their coronations, tournaments, and their celebrations of Christmas, Easter, and Whitsuntide. The great councils of the Norman reigns which assembled at Christmas and the other great festivals, were in appearance a continuation of the Witenagemots, but the power of the barons became very formal in the presence of such despotic monarchs as William the Conqueror and his sons. At the Christmas festival all the prelates and nobles of the kingdom were, by their tenures, obliged to attend their sovereign to assist in the administration of justice and in deliberation on the great affairs of the kingdom. On these occasions the King wore his crown, and feasted his nobles in the great hall of his palace, and made them presents as marks of his royal favour, after which they proceeded to the consideration of State affairs. Wherever the Court happened to be, there was usually a large assemblage of gleemen, who were jugglers and pantomimists as well as minstrels, and were accustomed to associate themselves in companies, and amuse the spectators with feats of strength and agility, dancing, tumbling, and sleight-of-hand tricks, as well as musical performances. Among the minstrels who came into England with William the Conqueror was one named Taillefer, who was present at the battle of Hastings, and rode in front of the Norman army, inspiriting the soldiers by his songs. He sang of Roland, the heroic captain of Charlemagne, tossing his sword in the air and catching it again as he approached the English line. He was the first to strike a blow at the English, but after mortally wounding one or two of King Harold's warriors, he was himself struck down.

At the Christmas feast minstrels played on various musical instruments during dinner, and sang or told tales afterwards, both in the hall and in the chamber to which the king and his nobles retired for amusement. Thus it is written of a court minstrel:—

"Before the King he set him down
And took his harp of merry soun,
And, as he full well can,
Many merry notes he began.
The king beheld, and sat full still,
To hear his harping he had good will.
When he left off his harping,
To him said that rich king,
To him said that rich king,
Minstrel, we liketh well thy glee,
What thing that thou ask of me
Largely I will thee pay;
Therefore ask now and asay." (*Sir Orpheo.*)

BLIND MINSTREL AT A FEAST.

After the Conquest the first entertainments given by William the Conqueror were those to his victorious warriors:—

"Every warrior's manly neck
Chains of regal honour deck,
Wreathed in many a golden link:
From the golden cup they drink
Nectar that the bees produce,
Or the grape's extatic juice.
Flush'd with mirth and hope they burn."

The Gododin.

In 1067 the Conqueror kept a grand Christmas in London. He had spent eight months of that year rewarding his warriors and gratifying his subjects in Normandy, where he had held a round of feasts and made a grand display of the valuable booty which he had won by his sword. A part of his plunder he sent to the Pope along with the banner of Harold. Another portion, consisting of gold, golden vases, and richly embroidered stuffs, was distributed among the abbeys, monasteries, and churches of his native duchy, "neither monks nor priests remaining without a guerdon." After spending the greater part of the year in splendid entertainments in Normandy, apparently undisturbed by the reports which had reached him of discontent and insurrection among his new subjects in England, William at length embarked at Dieppe on the 6th of December, 1067, and returned to London to celebrate the approaching festival of Christmas. With the object of quieting the discontent which prevailed, he invited a considerable number of the Saxon chiefs to take part in the Christmas festival, which was kept with unusual splendour; and he also caused a proclamation to be read in all the churches of the capital declaring it to be his will that "all the citizens of London should enjoy their national laws as in the days of King Edward." But his policy of friendship and conciliation was soon changed into one of cruelty and oppression.

At the instigation of Swein, the King of Denmark, who appeared in the Humber with a fleet, the people in the north of England and in some other parts rose in revolt against the rule of the Conqueror in 1068. So skilfully had the revolt been planned that even William was taken by surprise. While he was hunting in the Forest of Dean he heard of the loss of York and the slaughter of his garrison of 3,000 Normans, and resolved to avenge the disaster. Proceeding to the Humber with his horsemen, by a heavy bribe he got the King of Denmark to withdraw his fleet; then, after some delay, spent in punishing revolters in the Welsh border, he attacked and took the city of York. The land in Durham and Northumberland was still quite unsubdued, and some of William's soldiers had fared badly in their attempts to take possession. At the Christmas feast of 1068 William made a grant of the earldom of Northumberland to Robert of Comines, who set out with a Norman army to take possession. But he fared no better than his predecessors had done. The men of the land determined to withstand him, but through the help of Bishop Æthelwine he entered Durham peaceably. But he let his men plunder, so the men of the city rose and slew him and his followers. And now, says Freeman,[16] William "did one of the most frightful deeds of his life. He caused all Northern England, beginning with Yorkshire, to be utterly laid waste, that its people might not be able to fight against him any more. The havoc was fearful; men were starved or sold themselves as slaves, and the land did not recover for many years. Then King William wore his crown and kept his Christmas at York" (1069).

Now the Conqueror set barons in different parts of the country, and each of them kept his own miniature court and celebrated Christmas after the costly Norman style. In his beautiful poem of "The Norman Baron" Longfellow pictures one of these Christmas celebrations, and tells how—

> "In the hall, the serf and vassal
> Held, that night, their Christmas wassail;
> Many a carol, old and saintly,
>   Sang the minstrels and the waits.
>
> And so loud these Saxon gleemen
> Sang to slaves the songs of freemen,
> That the storm was heard but faintly
>   Knocking at the castle-gates.
>
> Till at length the lays they chaunted
> Reached the chamber terror-haunted,
> Where the monk, with accents holy,
>   Whispered at the baron's ear.

Tears upon his eyelids glistened
As he paused awhile and listened,
And the dying baron slowly
    Turned his weary head to hear.

'Wassail for the kingly stranger
Born and cradled in a manger!
King, like David, priest, like Aaron,
    Christ is born to set us free!'"

MINSTRELS' CHRISTMAS SERENADE AT AN OLD BARONIAL HALL.

According to Strutt, the popular sports and pastimes prevalent at the close of the Saxon era were not subjected to any material change by the coming of the Normans. But William and his immediate successors restricted the privileges of the chase, and imposed great penalties on those who presumed to destroy the game in the royal forests without a proper license. The wild boar and the wolf still afforded sport at the Christmas season, and there was an abundance of smaller game. Leaping, running, wrestling, the casting of darts, and other pastimes which required bodily strength and agility were also practised, and when the frost set in various games were engaged in upon the ice. It is not known at what time skating made its first appearance in England, but we find some traces of such an exercise in the thirteenth century, at which period, according to Fitzstephen, it was customary in the winter, when the ice would bear them, for the young citizens of London to fasten the leg bones of animals under the soles of their feet by tying them round their ankles; and then, taking a pole shod with iron into their hands, they pushed themselves forward by striking it against the ice, and moved with celerity equal, says the author, to a bird flying through the air, or an arrow from a cross-bow; but some allowance, we presume, must be made for the poetical figure: he then adds, "At times, two of them thus furnished agree to start opposite one to another, at a great distance; they meet, elevate their poles, attack, and strike each other, when one or both of them fall, and not without some bodily hurt; and, even after their fall, are carried a great distance from each other, by the rapidity of the motion, and whatever part of the head comes upon the ice it is sure to be laid bare."

The meetings of the King and his Wise Men for the consideration of state affairs were continued at the great festivals, and that held at Christmas in 1085 is memorable on account of the resolution then passed to make the Domesday survey, in reference to which Freeman says: "One of the greatest acts of William's reign, and that by which we come to know more about England in his time than from any other source, was done in the assembly held at Gloucester at the Christmas of 1085. Then the King had, as the Chronicle says, 'very deep speech with his Wise Men.' This 'deep speech' in English is in French *parlement*, and so we see how our assemblies came by their later name. And the end of the deep speech was that commissioners were sent through all England, save only the Bishopric of Durham and the earldom of Northumberland, to make a survey of the land. They were to set down by whom every piece of land, great and small, was held then, by whom it was held in King Edward's day, what it was worth now, and what it had been worth in King Edward's day. All this was written in a book kept at Winchester, which men called *Domesday Book*. It is a most wonderful record, and tells us more of the state of England just at that moment than we know of it for a long time before or after."

The Domesday Book was completed in 1086, and the following year (1087) William the Conqueror died, and his son, William Rufus, succeeded him.

THE CORONATION OF WILLIAM THE RED

took place at Westminster on September 26, 1087, Archbishop Lanfranc officiating. The King kept his first Christmas sumptuously at Westminster, and, Freeman says, "it seems to have been then that he gave back the earldom of Kent to his uncle, Bishop Odo." The character of the Royal Christmases degenerated during the reign of Rufus, whose licentiousness fouled the festivities. In the latter part of his reign Rufus reared the spacious hall at Westminster, where so many Royal Christmases were afterwards kept, and which Pope calls

"Rufus's roaring hall."

WESTMINSTER HALL.

It is a magnificent relic of the profuse hospitality of former times. Richard the Second heightened its walls and added its noble roof of British oak, which shows the excellence of the wood carving of that period. Although Sir Charles Barry has shortened the Hall of its former proportions to fit it as a vestibule to the

New Houses of Parliament, it is still a noble and spacious building, and one cannot walk through it without in imagination recalling some of the Royal Christmases and other stately scenes which have been witnessed there. The last of these festal glories was the coronation of George the Fourth, which took place in 1821. This grand old hall at Westminster was the theatre of Rufus's feasting and revelry; but, vast as the edifice then was, it did not equal the ideas of the extravagant monarch. An old chronicler states that one of the King's courtiers, having observed that the building was too large for the purposes of its construction, Rufus replied, "This halle is not begge enough by one half, and is but a bedchamber in comparison of that I mind to make." Yet this hall was for centuries the largest of its kind in Europe, and in it the Christmas feasts were magnificently kept.

After a reign of thirteen years the vicious life of William Rufus met with a tragical close. His dead body was found by peasants in a glade of the New Forest with the arrow either of a hunter or an assassin in his breast. Sir Walter Tyrrel, a Norman knight, who had been hunting with the king just before his death, fled to Normandy immediately afterwards, and was suspected of being a regicide. The body of Rufus was buried in Winchester Cathedral.

CHRISTMAS IN THE REIGN OF HENRY I.

Henry the First's Christmas festival at Windsor, in 1126, was a memorable one. In that year Henry's daughter Matilda became a widow by the death of her husband, Henry V. of Germany, and King Henry determined to appoint her his successor to the throne of England and the Dukedom of Normandy. On Christmas Day, 1126, a general assembly of the nobles and higher ecclesiastics of the kingdom was held at Windsor for the purpose of declaring the Empress Matilda (as she was still called) the legitimate successor of Henry I., and the clergy and Norman barons of both countries swore allegiance to her in the event of the king's death. This appointment of Matilda was made by Henry in consequence of the calamity which occurred just before Christmas, in 1120, when he lost his much-loved son, Prince William—the only male legitimate issue of Henry—through the wreck of *La Blanche Nef* (the White Ship). On board the vessel were Prince William, his half-brother Richard, and

Henry's natural daughter the Countess of Perche, as well as about a hundred and forty young noblemen of the most distinguished families in England and Normandy, all of whom were lost in their passage home, only a few hours after the safe arrival of the king in England. Henry is said to have swooned at the intelligence, and was never afterwards seen to smile. He had returned home anticipating a joyous Christmas festival, a season of glad tidings, but he was closely followed by this sad news of the death of the heir apparent. The incident has called forth one of the most beautiful poems of Mrs. Hemans, from which we quote two verses:—

> "The bark that held a prince went down,
>   The sweeping waves rolled on;
> And what was England's glorious crown
>   To him that wept a son?
> He lived—for life may long be borne,
>   Ere sorrow break its chain:
> Why comes not death to those who mourn?
>   He never smiled again!
>
> He sat where festal bowls went round,
>   He heard the minstrel sing;
> He saw the tourney's victor crowned,
>   Amidst the kingly ring;
> A murmur of the restless deep
>   as blent with every strain,
> A voice of winds that would not sleep,—
>   He never smiled again!"

In 1127 Henry invited the king of the Scots to Windsor to join in the royal celebration of Christmas, but the festivities were marred by an unseemly quarrel between the two primates. Thurstan, Archbishop of York, encroaching upon the privileges of his brother of Canterbury (William de Corbeuil), insisted upon placing the crown upon the king's head ere he set out for church. This the partisans of Canterbury would not allow, settling the matter by turning Thurstan's chaplain and followers out of doors, and thereby causing such strife between the heads of the Church that they both set off to Rome to lay their grievances before the

Pope. And, subsequently, appeals to Rome became frequent, until a satisfactory adjustment of the powers and privileges of the two archbishops was arrived at. The Archbishop of Canterbury was acknowledged Primate of all England and Metropolitan; but, while the privilege of crowning the sovereign was reserved for the Archbishop of Canterbury, that of crowning the Queen Consort was given to the Archbishop of York.

STRANGE OLD STORIES OF CHRISTMASTIDE.

The progress of literature under the Conqueror and his sons was very great, many devoting themselves almost entirely to literary pursuits. Lanfranc and Anselm, the Archbishops of Canterbury, had proved themselves worthy of their exalted station. Their precepts and examples had awakened the clergy and kindled an ardour for learning unknown in any preceding age. Nor did this enthusiasm perish with its authors: it was kept alive by the honours which were lavished on all who could boast of literary acquirements. During the reign of Henry I. Geoffrey of Monmouth published his History of the Britons, and William of Malmesbury assures us that every poet hastened to the court of Henry's Queen Matilda, at Westminster, to read his verses to the Queen and partake of her bounty. William of Malmesbury carefully collected the lighter ballads which embodied the popular traditions of the English kings, and he tells an amusing story which is connected with the festival of Christmas. In early times dancing developed into a sort of passion, men and women continually dancing and singing together, holding one another by the hands, and concluding the dances with kisses. These levities were at first encouraged by the Church, but afterwards, seeing the abuse of them, the priests were compelled to reprimand and restrain the people. And the story told by William of Malmesbury describes the singular punishment which came upon some young men and women for disturbing a priest who was performing mass on the eve of Christmas. "I, Othbert, a sinner," says the story, "have lived to tell the tale. It was the vigil of the Blessed Virgin, and in a town where was a church of St. Magnus. And the priest, Rathbertus, had just begun the mass, and I, with my comrades, fifteen young women and seventeen young men, were dancing outside the church. And we were singing so loud that our songs were distinctly heard inside the building, and interrupted the service of the mass. And the priest came out and told us to desist; and when we did not, he prayed God and St. Magnus that we might dance as our punishment for a year to come. A youth, whose sister was dancing with us, seized her by the arm to drag her away, but it came off in his hand, and she danced on. For a whole year we continued. No rain fell on us; cold, nor heat, nor hunger, nor thirst, nor fatigue affected us; neither our shoes nor our clothes wore out; but still we went on dancing. We trod the earth down to our knees, next to our middles, and at last were dancing in a pit. At the end of the year release came."

Giraldus Cambrensis, amongst many ridiculous Christmas stories of miracles, visions, and apparitions, tells of one devil who acted a considerable time as a gentleman's butler with great prudence and probity; and of another who was a very diligent and learned clergyman, and a mighty favourite of his archbishop. This last clerical devil was, it seems, an excellent historian, and used to divert the Archbishop with telling him old stories, some of which referred to the incarnation of our Saviour, and were related at the Christmas season. "Before the incarnation of our Saviour," said the Archbishop's historian, "the devils had great power over mankind, but after that event their power was much diminished and they were obliged to fly. Some of them threw themselves into the sea; some concealed themselves in hollow trees, or in the clefts of rocks; and I myself plunged into a certain fountain. As soon as he had said this, finding that he had discovered his secret, his face was covered with blushes, he went out of the room, and was no more seen."

The following cut (taken from MS. Harl., No. 4751, of the end of the twelfth century) represents an elephant, with its castle and armed men, engaged in battle. The bestiaries relate many strange things of the elephant. They say that, though so large and powerful, and so courageous against larger animals, it is afraid of a mouse; that its nature is so cold that it will never seek the company of the female until, wandering in the direction of Paradise, it meets with the plant called the mandrake, and eats of it, and that each female bears but one young one in her life.

Absurd as we consider such stories, they were believed by the Normans, who were no less credulous than the Anglo-Saxons. This is evident from the large number of miracles, revelations, visions, and enchantments which are related with great gravity by the old chroniclers.

THE MISRULE OF KING STEPHEN.

Stephen of Blois was crowned at Westminster Abbey during the Christmas festival (December 26, 1135). As a King of Misrule, he was fitly crowned at Christmastide, and it would have been a good thing for the nation if his reign had been of the ephemeral character which was customary to Lords of Misrule. The nineteen years of his reign were years of disorder unparalleled in any period of our history. On the landing of Henry the First's daughter, "the Empress Matilda," who claimed the English crown for her son Henry, a long struggle ensued, and the country was divided between the adherents of the two rivals, the West supporting Matilda, and London and the East Stephen. For a time the successes in war alternated between the two parties. A defeat at Lincoln left Stephen a prisoner in the hands of his enemies; but after his escape he laid siege to the city of Oxford, where Matilda had assembled her followers. "The Lady" of the English (as Matilda was then called) had retreated into the castle, which, though a place of great strength, proved to be insufficiently victualled. It was surrounded and cut off from all supplies without, and at Christmastide (1142), after a siege of three months, Matilda consulted her own safety by taking flight. On a cold December night, when the ground was covered with snow, she quitted the castle at midnight, attended by four knights, who as well as herself were clothed in white, in order that they might pass unobserved through the lines of their enemies. The adventurous "Lady" made good her escape, and crossing the river unnoticed on the ice, found her way to Abingdon. The long anarchy was ended by the Treaty of Wallingford (1153), Stephen being recognised as king during his life, and the succession devolving upon Matilda's son Henry. A year had hardly passed from the signing of the treaty, when Stephen's death gave Henry the crown, and his coronation took place at Christmastide, 1154, at Westminster.

THE REIGN OF HENRY II.,

it has been truly said, "initiated the rule of law," as distinct from despotism, whether personal or tempered by routine, of the Norman kings. And now the despotic barons began gradually to be shorn of their power, and the dungeons of their "Adulterine" castles to be stripped of their horrors, and it seemed more appropriate to celebrate the season of glad tidings. King Henry the Second kept his first Christmas at Bermondsey with great solemnity, marking the occasion by passing his royal word to expel all foreigners from the kingdom, whereupon William of Ypres and his Flemings decamped without waiting for further notice. In 1158 Henry, celebrating the Christmas festival at Worcester, took the crown from his head and placed it upon the altar, after which he never wore it. But he did not cease to keep Christmas. In 1171 he went to Ireland, where the chiefs of the land displayed a wonderful alacrity in taking the oath of allegiance, and were rewarded by being entertained in a style that astonished them. Finding no place in Dublin large enough to contain his own followers, much less his guests, Henry had a house built in Irish fashion of twigs and wattles in the village of Hogges, and there held high revelry during Christmastide, teaching his new subjects to eat cranes' flesh, and take their part in miracle plays, masques, mummeries, and tournaments. And a great number of oxen were roasted, so that all the people might take part in the rejoicings.

CHRISTMAS ENTERTAINMENTS AT CONSTANTINOPLE.

In his description of Christian Constantinople, Benjamin of Tudela, a Spanish Jew, who travelled through the East in the twelfth century (1159 or 1160), describes a "place where the king diverts himself, called the hippodrome, near to the wall of the palace. There it is that every year, on the day of the birth of Jesus the Nazarene, the king gives a grand entertainment. There are represented by magic arts before the king and queen, figures of all kinds of men that exist in the world; thither also are taken lions, bears, tigers, and wild asses, which are made to fight together; as well as birds. There is no such sight to be seen in all the world." At Constantinople, on the marriage of the Emperor Manuel with Mary, daughter of the Prince of Antioch, on Christmas Day, 1161, there were great rejoicings, and similar spectacular entertainments to those described by Benjamin of Tudela.

AN ARCHBISHOP MURDERED AT CHRISTMASTIDE.

During the Christmas festival of 1170 (December 29th) occurred an event memorable in ecclesiastical history—the murder of Thomas Becket, Archbishop of Canterbury. In 1162 Becket (who had previously been Chancellor to Henry II.) was made Archbishop, in succession to Archbishop Theobald. The King soon found that he who had served him faithfully as Chancellor would oppose him doggedly as Archbishop. Henry determined to subject the Church as well as the State to the supremacy of the law; and Becket determined to resist the King to the end, thus manifesting his desire for martyrdom in the cause of the Church. Henry had greatly offended the Archbishop by causing his eldest son to be crowned by the Archbishop of York. For this violation of the rights of Canterbury Becket threatened to lay the country under an interdict, which he had the power from the Pope to pronounce. A sort of reconciliation was effected between the King and the Archbishop at Freteval on July 21, 1170, but a further dispute arose on Becket delaying his return to England, the King being anxious to get him out of France. The Archbishop was full of complaints against Henry for the injuries he had done to his see, and the King stood upon his dignity, regardless of the threatened interdiction. The Archbishop returned to England on the 1st of December, and was joyfully received by the people. His enemies, however, and especially the family of De Broc, did all they could to annoy him; and on Christmas Day he uttered a violent anathema against them. He preached from the text, "I come to die among you," evidently anticipating what might be the personal consequences of his action. He told his congregation that one of the archbishops had been a martyr, and they would probably soon see another; but before he departed home he would avenge some of the wrongs the Church had suffered during the previous seven years. Then he thundered forth his sentence of excommunication against Ranulph and Robert de Broc, and Nigellus, rector of Harrow. Meanwhile news had reached the King that Becket had excommunicated certain bishops who had taken part in his son's coronation. In a fit of exasperation the King uttered some hasty words of anger against the Archbishop. Acting upon these, four of Henry's knights—Hugh de Morville, Reginald FitzUrse, William de Tracy, and Richard Brito—crossed to England, taking with them Ranulf de Broc and a band of men, and murdered the Archbishop in Canterbury Cathedral. In the altercation which took place before the consummation of the terrible deed, the Primate was asked to absolve the bishops whom he had excommunicated, but he refused in a defiant and insulting manner. "Then die," exclaimed FitzUrse, striking at Becket's head with his weapon; but the devoted cross-bearer warded off the blow with his own arm, which was badly cut, so that the Archbishop was but slightly injured. One of the attacking party then called out, "Fly, or thou diest!" The Archbishop, however, clasped his hands, and, with the blood streaming down his face, fervently exclaimed, "To God, to St. Mary, to the holy patrons of this Church, and to St. Denis I commend my soul and the Church's cause." He was then struck down by a second blow, and the third completed the tragedy; whereupon one of the murderers, putting his foot on the dead prelate's neck, cried, "Thus dies a traitor!" In 1173 the Archbishop was canonised, and his festival was appointed for the day of his martyrdom; and for three centuries after his death the shrine of St. Thomas at Canterbury was a favourite place of pilgrimage, so great was the impression that his martyrdom made on the minds of the English people. As early as the Easter of 1171 Becket's sepulchre was the scene of many miracles, if Matthew Paris, the historian, is to be believed. What must have been the credulity of the people in an age when an historian could gravely write, as Matthew Paris did in 1171? "In this year, about Easter, it pleased the Lord Jesus Christ to irradiate his glorious martyr Thomas Becket with many miracles, that it might appear to all the world he had obtained a victory suitable to his merits. None who approached his sepulchre in faith returned without a cure. For strength was restored to the lame, hearing to the deaf, sight to the blind, speech to the dumb, health to the lepers, and life to the dead. Nay, not only men and women, but even birds and beasts were raised from death to life."

Royal Christmases at Windsor.

Windsor Castle appears to have been the favourite residence of Henry II. When, in 1175, he had united with him his son Henry in his crown and prerogatives, the two kings held an assembly at Windsor, attended by the judges, deputies of counties and districts, and all the great officers of state. Henry also kept his ensuing Christmas with the magnificence and display peculiar to the times, and all the ancient sports and usages; in which the nobles and gentry of the surrounding country assisted with much splendour at the hunt and tourney, and bestowed lavish gifts on the spectators and the people. After the kingdom was parcelled out into four jurisdictions, another assembly was held at the castle, in 1179, by the two kings; and, in 1184, Henry for the last time celebrated his Christmas in the same hall of state: his son, who had shared the throne with him, being then dead.

For the festivals of this period the tables of princes, prelates, and great barons were plentifully supplied with many dishes of meat dressed in various ways. The Normans sent agents into different countries to collect the most rare dishes for their tables, by which means, says John of Salisbury, this island, which is naturally productive of plenty and variety of provisions, was overflowed with everything that could inflame a luxurious appetite. The same writer says he was present at an entertainment which lasted from three o'clock in the afternoon to midnight; at which delicacies were served up which had been brought from Constantinople, Babylon, Alexandria, Palestine, Tripoli, Syria, and Phœnicia. The sumptuous entertainments which the kings of England gave to their nobles and prelates at the festivals of Christmas, Easter, and Whitsuntide diffused a taste for profuse and expensive banqueting; for the wealthy barons, prelates, and gentry, in their own castles and mansions, imitated the splendour of the royal entertainments. Great men had some kinds of provisions at their tables which are not now to be found in Britain. When Henry II. entertained his own court, the great officers of his army, and all the kings and great men in Ireland, at the feast of Christmas, 1171, the Irish princes and chieftains were quite astonished at the profusion and variety of provisions which they beheld, and were with difficulty prevailed on by Henry to eat the flesh of cranes, a kind of food to which they had not been accustomed. Dellegrout, maupigyrum, karumpie, and other dishes were then used, the composition of which is now unknown, or doubtful. Persons of rank and wealth had variety of drinks, as well as meats; for, besides wines of various kinds, they had pigment, morat, mead, hypocras, claret, cider, perry, and ale. The claret of those times was wine clarified and mixed with spices, and hypocras was wine mixed with honey.

A COOK OF THE PERIOD.

The profusion of viands and drinks, obtained at great expense from different parts of the world for the gratification of the animal appetites at such festivals as have been described, naturally led to

EXCESSES IN EATING AND DRINKING,

and from the statements and illustrations in old manuscripts it would appear that "the merry monks" were prominent in gastronomical circles. And extant records also state that the abbots of some of the monasteries found it necessary to make regulations restraining the monks, and to these regulations the monks objected. Consequently the monks of St. Swithin at Winchester made a formal complaint to Henry II. against their abbot for taking away three of the thirteen dishes they used to have at dinner. The monks of Canterbury were still more luxurious, for they had at least seventeen dishes every day besides a dessert; and these dishes were dressed with spices and sauces which excited the appetite as well as pleased the taste. And of course the festive season of Christmas was an occasion of special indulgence. Sometimes serious excesses were followed by severe discipline, administered after the manner shown in the ancient illustration which is reproduced here.

But these excesses were by no means confined to the monks. The Norman barons and gentry adopted many of the manners of the English among whom they lived, and especially was this the case in regard to the drinking customs of Christmastide. Instead of commending the Normans of his time for their sobriety, as he might have done their ancestors, Peter of Blois, who was chaplain to Henry II., says: "When you behold our barons and knights going upon a military expedition you see their baggage horses loaded, not with iron but wine, not with lances but cheeses, not with swords but bottles, not with spears but spits. You would imagine they were going to prepare a great feast rather than to make war. There are even too many who boast of their excessive drunkenness and gluttony, and labour to acquire fame by swallowing great quantities of meat and drink." The earliest existing carol known to antiquaries is in the Anglo-Norman language, and contains references to the drinking customs of the period:—

> "To English ale, and Gascon wine,
> And French, doth Christmas much incline—
>   And Anjou's too;
> He makes his neighbour freely drink,
> So that in sleep his head doth sink
>   Often by day.
> May joys flow from God above
> To all those who Christmas love.

Lords, by Christmas and the host
Of this mansion hear my toast—
    Drink it well—
Each must drain his cup of wine,
And I the first will toss off mine:
    Thus I advise,
Here then I bid you all Wassail,
Cursed be he who will not say Drinkhail."[17]

WASSAILING AT CHRISTMASTIDE.

Proceeding with our historical narrative we come now to
THE ROMANTIC REIGN OF RICHARD THE FIRST,

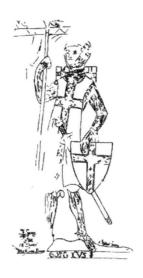

surnamed Cœur de Lion, the second son of Henry II. and Eleanor of Aquitaine, who succeeded to the English throne on the death of his father in 1189. Richard is generally supposed to have derived his surname from a superiority of animal courage; but, if the metrical romance bearing his name, and written in the thirteenth century, be entitled to credit, he earned it nobly and literally, by plucking out the heart of a lion, to whose fury he had been exposed by the Duke of Austria for having slain his son with a blow of his fist. In the numerous descriptions afforded by the romance Richard is a most imposing personage. He is said to have carried with him to the Crusades, and to have afterwards presented to Tancred, King of Sicily, the wonder-working sword of King Arthur—

> "The gude sword that
> Arthur luffed so well."

He is also said to have carried a shaft, or lance, 14 feet in length, and

> "An axe for the nones,
> To break therewith the Sarasyns bones.

> The head was wrought right wele,
> Therein was twenty pounds of steel."

But, without attempting to follow Richard through all the brilliant episodes of his romantic career, there can be no doubt that he was a king of great strength and courage, and that his valorous deeds won the admiration of poets and chroniclers, who have surrounded him with a splendid halo of romance. Contemporary writers tell us that while Richard kept magnificent Christmases abroad with the King of Sicily and other potentates, his justiciars (especially the extravagant William Longchamp, Bishop of Ely) were no less lavish in their expenditure for festive entertainments at home. And the old romance of "Richard Cœur de Lion" assures us that—

> "Christmas is a time full honest;
> Kyng Richard it honoured with gret feste.
> All his clerks and barouns
> Were set in their pavylouns,
> And seryed with grete plenté
> Of mete and drink and each dainté."

There is no doubt that the Crusades had a vast influence upon our literary tastes, as well as upon the national manners and the festivities of Christmastide. On their return from the Holy Land the pilgrims and Crusaders brought with them new subjects for theatrical representation, founded on the objects of their devotion and the incidents in their wars, and these found expression in the early mysteries and other plays of Christmastide—that of St. George and the Dragon, which survived to modern times, probably owing its origin to this period. It is to Richard Cœur de Lion that we are indebted for the rise of chivalry in England. It was he who developed tilts and tournaments, and under his auspices these diversions assumed a military air, the genius of poetry flourished, and the fair sex was exalted in admiration. How delightful was it then, beneath the inspiring gaze of the fair—

> "Sternly to strike the quintin down;
> Or fiercely storm some turf-formed town;

To rush with valour's doughty sway,
Against a Babylon of clay;
A Memphis shake with furious shock,
Or raze some flower-built Antioch!"[18]

On the death of Richard, in 1199, his brother

The youngest and favourite son of Henry II., John, was humoured in childhood and grew to be an arrogant and petulant man, and was one of the worst of English kings. He possessed ability, but not discipline. He could neither govern himself nor his kingdom. He was tyrannical and passionate, and spent a good deal of time in the gratification of his animal appetites. He was fond of display and good living, and extravagant in his Christmas entertainments. When, in 1201, he kept Christmas at Guildford he taxed his purse and ingenuity in providing all his servitors with costly apparel, and he was greatly annoyed because the Archbishop of Canterbury, in a similar fit of sumptuary extravagance, sought to outdo his sovereign. John, however, cunningly concealed his displeasure at the time, but punished the prelate by a costly celebration of the next Easter festival at Canterbury at the Archbishop's expense. In consequence of John's frequent quarrels with his nobles the attendance at his Christmas feasts became smaller every year, until he could only muster a very meagre company around his festive board, and it was said that he had almost as many enemies as there were nobles in the kingdom.

In 1205 John spent his Christmas at the ancient town of Brill, in the Vale of Aylesbury, and in 1213 he kept a Royal Christmas in the great hall at Westminster.

MAGNA CHARTA DEMANDED AT A CHRISTMAS FESTIVAL.

The Christmas of 1214 is memorable in English history as the festival at which the barons demanded from King John that document which as the foundation of our English liberties is known to us by the name of *Magna Charta*, that is, the Great Charter. John's tyranny and lawlessness had become intolerable, and the people's hope hung on the fortunes of the French campaign in which he was then engaged. His defeat at the battle of Bouvines, fought on July 27, 1214, gave strength to his opponents; and after his return to England the barons secretly met at St. Edmundsbury and swore to demand from him, if needful by force of arms, the restoration of their liberties by charter under the king's seal. Having agreed to assemble at the Court for this purpose during the approaching festival of Christmas they separated. When Christmas Day arrived John was at Worcester, attended only by a few of his immediate retainers and some foreign mercenaries. None of his great vassals came, as was customary at Christmas, to offer their congratulations. His attendants tried in vain to assume an appearance of cheerfulness and festivity; but John, alarmed at the absence of the barons, hastily rode to London and there shut himself up in the house of the Knights Templars. On the Feast of the Epiphany the barons assembled in great force at London and presenting themselves in arms before the King formally demanded his confirmation of the laws of Edward the Confessor and Henry I. At first John assumed a bold and defiant air and met the barons with an absolute refusal and threats; but, finding the nobles were firm, he sank to the meanness of subterfuge, and pleaded the necessity of time for the consideration of demands so weighty. With some reluctance the barons granted the delay, and ultimately, in 1215, the tyrant bowed to the inevitable, called the barons to a conference at Runnymede, and there signed the Great Charter, whose most important clauses protect the personal liberty and property of every freeman in the kingdom by giving security from arbitrary imprisonment and unjust exactions.

16   "Short History of the Norman Conquest."
17   Wassail and Drinkhail are both derived from the Anglo-Saxon. They were the
      common drinking pledges of the age. Wassail is equivalent to the phrase, "Your
      health," of the present day. Drinkhail, which literally signifies "drink health," was
      the usual acknowledgment of the other pledge. The carol from which the verses
      are quoted was evidently sung by the wandering minstrels who visited the castles
      of the Norman nobility at the festive season of Christmas.
18   Grattan.

CHAPTER V.

CHRISTMAS, FROM MAGNA CHARTA TO THE END OF THE WARS OF THE ROSES.

(1215-1485.)

Soon after the disaster which overtook John's army at the Wash the King ended his wretched career by death. He died on October 18, 1216, in the castle of Newark on the Trent, and the old chroniclers describe him as dying in an extremity of agony and remorse.

Henry the Third,

sometimes called "Henry of Winchester," came to the throne in troublous times, before he was ten years of age. The tyranny of his father had alienated every class of his subjects, and the barons who had obtained Magna Charta from King John had called in Louis of France. But through the conciliatory measures of the Regent Pembroke towards the barons, and the strong support which the Roman Church gave the boy-king (whose father had meanly done homage to the Pope), the foreigners were expelled, and the opposition of the barons was suppressed for a time, though in later years they again struggled with the crown for supremacy of power. When Henry had grown to manhood and the responsibility of government rested upon his own shoulders, he still exulted in the protection of the Holy See, which found in him a subservient vassal. He fasted during Lent, but feasted right royally both at

Christmas and Easter. In 1234 he kept a grand Christmas in the Great Hall at Westminster, and other royal Christmases were celebrated at Windsor Castle and at his palace at Winchester. He made large additions to Windsor Castle, and some of his mandates giving minute directions for the decoration of his palace at Winchester are still preserved. He enjoyed the old plays and ballets of Christmastide introduced from France at this period.

Henry the Third's most splendid Christmas was in the twentieth year of his reign, when he welcomed Eleanor, daughter of the Count of Provence, to whom he was married on January 14, 1236. The youthful princess left Provence amidst the rejoicings

ROYAL PARTY DINING IN STATE.

of the whole kingdom. She was accompanied by Henry's ambassadors and a grand cavalcade, in which were more than three hundred ladies on horseback. Her route lay through Navarre and France. On reaching England, at Dover, the princess and her train proceeded to Canterbury, where Henry awaited their coming. It was in that ancient city that the royal pair were married by the Archbishop Edmund and the prelates who accompanied Eleanor. From Canterbury the newly-wedded king and queen set out for London, attended by a splendid array of nobles, prelates, knights and ladies. On the 20th of January, Eleanor was crowned at Westminster with great splendour. Matthew Paris, the historian, gives an interesting description of the royal procession, and the loyal welcome of the citizens of London: "There had assembled together so great a number of the nobility of both sexes, so great a number of religious orders, so great a concourse of the populace, and so great a variety of players, that London could scarcely contain them in her capacious bosom. Therefore was the city adorned with silk hangings, and with banners, crowns, palls, tapers, and lamps, and with certain marvellous ingenuities and devices; all the streets being cleaned from dirt, mud, sticks and everything offensive. The citizens of London going to meet the king and queen, ornamented and trapped and wondrously sported their swift horses; and on the same day they went from the City to Westminster, that they might discharge the service of butler to the king in his coronation, which is acknowledged to belong to them of ancient right. They went in well-marshalled array, adorned in silken vestments, wrapped in gold-woven mantles, with fancifully-devised garments, sitting on valuable horses refulgent with new bits and saddles: and they bore three hundred and sixty gold and silver cups, the king's trumpeters going before and sounding their trumpets; so that so wonderful a novelty produced a laudable astonishment in the spectators." The literary monk of St. Albans also describes the splendour of the feast, and the order of the service of the different vassals of the crown, many of whom were called upon at the coronation to perform certain peculiar services. According to the ancient City records, "these served in order in that most elegant and unheard-of feast: the Bishop of Chichester, the Chancellor, with the cup of precious stones, which was one of the ancient regalia of the king, clothed in his pontificals, preceded the king, who was clad in royal attire, and wearing the crown. Hugh de Pateshall walked before with the patine, clothed in a dalmatica; and the Earls of Chester, Lincoln, and Warren, bearing the swords, preceded him. But the two renowned knights, Sir Richard Siward and Sir Nicholas de Molis, carried the two royal sceptres before the king; and the square purple cloth of silk, which was supported upon four silver lances, with four little bells of silver gilt, held over the king wherever he walked, was carried by the barons of the Cinque Ports; four being assigned to each lance, from the diversity of ports, that one port should not seem to be preferred before the other. The same in like manner bore a cloth of silk over the queen, walking behind the king, which said cloths they claimed to be theirs by right, and obtained them. And William de Beauchamp of Bedford, who had the office of almoner from times of old, found the striped cloth or *burel*, which was laid down under the king's feet as he went from the hall as far as the pulpit of the Church of Westminster; and that part of the cloth that was *within* the Church always fell to the sexton in whatever church the king was crowned; and all that was *without* the church was distributed among the poor, by the hands of William the almoner." The ancient records contain many other particulars respecting the ceremonies which graced the marriage feast of Henry and Eleanor of Provence, but enough has been quoted to show the magnificence of the celebration.

Year by year, as the Christmas festival came round, it was royally celebrated wherever the Court happened to be, even though the king had to pledge his plate and jewels with the citizens of London to replenish his exchequer. But Henry's Royal Christmases did not allay the growing disaffection of his subjects on account of his showing too much favour to foreigners; and some of the barons who attended the Royal Christmas at Westminster in 1241, left in high dudgeon, because the place of honour at the banquet was occupied by the papal legate, then about to leave England, "to the sorrow of no man but the king." In 1252, Henry gave in marriage his beautiful daughter Margaret, to Alexander, King of the Scots, and held his Christmas at the same time. The city of York was the scene of the regal festivities. The marriage took place on Christmas Day, the bridegroom and many of his nobles receiving knighthood at the hands of the English king. Henry seems to have conciliated the English barons for a time, for most of them were present at the marriage festivities, and he counted a thousand knights in his train; while Alexander brought sixty splendidly-attired Scottish knights with him. That the banqueting was on no mean scale is evident from the fact that six hundred fat oxen were slaughtered for the occasion, the gift of the Archbishop of York, who also subscribed four thousand marks (£2,700) towards the expenses. The consumption of meats and drinks at such feasts was enormous. An extant order of Henry's, addressed to his keeper of wines, directs him to deliver two tuns of white and one of red wine, to make garhiofilac and claret 'as usual,' for the king at Christmas; and upon another occasion the Sheriffs of Gloucestershire and

Sussex were called upon to supply part of the necessary provisions; the first named being directed to get twenty salmon, and make pies of them; while the latter was instructed to send ten peacocks, ten brawns with their heads, and other things. And all this provision was necessary, for while Henry feasted the rich, he did not forget the poor. When he kept his Christmas at Winchester in 1248, he ordered his treasurer to fill Westminster Hall with poor people, and feast them there for a week. Twenty years afterwards, he kept his Royal Christmas in London for fifteen days, opening a fair meantime at Westminster, and forbidding any shop to be opened in London as long as the festival lasted. This prohibition of business naturally displeased the citizens of London, but the king would not withdraw his prohibition until they agreed to make him a present of two thousand pounds, upon the receipt of which the prohibition was withdrawn.

We cannot pass over this period without reference to the summoning of

The First English Parliament,

which was a great event of Christmastide.

The Barons' Wars interfered seriously with the Christmas festivities, but they solved the problem of how to ensure the government of the realm in accordance with the provisions of the Great Charter. The King (Henry III.) had sworn again and again to observe the Charter, but his oath was no sooner taken than it was unscrupulously broken. The barons, with the patriotic Simon de Montfort at their head, were determined to uphold the rights of the people, and insisted on the king's compliance with the provisions of the Charter; and this struggle with the Crown yielded one of the greatest events of Christmastide: the summoning of the first national Parliament. By summoning the representatives of the cities and boroughs to sit beside the knights of the shires, the barons and the bishops in the Parliament of the realm, Simon de Montfort created a new force in English politics. This first national assembly met at Westminster, in January, 1265, while the king was a prisoner of Earl Simon. The form of national representation thus inaugurated had an immense influence on the rising liberties of the people, and has endured to our own times. It is not surprising, therefore, that the adoption of this measure by the great Earl of Leicester invested his memory with a lustre which has not been dimmed by the lapse of centuries. The paltering of the king called forth the patriotism of the people. "So may a glory from defect arise." The sevenfold lustre of the rainbow is only seen when there is rain as well as sun.

> "Only the prism's obstruction shows aright
> The secret of a sunbeam, breaks its light
> Into the jewelled bow from blankest white;
> So may a glory from defect arise."[19]

THE DEATH OF ROBIN HOOD ON CHRISTMAS EVE.

The famous freebooter, Robin Hood, who, according to tradition, flourished in Sherwood Forest in the distracted reign of Henry the Third, is said to have died on Christmas Eve, in the year 1247. The career of this hero of many popular ballads is not part of our subject, though Hone[20] records his death as a Christmas event; and Stowe, writing in 1590, evidently believes in Robin Hood as an historical personage, for he says, "he suffered no woman to be oppressed… poor men's goods he spared, abundantly relieving them with that which by theft he got from the abbeys, and the houses of rich old earles."

From the doubtful doings of the romantic chief and his band of freebooters, we now pass on to the

Edward the First was in the truest sense a national king. He was English to the core, and he won the love of his people by his bravery, justice, and good government. He joined freely in the national sports and pastimes, and kept the Christmas festival with great splendour. There was much of the chivalric in his character, and he shared to the full his people's love of hard fighting. He was invested with the honour of knighthood and went to foreign courts to display his prowess. Matthew of Westminster states that while Edward was travelling in France, he heard that a lord of Burgundy was continually committing outrages on the persons and property of his neighbours. In the true spirit of chivalry Edward attacked the castle of the uncourteous baron. His prowess asserted the cause of justice, and he bestowed the domains which he had won upon a nobler lord. For the sake of acquiring military fame he exposed himself to great dangers in the Holy Land, and, during his journey homeward, saved his life by sheer fighting in a tournament at Challon. At his "Round Table of Kenilworth" a hundred lords and ladies "clad all in silk" renewed the faded glories of Arthur's Court, and kept Christmas with great magnificence. In 1277, Llewellyn, Prince of Wales, bidden from his mountain fastnesses "with a kiss of peace," sat a guest at the Christmas feast of Edward, but he was soon to fall the last defender of his weeping country's independence in unequal battle with the English King. In 1281-2, Edward kept his feast of Christmas at Worcester, and there was "such a frost and snow as no man living could remember the like." Rivers were frozen over, even including the Thames and Severn; fish in ponds, and birds in woods died for want of food; and on the breaking up of the ice five of the arches of old London bridge were carried away by the stream, and the like happened to many other bridges.

In 1286 Edward kept his Christmas at Oxford, but the honour was accompanied by an unpleasant episode in the hanging of the Mayor by the King's command. In 1290, 1292, and 1303, Edward the First kept Royal Christmases in the great hall at Westminster. On his way to Scotland, in the year 1299, the King witnessed the Christmas ceremonial of the Boy Bishop. He permitted one of the boy bishops to say vespers before him in his chapel at Heton, near Newcastle-upon-Tyne, and made a present to the performers of forty shillings, no inconsiderable sum in those days. During his Scotch wars, in 1301, Edward, on the approach of winter, took up his quarters in Linlithgow, where he built a castle and kept his Christmas; and during his reign he celebrated the festival at other places not usually so honoured—namely, Bury, Ipswich, Bristol, Berwick, Carlisle, and Lincoln.

EDWARD THE SECOND

succeeded his father in 1307, being the fourth son of Edward I. and Eleanor of Castile. He took great delight in the Christmas revels and expended large sums of money in the entertainment of his court favourites. In 1311 he kept his Christmas at York, rejoicing in the presence of Piers Gaveston, whom he had recalled from banishment in utter disregard of advice given to him by his father (Edward I.) on his death-bed. Edward II. kept his Christmas in the great hall at Westminster in 1317, when, however, few nobles were present, "because of discord betwixt them and the King;" but in 1320 the Royal Christmas was kept at Westminster "with great honour and glorie." In 1324-5 the King's Christmas was sumptuously observed at Nottingham, but the following year found Edward a prisoner at Kenilworth, while his wife, who had successfully intrigued with Roger Mortimer, leader of the Barons, observed the Christmas festivities with her son at Wallingford, glad at the downfall of her husband. Edward was an irresolute and weak-minded king. He displayed singular incapacity for government, wasting almost all his time in frivolous amusements. The chief characteristics of his reign were defeat and disgrace abroad, and misrule ending in misery at home. Instead of following the example of his noble father, Edward I., who has been deservedly styled "the greatest of the Plantagenets," he proved himself the weakest of that line of kings, spending his time in such trifling diversions as "cross and pile," a game of chance with coins. He was so utterly devoid of self-respect that he even borrowed money of his barber to carry on this frivolous pastime, such items as the following being found in his wardrobe rolls:—"Item, paid to Henry, the king's barber, for money which he lent the king to play at cross and pile, five shillings. Item, paid to Pires Barnard, usher of the king's chamber, money which he lent the king, and which he lost at cross and pile; to Monsieur Robert Wattewille eightpence." At length the barons, tired of Edward's misgovernment, revolted, and made the king a prisoner. During the Christmas festival of 1326, Edward imprisoned in Kenilworth Castle. While there he was informed that in a Parliament held at Westminster, during Christmas 1326-7, he was deposed, and his son Edward, then only fourteen years of age, elected in his stead. On the 21st of September in the same year Edward II. ended his miserable career in Berkeley Castle, being, it is supposed, cruelly murdered by his keepers.

EDWARD THE THIRD'S CORONATION

festivities were a sumptuous enlargement of the Christmas celebration, which usually extended over Twelfth Night. It is said that the banqueting cost the equivalent of forty thousand pounds of our money; and before the young king there appeared quite a multitude of minstrels, mimics, and gleemen. Professor Henry Morley[21] gives a specimen of the metrical romances which were translated from the French for recitation at the royal and noble banquets of this period. They were "busy with action, and told with a lively freedom;" and, in the one quoted, "The Fabliau of Sir Cleges," we catch some interesting references to the celebration of Christmas:—

> "Every year Sir Cleges would
> At Christmás a great feast hold
>   In worship of that day,
> As royál in allé thing
> As he haddé been a king

For sooth as I you say.
Rich and poor in the country about
Should be there withouten doubt;
    There would no man say nay.
Minstrels would not be behind,
For there they might most mirthés find
    There would they be aye.

"Minstrels when the feast was done
Withouten giftés should not gon,
    And that both rich and good:
Horsé, robes and riché ring,
Gold, silver, and other thing,
    To mend with their mood.
Ten yearé such feast be held,
In the worship of Mary mild
    And for Him that died on the rood.
By that his good began to slake
For the great feasts that he did make.
    The knight gentil of blood."

"KEPE OPEN COURT" AT CHRISTMAS.

Froissart, in Cap. XIIII. of his "Chronicles,"[22] gives the
following account of the Christmas Celebration at which Edward
the Third was crowned:—

"After that the most part of the company of Heynaulte were
departed, and syr John Heynaulte lorde of Beamonde taryed, the
Quene gave leve to her people to departe, savynge a certayne noble
knightis the whiche she kept styl about her and her sône, to counsell
them, and commaunded all them that departed, to be at London
the next Christmas, for as than she was determyned to kepe open
court, and all they promysed her so to do. And whan Christmas
was come, she helde a great court. And thyther came dukes, erles,
barons, knightis, and all the nobles of the realme, with prelates, and
burgesses of good townes, and at this assemble it was advised that
the realme coud nat long endure without a head and a chief lord.
Than they put in wrytynge all the dedis of the kyng who was in
prison, and all that he had done by evyll counsell, and all his usages,

and evyll behavyngis, and how evyll he had governed his realme, the which was redde openly in playn audience, to thentent that the noble sagis of the realme might take therof good advyce, and to fall at acorde how the realme shuld be governed from thensforth; and whan all the cases and dedis that the kyng had done and côsented to, and all his behavyng and usages were red, and wel understand, the barons and knightis and al ye coûsels of the realme, drew them aparte to coûsell, and the most part of them accorded, and namely the great lordes and nobles, with the burgesses of ye good townes, accordyng as they had hard say, and knew themselfe the most parte of his dedis. Wherfore they côcluded that such a man was nat worthy to be a kyng. But they all accorded that Edward his eldeste son who was ther present, and was ryghtful heyre, shuld be crowned kyng in stede of his father, so that he would take good counsell, sage and true about hym, so that the realme from thensforth myght be better governed than it was before, and that the olde kyng his father shuld be well and honestly kept as long as he lyved accordyng to his astate; and thus as it was agreed by all the nobles, so it was accomplysshed, and than was crowned with a crowne royall at the palaice of Westminster, beside Lôdon, the yong kyng Edward the III. who in his dayes after was right fortunate and happy in armes. This coronacion was in the yere of our Lorde MCCCXXVI, on Christymas day, and as than the yong kyng was about the age of XVI., and they held the fest tyl the côvercion of saynt Paule followyng: and in the mean tyme greatly was fested sir John of Heynaulte and all the princis and nobles of his coûtre, and was gyven to hym, and to his company, many ryche jewels. And so he and his company in great feast and solas both with lordis and ladyes taried tyll the XII. day."

EDWARD BALLIOL, OF SCOTLAND, DEFEATED AT CHRISTMAS.

The Christmas of 1332 is memorable in Scottish annals as the time of the defeat of Edward Balliol, the "phantom king" of Scotland. His success was as unreal as a dream. He was solemnly crowned at Scone in the month of September, 1332, fondly imagining that he had permanently conquered the patriotic Scottish nobles who had opposed him. His reign, however, only lasted for a few months. The leaders of the national party suddenly assembled a force, and attacked him, while he was feasting at Annan, in Dumfriesshire, where he had gone to keep his Christmas. A body of horse under Sir Archibald, the young Earl of Moray, and Sir Simon Fraser, made a dash into the town to surprise Balliol, and he escaped only by springing upon a horse without any saddle, leaving behind him his brother Henry slain. Balliol escaped to England and was kindly received by Edward III., who afterwards made fresh expeditions into Scotland to support him. "Whenever the English king appeared the Scots retired to their mountain fastnesses, while Edward and his army overran the country with little opposition, burnt the houses, and laid waste the lands of those whom he styled rebels; but whenever he returned to England they came forth again, only the more embittered against the contemptible minion of the English king, the more determined against the tyranny of England. The regent, Sir Andrew Murray, pursued, with untiring activity, Balliol and his adherents. When Edward marched homeward to spend in London the Christmas of 1336, he left Scotland to all appearance prostrate, and flattered himself that it was completely subdued. Never was it further from such a condition. Only one spirit animated the Scottish nation—that of eternal resistance to the monarch who had inflicted on it such calamities, and set a slave on its throne."[23]

COTTAGE CHRISTMAS-KEEPING IN THE FOURTEENTH CENTURY.

At this period the greatest of the Bishops of Winchester, William of Wykeham, was a schoolboy. He was born of humble parents, educated at Winchester school, and afterwards became secretary to Uvedale, Lord of Wickham Manor, through whom he was introduced to King Edward III. In his interesting "Story of the Boyhood of William of Wykeham," the Rev. W. A. C. Chevalier thus pictures William's Christmas holidays:—

"Three days after William's arrival home was Christmas-eve. There were great preparations in the cottage for spending Christmas worthily, for if there was one thing more than another that John Longe believed in, it was the proper keeping of Christmas. It was a part of the worthy yeoman's faith. He was a humble and thorough believer in all the tenets of Christianity, he worshipped the Saviour and adored His Nativity, but his faith was a cheerful one, and he thought he best honoured his Master by enjoying the good gifts which He sent. Hence it was a part of his creed to be jovial at Christmas-tide. And so Dame Alice had been busy all that day, and a part of the day before, making Christmas pies, dressing Christmas meats, and otherwise making ready for the great festival. John Longe, too, had not been idle. He and his men had been working hard all day getting in huge Yule-logs for the great kitchen fire, whilst William and little Agnes had been employed in decorating the kitchen with evergreens and mistletoe, displaying in great profusion the red berries of the holly bushes. Everything was decked with evergreens, from the cups and platters on the shelves to the hams and bacon hanging from the ceiling."

At length the preparations were completed; then came the telling of tales and cheerful gossip round the blazing fire on Christmas Eve, and the roasting of chestnuts on the embers. "Christmas Day passed at the little homestead with all the social and religious honours that the honest yeoman could think of. The little household attended the service of Mass in the morning, and then, with clear consciences and simple hearts, spent the rest of the day in domestic and convivial enjoyment."

Returning to royalty, we next see illustrated Froissart's statement that "Edward the third was right fortunate and happy in armes."

EDWARD THE THIRD'S VICTORIES AND FESTIVITIES.

During the invasion of France, Edward III. raised the martial glory of England by his splendid victories at Crecy, Poictiers, and other places; and he kept Christmas right royally with his soldiers on French soil. After the battle of Crecy, at which the Prince of Wales gained the celebrated title of the Black Prince, Edward marched upon Calais, and laid siege to it; and at length he took the place. During Edward's absence, England was invaded by David II. of Scotland, who was defeated and taken prisoner by the army under Philippa, Edward's Queen. The brave Queen then joined King Edward on the French battle-ground, and they kept the Christmas of 1346 with much rejoicing.

During the Christmas festivities of this period the most noble Order of the Garter was instituted by King Edward III. to excite emulation amongst the aristocratic warriors of the time, in imitation of orders of a similar kind, both religious and military, which had been instituted by different monarchs of Europe; and that those who were admitted to the order were enjoined to exalt the religion of Christ is evident from some lines which Chaucer addressed to the Lords and Knights—

> "Do forth, do forth, continue your succour,
> Hold up Christ's banner, let it not fall."

And again—

> "Ye Lordis eke, shining in noble fame,
> To which appropered is the maintenance
> Of Christ 'is cause; in honour of his name,
> Shove on, and put his foes to utterance."

In imitation of King Arthur, Edward III. set up at Windsor a Round Table, which was consecrated with feasts and tournaments, and baptized with the blood of the brave. On New Year's Day, 1344, he issued his royal letters of protection for the safe-coming and return of foreign knights to the solemn jousts which he appointed to be held at Windsor on St. Hilary's Day, in extension of the Christmas festivities. The festival was opened with a splendid supper; and the next day, and until Lent, all kinds of knightly feats of arms were performed. "The queen and her ladies," says an old historian, "that they might with more convenience behold this spectacle, were orderly seated upon a firm ballustrade, or scaffold, with rails before it, running all round the lists. And certainly their extraordinary beauties, set so advantageously forth with excessive riches of apparel, did prove a sight as full of pleasant encouragement to the combatants, as the fierce hacklings of men and horses, gallantly armed, were a delightful terror to the feminine beholders."

LADIES LOOKING FROM THE HUSTINGS UPON THE TOURNAMENT.

In 1348 Edward III. kept a grand Christmas at Guildford. "Orders were given to manufacture for the Christmas sports eighty tunics of buckram of different colours, and a large number of masks—some with faces of women, some with beards, some like angel heads of silver. There were to be mantles embroidered with heads of dragons, tunics wrought with heads and wings of peacocks, and embroidered in many other fantastic ways. The celebration of Christmas lasted from All Hallow's Eve, the 31st of October, till the day after the Purification, the 3rd of February. At the court a lord of misrule was appointed, who reigned during the whole of this period, and was called 'the master of merry disports.' He ruled over and organised all the games and sports, and during the period of his rule there was nothing but a succession of masques, disguisings, and dances of all kinds. All the nobles, even the Mayor of London, had an officer of this kind chosen in their households. Dancing was a very favourite amusement. It was practised by the nobility of both sexes. The damsels of London spent their evenings in dancing before their masters' doors, and the country lasses danced upon the village green."[24]

THE LORD OF MISRULE.

A Royal Christmas was kept at Westminster, with great splendour, in 1358, when King Edward had two crowned guests at his feast; but these were present from no choice of their own: they were the victims to the fortune of war at Poictiers and Neville's Cross. And in 1362, King David of Scotland and the King of Cyprus met at King Edward's grand entertainments. The later years of his life were spent by this great warrior-king in partial retirement from public affairs, and under the influence of his mistress, Alice Perrers, while John of Gaunt took a leading part in the government of the state. In 1376 Edward the Black Prince died, and the same year King Edward III. kept his last Christmas at Westminster, the festival being made memorable by all the nobles of the realm attending to swear fealty to the son of the Black Prince, who, by the King's desire, took precedence of his uncles at the banquet as befitted the heir apparent to the crown. The King died on the 21st of June, 1377, having reigned for just over half a century.

The old chronicler, Stowe, refers to a

which he says occurred in 1362: "The King held his Christmas at Windsore, and the XV. day following a sore and vehement southwest winde brake forth, so hideous that it overthrew high houses, towers, steeples, and trees, and so bowed them, that the residue which fell not, but remained standing, were the weaker."

King Edward the Third's wardrobe accounts witness to the

COSTLY CHRISTMAS ROBES

that were worn at this period. And these accounts also show that Alice Perrers was associated with the King's daughter and granddaughter in the Christmas entertainments. There are items in 1376 stating that the King's daughter Isabella (styled Countess of Bedford), and her daughter (afterwards wife of Vere, Earl of Oxford), were provided with rich garments trimmed with ermine, in the fashion of the robes of the Garter, and with others of shaggy velvet, trimmed with the same fur, for the Christmas festival; while articles of apparel equally costly are registered as sent by the King to his chamber at Shene, to be given to Alice Perrers. And at a festival at Windsor the King caused twelve ladies (including his daughters and Alice Perrers) to be clothed in handsome hunting suits, with ornamented bows and arrows, to shoot at the King's deer; and a very attractive band of foresters they made. We have also seen that eighty costly tunics were provided for the Christmas sports and disguisings at Guildford.

We now come to a

COMICALLY CRUEL CHRISTMAS INCIDENT,

recorded by Sir John Froissart, and which he says gave "great joye" to the hilarious "knightes and squyers" who kept the festival with "the Erle of Foiz":—

"So it was on a Christmas day the Erle of Foiz helde a great feest, and a plentifull of knightes and squyers, as it is his usage; and it was a colde day, and the erle dyned in the hall, and with him great company of lordes; and after dyner he departed out of the hall, and went up into a galarye of xxiiii stayres of heyght, in which galarye ther was a great chymney, wherin they made fyre whan therle was ther; and at that tyme there was but a small fyre, for the erle loved no great fyre; howbeit, he hadde woode ynoughe there about, and in Bierne is wode ynoughe. The same daye it was a great frost and very colde: and when the erle was in the galarye, and saw the fyre so lytell, he sayde to the knightes and squiers about hym, Sirs, this is but a small fyre, and the day so colde: than Ernalton of Spayne went downe the stayres, and beneth in the courte he sawe a great meny of asses, laden with woode to serve the house: than he went and toke one of the grettest asses, with all the woode, and layde hym on his backe, and went up all the stayres into the galary, and dyde cast downe the asse with all the woode into the chymney, and the asses fete upward; wherof the erle of Foiz had great joye, and so hadde all they that were there, and had marveyle of his strength howe he alone came up all the stayres with the asse and the woode in his necke."

Passing on to

THE REIGN OF RICHARD THE SECOND,

the son of Edward the Black Prince and Joan of Kent, who came to the throne (in tutelage) on the death of his grandfather, Edward III. (1377), we find that costly banquetings, disguisings, pageants, and plays continued to be the diversions of Christmastide at court. From the rolls of the royal wardrobe, it appears that at the Christmas festival in 1391, the sages of the law were made subjects for disguisements, this entry being made: "Pro XXI *coifs* de tela linea pro hominibus de lege contrafactis pro Ludo regis tempore natalis Domini anno XII." That is, for twenty-one linen coifs for counterfeiting men of the law in the King's play at Christmas. And Strutt[25] says that in the same year (1391) the parish clerks of London put forth a play at Skinners' Wells, near Smithfield, which continued three days: the king, queen, and many of the nobility, being present at the performance.

MONETA NOVA ADRIANI STVLTORV PAPE.

[On one side is the legend, MONETA NOVA ADRIANI STVLTORV PAPE, the last E being in the field of the piece, on which is represented the Pope, with his double cross and tiara, with a fool in full costume approaching his bauble to the pontifical cross, and two persons behind, who form part of his escort. On the reverse is a "mother fool," with her bauble, attended by a grotesque person with a cardinal's hat, with the oft-recurring legend, STVLTORV INFINITVS EST NVMERVS.

But the miracle plays and mysteries performed by the Churchmen differed greatly from the secular plays and interludes which at this period "were acted by strolling companies of minstrels, jugglers, tumblers, dancers, bourdours, or jesters, and other performers properly qualified for the different parts of the entertainment, which admitted of a variety of exhibitions. These pastimes are of higher antiquity than the ecclesiastical plays; and they were much relished not only by the vulgar part of the people, but also by the nobility. The courts of the kings of England, and the castles of the great earls and barons, were crowded with the performers of the secular plays, where they were well received and handsomely rewarded; vast sums of money were lavishly bestowed upon these secular itinerants, which induced the monks and other ecclesiastics to turn actors themselves, in order to obtain a share of the public bounty. But to give the better colouring to their undertaking, they took the subjects of their dialogues from the holy writ, and performed them in the churches. The secular showmen, however, retained their popularity notwithstanding the exertions of their clerical rivals, who diligently endeavoured to bring them into disgrace, by bitterly inveighing against the filthiness and immorality of their exhibitions. On the other hand, the itinerant players sometimes invaded the province of the churchmen, and performed their mysteries, or others similar to them, as we find from a petition presented to Richard II. by the scholars of St. Paul's School, wherein complaint is made against the secular actors, because they took upon themselves to act plays composed from the Scripture history, to the great prejudice of the clergy, who had been at much expense to prepare such performances for public exhibition at the festival of Christmas."

A COURT FOOL.

In his Christmas feasts Richard the Second outdid his predecessors in prodigal hospitality. He delighted in the neighbourhood of Eltham, and spent much of his time in feasting with his favourites at the royal palace there. In 1386 (notwithstanding the still prevalent distress, which had continued from the time of the peasant revolt) Richard kept the Christmas festivities at Eltham with great extravagance, at the same time entertaining Leon, King of Armenia, in a manner utterly unjustified by the state of the royal exchequer, which had been replenished by illegal methods. And, on the completion of his enlargements and embellishments of Westminster Hall, Richard reopened it with "a most royal Christmas feast" of twenty-eight oxen and three hundred sheep, and game and fowls without number, feeding ten thousand guests for many days. Yet but a few years afterwards (such is the fickleness of fortune and the instability of human affairs) this same king, who had seen the "Merciless Parliament," who had robbed Hereford of his estates, who had been robed in cloth of gold and precious stones, and who had alienated his subjects by his own extravagance, was himself deposed and sentenced to lifelong banishment, his doom being pronounced in the very hall which he had reared to such magnificence for his own glory. Thus ingloriously Richard disappears from history, for nothing certain is known of the time, manner, or place of his death, though it is conjectured that he was speedily murdered. How history repeats itself! Richard's ignominious end recalls to mind the verse in which an English poet depicts the end of an Eastern king who was too fond of revelling:—

> "That night they slew him on his father's throne,
> The deed unnoticed and the hand unknown:
> Crownless and sceptreless Belshazzar lay,
> A robe of purple round a form of clay!"

GRAND CHRISTMAS TOURNAMENT.

An example of the tournaments which were favourite diversions of kings and nobles at this period is found in that held at Christmastide in London in 1389. Richard II., his three uncles, and the greater barons having heard of a famous tournament at

Paris at the entry of Isabel, Queen of France, resolved to hold one of equal splendour at London, in which sixty English knights, conducted to the scene of action by sixty ladies, should challenge all foreign knights. They therefore sent heralds into all parts of England, Scotland, Germany, Italy, Flanders, Brabant, Hainault, and France to proclaim the time, place, and other circumstances of the proposed gathering, and to invite all valorous knights and squires to honour it with their presence. This, says the historian, excited a strong desire in the knights and squires of all these countries to attend to see the manners and equipages of the English, and others to tourney. The lists were prepared in Smithfield, and chambers erected around them for the accommodation of the king, queen, princes, lords, ladies, heralds, and other spectators. As the time approached many important personages of both sexes, attended by numerous retinues, arrived in London. On the first day of the tournament (Sunday) sixty-five horses, richly furnished for the jousts, issued one by one from the Tower, each conducted by a squire of honour, and proceeded in a slow pace through the streets of London to Smithfield, attended by a numerous band of trumpeters and other minstrels. Immediately after, sixty young ladies, elegantly attired and riding on palfreys, issued from the same place, and each lady leading a knight completely armed by a silver chain, they proceeded slowly to the field. When they arrived there the ladies were lifted from the palfreys and conducted to the chambers provided for them; the knights mounted their horses and began the jousts, in which they exhibited such feats of valour and dexterity as won the admiration of the spectators. When the approach of night put an end to the jousts the company repaired to the palace of the Bishop of London, in St. Paul's Street, where the king and queen then staying, the supper was prepared. The ladies, knights, and heralds who had been appointed judges awarded one of the prizes, a crown of gold, to the Earl of St. Paul as the best performer among the foreign knights, and the other, a rich girdle adorned with gold and precious stones, to the Earl of Huntingdon as the best performer of the English. After a sumptuous supper the ladies and knights spent the remainder of the night in dancing. The tournaments were continued in a similar manner on Monday, Tuesday, Wednesday, Thursday, and Friday, and on Saturday the Court, with all the company, removed to Windsor, where the jousts, feasting, and other diversions were renewed, and lasted several days longer. Subsequently the king presented the foreign ladies, lords, and knights with valuable gifts, and they returned to their own countries highly pleased with the entertainment which they had enjoyed in England.

King Henry the Fourth

was born at Bolingbroke, in Lincolnshire, being the eldest son of John of Gaunt and of his first wife, the heiress of the house of Lancaster, and a grandson of Edward III. On the death of John of Gaunt in 1399, Richard II. seized his lands, having in the previous year banished Henry of Bolingbroke. On Henry hearing what had occurred, knowing his own popularity and Richard's unpopularity, Henry returned from banishment, and succeeded in an attack on Richard, whom he made a prisoner. Then summoning a Parliament, at which Richard was formally deposed and himself made king, Henry came to the throne with the title of Henry IV. Soon, however, he found himself menaced by danger. Some of the lords who had been stripped of the honours and wealth heaped upon them by Richard entered into a conspiracy to assassinate Henry the usurper. During the Christmas holidays they met frequently at the lodgings of the Abbot of Westminster to plan the king's destruction. After much deliberation they agreed to hold a splendid tournament at Oxford on the 3rd of January, 1400. Henry was to be invited to preside, and while intent on the spectacle a number of picked men were to kill him and his sons. The king was keeping his Christmas at Windsor, whither the Earl of Huntingdon presented himself and gave him the invitation. Henry accepted it, but on the 2nd of January, the day previous to the tournament, the Earl of Rutland, who was privy to the plot, went secretly to Windsor and informed the king of the arrangements which had been made for his assassination. The same evening, after dusk, the king proceeded to London; and the next day when the conspirators assembled at Oxford they were surprised to find that neither the king nor their own accomplice, Rutland, had arrived. Suspecting treachery they resolved to proceed at once to Windsor and surprise Henry, but arrived only to find that he had escaped. They afterwards raised the standard of revolt, but their insurrection proved abortive, and the fate of the leaders was summary and sanguinary.

The favourite palace of Henry the Fourth was at Eltham, where, in the second year of his reign, he kept a grand Christmas, and entertained the Emperor of Constantinople. At this festival the men of London made a "gret mummyng to him of XII. Aldermen and theire sones, for which they had gret thanke." Similar festivities were observed at several subsequent festivals; then the king's health gave way, and he passed the last Christmas of his life in seclusion at Eltham, suffering from fits of epilepsy, and lying frequently for hours in an unconscious state. After Candlemas he was so much better as to be able to return to his palace at Westminster, but he died there on the 20th of March the same year (1413). The final scene and the parting words of the king to his son, who became Henry V., have been beautifully depicted by Shakespeare.

King Henry the Fifth.

In connection with the Christmas festival in 1414 a conspiracy to murder the king is alleged against the Lollards, but the charge has never been satisfactorily proved. "If we are to believe the chroniclers of the times the Lollards resolved to anticipate their enemies, to take up arms and to repel force by force. Seeing clearly that war to the death was determined against them by the Church, and that the king had yielded at least a tacit consent to this iniquitous policy, they came to the conclusion to kill not only the bishops, but the king and all his kin. So atrocious a conspiracy is not readily to be credited against men who contended for a greater purity of gospel truth, nor against men of the practical and military knowledge of Lord Cobham. But over the whole of these transactions there hangs a veil of impenetrable mystery, and we can only say that the Lollards are charged with endeavouring to surprise the king and his brother at Eltham, as they were keeping their Christmas festivities there, and that this attempt failed through the Court receiving intimation of the design and suddenly removing to Westminster."[26] Lord Cobham was put to death by cruel torture in St. Giles's Fields, London, on Christmas Day, 1418.

In the early part of his reign Henry invaded France and achieved a series of brilliant successes, including the famous victory at Agincourt. The hero of this great battle did not allow the holiday season to interfere with his military operations; but he did generously suspend proceedings against Rouen upon Christmas Day and supply his hungry foes with food for that day only, so that they might keep the feast of Christmas. After his military successes in France Henry married the Princess Katherine, the youngest daughter of Charles VI., King of France, and the king and queen spent their first Christmas of wedded life at Paris, the festival being celebrated by a series of magnificent entertainments. Henry's subsequent journey to England was "like the ovation of an ancient conqueror." He and his queen were received with great festivity at the different towns on their way, and on the 1st of February they left Calais, and landed at Dover, where, according to Monstrelet, "Katherine was received as if she had been an angel of God." All classes united to make the reception of the hero of Agincourt and his beautiful bride a most magnificent one. They proceeded first to Eltham, and thence, after due rest, to London, where Katherine was crowned with great rejoicing on the 24th of February, 1421. Henry's brilliant career was cut short by his death on the last day of August, 1422.

> "Small time, but, in that small, most greatly liv'd
>   This star of England: fortune made his sword;
> By which the world's best garden he achiev'd,
>   And of it left his son imperial lord."[27]

Fabian's account of the stately feast at the coronation of Henry the Fifth's newly-wedded consort is an interesting picture of the

COURT LIFE AND CHRISTMAS FESTIVITIES OF THE PERIOD.

Queen Katherine was conveyed to the great hall at Westminster and there set to dinner. Upon her right hand, at the end of the table, sat the Archbishop of Canterbury, and Henry, surnamed the rich Cardinal of Winchester; and upon her left hand the King of Scotland in his royal robes; near the end sat the Duchess of York and the Countess of Huntingdon. The Earl of March, holding a sceptre, knelt upon her right side, and the Earl-Marshal upon her left; his Countess sat at the Queen's left foot under the table, and the Countess of Kent at her right foot. Humphrey, Duke of Gloucester, was overlooker, and stood before the Queen bareheaded; Sir Richard Nevill was carver, the Earl of Suffolk's brother cupbearer, Sir John Steward server, Lord Clifford panterer, Lord Willoughby butler, Lord Grey de Ruthyn naperer, the Lord Audley almoner, and the Earl of Worcester, Earl-Marshal, rode about the hall during dinner on a charger, with a number of constables to keep order.

The bill of fare consisted of: *First course*—Brawn and mustard, dedells in burneaux, frument with balien, pike in erbage (pike stuffed with herbs), lamprey powdered, trout, codling, fried plaice and marling, crabs, leche lumbard flourished, and tarts. Then came a subtlety representing a pelican sitting on her nest with her young and an image of St. Katherine bearing a book and disputing with the doctors, bearing a reason (motto) in her right hand, saying, in the French apparently of Stratford-at-the-Bow, "Madame le Royne," and the pelican as an answer—

> "Ce est la signe
> Et lu Roy Pur tenir ioy
> Et a tout sa gent,
> Elle mete sa entent."

Second course—Jelly coloured with columbine flowers, white potage, or cream of almonds, bream of the sea, conger, soles, cheven, barbel with roach, fresh salmon, halibut, gurnets, broiled roach, fried smelt, crayfish or lobster, leche damask with the king's word or proverb flourished "*une sanz plus.*" Lamprey fresh baked, flampeyn flourished with an escutcheon royal, therein three crowns of gold, planted with flowers de luce, and flowers of camomile wrought of confections. Then a subtlety representing a panther with an image of St. Katherine having a wheel in one hand and a roll with a reason in the other, saying—

> "La royne ma file,
> In ceste ile,
> Par bon reson
> Alues renoun."

Third course—Dates in composite, cream mottled, carp, turbot, tench, perch, fresh sturgeon with whelks, porpoise roasted, memis fried, crayfish, prawns, eels roasted with lamprey, a leche called the white leche flourished with hawthorn leaves and red haws, and a march pane, garnished with figures of angels, having among them an image of St. Katherine holding this reason—

> "Il est ecrit,
> Pour voir et dit
> Per mariage pur
> C'est guerre ne dure."

And lastly, a subtlety representing a tiger looking into a mirror, and a man sitting on horseback fully armed, holding in his arms a tiger's whelp, with this reason, "Par force sanz reson il ay pryse ceste beste," and with his one hand making a countenance of throwing mirrors at the great tiger, the which held this reason—

> "Gile de mirror,
> Ma fete distour."

MARBLE PANEL FLORENTINE 1420, S.KENSINGTON MUSEUM.

became king in 1422, before he was nine months old, and although the regency of the two kingdoms to which he was heir had been arranged by Henry V. before his death, the reign of the third king of the House of Lancaster saw the undoing of much that had been accomplished in the reigns of his father and grandfather. It was during the reign of Henry VI. that Joan of Arc came forward alleging her Divine commission to rescue France from the English invader. But it is not part of our subject to describe her heroic career. The troublous times which made the French heroine a name in history were unfavourable to Christmas festivities. The Royal Christmases of Henry the Sixth were less costly than those of his immediate predecessors. But as soon as he was old enough to do so he observed the festival, as did also his soldiers, even in time of war. Mills[28] mentions that, "during the memorable siege of Orleans [1428-9 , at the request of the English the festivities of Christmas suspended the horrors of war, and the nativity of the Saviour was commemorated to the sound of martial music. Talbot, Suffolk, and other ornaments of English chivalry made presents of fruits to the accomplished Dunois, who vied with their courtesy by presenting to Suffolk some black plush he wished for as a lining for his dress in the then winter season. The high-spirited knights of one side challenged the prowest knights of the other, as their predecessors in chivalry had done. It is observable, however, that these jousts were not held in honour of the ladies, but the challenge always declared that if there were in the other host a knight so generous and loving of his country as to be willing to combat in her defence, he was invited to present himself."

HENRY IV.'S CRADLE.

In 1433 Henry kept his Christmas at Bury, and in 1436 at Kenilworth Castle. Nothing remarkable, however, is recorded respecting these festivities. But some interesting particulars have been preserved of a

Christmas Play Performed in 1445

at Middleton Tower, Norfolk, the family seat of Lord Scales, one of the early owners of Sandringham, which is now a residence of the Prince of Wales. Mrs. Herbert Jones[29] says:—

"One winter, when he was about forty-six years old, in a quiet interval soon after Henry the Sixth's marriage to Margaret of Anjou, Lord Scales and his wife were living at Middleton. In a south-east direction lay the higher ground where rose the Blackborough Priory of nuns, founded by a previous Lady Scales; west of them, at three miles' distance, bristling with the architecture of the Middle Ages in all its bloom and beauty, before religious disunion had defaced it, prosperous in its self-government, stood the town of Lynn.

"The mayor and council had organised a play to be acted on Christmas Day, 1445, before the Lord Scales at Middleton, representing scenes from the Nativity of our Lord. Large sums were paid by order of the mayor for the requisite dresses, ornaments, and scenery, some of which were supplied by the 'Nathan' of Lynn, and others prepared and bought expressly. 'John Clerk' performed the angel Gabriel, and a lady of the name of Gilbert the Virgin Mary. Their parts were to be sung. Four other performers were also paid for their services, and the whole party, headed by the mayor, set off with their paraphernalia in a cart, harnessed to four or more horses, for Middleton on Christmas morning. The breakfast of the carters was paid for at the inn by the town, but the magnates from Lynn and the actors were entertained at the castle.[30]

"It was in the courtyard that this quaint representation took place; the musical dialogues, the songs and hymns, the profusion of ornaments, personal and otherwise, recorded as pressed on to the stage, the grotesque angel and virgin, must have furnished a lively hour under the castle walls on that long-ago Christmas Day."

During the destructive wars of York and Lancaster the festivities of Christmas were frequently interrupted by hostilities, for some of the most bloody encounters (as, for example, the terrible battle of Wakefield) occurred at Christmastide. The wars of the contending factions continued throughout the reign of Henry VI., whose personal weakness left the House of Lancaster at the mercy of the Parliament, in which the voice of the Barons was paramount. That the country was in a state of shameful misgovernment was shown by the attitude of the commercial class and the insurrection under John Cade; yet Henry could find time for amusement. "Under pretence of change of air the court removed to Coventry that the king might enjoy the sports of the field."[31]

The Christmases of Henry were not kept with the splendour which characterised those of his rival and successor, Edward IV. Henry's habits were religious, and his house expenses parsimonious—sometimes necessarily so, for he was short of money. From the introduction to the "Paston Letters" (edited by Mr. James Gairdner) it appears that the king was in such impecunious circumstances in 1451 that he had to borrow his expenses for Christmas: "The government was getting paralysed alike by debt and by indecision. 'As for tidings here,' writes John Bocking, 'I certify you all that is nought, or will be nought. The king borroweth his expenses.'" Henry anticipated what Ben Jonson discovered in a later age, that—

> "Christmas is near;
> And neither good cheer,
> Mirth, fooling, nor wit,
> Nor any least fit
> Of gambol or sport
> Will come at the
> Court, If there be no money."

And so rather than leave Christmas unobserved the poor king "borrowed his expenses." Subsequently Henry's health failed, and then later comes the record: "At Christmas [1454, to the great joy of the nation, the king began to recover from his painful illness. He woke up, as it were, from a long sleep. So decidedly had he regained his faculties that on St. John's Day (27th December) he commanded his almoner to ride to Canterbury with an offering, and his secretary to present another at the shrine of St. Edward."[32]

The terrible battle of Wakefield at Christmastide, 1460, was one of the most important victories won by the Lancastrians during the Wars of the Roses. The king, Henry VI., had secretly encouraged Richard, Duke of York, that the nation would soon be ready to assent to the restoration of the legitimate branch of the royal family. Richard was the son of Anne Mortimer, who was descended from Philippa, the only daughter of the Duke of Clarence, second son of Edward III.; and consequently he stood in the order of succession before the king actually on the throne, who was descended from John of Gaunt, a younger son of Edward III. The Duke of York at length openly advanced his title as the true heir to the crown, and urged Parliament to confer it upon him. As, however, the Lancastrian branch of the royal family had enjoyed the crown for three generations it was resolved that Henry VI. should continue to reign during his life and that Richard should succeed him. This compromise greatly displeased the queen, Margaret, who was indignant at the injury it inflicted on her son. She therefore urged the nobles who had hitherto supported her husband to take up arms on behalf of his son. Accordingly the Earl of Northumberland, with Lords Dacre, Clifford, and Nevil, assembled an army at York, and were soon joined by the Duke of Somerset and the Earl of Devon. "Parliament being prorogued in December, the Duke of York and the Earl of Salisbury hastened from London with a large armed force towards York, but coming unexpectedly upon the troops of the Duke of Somerset at Worksop, their vanguard was destroyed. On the 21st of December, however, they reached Sandal Castle with six thousand men, and kept their Christmas there, notwithstanding that the enemy under the Duke of Somerset and the Earl of Northumberland were close by at Pontefract" (*William Wyrcester*). On the 30th of December the opposing forces met at Wakefield, and in the terrible battle which ensued Richard, Duke of York was slain, his son, Lord Rutland, was murdered by Lord Clifford while escaping from the battlefield, and the Earl of Salisbury and others were taken as prisoners to Pontefract, where they were beheaded.

Edward, son of Richard Duke of York, was afterwards joined by his cousin, Richard, Earl of Warwick, the famous "kingmaker." They hastened northwards and met the Lancastrians at Towton, where a decisive battle was fought, and won by the Yorkists. Edward was then recognised by Parliament and proclaimed king as Edward IV., and Henry VI. was attainted of high treason.

called his first Parliament at Westminster, and concluded the session by the unusual but popular measure of a speech from the throne to the Commons delivered by himself. It was during this session that the statute was passed prohibiting the great and rich from giving or wearing any liveries or signs of companionship, except while serving under the king; from receiving or maintaining plunderers, robbers, malefactors, or unlawful hunters; and from allowing dice and cards in their houses beyond the twelve days of Christmas (Parl. Rolls, 488).

The Christmas festival was kept by Edward IV. with great magnificence, the king's natural inclinations leading him to adopt whatever was splendid and costly. "At the Christmas festivities he appeared in a variety of most costly dresses, of a form never seen before, which he thought displayed his person to considerable advantage" (*Croyland Chronicler*). Sir Frederick Madden's narrative of the visit of the Lord of Granthuse, Governor of Holland, to Edward, in 1472, paints in glowing colours the luxury of the English Court. On his arrival at Windsor he was received by Lord Hastings, who conducted him to the chambers of the King and Queen. These apartments were richly hung with cloth of gold arras. When he had spoken with the King, who presented him to the Queen's Grace, the Lord Chamberlain, Hastings, was ordered to conduct him to his chamber, where supper was ready for him. "After he had supped the King had him brought immediately to the Queen's own chamber, where she and her ladies were playing at the marteaux [a game played with small balls of different colours ; and some of her ladies were playing at closheys [ninepins of ivory, and dancing, and some at divers other games: the which sight was full pleasant to them. Also the King danced with my Lady Elizabeth, his eldest daughter. In the morning when Matins was done, the King heard, in his own chapel, Our Lady-Mass, which was most melodiously chaunted, the Lord Granthuse being present. When the Mass was done, the King gave the said Lord Granthuse a cup of gold, garnished with pearl. In the midst of the cup was a great piece of unicorn's horn, to my estimation seven inches in compass; and on the cover of the cup a great sapphire." After breakfast the King came into the Quadrangle. "My Lord Prince, also, borne by his Chamberlain, called Master Vaughan, which bade the Lord of Granthuse welcome. Then the King had him and all his company into the little Park, where he made him have great sport; and there the King made him ride on his own horse, on a right fair hobby, the which the King gave him." The King's dinner was "ordained" in the Lodge, Windsor Park. After dinner they hunted again, and the King showed his guest his garden and vineyard of pleasure. Then "the Queen did ordain a great banquet in her own chamber, at which King Edward, her eldest daughter the Lady Elisabeth, the Duchess of Exeter, the Lady Rivers, and the Lord of Granthuse, all sat with her at one mess; and, at the same table, sat the Duke of Buckingham, my Lady, his wife, with divers other ladies, my Lord Hastings, Chamberlain to the King, my Lord Berners, Chamberlain to the Queen, the son of Lord Granthuse, and Master George Barthe, Secretary to the Duke of Burgundy, Louis Stacy, Usher to the Duke of Burgundy, George Martigny, and also certain nobles of the King's own court. There was a side table, at which sat a great view (*show*) of ladies, all on the one side. Also, in the outer chamber, sat the Queen's gentlewomen, all on one side. And on the other side of the table, over against them, as many of the Lord Granthuse's servants, as touching to the abundant welfare, like as it is according to such a banquet. And when they had supped my Lady Elizabeth, the King's eldest daughter, danced with the Duke of Buckingham and divers other ladies also. Then about nine of the clock, the King and the Queen, with her ladies and gentlewomen, brought the said Lord of Granthuse to three chambers of plesance, all hanged with white silk and linen cloth, and all the floors covered with carpets. There was ordained a bed for himself of as good down as could be gotten. The sheets of Rennes cloth and also fine fustians; the counterpane, cloth of gold, furred with ermines. The tester and ceiler also shining cloth of gold; the curtains of white sarcenet; as for his head-suit and pillows, they were of the Queen's own ordonnance. In the second chamber was likewise another state-bed, all white. Also, in the same chamber, was made a couch with feather beds, and hanged with a tent, knit like a net, and there was a cupboard. In the third chamber was ordained a bayne (*bath*) or two, which were covered with tents of white cloth. And, when the King and the Queen with all her ladies and gentlemen had showed him these chambers, they turned again to their own chambers, and left the said Lord Granthuse there, accompanied with the Lord Chamberlain (Hastings), who undressed him, and they both went together to the bath.—And when they had been in their baths as long as was their pleasure, they had green ginger, divers syrups, comfits, and ipocras, and then they went to bed. And in the morning he took his cup with the King and Queen, and returned to Westminster again."

In 1465 Edward the Fourth and his Queen kept Christmas in the Abbey at Coventry, and for six days (says *William Wyrcester*) "the Duke of Clarence dissembled there."

In 1478 the King celebrated the Christmas festival at Westminster with great pomp, wearing his crown, feasting his nobles, and making presents to his household; and in 1482-3 he kept a splendid Christmas at Eltham, more than two thousand people being fed at his expense every day. Edward almost entirely rebuilt Eltham Palace, of which the hall was the noblest part. In that hall he kept the Christmas festival, "with bountiful hospitality for high and low, and abundance of mirth and sport."

One of the continental visitors who participated in the royal festivities of this period was Leo von Rozmital, brother of George, King of Bohemia. His retinue included Tetzel, who, in describing the Court of Edward the Fourth, after remarking upon Edward's own handsome person, says, "The king has the finest set of courtiers that a man may find in Christendom. He invited my Lord Leo and all his noble companions, and gave them a very costly feast, and also he gave to each of them the medal of his order, to every knight a golden one, and to every one who was not a knight a silver one; and he himself hung them upon their necks. Another day the king called us to court. In the morning the queen (Elizabeth Woodville) went from child-bed to church with a splendid procession of many priests, bearing relics, and many scholars, all singing, and carrying burning candles. Besides there was a great company of women and maidens from the country and from London, who were bidden to attend. There were also a great number of trumpeters, pipers, and other players, with forty-two of the king's singing men, who sang very sweetly. Also, there were four and twenty heralds and pursuivants, and sixty lords and knights. Then came the queen, led by two dukes, and with a canopy borne over her. Behind her followed her mother and above sixty ladies and maidens. Having heard the service sung, and kneeled down in the church, she returned with the same procession to her palace. Here all who had taken part in the procession were invited to a feast, and all sat down, the men and the women, the clergy and the laity, each in his rank, filling four large rooms. Also, the king invited my lord and all his noble attendants to the table where he usually dined with his courtiers. And one of the king's greatest lords must sit at the king's table upon the king's stool, in the place of the king; and my lord sat at the same table only two steps below him. Then all the honours which were due to the king had to be paid to the lord who sat in his place, and also to my lord; and it is incredible what ceremonies we observed there. While we were eating, the king was making presents to all the trumpeters, pipers, players, and heralds; to the last alone he gave four hundred nobles, and every one, when he received his pay, came to the tables and told aloud what the king had given him. When my lord had done eating, he was conducted into a costly ornamented room, where the queen was to dine, and there he was seated in a corner that he might see all the expensive provisions. The queen sat down on a golden stool alone at her table, and her mother and the queen's sister stood far below her. And when the queen spoke to her mother or to the king's sister, they kneeled down every time before her, and remained kneeling until the queen drank water. And all her ladies and maids, and those who waited upon her, even great lords, had to kneel while she was eating, which continued three hours(!). After dinner there was dancing, but the queen remained sitting upon her stool, and her mother kneeled before her. The king's sister danced with two dukes, and the beautiful dances and reverences performed before the queen—the like I have never seen, nor such beautiful maidens. Among them were eight duchesses, and above thirty countesses and others, all daughters of great people. After the dance the king's singing men came in and sang. When the king heard mass sung in his private chapel my lord was admitted: then the king had his relics shown to us, and many sacred things in London. Among them we saw a stone from the Mount of Olives, upon which there is the footprint of Jesus Christ, our Lady's girdle, and many other relics."

The amusements of the people in the fifteenth century are referred to by Thomas Wright, Esq., M.A., F.S.A., who says: "In England, in the third year of the reign of Edward IV. (1463), the importation of playing-cards, probably from Germany, was forbidden, among other things, by Act of Parliament; and as that Act is understood to have been called for by the English manufacturers, who suffered by the foreign trade, it can hardly be doubted that cards were then manufactured in England on a rather extensive scale. Cards had then, indeed, evidently become very popular in England; and only twenty years afterwards they are spoken of as the common Christmas game, for Margery Paston wrote as follows to her husband, John Paston, on the 24th of December in 1483:— 'Please it you to weet (*know*) that I sent your eldest son John to my Lady Morley, to have knowledge of what sports were used in her house in the Christmas next following after the decease of my lord her husband; and she said that there were none disguisings, nor harpings, nor luting, nor singing, nor none loud disports, but playing at the tables, and the chess, and *cards*—such disports she gave her folks leave to play, and none other... I sent your younger son to the lady Stapleton, and she said according to my lady Morley's saying in that, and as she had seen used in places of worship (*gentlemen's houses*) there as she had been.'... After the middle of the fifteenth century, cards came into very general use; and at the beginning of the following century, there was such a rage for card-playing, that an attempt was made early in the reign of Henry VIII. to restrict their use by law to the period of Christmas. When, however, people sat down to dinner at noon, and had no other occupation for the rest of the day, they needed amusement of some sort to pass the time; and a poet of the fifteenth century observes truly—

'A man may dryfe forthe the day that long tyme dwellis
With harpyng and pipyng, and other mery spellis,
With gle, and wyth game.'"

LADY MUSICIAN OF THE 15TH CENTURY.

Another book well known to bibliomaniacs ("Dives and Pauper," ed. W. de Worde; 1496) says: "For to represente in playnge at Crystmasse herodes and the thre kynges and other processes of the gospelles both then and at Ester and other tymes also it is lefull and cômendable."

RUSTIC CHRISTMAS MINSTREL WITH PIPE AND TABOR.

succeeded his father, Edward IV., in the dangerous days of 1483. He was at Ludlow when his father died, being under the guardianship of his uncle, Earl Rivers, and attended by other members of the Woodville family. Almost immediately he set out for London, but when he reached Stony Stratford, on April 29th, he was met by his uncle Richard, Duke of Gloucester, who had arrested Lord Rivers and Lord Richard Grey. The young king (a boy of thirteen) renewed his journey under Gloucester's charge, and on reaching London was lodged in the Tower. His mother, on hearing of the arrest of Rivers and Grey, had taken sanctuary at Westminster. Lord Hastings, a supporter of the king, was arrested and executed because he would not sanction Gloucester's nefarious schemes for obtaining the throne. About the same time Rivers and Grey were beheaded at Pontefract, whither they had been taken by Gloucester's orders. Soon afterwards the Queen was compelled to deliver up the young Duke of York to Richard, who sent him to join his brother in the Tower. On June 22nd, at the request of Richard, Dr. Shaw, brother of the Lord Mayor of London, delivered a sermon at St. Paul's Cross, in which he insisted on the illegitimacy of Edward V. and his brother. On June 25th a deputation of nobles and citizens of London offered the crown to Richard. He accepted it, and began to reign as Richard III. And, according to a confession afterwards made by Sir James Tyrell, one of Richard's officers, the two young princes remained in the Tower, being put to death by their Uncle Richard's orders. Thus, atrociously, began the reign of the murderous usurper,

RICHARD THE THIRD.

The King kept his first Christmas at Kenilworth Castle, having previously visited the city of Coventry, at the festival of *Corpus Christi*, to see the plays. The accounts of Kenilworth Castle show that in 1484 John Beaufitz was paid £20 "for divers reparacions made in the Castell of Kyllingworth" by order of Richard III. At this time, says Philip de Comines, "he was reigning in greater splendour and authority than any king of England for the last hundred years." The following year Richard kept Christmas in the great hall at Westminster, celebrating the festival with great pomp and splendour, encouraging the recreations usual at the season, and so attentively observing the ancient customs that a warrant is entered for the payment of "200 marks for certain new year's gifts bought against the feast of Christmas." The festivities continued without interruption until the day of the Epiphany, when they terminated with an entertainment of extraordinary magnificence given by the monarch to his nobles in Westminster Hall—"the King himself wearing his crown," are the words of the Croyland historian, "and holding a splendid feast in the great hall, similar to that of his coronation." "Little did Richard imagine that this would be the last feast at which he would preside—the last time he would display his crown in peace before his assembled peers."[33] An allusion to this Christmas festival, and to the King's wicked nature, is contained in a note to Bacon's "Life of King Henry VII.," which says: "Richard's wife was Anne, the younger daughter of Warwick the King-maker. She died 16th March, 1485. It was rumoured that her death was by poison, and that Richard wished to marry his niece Elizabeth of York, eldest daughter of Edward IV. It is said that in the festivities of the previous Christmas the Princess Elizabeth had been dressed in robes of the same fashion and colour as those of the Queen. Ratcliffe and Catesby, the King's confidants, are credited with having represented to Richard that this marriage of so near a kinswoman would be an object of horror to the people, and bring on him the condemnation of the clergy."

At a Christmas festival at Rhedon, in Brittany, Henry of Richmond met English exiles to the number of 500, and swore to marry Elizabeth of York as soon as he should subdue the usurper; and thereupon the exiles unanimously agreed to support him as their sovereign. On the 1st of August, 1485, Henry set sail from Harfleur with an army of 3,000 men, and a few days afterwards landed at Milford Haven. He was received with manifest delight, and as he advanced through Wales his forces were increased to upwards of 6,000 men. Before the close of the month he had encountered the royal army and slain the King at Bosworth Field, and by this memorable victory had terminated the terrible Wars of the Roses and introduced into England a new dynasty.

19   Browning.

20   "Every-day Book," vol. ii. p. 1635.

21   "Shorter Poems."

22   Sir John Froissart's Chronicles of England, France, Spain, Portugal, Scotland, Brittany, Flanders, and the adjoining countries; translated from the original French, at the command of King Henry the Eighth, by John Bourchier, Lord Berners. London edition, 1812.

23   Cassell's "History of England."

24   Creighton's "Life of Edward the Black Prince."

25   "Sports and Pastimes."

26   Cassell's "History of England."

27   Shakespeare.

28   "History of Chivalry."

29   "Sandringham Past and Present, 1888."

30   King's Lynn Chamberlains' Accounts Rolls, 23rd of Henry VI.

31   "Chronicles of the White Rose of York."

32   "Paston Letters."

33   Halstead's "Life of Richard III."

CHAPTER VI.

CHRISTMAS UNDER HENRY VII. AND HENRY VIII.

(1485-1547.)

HENRY THE SEVENTH

Was the son of Edmund Tudor, Earl of Richmond, son of Owen Tudor, a Welsh gentleman who had married the widow of Henry V. His mother, Margaret, was a great-granddaughter of John of Gaunt by Catherine Swynford. In early life Henry was under the protection of Henry VI.; but after the battle of Tewkesbury he was taken by his uncle, Jasper Tudor, Earl of Pembroke, to Brittany for safety. Edward IV. made several unsuccessful attempts to get him into his power, and Richard III. also sent spies into Brittany to ascertain his doings. On Christmas Day, 1483, the English exiles, who gathered round Henry in Brittany, took an oath in the Cathedral of Rheims to support him in ousting Richard and succeeding him to the English throne. Henry, on his part, agreed to reconcile the contending parties by marrying Elizabeth of York, eldest daughter and co-heir of Edward IV., and this promise he faithfully kept. After his defeat of Richard the Third at Bosworth he assumed the royal title, advanced to London, and had himself crowned King of England; and at the following Christmas festival he married Elizabeth of York. The Archbishop who married them (Archbishop Bourchier) had crowned both Richard III. and Henry VII., and Fuller quaintly describes this last official act of marrying

King Henry to Elizabeth of York as the holding of "the posie on which the White Rose and the Red Rose were tied together." And Bacon says, "the so-long-expected and so-much-desired marriage between the King and the Lady Elizabeth was celebrated with greater triumph and demonstrations, especially on the people's part, of joy and gladness, than the days either of his entry or coronation."

The Christmas festivities were attended to with increasing zest during the reign of Henry VII., for the King studied magnificence quite as much as his predecessors had done. His riding dress was "a doublet of green or white cloth of gold satin, with a long gown of purple velvet, furred with ermine, powdered, open at the sides, and purpled with ermine, with a rich sarpe (scarf) and garter." His horse was richly caparisoned, and bore a saddle of estate, covered with gold. His Majesty was attended by seven henchmen, clothed in doublets of crimson satin, with gowns of white cloth of gold. The Queen appeared with equal splendour, "wearing a round circle of gold, set with pearls and precious stones, arrayed in a kirtle of white damask cloth of gold, furred with miniver pure, garnished, having a train of the same, with damask cloth of gold, furred with ermine, with a great lace, and two buttons and tassels of white silk, and gold at the breast above." And the royal apartments were kept with great splendour. At his ninth Christmas festival (Dec. 31, 1494) the King established new rules for the government of the royal household (preserved among the Harleian MSS.), which he directed should be kept "in most straightest wise." The Royal Household Book of the period, in the Chapter-house at Westminster, contains numerous disbursements connected with Christmas diversions. In the seventh year of this reign is a payment to Wat Alyn (Walter Alwyn) in full payment for the disguising made at Christmas, £14 13s. 4d., and payments for similar purposes occur in the following years. Another book, also in the Chapter-house, called "The Kyng's boke of paymentis," contains entries of various sums given to players and others who assisted to amuse the King at Christmas, and among the rest, to the Lord of Misrule (or Abbot as he is sometimes called), for several years, "in rewarde for his besynes in Crestenmes holydays, £6 13s. 4d." The plays at this festival seem to have been acted by the "gentlemen of the King's Chapell," as there are several liberal payments to certain of them for playing on Twelfth Night; for instance, an entry on January 7th, 23 Henry VII., of a reward to five of them of £6 13s. 4d., for acting before the King on the previous night; but there was a distinct set of players for other times.

Leland, speaking of 1489, says: "This Cristmas I saw no disgysyngs, and but right few plays. But ther was an Abbot of Misrule, that made much sport and did right well his office." In the following year, however, "on neweres day at nyght, there was a goodly disgysyng," and "many and dyvers pleyes."

That the Christmas festival did not pass unobserved by the men of this period who navigated the high seas we know from the name of a Cuban port which was

A Christmas Discovery by Christopher Columbus.

On Christmas Day, 1492, Christopher Columbus, the celebrated Genoese navigator, landed at a newly-discovered port in Cuba, which he named Navidad, because he landed there on Christmas Day.

The Fire at the Royal Residence, Shene,

was the event of Christmas, 1497. It broke out in the palace, on the evening of December 21st, while the royal family were there, and for three hours raged fiercely, destroying, with the fairest portion of the building, the rich furniture, beds, tapestry, and other decorations of the principal chambers. Fortunately an alarm was given in time, and the royal and noble personages of the Court escaped to a place of safety. In consequence of this fire the King built the fine new palace of Richmond.

Royal Christmases

were kept by Henry VII. at Westminster Hall with great hospitality, the King wearing his crown, and feasting numerous guests, loading the banquet-table with peacocks, swans, herons, conger, sturgeon, brawn, and all the delicacies of the period. At his ninth Christmas festival the Mayor and Aldermen of London were feasted with great splendour at Westminster, the King showing them various sports on the night following in the great hall, which was richly hung with tapestry: "which sports being ended *in the morning*, the king, queen, and court sat down at a table of stone, to 120 dishes, placed by as many knights and esquires, while the Mayor was served with twenty-four dishes and abundance of wine. And finally the King and Queen being conveyed with great lights into the palace, the Mayor, with his company in barges, returned to London by break of the next day."

From the ancient records of the Royal Household it appears that on the morning of New Year's Day, the King "sitting in his foot-sheet," received according to prescribed ceremony a new year's gift from the Queen, duly rewarding the various officers and messengers, according to their rank. The Queen also "sat in her foot-sheet," and received gifts in the same manner, paying a less reward. And on this day, as well as on Christmas Day, the King wore his kirtle, his surcoat and his pane of arms; and he walked, having his hat of estate on his head, his sword borne before him, with the chamberlain, steward, treasurer, comptroller, preceding the sword and the ushers; before whom must walk all the other lords except those who wore robes, who must follow the King. The highest nobleman in rank, or the King's brother, if present, to lead the Queen; another of the King's brothers, or else the Prince, to walk with the King's train-bearer. On Twelfth Day the King was to go "crowned, in his royal robes, kirtle, and surcoat, his furred hood about his neck, and his ermines upon his arms, of gold set full of rich stones with balasses, sapphires, rubies, emeralds, and pearls." This ornament was considered so sacred, that "no temporal man" (none of the laity) but the King was to presume to touch it; an esquire of the body was to bring it in a fair handkerchief, and the King was to put it on with his own hands; he must also have his sceptre in his right hand, the ball with the cross in his left hand, and must offer at the altar gold, silver, and incense, which offering the Dean of the Chapel was to send to the Archbishop of Canterbury, and this was to entitle the Dean to the next vacant benefice. The King was to change his mantle when going to meat, and to take off his hood and lay it about his neck, "clasping it before with a rich *owche*." The King and the Queen on Twelfth Night were to take the *void* (evening repast) in the hall; as for the wassail, the steward and treasurer were to go for it, bearing their staves; the chapel choir to stand on the side of the hall, and when the steward entered at the hall door he was to cry three times, "Wassail! Wassail! Wassail!" and the chapel to answer with a good song; and when all was done the King and Queen retired to their chamber.

Among the special features of the banquets of this period were the devices for the table called subtleties, made of paste, jelly, or blanc-mange, placed in the middle of the board, with labels describing them; various shapes of animals were frequent; and on a saint's day, angels, prophets, and patriarchs were set upon the table in plenty. Certain dishes were also directed as proper for different degrees of persons; as "conies parboiled, or else rabbits, for they are better for a lord"; and "for a great lord take squirrels, for they are better than conies"; a whole chicken for a lord; and "seven mackerel in a dish, with a dragge of fine sugar," was also a dish for a lord. But the most famous dish was "the peacock enkakyll, which is foremost in the procession to the king's table." Here is the recipe for this royal dish: Take and flay off the skin with the feathers, tail, and the neck and head thereon; then take the skin, and all the feathers, and lay it on the table abroad, and strew thereon ground cinnamon; then take the peacock and roast him, and baste him with raw yolks of eggs; and when he is roasted, take him off, and let him cool awhile, and take him and sew him in his skin, and gild his comb, and so serve him with the last course.

CARD-PLAYING WAS FORBIDDEN EXCEPT AT CHRISTMAS,

by a statute passed in the reign of Henry VII. A Scotch writer,[34] referring to this prohibition, says: "A universal Christmas custom of the olden time was playing at cards; persons who never touched a card at any other season of the year felt bound to play a few games at Christmas. The practice had even the sanction of the law. A prohibitory statute of Henry VII.'s reign, forbade card-playing save during the Christmas holidays. Of course, this prohibition extended only to persons of humble rank; Henry's daughter, the Princess Margaret, played cards with her suitor, James IV. of Scotland; and James himself kept up the custom, receiving from his treasurer, at Melrose, on Christmas Night, 1496, thirty-five unicorns, eleven French crowns, a ducat, a *ridare*, and a *leu*, in all about equal to £42 of modern money, to use at the card-table." Now, as the Scottish king was not married to the English princess until 1503, it is quite clear that he had learned to play cards long before his courtship with Margaret; for in 1496, when he received so much card-money from his treasurer, the English princess was but seven years of age. James had evidently learned to play at cards with the Scottish barons who frequented his father's Court, and whose lawlessness led to the revolt which ended in the defeat and melancholy fate of James III. (1488), and gave the succession to his son, James IV., at the early age of fifteen years. The no less tragic end of James IV. at Flodden Field, in 1513, is strikingly depicted by Sir Walter Scott, who tells:—

> "Of the stern strife, and carnage drear,
>   Of Flodden's fatal field,
> Where shiver'd was fair Scotland's spear,
>   And broken was her shield."

THE REIGN OF HENRY THE EIGHTH.

On the death of Henry VII., who had given England peace and prosperity, and established firmly his own house on the English throne, in 1509, his son Henry became king as Henry VIII. He was a handsome and accomplished young man, and his accession was an occasion of great rejoicing. Henry kept his first with great magnificence. Proclaimed king on the 22nd of April at the age of eighteen, and married on the 3rd of June to Katherine of Arragon, widow of his deceased brother Arthur, Prince of Wales, the youthful Monarch and his Queen were afterwards crowned at Westminster Abbey by the Archbishop of Canterbury, and spent the first Christmas of their wedded life at Richmond. "And a very pleasant time it ought to have been to the Queen, for every species of entertainment was there got up by the handsome young king and his gallant company of courtiers, for her particular gratification. There was a grand tournament on the green, before the palace, which was rendered brilliant with pavilions, and the other gay structures always erected for these chivalrous ceremonies. The King and Queen took their places in the customary elevated position, surrounded by the nobles and beauties of the Court, to witness the feats of arms of the many gallant knights who had thronged to display their prowess before their sovereign; these, with their esquires, the heralds, pages, and other attendants, mounted and on foot, clad in their gay apparel, the knights wearing handsome suits of armour, and careering on gaily caparisoned horses, made a very inspiriting scene, in which the interest deepened when the usual combats between individuals or select companies commenced."[35]

> "For every knight that loved chivalry,
> And would his thanks have a passant name,
> Hath prayed that he might be of that game,
> And well was him that thereto chosen was."[36]

The spectacle presented was one of great splendour; for "the commencement of the reign of Henry VIII., who was then styled by his loving subjects 'the rose without a thorn,' witnessed a remarkable revival of magnificence in personal decoration. So brilliant were the dresses of both sexes at the grand entertainment over which the King and Queen presided at Richmond, that it is difficult to convey an adequate idea of their splendour. But in the first half of the sixteenth century the principal Courts of Europe were distinguished by a similar love of display, which, though it fostered habits of luxury, afforded an extraordinary impulse towards art."[37]

In England the love of finery became so general among the people that several statutes were passed during Henry's reign to restrain it. But while the King was quite willing that his subjects should observe due propriety in regard to their own dress and adornments, not exceeding the regulations laid down for their particular rank or station in life, he was lavish in his own expenditure, and it pleased the people to see Henry dressed in kingly fashion. He greatly increased his own popularity by taking part in the tournaments, in which "he did exceedingly well"; and he also assisted in the several curious and picturesque masques of Christmastide.

On one occasion the King with some of the chief nobles of his Court appeared apparelled as Robin Hood and his foresters, in which disguise he entered unexpectedly into the Queen's chamber, "whereat," says Holinshed, "the Queen and her ladies were greatly amazed, as well for the strange sight as for the sudden appearance."

The splendour of the Court festivities necessitated

INCREASED EXPENDITURE FOR CHRISTMAS-KEEPING,

notwithstanding that the King's domestic affairs were managed by "a good number of honourable, virtuous, wise, expert, and discreet persons of his Council." The preserved bills of fare show that the Court diet was liberal generally, but especially sumptuous at the grand entertainments of Christmas. And the Royal Household Accounts also show increased expenditure for the diversions, as well as for the banquetings, of the festival. For instance, the payments to the Lord of Misrule, which in Henry the Seventh's time never exceeded £6 13s. 4d., were raised by Henry the Eighth in his first year to £8 6s. 8d., and subsequently to £15 6s. 8d. In the first year is a payment to "Rob Amadas upon his bill for certain plate of gold stuf bought of him for the disguisings," £451 12s. 2d.; and another to "Willm. Buttry upon his bill for certen sylks bought of him for the disguisings," £133 7s. 5d. In the sixth year are charges "To Leonard Friscobald for diverse velvets, and other sylks, for the disguising," £247 12s. 7d.; and "To Richard Gybson for certen apparell, &c., for the disguysing at the fest of Cristemes last," £137 14s. ½d. Considerable payments are made to the same Gybson in after years for the same purpose, particularly in the eleventh, for revels, called a Maskelyn. In the tenth year large rewards were given to the gentlemen and children of the King's Chapel; the former having £13 6s. 8d. "for their good attendance in Xtemas"; and "Mr. Cornisse for playing affore the King opon newyeres day at nyght with the children," £6 13s. 4d.

Hall, in his Chronicle, Henry VIII. folio 15b, 16a, gives the following account of a

Royal Masquerade at Greenwich,

where the King was keeping his Christmas in 1512: "On the daie of the Epiphanie, at night, the King with XI others, wer disguised after the maner of Italie, called a maske, a thing not seen afore in England; thei were appareled in garments long and brode, wrought all with gold, with visers and cappes of gold; and after the banket doen, these maskers came in with six gentlemen disguised in silke, bearing staffe torches, and desired the ladies to daunce: some were content, and some that new the fashion of it refused, because it was a thing not commonly seen. And after thei daunced and communed together, as the fashion of the maske is, thei tooke their leave and departed, and so did the quene and all the ladies."

In 1521 the King kept his Christmas at Greenwich "with great nobleness and open court," and again in 1525. In 1527, he received the French Embassy here, and also kept his Christmas "with revels, masks, disguisings, and banquets royal;" as he did again in 1533, in 1537, and in 1543; the last-mentioned year "he entertained twenty-one of the Scottish nobility whom he had taken prisoners at Salom Moss, and gave them their liberty without ransom."[38]

On all these occasions Henry diverted his guests right royally, spending vast sums on the masques and disguisings; but none of the Christmas diversions proved greater attractions than

The King's Tournament Displays.

To these splendid exercises Henry gave unremitting attention, and not to display proficiency in them was almost to lose his favour; yet some discretion was required to rival, but not to excel the King, whose ardent temper could not brook superiority in another. But, although victory was always reserved for royalty, it is but fair to allow that the King was no mean adept in those pursuits for which his bodily powers and frequent exercise had qualified him.

Among the most distinguished Knights of Henry's Court Charles Brandon was pre-eminent, not only for his personal beauty and the elegance that attended every movement which the various evolutions of the game required, but for his courage, judgment, and skill, qualities which he displayed to great advantage at the royal festivities. This celebrated man was the son of Sir William Brandon, who, bearing the standard of Henry the Seventh, was slain by Richard the Third at Bosworth Field. Three sons of the Howard family were also distinguished at the royal tournaments. Lord Thomas Howard was one of the most promising warriors, and, unfortunately, one of the most dissolute men at the Court of Henry. Sir Edward and Sir Edmund Howard, the one famed for naval exploits, the other less remarkable, but not without celebrity for courage. Sir Thomas Knevet, Master of the Horse, and Lord Neville, brother to the Marquis of Dorset, were also prominent in the lists of combat. The trumpets blew to the field the fresh, young gallants and noblemen, gorgeously apparelled with curious devices of arts and of embroideries, "as well in their coats as in trappers for their horses; some in gold, some in silver, some in tinsel, and divers others in goldsmith's work goodly to behold." Such was the array in which the young knights came forth at Richmond, in the splendid tournament which immediately succeeded Henry's coronation, "assuming the name and devices of the knights or scholars of Pallas, clothed in garments of green velvet, carrying a crystal shield, on which was pourtrayed the goddess Minerva, and had the bases and barbs of their horses embroidered with roses and pomegranates of gold; those of Diana were decorated with the bramble-bush, displayed in a similar manner. The prize of valour was the crystal shield. Between the lists the spectators were amused with a pageant, representing a park enclosed with pales, containing fallow deer, and attended by foresters and huntsmen. The park being moved towards the place where the queen sat, the gates were opened, the deer were let out, pursued by greyhounds, killed and presented by Diana's champions to the Queen and the ladies. Thus were they included in the amusement, not only as observers, but as participators; nor were the populace without their share of enjoyments; streams of Rhenish wine and of claret, which flowed from the mouths of animals sculptured in stone and wood, were appropriated to their refreshment. Night closed on the joyous scene; but before its approach the King, perceiving that the ardour of the combatants had become intemperate and dangerous, wisely limited the number of strokes, and closed the tourney.

"It was about this period that the tournament ceased to be merely a chivalric combat; and, united with the pageant, acquired more of the dramatic character. The pageant consisted of a temporary building, moved on biers, generally representing castles, rocks, mountains, palaces, gardens, or forests. The decoration of these ambulating scenes was attended with considerable expense, but was seldom conducted with taste or consistency. They generally contained figures, personating a curious medley of nymphs, savages, heathen gods, and Christian saints, giants and the nine worthies, who descended and danced among the spectators.

"On the night of the Epiphany (1516) a pageant was introduced into the hall at Richmond, representing a hill studded with gold and precious stones, and having on its summit a tree of gold, from which hung roses and pomegranates. From the declivity of the hill descended a lady richly attired, who, with the gentlemen, or, as they were then called, children of honour, danced a morris before the King.

"On another occasion, in the presence of the Court, an artificial forest was drawn in by a lion and an antelope, the hides of which were richly embroidered with golden ornaments; the animals were harnessed with chains of gold, and on each sat a fair damsel in gay apparel. In the midst of the forest, which was thus introduced, appeared a gilded tower, at the gates of which stood a youth, holding in his hands a garland of roses, as the prize of valour in a tournament which succeeded the pageant."[39]

CHRISTMAS FESTIVITIES OF NOBLEMEN AND OTHERS.

The royal magnificence was imitated by the nobility and gentry of the period, who kept the Christmas festival with much display and prodigality, maintaining such numerous retinues as to constitute a miniature court. The various household books that still exist show the state in which they lived. From that of the Northumberland family (1512), it appears that the "Almonar" was often "a maker of Interludys," and had "a servaunt to the intent for writynge the parts." The persons on the establishment of the Chapel performed plays from some sacred subject during Christmas; as "My lorde usith and accustomyth to gyf yerely, if his lordship kepe a chapell and be at home, them of his lordschipes chapell, if they doo play the Play of the Nativitie uppon Cristynmes day in the mornnynge in my lords chapell befor his lordship, xxs." Other players were also permitted and encouraged, and a Master of the Revells appointed to superintend. And "My lorde useth and accustomyth yerly to gyf hym which is ordynede to be Master of the Revells yerly in my lordis hous in Cristmas for the overseyinge and orderinge of his lordschips Playes, Interludes, and Dresinge that is plaid befor his lordship in his hous in the XII dayes of Christenmas, and they to have in rewarde for that caus yerly, xxs." Another entry shows that 13s. 4d. was the price paid to the chaplain, William Peres, in the 17th Henry VIII., "for makyng an Enterlued to be playd this next Christenmas."

In this reign the working classes were allowed greater privileges at Christmas than at any other part of the year. The Act of 11 Henry VII. c. 2, against unlawful games, expressly forbids Artificers, Labourers, Servants, or Apprentices, to play at any such games, except at Christmas, and then only in their masters' houses by the permission of the latter; and a penalty of 6s. 8d. was incurred by any householder allowing such games, except during those holidays; which, according to Stow, extended from All-hallows evening to the day after Candlemas Day. The Act of 33 Henry VIII. c. 9, enacts more particularly, "That no manner of Artificer or Craftsman of any handicraft or occupation, Husbandman, Apprentice, Labourer, Servant at husbandry, Journeyman, or Servant of Artificer, Mariners, Fishermen, Watermen, or any Serving-man, shall from the said feast of the Nativity of *St. John Baptist*, play at the Tables, Tennis, Dice, Cards, Bowls, Clash, Coyting, Logating, or any other unlawful Game, out of *Christmas*, under the pain of xxs. to be forfeit for every time; and in *Christmas* to play at any of the said Games in their Masters' houses, or in their Masters' presence."

In his description of the "mummings and masquerades" of this period, Strutt[40] says that the "mummeries" practised by the lower classes of the people usually took place at the Christmas holidays; and such persons as could not procure masks rubbed their faces over with soot, or painted them; hence Sebastian Brant, in his "Ship of Fools" (translated by Alexander Barclay, and printed by Pynson, in 1508) alluding to this custom, says:

> "The one hath a visor ugley set on his face,
> Another hath on a vile counterfaite vesture,
> Or painteth his visage with fume in such case,
> That what he is, himself is scantily sure."

Sandys,[41] in reference to this period, says: "The lower classes, still practising the ceremonies and superstitions of their forefathers, added to them some imitations of the revelries of their superiors, but, as may be supposed, of a grosser description; and many abuses were committed. It was, therefore, found necessary by an Act passed in the 3rd year of Henry VIII. to order that no person should appear abroad like mummers, covering their faces with vizors, and in disguised apparel, under pain of three months' imprisonment; and a penalty of 20s. was declared against such as kept vizors in their house for the purpose of mumming. It was not intended, however, to debar people from proper recreations during this season, but, on the contrary, we have reason to believe that many indulgencies were afforded them, and that landlords and masters assisted them with the means of enjoying the customary festivities; listening to their tales of legendary lore, round the yule block, when weary of more boisterous sports, and encouraging them by their presence."

KING HENRY VIII.'S "STILL CHRISTMAS."

In the 17th year of his reign, in consequence of the prevalence of the plague in London, the King kept his Christmas quietly in the old palace at Eltham, whence it was called the "still Christmas." This suppression of the mirth and jollity which were the usual concomitants of the festive season did not satisfy the haughty Cardinal Wolsey, who "laye at the Manor of Richemond, and there kept open householde, to lordes, ladies, and all other that would come, with plaies and disguisyng in most royall maner; whiche sore

greved the people, and in especiall the Kynges servauntes, to se
hym kepe an open Court and the Kyng a secret Court."[42]

subsequently kept, however, made amends for the cessation
of festivities at the Kyng's "Still Christmas," especially the royal
celebrations at Greenwich. In 1527 the "solemne Christmas" held
there was "with revels, maskes, disguisings, and banquets; and on
the thirtieth of December and the third of January were solemne
Justs holden, when at night the King and fifteen other with him,
came to Bridewell, and there putting on masking apparell, took his
barge, and rowed to the Cardinall's (Woolsey) place, where were at
supper many Lords and Ladyes, who danced with the maskers, and
after the dancing was made a great Banquet."[43]

During the girlhood of the Princess (afterwards Queen)
Mary, entertainments were given for her amusement, especially
at Christmastide; and she gave presents to the King's players,
the children of the Chapel, and others. But, Sandys says, that "as
she grew up, and her temper got soured, she probably lost all
enjoyment of such scenes." Ellis, in his "Original Letters," gives
a curious application from the Council for the household of the
Lady Mary to the Cardinal Wolsey, to obtain his directions and
leave to celebrate the ensuing Christmas. In this letter the reader is
reminded of the long train of sports and merriment which made
Christmas cheerful to our ancestors. The Cardinal, at the same time
that he established a household for the young Duke of Richmond,
had also "ordained a council, and stablished another household for
the Lady Mary, then being *Princess of the Realm*."[44] The letter which
seems to have been written in the same year in which the household
was established, 1525, is as follows:—

"Please it youre Grace for the great repaire of straungers
supposed unto the Pryncesse honorable householde this solempne
fest of Cristmas, We humbly beseche the same to let us knowe
youre gracious pleasure concernyng as well a ship of silver for the
almes disshe requysite for her high estate, and spice plats, as also
for trumpetts and a rebek to be sent, and whither we shall appoynte
any Lord of Mysrule for the said honorable householde, provide

for enterluds, disgysyngs, or pleyes in the said fest, or for banket on twelf nyght. And in likewise whither the Pryncesse shall sende any newe yeres gifts to the Kinge, the Quene, your Grace, and the Frensshe Quene, and of the value and devise of the same. Besechyng yowre Grace also to pardon oure busy and importunate suts to the same in suche behalf made. Thus oure right syngler goode lorde we pray the holy Trynyte have you in his holy preservacion. At Teoxbury, the xxvij day of November.

Youre humble orators,
JOHN EXON
JEILEZ GREVILE
PETER BURNELL
JOHN SALTER
G. BROMLEY
THOMAS AUDELEY.

"To the most reverent Father in God the Lord Cardinall his good Grace."

CHRISTMAS AND THE REFORMATION.

The great Reformer, Martin Luther, took much interest in the festivities of Christmastide, including, of course, the Christmas-tree. One of his biographers[45] tells how young Luther, with other boys of Mansfeld, a village to the north-west of Eisleben, sang Christmas carols "in honour of the Babe of Bethlehem." And the same writer says, "Luther may be justly regarded as the central representative of the Reformation in its early period, for this among other reasons—that he, more powerfully than any other, impressed upon the new doctrine the character of glad tidings of great joy." On Christmas Day, 1521, Martin Luther "administered the communion in both kinds, and almost without discrimination of applicants," in the parish church of Eisenach, his "beloved town."

MARTIN LUTHER AND THE CHRISTMAS TREE.

In England, the desire for some reform in the Church was recognised even by Cardinal Wolsey, who obtained from the Pope permission to suppress thirty monasteries, and use their revenues for educational purposes; and Wolsey's schemes of reform might have progressed further if Henry VIII. had not been fascinated by Anne Boleyn. But the King's amour with the "little lively brunette" precipitated a crisis in the relations between Church and State. Henry, who, by virtue of a papal dispensation, had married his brother's widow, Katherine, now

needed papal consent to a divorce, that he might marry Anne Boleyn, and when he found that he could not obtain it, he resolved to be his own Pope, "sole protector and supreme head of the Church and clergy of England." And among the events

THE LITTLE ORLEANS MADONNA OF RAPHAEL.

of Christmastide may be mentioned the resolution of the King's minister, Thomas Cromwell, and his party, in 1533, to break the ecclesiastical connection with Rome, and establish an independent Church in England. The necessary Bills were framed and introduced to Parliament soon after the Christmas holidays by Cromwell, who for his successful services was made Chancellor of the Exchequer for life. Authority in all matters ecclesiastical, as well as civil, was vested solely in the Crown, and the "courts spiritual" became as thoroughly the King's courts as the temporal courts at Westminster. The enslavement of the clergy, the dissolution of the monasteries, and the gagging of the pulpits followed, the years of Cromwell's administration being an English reign of terror. But the ruthless manner in which he struck down his victims sickened the English people, and they exhibited their disapprobation in a manner which arrested the attention of the King. The time of Cromwell himself was coming, for the block was the goal to which Henry's favourite minister was surely hastening; and it is only anticipating events by very few years, to say that he was beheaded on Tower Hill, July 28, 1540.

ANOTHER ROYAL CHRISTMAS.

That following the execution of Anne Boleyn (1536), Henry spent in the company of his third Queen, Jane Seymour, at Richmond Palace, with a merry party, and subsequently crossed the frozen Thames to Greenwich. During the following summer the Queen went with her husband on a progress, and in the autumn retired to Hampton Court, where she gave birth to a son (who became Edward VI.), and died twelve days afterwards, on the 14th of October, 1537.

During the married life of Queen Jane, the Princess Mary was often with the Court at Richmond, affecting affectionate attachment for the Queen, apparently to conciliate her father. The birth of a prince, followed by the death of the queen, it might have been thought would have a chastening effect upon Mary, as somewhat altering her prospects; but after acting as chief mourner to her friendly stepmother, she spent a pleasant Christmas at Richmond, where she remained till February. Her losses at cards during the Christmas festivities were very considerable, for she was fond of gambling. And she appears to have also amused herself a good deal with her attendant, "Jane the Fool," to whose maintenance she contributed while staying at Richmond. One curious entry in the Household Book of the Princess Mary is: "Item, for shaving Jane fooles hedde, iiiid." Another is: "Item, geven Heywood, playeng an enterlude with his children before my Ladye's grace xls."

The great event of Christmas, 1539, was

THE LANDING OF ANNE OF CLEVES,

at Deal, on the 27th of December. King Henry had become alarmed at the combination between France and Spain, and his unprincipled Chancellor, Cromwell, desirous of regaining his lost influence with the King, recommended a Protestant marriage. He told Henry that Anne, daughter of John III., Duke of Cleves, was greatly extolled for her beauty and good sense, and that by marrying her he would acquire the friendship of the Princes of Germany, in counterpoise to the designs of France and Spain. Henry despatched Hans Holbein to take the lady's portrait, and, being delighted with the picture produced, soon concluded a treaty of marriage, and sent the Lord Admiral Fitzwilliam, Earl of Southampton, to receive the Princess at Calais, and conduct her to England. On her arrival Henry was greatly disappointed. He did not think the Princess as charming as her portrait; and, unfortunately for her, she was unable to woo him with winning words, for she could speak no language but German, and of that Henry did not understand a word. Though not ugly (as many contemporaries testify), she was plain in person and manners, and she and her maidens, of whom she brought a great train, are said to have been as homely and awkward a bevy as ever came to England in the cause of Royal matrimony. The Royal Bluebeard, who had consorted with such celebrated beauties as Anne Boleyn and Jane Seymour, recollecting what his queens had been, and what Holbein and Cromwell had told him should again be, entered the presence of Anne of Cleves with great anticipation, but was thunderstruck at the first sight of the reality. Lord John Russell, who was present, declared "that he had never seen his highness so marvellously astonished and abashed as on that occasion." The marriage was celebrated on the 6th of January, 1540, but Henry never became reconciled to his German queen; and he very soon vented his anger upon Cromwell for being the means of bringing him, not a wife, but "a great Flanders mare."

CHRISTMAS AT THE COLLEGES.

The fine old tower of Magdalen College, embowered in verdure (as though decorated for Christmas), is one of the most picturesque of the venerable academical institutions of Oxford. It stands on the east side of the Cherwell, and is the first object of interest to catch the eye of the traveller who enters the city from the London Road. This college was the scene of many Christmas festivities in the olden time, when it was the custom of the several colleges to elect a "Christmas Lord, or Lord of Misrule, styled in the registers *Rex Fabarum* and *Rex Regni Fabarum*, which custom continued till the Reformation of Religion, and then that producing Puritanism, and Puritanism Presbytery, the profession of it looked upon such laudable and ingenious customs as Popish, diabolical and anti-Christian."[46] Queen's College, Oxford (whose members have from time immemorial been daily summoned to dine in hall by sound of trumpet, instead of by bell as elsewhere), is noted for its ancient Christmas ceremony of ushering in the boar's head with the singing of the famous carol—

> "*Caput afri differo Reddens laudes*
> *Domino.* The boar's head in hand bring I,
> With garlands gay and rosemary,
> I pray you all sing merrily
> *Qui estis in convivio.*"

Tradition says that this old custom commemorates the deliverance of a student of the college, who, while walking in the country, studying Aristotle, was attacked by a wild boar from Shotover Forest, whereupon he crammed the philosopher down the throat of the savage, and thus escaped from its tusks.

MAGDALEN COLLEGE, OXFORD.

Warton[47] mentions that, "in an original draught of the Statutes of Trinity College, at Cambridge, founded in 1546, one of the chapters is entitled *De Præfecto Ludorum qui Imperator dicitur*, under whose direction and authority Latin Comedies and Tragedies are to be exhibited in the hall at Christmas. With regard to the peculiar business and office of Imperator it is ordered that one of the Masters of Arts shall be placed over the juniors, every Christmas, for the regulation of their games and diversions at that season of festivity. At the same time, he is to govern the whole society in the hall and chapel, as a republic committed to his special charge by a set of laws which he is to frame in Latin and Greek verse. His sovereignty is to last during the twelve days of Christmas, and he is to exercise the same power on Candlemas. His fee amounted to forty shillings. Similar customs were observed at other colleges during Christmastide. In a subsequent chapter of this work will be found an account of a grand exhibition of the Christmas Prince, at St. John's College, Oxford, in the year 1607.

BRINGING IN THE BOAR'S HEAD WITH MINSTRELSY.

CHRISTMAS AT THE INNS OF COURT AND GREAT HOUSES.

In the time of Henry the Eighth the Christmases at the Inns of Court became celebrated, especially those at Lincoln's Inn, which had kept them as early as the reign of Henry VI. The Temples and Gray's Inn afterwards disputed the palm with it. Every Corporation appointed a Lord of Misrule or Master of Merry Disports, and, according to Stow, there was the like "in the house of every nobleman of honour or good worship, were he spiritual or temporal." And during the period of the sway of the Lord of Misrule, "there were fine and subtle disguisings, masks, and mummeries, with playing at cards for counters, nails, and points in every house, more for pastime than for gain." Town and country would seem to have vied with each other as to which should exhibit the greatest extravagance in the Christmas entertainments, but (as in the days of Massinger the poet), the town carried off the palm:—

> "Men may talk of country Christmasses—
> Their thirty-pound buttered eggs, their pies of carps'
>   tongues,
> Their pheasants drenched with ambergris, the carcases
> Of three fat wethers bruised for gravy; to
> Make sauce for a single peacock; yet their feasts
> Were fasts, compared with the city's."

The earliest particular account of the regulations for conducting one of these grand Christmases is in the 9th of Henry VIII.,[48] when, besides the King for Christmas Day, the Marshal and the Master of the Revels, it is ordered that the King of Cockneys, on Childermas Day, should sit and have due service, and "that Jack Straw, and all his adherents, should be thenceforth utterly banished, and no more to be used in this house, upon pain to forfeit for every time five pounds, to be levied on every fellow hapning to offend against this rule." "Jack Straw" was a kind of masque, which was very much disliked by the aristocratic and elder part of the community, hence the amount of the fine imposed. The Society of Gray's Inn, however, in 1527, got into a worse scrape than permitting Jack Straw and his adherents, for they acted a play (the first on record at the Inns of Court) during this Christmas, the effect whereof was, that Lord Governance was ruled by Dissipation and Negligence, by whose evil order Lady Public Weal was put from Governance. Cardinal Wolsey, conscience-smitten, thought this to be a reflection on himself, and deprived the author, Sergeant Roe, of his coif, and committed him to the Fleet, together with Thomas Moyle, one of the actors, until it was satisfactorily explained to him.

It was found necessary from time to time to make regulations to limit the extent of these revels and plays, and to provide for the expenses, which were considerable, and they were therefore not performed every year. In 1531 the Lincoln's Inn Society agreed that if the two Temples kept Christmas, they would also do so, not liking to be outdone. And later an order was made in Gray's Inn that no Comedies, commonly called Interludes, should be acted in the refectory in the intervals of vacation, except at the celebration of Christmas; and that then the whole body of students should jointly contribute towards the dresses, scenes, and decorations.

As an example of the Christmas hospitality of the period, we refer to the establishment of John Carminow, whose family was of high repute in the county of Cornwall in the time of Henry the Eighth. Hals says that "he kept open house for all comers and goers, drinkers, minstrells, dancers, and what not, during the Christmas time, and that his usual allowance of provision for those twelve days, was twelve fat bullocks, twenty Cornish bushels of wheat (*i.e.*, fifty Winchesters), thirty-six sheep, with hogs, lambs, and fowls of all sort, and drink made of wheat and oat-malt proportionable; for at that time barley-malt was little known or used in those parts."

That the beneficed clergy of this period also "made merry" with their parishioners is quite clear from the writings of "Master Hugh Latimer," who, in Henry's reign, held the benefice of West Kington, in Wiltshire. A citation for heresy being issued against Latimer, he wrote with his peculiar medley of humour and pathos: "I intend to make merry with my parishioners this Christmas, for all the sorrow, lest perchance I may never return to them again."

One of the most celebrated personages of this period was

WILL SOMERS, THE KING'S JESTER.

This famous fool enlivened the Christmas festivities at the Court of Henry the Eighth, and many quaint stories are told of his drolleries and witticisms. Though a reputed fool, his sarcastic wit and sparkling talents at repartee won him great celebrity. Very little is known of his actual biography, but some interesting things are told about him in a scarce tract, entitled "A pleasant History of the Life and Death of Will Somers," &c. (which was first published in 1676, and a great part of which is said to have been taken from

Andrew Borde's collection of "The Merry Jests and Witty Shifts of Scoggin"). "And now who but Will Sommers, the King's Fool? who had got such an interest in him by his quick and facetious jests, that he could have admittance to his Majesty's Chamber, and have his ear, when a great nobleman, nay, a privy counsellor, could not be suffered to speak with him: and farther, if the King were angry or displeased with anything, if no man else durst demand the cause of his discontent, then was Will Sommers provided with one pleasant conceit or another, to take off the edge of his displeasure. Being of an easy and tractable disposition he soon found the fashions of the court, and obtained a general love and notice of the nobility; for he was no carry-tale, nor flattering insinuator to breed discord and dissension, but an honest, plain, downright [man , that would speak home without halting, and tell the truth of purpose to shame the devil—so that his plainness, mixed with a kind of facetiousness, and tartness with pleasantry, made him acceptable into the company of all men." There cannot, perhaps, be a greater proof of the estimation in which Somers was held by King Henry, than the circumstance of his portrait having been twice introduced into the same piece with that of the King; once in the fine picture by Holbein of Henry VIII. and his family, and again, in an illuminated Psalter which was expressly written for the King, by John Mallard, his chaplain and secretary ("*Regis Orator et Calamo*"), and is now preserved in the British Museum. According to an ancient custom, there is prefixed to Psalm lii., "*dixit incipens*" in the Psalter, a miniature illumination of King David and a Fool, whose figures, in this instance, are portraits of Henry VIII. and his favourite Will Somers. The King is seated at a kind of altar table, and playing on the harp, whilst Somers who is standing near him, with his hands clasped over his breast, appears to listen with admiration. The King wears a round flat cap, furred, and a vest of imperial purple striped with gold, and fluted at bottom; his doublet is red, padded with white; his hose crimson; on his right leg is a blue garter. Somers is in a vest, with a hood thrown over the back; his stockings are blue; at his girdle is a black pouch.

When Henry VIII. became old and inactive, his Christmases grew gradually duller, until he did little more than sit out a play or two, and gamble with his courtiers, his Christmas play-money requiring a special draught upon the treasury, usually for a hundred pounds. He died on January 28, 1547.

34   "Book of Days," Edinburgh.

35   Williams's "Domestic Memoirs of the Royal Family and of the Court of England."

36   Chaucer.

37   "William's Domestic Memoirs."

38   Nichols's "Progresses of Queen Elizabeth."

39   "Recollections of Royalty," by Mr. Charles C. Jones, 1828.

40   "Sports and Pastimes."

41   Introduction to "Christmas Carols."

42   Hall's "Chronicle."

43   Baker's "Chronicle."

44   Hall's "Chronicle."

45   Peter Bayne, LL. D.

46   Wood's "Athenæ Oxonienses."

47   "History of English Poetry."

48   Dugdale, "Origines Juridiciales."

CHAPTER VII.

CHRISTMAS UNDER EDWARD VI., MARY, AND ELIZABETH.

(1547-1603.)

During the short reign of the youthful monarch Edward the Sixth (1547-1553), the splendour of the Royal Christmases somewhat abated, though they were still continued; and the King being much grieved at the condemnation of the Duke of Somerset, his uncle and Protector, it was thought expedient to divert his mind by additional pastimes at the Christmas festival, 1551-2. "It was devised," says Holinshed, "that the feast of Christ's nativitie, commonlie called Christmasse, then at hand, should be solemnlie kept at Greenwich, with open houshold, and franke resort to Court (which is called keeping of the hall), what time of old ordinarie course there is alwaise one appointed to make sport in the court, commonlie Lord of Misrule; whose office is not unknown to such as have been brought up in noblemen's houses, and among great housekeepers, who use liberall feasting in that season. There was therefore by order of the Councell, a wise gentleman, and learned, named George Ferrers, appointed to that office for this yeare; who, being of better credit and estimation than comonlie his predecessors had been before, received all his commissions and warrants by the name of the maister of the King's pastimes. Which gentleman so well supplied his office, both in show of sundry sights and devices of rare inventions, and in act of diverse interludes, and matters of pastime plaied by persons, as not onlie satisfied the common sort, but also were verie well liked and allowed by the Councell, and other of skill in the like pastimes; but best of all by the young King himselfe, as appeered by his princelie liberalitie in rewarding that service." The old chronicler quaintly adds, that "Christmas being thus passed with much mirth and pastime, it was thought now good to proceed to the execution of the judgment against the Duke of Somerset." The day of execution was the 22nd of January, 1552, six weeks after the passing of the sentence.

King Edward took part in some of the Christmas masques performed at his Court, with other youths of his age and stature, all the performers being suitably attired in costly garments. Will Somers also figured in some of these masques. The young King seems to have found more amusement in the pageants superintended by Master Ferrers than he had gained from some of the solemnities of the state in which he had been obliged to play a prominent part; but none of the diversions restored him to good health. Large sums of money were expended on these Christmas entertainments, and the King handsomely rewarded the Master of his pastimes.

George Ferrers, who was a lawyer, a poet, and an historian, was certainly well qualified for his task, and well supplied with the means of making sport, as "Master of the King's Pastimes." He complained to Sir Thomas Cawarden that the dresses provided for his assistants were not sufficient, and immediately an order was given for better provision. He provided clowns, jugglers, tumblers, men to dance the fool's dance, besides being assisted by the "Court Fool" of the time—John Smyth. This man was newly supplied for the occasion, having a long fool's coat of yellow cloth of gold, fringed all over with white, red, and green velvet, containing 7½ yards at £2 per yard, guarded with plain yellow cloth of gold, 4 yards at 33s. 4d. per yard; with a hood and a pair of buskins of the same figured gold containing 2½ yards at £5, and a girdle of yellow sarsenet containing one quarter 16d., the whole value of "the fool's dress" being £26 14s. 8d. Ferrers, as the "Lord of Misrule" wore a robe of rich stuff made of silk and golden thread containing 9 yards at 16s. a yard, guarded with embroidered cloth of gold, wrought in knots,

14 yards at 11s. 4d. a yard; having fur of red feathers, with a cape of camlet thrum. A coat of flat silver, fine with works, 5 yards at 50s., with an embroidered garb of leaves of gold and coloured silk, containing 15 yards at 20s. a yard. He wore a cap of maintenance, hose buskins, panticles of Bruges satin, a girdle of yellow sarsenet with various decorations, the cost of his dress being £52 8s. 8d., which, considering the relative value of money, must be considered a very costly dress.

The office which George Ferrers so ably filled had been too often held by those who possessed neither the wit nor the genius it required; but, originally, persons of high rank and ability had been chosen to perform these somewhat difficult duties. Ferrers received £100 for the charges of his office; and afterwards the Lord Mayor, who probably had been at the Royal festival, entertained him in London. The cost of the Royal festivities exceeded £700.

Stowe, in his "Annals," thus refers to the celebration: "The King kept his Christmasse with open houshold at Greenwich, George Ferrers, Gentleman of Lincolnes Inne, being Lord of the merry Disports all the 12 dayes, who so pleasantly and wisely behaved himselfe, that the King had great delight in his pastimes. On Monday the fourth of January, the said Lord of Merry Disports came by water to London, and landed at the Tower-wharfe, entered the Tower, and then rode through the Tower-streete, where he was received by Sergeant Vawce, Lord of Misrule to John Mainard, one of the Sheriffes of London, and so conducted through the Citie with a great company of young Lords and gentlemen, to the house of Sir George Barne, Lord Maior; where he, with the chiefe of his company dined, and after had a great banquet; and, at his departure, the Lord Maior gave him a standing cup, with a cover of silver and gilt, of the value of ten pounds, for a reward; and also set a hogs-head of wine, and a barrell of beere, at his gate, for his traine that followed him; the residue of his gentlemen and servants dined at other Aldermen's houses, and with the sheriffes, and so departed to the Tower wharfe againe, and to the Court by water, to the great commendation of the Maior and Aldermen, and highly accepted of the King and Councell."

occupied public attention throughout the reign of Edward VI. The young king was willing to support the reforming projects of Archbishop Cranmer, and assented to the publication of the new Liturgy in the Prayer Book of 1549, and the Act of Uniformity. And with the sanction of the sovereign, Cranmer, in 1552, issued a revised Liturgy, known as the Second Prayer Book of King Edward VI., and the Forty-two Articles, which were markedly Protestant in tendency. On his health failing, the King, acting on the advice of the Duke of Northumberland, altered the settlement of the crown as arranged in the will of Henry VIII., and made a will excluding Mary and Elizabeth from the succession in favour of Lady Jane Grey, daughter-in-law of Northumberland, which was sanctioned by Archbishop Cranmer and the Privy Council. Although Cranmer had sanctioned this act with great reluctance, and on the assurance of the judges, it sufficed to secure his condemnation for high treason on Mary's accession. Edward sank rapidly and died on July 6, 1553.

The Duke of Northumberland then

PROCLAIMED LADY JANE GREY QUEEN,

but the people refused to recognise the usurpation. After a brief reign of eleven days,

THE CROWN WAS TRANSFERRED TO MARY,

daughter of Henry VIII. and Catherine of Arragon, and Lady Jane Grey and her husband were sent to the Tower, and subsequently condemned to death. They were kept in captivity for some time, and were not executed until after Wyatt's rebellion in 1554.

VIRGIN & CHILD, CHIRBURY.

Mary was a firm Roman Catholic, and she looked to her uncle, Charles V. of Spain, for assistance and support. In January, 1554, much to the disappointment of her subjects, she concluded a treaty of marriage with Philip of Spain, son of Charles V. Afterwards her reign was disturbed by insurrections, and also by the persecution of Protestants by Cardinal Pole, who came over to England to push forward the Roman Catholic reaction.

THIS TROUBLED REIGN

was not congenial to Christmas festivities, though they were still kept up in different parts of the country. During the Christmas festival (January 2, 1554) a splendid embassy, sent by the Emperor, Charles the Fifth, headed by the Counts Egmont and Lalain, the Lord of Courrieres, and the Sieur de Nigry, landed in Kent, to arrange the marriage between Queen Mary and Philip. The unpopularity of the proceeding was immediately manifested, for the men of Kent, taking Egmont for Philip, rose in fury and would have killed him if they could have got at him. Although an attempt was made to allay the fears of the English, within a few days three insurrections broke out in different parts of the kingdom, the most formidable being that under Sir Thomas Wyatt, who fixed his headquarters at Rochester. In city and court alike panic prevailed. The lawyers in Westminster Hall pleaded in suits of armour hidden under their robes, and Dr. Weston preached before the Queen in Whitehall Chapel, on Candlemas Day, in armour under his clerical vestments. Mary alone seemed calm and self-possessed. She mounted her horse, and, attended by her ladies and her Council, rode into the City, where, summoning Sir Thomas White, Lord Mayor, and the Aldermen, who all came clad in armour under their civic livery, she ascended a chair of State, and with her sceptre in her hand addressed them, declaring she would never marry except with the leave of her Parliament. Her courage gained the day. The rebellion was speedily quelled and the ringleaders put to death; and the following July the marriage took place. Mary's subsequent reign was a "reign of terror, a time of fire and blood, such as has no parallel in the history of England."[49]

Christmas Diversions of Queen Mary.

During her "reign of terror" Queen Mary was diverted by Christmas plays and pageants, and she showed some interest in the amusements of the people. Strutt's "Sports and Pastimes," in an article on the "Antiquity of Tumbling," says: "It would seem that these artists were really famous mirth-makers; for one of them had the address to excite the merriment of that solemn bigot Queen Mary. 'After her Majesty,' observes Strype, 'had reviewed the royal pensioners in Greenwich Park, there came a tumbler, and played many pretty feats, the Queen and Cardinal Pole looking on; whereat she was observed to laugh heartily.'" Strutt also mentions that "when Mary visited her sister, the Princess Elizabeth, during her confinement at Hatfield House, the next morning, after mass, a grand exhibition of bear-baiting was made for their amusement, with which, it is said, 'their highnesses were right well content.'" The idle pageantry of the Boy-bishop, which had been formally abrogated by proclamation from the King, in the thirty-third year of Henry VIII., was revived by his daughter Mary. Strutt says that "in the second year of her reign an edict, dated November 13,

1554, was issued from the Bishop of London to all the clergy of his diocese, to have a Boy-bishop in procession. The year following, 'the child Bishop, of Paules Church, with his company,' were admitted into the Queen's privy chamber, where he sang before her on Saint Nicholas Day, and upon Holy Innocents Day. After the death of Mary this silly mummery was totally discontinued."

The Christmas entertainments of Philip and Mary at Richmond are thus described by Folkstone Williams:[50] "The Queen strove to entertain her Royal husband with masques, notwithstanding that he had seen many fair and rich beyond the seas; and Nicholas Udall, the stern schoolmaster, was ordered to furnish the drama. An idea of these performances may be gathered from the properties of a masque of patrons of gallies like Venetian senators with galley-slaves for their torch-bearers, represented at Court in Christmas of the first and second years of Philip and Mary, with a Masque of six Venuses, or amorous ladies, with six Cupids, and as many torch-bearers. Among them were lions' heads, sixteen other headpieces, made in quaint fashion for the Turkish magistrates, as well as eight falchions for them, the sheaths covered with green velvet, and bullioned with copper. There were eight headpieces for women-masks, goddesses and huntresses. A masque of eight mariners, of cloth of gold and silver, and six pairs of chains for the galley slaves. Another mask of goddesses and huntresses, with Turks, was performed on the following Shrovetide; and one of six Hercules, or men of war, coming from the sea with six Mariners to their torch-bearers, was played a little later. Besides which, we find mention of a masque of covetous men with long noses—a masque of men like Argus—a masque of women Moors—a masque of Amazons—one of black and tawney tinsel, with baboons' faces—one of Polanders, and one of women with Diana hunting."

Nichols ("Progresses," vol. i. p. 18) says that in 1557 the Princess Elizabeth was present at a Royal Christmas kept with great solemnity by Queen Mary and King Philip at Hampton Court. "On Christmas Eve, the great hall of the palace was illuminated with a thousand lamps curiously disposed. The Princess supped at the same table in the hall with the King and Queen, next the cloth of state; and after supper, was served with a perfumed napkin and plates of confects by the Lord Paget. But she retired to her ladies before the revels, maskings, and disguisings began. On St. Stephen's day she heard mattins in the Queen's closet adjoining to the chapel, where she was attired in a robe of white sattin, strung all over with large pearls. On the 29th day of December she sate with their majesties and the nobility at a grand spectacle of justing, when two hundred spears were broken. Half of the combatants were accoutred in the Almaine and half in the Spanish fashion. Thus our chronicler, who is fond of minute description. But these and other particularities, insignificant as they seem, which he has recorded so carefully, are a vindication of Queen Mary's character in the treatment of her sister; they prove that the Princess, during her residence at Hatfield, lived in splendour and affluence; that she was often admitted to the diversions of the Court; and that her present situation was by no means a state of oppression and imprisonment, as it has been represented by most of our historians."

THE ROMISH PRIESTLY PRACTICES

on "Christmass-daye," at this period, are referred to in the following translation from Naogeorgus, by Barnaby Googe:—

"Then comes the day wherein the Lorde did bring his birth
    to passe;
Whereas at midnight up they rise, and every man to Masse,
This time so holy counted is, that divers earnestly

Do think the waters all to wine are chaunged sodainly;

In that same houre that Christ Himselfe was borne, and
came to light,

And unto water streight againe transformde and altred
quight.

There are beside that mindfully the money still do watch,

That first to aultar commes, which then they privily do
snatch.

The priestes, least other should it have, take oft the same
away,

Whereby they thinke throughout the yeare to have good
lucke in play,

And not to lose: then straight at game till day-light do they
strive,

To make some present proofe how well their hallowde
pence wil thrive.

Three Masses every priest doth singe upon that solemn
day,

With offrings unto every one, that so the more may play.

This done, a woodden childe in clowtes is on the aultar
set,

About the which both boyes and gyrles do daunce and
trymly jet;

And Carrols sing in prayse of Christ, and, for to helpe them
heare,

The organs aunswere every verse with sweete and solemne
cheare.

The priestes do rore aloude; and round about the parentes
stande

To see the sport, and with their voyce do helpe them and
their hande."

THE CHRISTMAS MUMMERS

played a prominent part in the festivities of this period, and the
following illustration shows how they went a-mumming.

RIDING A-MUMMING AT CHRISTMASTIDE.

Queen Mary died on November 17, 1558, and her half-sister,

ELIZABETH, CAME TO THE THRONE

in perilous times, for plots of assassination were rife, and England
was engaged on the side of Spain in war with France. But the alliance
with Spain soon came to an end, for Queen Elizabeth saw that the
defence of Protestantism at home and peace with France abroad
were necessary for her own security and the good of her subjects.
She began her reign by regarding the welfare of her people, and she
soon won and never lost their affection.

With the accession of Queen Elizabeth there was a revival of
the courtly pomp and pageantry which were marked characteristics
of her father's reign. Just before the Christmas festival (1558) the
new queen made a state entry into the metropolis, attended by a
magnificent throng of nobles, ladies, and gentlemen, and a vast
concourse of people from all the country round. At Highgate she
was met by the bishops, who kneeled by the wayside and offered
their allegiance. She received them graciously and gave them all
her hand to kiss, except Bonner, whom she treated with marked
coldness, on account of his atrocious cruelties: an intimation of
her own intentions on the score of religion which gave satisfaction

to the people. In the pageantry which was got up to grace her entry into London, a figure representing "Truth" dropped from one of the triumphal arches, and laid before the young Queen a copy of the Scriptures. Holinshed says she revived the book with becoming reverence, and, pressing it to her bosom, declared that of all the gifts and honours conferred upon her by the loyalty of the people this was the most acceptable. Yet Green,[51] in describing Elizabeth's reign, says: "Nothing is more revolting in the Queen, but nothing is more characteristic, than her shameless mendacity. It was an age of political lying, but in the profusion and recklessness of her lies Elizabeth stood without a peer in Christendom."

Sir William Fitzwilliam, writing to Mr. More, of Loseley, Surrey, a few weeks after the accession of Elizabeth, as an important piece of Court news, says: "You shall understand that yesterday, being Christmas Day, the Queen's Majesty repaired to her great closet with her nobles and ladies, as hath been accustomed in such high feasts; and she, perceiving a bishop preparing himself to mass, all in the old form, tarried there until the gospel was done, and when all the people looked for her to have offered according to the old fashion, she with her nobles returned again from the closet and the mass, on to her privy chamber, which was strange unto divers. Blessed be God in all His gifts."

During the Christmas festival (1558) preparations went on for the coronation of Elizabeth, which was to take place on the 15th of January. On the 12th of that month she proceeded to the Tower by water, attended by the lord mayor and citizens, and greeted with peals of ordnance, with music and gorgeous pageantry—a marked contrast to her previous entrance there as a suspected traitor in imminent peril of her life. Two days later the Queen rode in state from the Tower to Westminster, "most honourably accompanied, as well with gentlemen, barons, and other the nobility of this realm, as also with a notable train of godly and beautiful ladies, richly appointed," and all riding on horseback. The streets through which the procession passed were adorned with stately pageants, costly decorations, and various artistic devices, and were crowded with enthusiastic spectators, eager to welcome their new sovereign, and to applaud "the signs they noticed in her of a most prince-like courage, and great readiness of wit." On the following day (Sunday, the 15th of January) Elizabeth was crowned in Westminster Abbey, by Dr. Oglethorpe, Bishop of

Carlisle, "Queen of England, France, and Ireland, Defender of the Faith." The ceremonials of the coronation were regulated according to ancient custom, and the entertainment in Westminster Hall was on a scale of great magnificence.

A DUMB SHOW IN THE TIME OF ELIZABETH.
(From Messrs. Cassels & Co.'s *"English Plays,"* by permission.)

Elizabeth was particularly fond of dramatic displays, and her first Royal Christmas was celebrated with plays and pageants of a most costly description. Complaints, however, being made of the expense of these entertainments, she determined to control them, and directed an estimate to be made in the second year of her reign for the masques and pastimes to be shown before her at Christmas and Shrovetide. Sir Thomas Cawarden was then, as he had for some time previous been, Master of the Revels. According to Collier, the estimate amounted to £227 11s. 2d., being nearly £200 less than the expenses in the former year. The control over the expenses, however, must soon have ceased, for in subsequent years the sums were greatly enlarged.

Nichols[52] mentions that on Twelfth Day, 1559, in the afternoon, the Lord Mayor and Aldermen, and all the crafts of London, and the Bachelors of the Mayor's Company, went in procession to St. Paul's, after the old custom, and there did hear a sermon. The same day a stage was set up in the hall for a play; and after the play was over, there was a fine mask; and, afterwards, a great banquet which lasted till midnight.

In this reign a more decorous and even refined style of entertainment had usurped the place of the boisterous feastings of former times, but there was no diminution in that ancient spirit of hospitality, the exercise of which had become a part of the national faith. This is evident from the poems of Thomas Tusser (born 1515—died 1580) and other writers, who show that the English noblemen and yeomen of that time made hospitality a prominent feature in the festivities of the Christmas season. In his "Christmas Husbandry Fare," Tusser says:—

"Good husband and housewife, now chiefly be glad
Things handsome to have, as they ought to be had,
They both do provide against Christmas do come,
To welcome their neighbour, good cheer to have some;
Good bread and good drink, a good fire in the hall,
Brawn pudding and souse, and good mustard withal.

Beef, mutton, and pork, shred pies of the best,
Pig, veal, goose, and capon, and turkey well dressed;
Cheese, apples, and nuts, jolly carols to hear,
As then in the country is counted good cheer.

What cost to good husband is any of this?
Good household provision only it is;
Of other the like I do leave out a many,
That costeth the husbandman never a penny."

GRAND CHRISTMAS OF THE INNER TEMPLE, 1561-2.

Professor Henry Morley[53] says the first English tragedy, "Gorboduc," was written for the Christmas festivities of the Inner Temple in the year 1561 by two young members of that

Inn—Thomas Norton, then twenty-nine years old, and Thomas Sackville, then aged twenty-five. And the play was performed at this "Grand Christmass" kept by the members of the Inner Temple. Before a "Grand Christmas" was kept the matter was discussed in a parliament of the Inn, held on the eve of St. Thomas's Day, December 21st. If it was resolved upon, the two youngest of those who served as butlers for the festival lighted two torches, with which they preceded the benchers to the upper end of the hall. The senior bencher there made a speech; officers were appointed for the occasion, "and then, in token of joy and good liking, the Bench and company pass beneath the hearth and sing a carol."[54] The revellings began on Christmas Eve, when three Masters of the Revels sat at the head of one of the tables. All took their places to the sound of music played before the hearth. Then the musicians withdrew to the buttery, and were themselves feasted. They returned when dinner was ended to sing a song at the highest table. Then all tables were cleared, and revels and dancing were begun, to be continued until supper and after supper. The senior Master of the Revels, after dinner and after supper, sang a carol or song, and commanded other gentlemen there present to join him. This form of high festivity was maintained during the twelve days of Christmas, closing on Twelfth Night. On Christmas Day (which in 1561 was a Thursday), at the first course of the dinner, the boar's head was brought in upon a platter, followed by minstrelsy. On St. Stephen's Day, December the 26th, the Constable Marshal entered the hall in gilt armour, with a nest of feathers of all colours on his helm, and a gilt pole-axe in his hand; with him sixteen trumpeters, four drums and fifes, and four men armed from the middle upward. Those all marched three times about the hearth, and the Constable Marshal, then kneeling to the Lord Chancellor, made a speech, desiring the honour of admission into his service, delivered his naked sword, and was solemnly seated. That was the usual ceremonial when a Grand Christmas was kept. At this particular Christmas, 1561, in the fourth year of Elizabeth, it was Lord Robert Dudley, afterwards Earl of Leicester, who was Constable Marshal, and with chivalrous gallantry, taking in fantastic style the name of Palaphilos, Knight of the Honourable Order of Pegasus, Pegasus being the armorial device of the Inner Temple, he contributed to the splendour of this part of the entertainment. After the seating of the Constable

Marshal, on the same St. Stephen's Day, December the 26th, the Master of the Game entered in green velvet, and the Ranger of the Forest in green satin; these also went three times about the fire, blowing their hunting-horns. When they also had been ceremoniously seated, there entered a huntsman with a fox and a cat bound at the end of a staff. He was followed by nine or ten couple of hounds, who hunted the fox and the cat to the glowing horns, and killed them beneath the fire. After dinner, the Constable Marshal called a burlesque Court, and began the Revels, with the help of the Lord of Misrule. At seven o'clock in the morning of St. John's Day, December the 27th (which was a Saturday in 1561) the Lord of Misrule was afoot with power to summon men to breakfast with him when service had closed in the church. After breakfast, the authority of this Christmas official was in abeyance till the after-dinner Revels. So the ceremonies went on till the Banqueting Night, which followed New Year's Day. That was the night of hospitality. Invitations were sent out to every House of Court, that they and the Inns of Chancery might see a play and masque. The hall was furnished with scaffolds for the ladies who were then invited to behold the sports. After the play, there was a banquet for the ladies in the library; and in the hall there was also a banquet for the Lord Chancellor and invited ancients of other Houses. On Twelfth Day, the last of the Revels, there were brawn, mustard, and malmsey for breakfast after morning prayer, and the dinner as on St. John's Day.

The following particulars of this "Grand Christmas" at the Inner Temple are from Nichols's "Progresses of Queen Elizabeth":—

"In the fourth year of Queen Elizabeth's reign there was kept a magnificent Christmas here; at which the Lord Robert Dudley (afterwards Earl of Leicester) was the chief person (his title Palaphilos), being Constable and Marshall; whose officers were as followeth:

Mr. Onslow, Lord Chancellour.
Anthony Stapleton, Lord Treasurer.
Robert Kelway, Lord Privy Seal.
John Fuller, Chief Justice of the King's Bench.
William Pole, Chief Justice of the Common Pleas.

Roger Manwood, Chief Baron of the Exchequer.

Mr. Bashe, Steward of the Household.

Mr. Copley, Marshall of the Household.

Mr. Paten, Chief Butler.

Christopher Hatton, Master of the Game. (He was afterwards Lord Chancellor of England.)

Mr. Blaston   }
Mr. Yorke   }
Mr. Penston   }   Masters of the Revells.
Mr. Jervise   }

Mr. Parker, Lieutenant of the Tower.

Mr. Kendall, Carver.

Mr. Martin, Ranger of the Forests.

Mr. Stradling, Sewer.

"And there were fourscore of the Guard; beside divers others not here named.

"Touching the particulars of this Grand Feast, Gerard Leigh, in his 'Accidence of Armory,' p. 119, &c., having spoken of the Pegasus borne for the armes of this Society, thus goes on: 'After I had travelled through the East parts of the unknown world, to understand of deedes of armes, and so arriving in the fair river of Thames, I landed within half a league from the City of London, which was (as I conjecture) in December last; and drawing neer the City, suddenly heard the shot of double canons, in so great a number, and so terrible, that it darkened the whole ayr; wherewith, although I was in my native country, yet stood I amazed, not knowing what it meant. Thus, as I abode in despair, either to return or to continue my former purpose, I chanced to see coming towards me an honest citizen, clothed in a long garment, keeping the highway, seeming to walk for his recreation, which prognosticated rather peace than perill; of whom I demanded the cause of this great shot; who friendly answered, "It is," quoth he, "a warning shot to the Constable Marshall of the Inner Temple, to prepare to dinner."

""Why," said I, "what, is he of that estate that seeketh no other means to warn his officers than with so terrible shot in so peaceable a country?" "Marry," saith he, "he uttereth himself the better to be that officer whose name he beareth."

"'I then demanded, "What province did he govern, that needed such an officer?" He answered me, "The province was not great in quantity, but antient in true nobility. A place," said he, "privileged by the most excellent Princess the High Governor of the whole Island, wherein are store of Gentlemen of the whole Realm, that repair thither to learn to rule and obey by Law, to yield their fleece to their Prince and Commonweal; as also to use all other exercises of body and mind whereunto nature most aptly serveth to adorn, by speaking, countenance, gesture, and use of apparel the person of a Gentleman; whereby amity is obtained, and continued, that Gentlemen of all countries, in their young years, nourished together in one place, with such comely order, and daily conference, are knit by continual acquaintance in such unity of minds and manners as lightly never after is severed, than which is nothing more profitable to the Commonweale."

"'And after he had told me thus much of honour of the place, I commended in mine own conceit the policy of the Governour, which seemed to utter in itself the foundation of a good Commonweal; for that, the best of their people from tender years trained up in precepts of justice, it could not choose but yield forth a profitable People to a wise Commonweal; wherefore I determined with myself to make proof of what I heard by report.

"'The next day I thought of my pastime to walk to this Temple, and entring in at the gates, I found the building nothing costly; but many comely Gentlemen of face and person, and thereto very courteous, saw I to pass to and fro, so as it seemed a Prince's port to be at hand; and passing forward, entred into a Church of antient building, wherein were many monuments of noble personages armed in knightly habit, with their cotes depainted in ancient shields, whereat I took pleasure to behold. Thus gazing as one bereft with the rare sight, there came unto me an Hereaught, by name Palaphilos, a King of Armes, who courteously saluted me, saying, "For that I was a stranger, and seeming by my demeanour a lover of honour, I was his guest of right," whose courtesy (as reason was) I obeyed; answering, "I was at his commandment."

"'"Then," said he, "ye shall go to mine own lodging here within the Palace, where we will have such cheer as the time and country will yield us;" where, I assure you I was so entertained, and no where I met with better cheer or company, &c.

"'—Thus talking, we entred the Prince his Hall, where anon we heard the noise of drum and fyfe. "What meaneth this drum?" said I. Quoth he, "This is to warn Gentlemen of the Houshold to repair to the dresser; wherefore come on with me, and ye shall stand where ye may best see the Hall served:" and so from thence brought me into a long gallery, that stretched itself along the Hall neer the Prince's table, where I saw the Prince set: a man of tall personage, a manly countenance, somewhat brown of visage, strongly featured, and thereto comely proportioned in all lineaments of body. At the nether end of the same table were placed the Embassadors of sundry Princes. Before him stood the carver, sewer, and cupbearer, with great number of gentlemen-wayters attending his person; the ushers making place to strangers, of sundry regions that came to behold the honour of this mighty Captain. After the placing of these honourable guests, the Lord Steward, Treasurer, and Keeper of Pallas Seal, with divers honourable personages of that Nobility, were placed at a side-table neer adjoining the Prince on the right hand: and at another table, on the left side, were placed the Treasurer of the Houshold, Secretary, the Prince his Serjeant at the Law, four Masters of the Revels, the King of Arms, the Dean of the Chappel, and divers Gentlemen Pensioners to furnish the same.

"'At another table, on the other side, were set the Master of the Game, and his Chief Ranger, Masters of Houshold, Clerks of the Green Cloth and Check, with divers other strangers to furnish the same.

"'On the other side against them began the table, the Lieutenant of the Tower, accompanied with divers Captains of foot-bands and shot. At the nether end of the Hall began the table, the High Butler, the Panter, Clerks of the Kitchen, Master Cook of the Privy Kitchen, furnished throughout with the souldiers and Guard of the Prince: all which, with number of inferior officers placed and served in the Hall, besides the great resort of strangers, I spare to write.

"'The Prince so served with tender meats, sweet fruits, and dainty delicates confectioned with curious cookery, as it seemed wonder a world to observe the provision: and at every course the trumpetters blew the couragious blast of deadly war, with noise of drum and fyfe, with the sweet harmony of violins, sack-butts, recorders, and cornetts, with other instruments of musick, as it seemed Apollo's harp had tuned their stroke.

"'Thus the Hall was served after the most ancient order of the Island; in commendation whereof I say, I have also seen the service of great Princes, in solemn seasons and times of triumph, yet the order hereof was not inferior to any.

"'But to proceed, this Herehaught Palaphilos, even before the second course came in, standing at the high table, said in this manner: "The mighty Palaphilos, Prince of Sophie, High Constable Marshall of the Knights Templars, Patron of the Honourable Order of Pegasus:" and therewith cryeth, "A Largess." The Prince, praysing the Herehaught, bountifully rewarded him with a chain to the value of an hundred talents.

"'I assure you I languish for want of cunning ripely to utter that I saw so orderly handled appertaining to service; wherefore I cease, and return to my purpose.

"'The supper ended, and tables taken up, the High Constable rose, and a while stood under the place of honour, where his achievement was beautifully embroidered, and devised of sundry matters, with the Ambassadors of foreign nations, as he thought good, till Palaphilos, King of Armes, came in, his Herehaught Marshal, and Pursuivant before him; and after followed his messenger and Calligate Knight; who putting off his coronal, made his humble obeysance to the Prince, by whom he was commanded to draw neer, and understand his pleasure; saying to him; in few words, to this effect: "Palaphilos, seeing it hath pleased the high Pallas, to think me to demerit the office of this place; and thereto this night past vouchsafed to descend from heavens to increase my further honour, by creating me Knight of her Order of Pegasus; as also commanded me to join in the same Society such valiant Gentlemen throughout her province, whose living honour hath best deserved the same, the choice whereof most aptly belongeth to your skill, being the watchman of their doings, and register of their deserts; I will ye choose as well throughout our whole armyes, as elsewhere, of such special gentlemen, as the gods hath appointed, the number of twenty-four, and the names of them present us: commanding also those chosen persons to appear in our presence in knightly habit, that with conveniency we may proceed in our purpose." This done, Palaphilos obeying his Prince's commandement, with twenty-four valiant Knights, all apparelled in long white vestures, with each man a scarf of Pallas colours, and them presented, with their names, to the Prince; who allowed well his choise, and commanded him to do his office. Who, after his duty to the Prince, bowed towards these worthy personages, standing every man in his antienty, as he had borne armes in the field, and began to shew his Prince's pleasure; with the honour of the Order.'"

"*Other Particulars touching these Grand Christmasses, extracted out of the Accompts of the House.*

"First, it hath been the duty of the Steward, to provide five fat brawns, vessels, wood, and other necessaries belonging to the kitchen: as also all manner of spices, flesh, fowl, and other cates for the kitchen.

"The office of the Chief Butler, to provide a rich cupboard of plate, silver and parcel gilt: seaven dozen of silver and gilt spoons: twelve fair salt-cellers, likewise silver and gilt: twenty candlesticks of the like.

"Twelve fine large table cloths, of damask and diaper. Twenty dozen of napkins suitable at the least. Three dozen of fair large towels; whereof the Gentleman Sewers, and Butlers of the House, to have every of them one at mealtimes, during their attendance. Likewise to provide carving knives; twenty dozen of white cups and green potts: a carving table; torches; bread, beer, and ale. And the chief of the Butlers was to give attendance on the highest table in the Hall, with wine, ale and beer: and all the other Butlers to attend at the other tables in like sort.

"The cupboard of plate is to remain in the Hall on Christmas Day, St. Stephen's Day and New Year's Day, from breakfast time ended untill after supper. Upon the banquetting night it was removed into the buttry; which in all respects was very laudably performed.

"The office of the Constable Marshall to provide for his employment, a fair gilt compleat harneys, with a nest of fethers in the helm; a fair pole-axe to bear in his hand, to be chevalrously ordered on Christmas Day and other days, as afterwards is shewed; touching the ordering and settling of all which ceremonies, during the said Grand Christmas, a solemn consultation was held at their Parliament in this house; in the form following:

"First, at the Parliament kept in their Parliament Chamber in this House, on the even at night of St. Thomas the Apostle, officers are to attend, according as they had been long before that time, at a former Parliament named and elected to undergo several offices for this time of solemnity, honour, and pleasance; of which officers these are the most eminent; namely, the Steward, Marshall, Constable Marshall, Butler and Master of the Game. These officers are made known and elected in Trinity Term next before; and to have knowledg thereof by letters, in the country, to the end they may prepare themselves against All-Hallow-tide; that, if such nominated officers happen to fail, others may then be chosen in their rooms. The other officers are appointed at other times nearer Christmas Day.

"If the Steward, or any of the said officers named in Trinity Term, refuse or fail, he or they were fined every one, at the discretion of the Bench; and the officers aforenamed agreed upon. And at such a Parliament, if it be fully resolved to proceed with such a Grand Christmas, then the two youngest Butlers must light two torches, and go before the Bench to the upper end of the Hall; who being set down, the antientest Bencher delivereth a speech briefly, to the whole society of Gentlemen then present, touching their consent as afore: which ended, the eldest Butler is to publish all the officers' names, appointed in Parliament; and then in token of joy and good-liking, the Bench and Company pass beneath the harth, and sing a carol, and so to boyer.

"*Christmas Eve.*—The Marshall at dinner is to place at the highest table's end, and next to the Library, all on one side thereof, the most antient persons in the company present: the Dean of the Chappel next to him; then an antient or Bencher, beneath him. At the other end of the table, the Sewer, Cup-bearer, and Carver. At the upper end of the bench-table, the King's Serjeant and Chief Butler; and when the Steward hath served in, and set on the table the first mess, then he is also to sit down.

"Also at the supper end of the other table, on the other side of the Hall, are to be placed the three Masters of the Revels; and at the lower end of the bench-table are to sit, the King's Attorney, the Ranger of the Forest, and the Master of the Game. And at the lower end of the table, on the other side of the Hall, the fourth Master of the Revels, the Common Serjeant, and Constable-

Marshall. And at the upper end of the Utter Barrister's table, the Marshal sitteth, when he hath served in the first mess; the Clark of the Kitchen also, and the Clark of the Sowce-tub, when they have done their offices in the kitchen, sit down. And at the upper end of the Clark's table, the Lieutenant of the Tower, and the attendant to the Buttery are placed.

"At these two tables last rehersed, the persons they may sit upon both sides of the table; but of the other three tables all are to sit upon one side. And then the Butlers or Christmas Servants, are first to cover the tables with fair linnen table-cloths; and furnish them with salt-cellers, napkins, and trenchers, and a silver spoon. And then the Butlers of the House must place at the salt-celler, at every the said first three highest tables, a stock of trenchers and bread; and at the other tables, bread onely without trenchers.

"At the first course the minstrels must sound their instruments, and go before; and the Steward and Marshall are next to follow together; and after them the Gentleman Sewer; and then cometh the meat. Those three officers are to make altogether three solemn curtesies, at three several times, between the skreen and the upper table; beginning with the first at the end of the Bencher's table; the second at the midst; and the third at the other end; and then standing by the Sewer performeth his office.

"When the first table is set and served, the Steward's table is next to be served. After him the Master's table of the Revells; then that of the Master of the Game. The High Constable-Marshall; then the Lieutenant of the Tower; then the Utter Barrister's table; and lastly the Clerk's table; all which time the musick must stand right above the harth side, with the noise of their musick; their faces direct towards the highest table; and that done, to return into the buttry, with their music sounding.

"At the second course every table is to be served as at the first course, in every respect; which performed the Servitors and Musicians are to resort to the place assigned for them to dine at; which is the Valects or Yeoman's table, beneath the skreen. Dinner ended the musicians prepare to sing a song, at the highest table: which ceremony accomplished, then the officers are to address themselves every one in his office, to avoid the tables in fair and decent manner, they beginning at the Clerk's table; thence proceed to the next; and thence to all the others till the highest table be solemnly avoided.

"Then, after a little repose, the persons at the highest table arise and prepare to revells: in which time, the Butlers, and other Servitors with them, are to dine in the Library.

"At both the doors in the hall are porters, to view the comers in and out at meal times; to each of them is allowed a cast of bread, and a caudle nightly after supper.

"At night before supper are revels and dancing, and so also after supper during the twelve daies of Christmas. The antientest Master of the Revels is, after dinner and supper, to sing a caroll or song; and command other gentlemen then there present to sing with him and the company; and so it is very decently performed.

"A repast at dinner is 8d.

"*Christmas Day.*—Service in the Church ended, the Gentlemen presently repair into the hall to breakfast, with brawn, mustard and malmsey.

"At dinner, the Butler appointed for the Grand Christmas, is to see the tables covered and furnished: and the Ordinary Butlers of the House are decently to set bread, napkins, and trenchers in good form, at every table; with spoones and knives.

"At the first course is served in a fair and large bore's-head, upon a silver platter, with minstralsye. Two Gentlemen in gowns are to attend at supper, and to bear two fair torches of wax, next before the Musicians and Trumpetters, and to stand above the fire with the musick till the first course be served in through the Hall. Which performed, they, with the musick, are to return into the buttery. The like course is to be observed in all things, during the time of Christmas. The like at supper.

"At service time, this evening, the two youngest Butlers are to bear two torches *Genealogia.*

"A repast at dinner is 12d. which strangers of worth are admitted to take in the Hall; and such are to be placed at the discretion of the Marshall.

"*St. Stephen's Day.*—The Butler, appointed for Christmas, is to see the tables covered, and furnished with salt-sellers, napkins, bread, trenchers, and spoons. Young Gentlemen of the House are to attend and serve till the latter dinner, and then dine themselves.

"This day the Sewer, Carver, and Cup-bearer are to serve as afore. After the first course served in, the Constable-Marshall cometh into the Hall, arrayed with a fair rich compleat harneys, white and bright, and gilt, with a nest of fethers of all colours upon his crest or helm, and a gilt pole-axe in his hand: to whom is associate the Lieutenant of the Tower, armed with a fair white armour, a nest of fethers in his helm, and a like pole-axe in his hand; and with them sixteen Trumpetters; four drums and fifes going in rank before them; and with them attendeth four men in white harneys, from the middle upwards, and halberds in their hands, bearing on their shoulders the Tower: which persons, with the drums, trumpets and musick, go three times about the fire. Then the Constable-Marshall, after two or three curtesies made, kneeleth down before the Lord Chancellor; behind him the Lieutenant; and they kneeling, the Constable-Marshall pronounceth an oration of a quarter of an hour's length, therby declaring the purpose of his coming; and that his purpose is to be admitted into his Lordship's service.

"The Lord Chancellor saith, 'He will take further advice therein.'

"Then the Constable-Marshall, standing up, in submissive manner delivereth his naked sword to the Steward; who giveth it to the Lord Chancellor: and thereupon the Lord Chancellor willeth the Marshall to place the Constable-Marshall in his seat: and so he doth, with the Lieutenant also in his seat or place. During this ceremony the Tower is placed beneath the fire.

"Then cometh the Master of the Game, apparelled in green velvet, and the Ranger of the Forest also, in a green suit of satten; bearing in his hand a green bow and divers arrows, with either of them a hunting horn about their necks; blowing together three blasts of venery, they pace round about the fire three times. Then the Master of the Game maketh three curtesies; as aforesaid; and kneeleth down before the Lord Chancellor, declaring the cause of his coming; and desireth to be admitted into his service, &c. All this time the Ranger of the Forest standeth directly behind him. Then the Master of the Game standeth up.

"This ceremony also performed, a Huntsman cometh into the Hall, with a fox and a purse-net; with a cat, both bound at the end of a staff; and with them nine or ten couple of hounds, with the blowing of hunting hornes. And the fox and cat are by the hounds set upon, and killed beneath the fire. This sport finished the Marshall placeth them in their several appointed places.

"Then proceedeth the second course; which done, and served out, the Common Serjeant delivereth a plausible speech to the Lord Chancellour, and his company at the highest table, how necessary a thing it is to have officers at this present; the Constable-Marshall and Master of the Game, for the better honour and reputation of the Commonwealth; and wisheth them to be received, &c.

"Then the King's Serjeant at Law declareth and inferreth the necessity; which heard the Lord Chancellor desireth respite of farther advice. Then the antientest of the Masters of the Revels singeth a song with the assistance of others there present.

"At Supper the Hall is to be served in all solemnity, as upon Christmas Day, both the first and second course to the highest table. Supper ended the Constable-Marshall presenteth himself with drums afore him, mounted upon a scaffold, born by four men; and goeth three times round about the harthe, crying out aloud, 'A Lord, a lord,' &c. Then he descendeth and goeth to dance, &c. And after he calleth his Court every one by name, one by one, in this manner:

"Sir *Francis Flatterer* of *Fowlehurst*, in the county of *Buckingham*.

"Sir *Randle Rakabite*, of *Rascall-Hall*, in the county of *Rakehell*.

"Sir *Morgan Mumchance*, of *Much Monkery*, in the county of *Mad Mopery*.

"Sir *Bartholomew Baldbreech*, of *Buttocks-bury*, in the county of *Brekeneck*.

"This done the Lord of Misrule addresseth himself to the banquet; which ended with some minstralsye, mirth and dancing every man departeth to rest.

"At every mess is a pot of wine allowed.

"Every repast is 6d.

"*St. John's Day.*—About seaven of the clock in the morning, the Lord of Misrule is abroad, and if he lack any officer or attendant, he repaireth to their chambers, and compelleth them to attend in person upon him after service in the church, to breakfast, with brawn, mustard, and malmsey. After breakfast ended, his Lordship's power is in suspense, until his personal presence at night; and then his power is most potent.

"At dinner and supper is observed the diet and service performed on St. Stephen's Day. After the second course served in, the King's Serjeant, orator-like, declareth the disorder of the Constable-Marshall, and of the Common-Serjeant: which complaint is answered by the Common-Serjeant; who defendeth himself and the Constable-Marshall with words of great efficacy. Hereto the King's Serjeant replyeth. They rejoyn, &c., and who so is found faulty is committed to the Tower, &c.

"If any officer be absent at dinner or supper times; if it be complained of, he that sitteth in his place is adjudged to have like punishment as the officer should have had being present: and then withal he is enjoyned to supply the office of the true absent officer, in all pointe. If any offendor escape from the Lieutenant into the Buttery, and bring into the Hall a manchet upon the point of a knife, he is pardoned: for the buttry in that case is a sanctuary. After cheese served to the table not any is commanded to sing.

"*Childermas Day.*—In the morning, as afore on Monday, the Hall is served; saving that the Sewer, Carver, and Cup-bearer, do not attend any service. Also like ceremony at supper.

"*Thursday.*—At breakfast, brawn, mustard, and malmsey. At dinner, roast beef, venison-pasties, with like solemnities as afore. And at supper, mutton and hens roasted.

"*New Year's Day.*—In the morning, breakfast as formerly. At dinner like solemnity as on Christmas Eve.

"*The Banquetting Night.*—It is proper to the Butler's office, to give warning to every House of Court, of this banquet; to the end that they and the Innes of Chancery, be invited thereto to see a play and mask. The hall is to be furnished with scaffolds to sit on, for Ladies to behold the sports, on each side. Which ended the ladyes are to be brought into the Library, unto the Banquet there; and a table is to be covered and furnished with all banquetting dishes, for the Lord Chancellor, in the Hall; where he is to call to him the Ancients of other Houses, as many as may be on the one side of the table. The Banquet is to be served in by the Gentlemen of the House.

"The Marshall and Steward are to come before the Lord Chancellour's mess. The Butlers for Christmas must serve wine;

and the Butlers of the House beer and ale, &c. When the banquet is ended, then cometh into the Hall the Constable-Marshall, fairly mounted on his mule; and deviseth some sport for passing away the rest of the night.

"*Twelf Day.*—At breakfast, brawn, mustard, and malmsey, after morning prayer ended. And at dinner, the Hall is to be served as upon St. John's Day."

* * * * *

The performance of "Gorboduc" at the Inner Temple was received with such great applause, and the services of Lord Robert Dudley, first favourite of the Queen, so highly appreciated at that particular "grand Christmasse," that Queen Elizabeth commanded a repetition of the play about a fortnight later, before herself, at her Court at Whitehall. A contemporary MS. note (Cotton MSS., Vit. F. v.) says of

THE PERFORMANCE BEFORE THE QUEEN,

that "on the 18th of January, 1562, there was a play in the Queen's Hall at Westminster by the gentlemen of the Temple after a great mask, for there was a great scaffold in the hall, with great triumph as has been seen; and the morrow after, the scaffold was taken down." An unauthorised edition of the play was first published, in September of that year, by William Griffith, a bookseller in St. Dunstan's Churchyard; but nine years afterwards an authorised and "true copy" of the play was published by John Day, of Aldersgate, the title being then altered from "Gorboduc" (in which name the spurious edition had been issued) to "Ferrex and Porrex." The title of this edition set forth that the play was "without addition or alteration, but altogether as the same was shewed on stage before the Queen's Majestie, by the gentlemen of the Inner Temple." The argument of the play was taken from Geoffrey of Monmouth's "History of British Kings," and was a call to Englishmen to cease from strife among themselves and become an united people, obedient to one undisputed rule:—

> "Within one land one single rule is best:
> Divided reigns do make divided hearts;
> But peace preserves the country and the prince."

It recalled the horrors of the civil wars, and forbade the like again:—

> "What princes slain before their timely hour!
> What waste of towns and people in the land!
> What treasons heap'd on murders and on spoils!
> Whose just revenge e'en yet is scarcely ceas'd:
> Ruthful remembrance is yet raw in mind.
> The gods forbid the like to chance again."

A good description of the play, with copious extracts, is published in Morley's "English Plays," from which it also appears that "Queen Mary's expenditure on players and musicians had been between two and three thousand pounds a year in salaries. Elizabeth reduced this establishment, but still paid salaries to interlude players and musicians, to a keeper of bears and mastiffs, as well as to the gentlemen and children of the chapel. The Master of the Children had a salary of forty pounds a year; the children had largesse at high feasts, and when additional use was made of their services; and each Gentleman of the Chapel had nineteenpence a day, with board and clothing. The Master of the Chapel who at this time had the training of the children was Richard Edwards, who had written lighter pieces for them to act before her Majesty, and now applied his skill to the writing of English comedies, and teaching his boys to act them for the pleasure of the Queen. The new form of entertainment made its way at Court and through the country."

THE FOOL OF THE OLD PLAY
(*From a print by Bruegel.*)

At this period

THE CHRISTMAS REVELS AT THE INNS OF COURT

were observed with much zest and jollity. Sandys (writing in 1833 of Elizabeth's time) says:—

"The order of the usual Christmas amusements at the Inns of Court at this period would cause some curious scenes if carried into effect in the present day. Barristers singing and dancing before the judges, serjeants and benchers, would 'draw a house' if spectators were admitted. Of so serious import was this dancing considered, that by an order in Lincoln's Inn of February, 7th James I., the under barristers were by decimation put out of commons because the whole bar offended by not dancing on Candlemas Day preceding, according to the ancient order of the society, when the judges were present; with a threat that if the fault were repeated, they should be fined or disbarred."

Sir William Dugdale makes the following reference to

"First, the solemn Revells (after dinner, and the play ended,) are begun by the whole House, Judges, Sergeants at Law, Benchers; the Utter and Inner Barr; and they led by the *Master of the Revells*: and one of the Gentlemen of the Utter Barr are chosen to sing a song to the Judges, Serjeants, or Masters of the Bench; which is usually performed; and in default thereof, there may be an amerciament. Then the Judges and Benchers take their places, and sit down at the upper end of the Hall. Which done, the *Utter-Barristers* and *Inner-Barristers*, perform a second solemn Revell before them. Which ended, the *Utter-Barristers* take their places and sit down. Some of the Gentlemen of the *Inner-Barr*, do present the House with dancing, which is called the *Post Revells*, and continue their Dances, till the Judges or Bench think meet to rise and depart."

The Hard Frost of 1564

gave the citizens of London an opportunity of keeping Christmas on the ice. An old chronicler says: "From 21st December, 1564, a hard frost prevailed, and on new year's eve, people went over and alongst the Thames on the ise from London Bridge to Westminster. Some plaied at the football as boldlie there, as if it had been on the drie land; divers of the Court, being then at Westminster shot dailie at prickes set upon the Thames, and tradition says, Queen Elizabeth herself walked upon the ise. The people both men and women, went on the Thames in greater numbers than in any street of the City of London. On the third daie of January, 1565, at night it began to thaw, and on the fifth there was no ise to be seene between London Bridge and Lambeth, which sudden thaw caused great floods, and high waters, that bore downe bridges and houses and drowned Manie people in England."

How Queen Elizabeth went to Worship, Christmas, 1565.

Nichols[55] gives the following particular account of Queen Elizabeth's attendance at Divine worship, at the "Chappell of

Whitehall, Westminster," Christmas Eve and Christmas Day, 1565:—

"Item, on Monday, the 24th of December, the Officers of Arms being there present, the Queen's Majesty came to the evening prayer, the sword borne by the Earle of Warwick, her trayn borne by the Lady Strange.

"Item, on Christmas Day her Majesty came to service very richly apparelled in a gown of purple velvet embroidered with silver very richly set with stones, with a rich collar set with stones; the Earl of Warwick bare the sword, the Lady Strange the trayn. After the Creed, the Queene's Majesty went down to the offering, and having a short forme with a carpet, and a cushion laid by a gentleman usher, the... taken by the Lord Chamberlain, her Majesty kneeled down, her offering given her by the Marquis of Northampton; after which she went into her traverse, where she abode till the time of the communion, and then came forth, and kneeled down at the cushion and carpet aforesaid; the Gentlemen Ushers delivered the towel to the Lord Chamberlain, who delivered the same to be holden by the Earl of Sussex on the right hand, and the Earl of Leicester on the left hand; the Bishop of Rochester served the Queen both of wine and bread; then the Queen went into the traverse again; and the Ladie Cicilie, wife of the Marquis of Baden, came out of the traverse, and kneeled at the place where the Queen kneeled, but she had no cushion, but one to kneel on; after she had received she returned to the traverse again; then the Archbishop of Canterbury and the Lord Chamberlain received the Communion with the Mother of the Maids; after which the service proceeded to the end, and the Queen returned again to the Chamber of presence strait, and not the closet. Her Majesty dined not abroad; the said Officers of Arms had a mess of meat of seven dishes, with bread, beer, ale, and wine."

ROYAL CHRISTMASES AT HAMPTON COURT.

In 1568, the Earl of Shrewsbury, writing from Hampton Court to his countess, says, "The Plage is disposed far abrode in London, so that the Queene kepes hur Kyrsomas her, and goth not to Grenwych as it was mete." Meet or not, Elizabeth kept many Christmases at Hampton Court, banqueting, dancing, and dicing—the last being a favourite amusement with her, because she generally won, thanks to her dice being so loaded as to throw up the higher numbers. Writing from Hampton Court at Christmas, 1572, Sir Thomas Smith says: "If ye would what we do here, we play at tables, dance, and keep Christmasse."

QUEEN ELIZABETH'S SINGERS AND PLAYERS.

The Christmas entertainments of Queen Elizabeth were enlivened by the beautiful singing of the children of her Majesty's Chapel. From the notes to Gascoigne's *Princely Pleasures* (1821) it appears that Queen Elizabeth retained on her Royal establishment four sets of singing boys; which belonged to the Cathedral of St. Paul, the Abbey of Westminster, St. George's Chapel, Windsor, and the Household Chapel. For the support and reinforcement of her musical bands, Elizabeth, like the other English Sovereigns, issued warrants for taking "up suche apt and meete children, as are fitt to be instructed and framed in the Art and Science of Musicke and Singing." Thomas Tusser, the well-known author of "Five Hundreth Points of Good Husbandrye," was in his youth a choir boy of St. Paul's. Nor is it astonishing, that although masses had ceased to be performed, the Queen should yet endeavour to preserve sacred melody in a high state of perfection; since, according to Burney, she was herself greatly skilled in musical learning. "If her Majesty," says that eminent author, "was ever able to execute any of the pieces that are preserved in a MS. which goes under the name of Queen Elizabeth's Virginal-book, she must have been a very great player, as some of the pieces which were composed by Tallis, Bird, Giles, Farnaby, Dr. Bull, and others, are so difficult that it would be hardly possible to find a master in Europe who would undertake to play any of them at the end of a month's practice."[56]

But the children of the chapel were also employed in the theatrical exhibitions represented at Court, for which their musical education had peculiarly qualified them. Richard Edwards, an eminent poet and musician of the sixteenth century, had written two comedies; Damon and Pythias, and Palemon and Arcite, which, according to Wood, were often acted before the Queen, both at Court and at Oxford.

THE ACTING OF ONE OF SHAKESPEARE'S PLAYS.

IN THE TIME OF QUEEN ELIZABETH.

(By permission, from Messr Cassell & Cos "Illustrated History of England")

With the latter of these Queen Elizabeth was so much delighted that she promised Edwards a reward, which she subsequently gave him by making him first Gentleman of her Chapel, and in 1561 Master of the Children on the death of Richard Bowyer. As the Queen was particularly attached to dramatic entertainments, about 1569 she formed the children of the Royal Chapel into a company of theatrical performers, and placed them under the superintendence of Edwards. Not long after she formed a second society of players under the title of the "Children of the Revels," and by these two companies all Lyly's plays, and many of Shakespeare's and Jonson's, were first performed. Jonson has celebrated one of the chapel children, named Salathiel Pavy, who was famous for his performance of old men, but who died about 1601, under the age of thirteen. In his beautiful epitaph of Pavy, Jonson says:—

> "'Twas a child that did so thrive
>   In grace and feature,
> As heaven and nature seem'd to strive
>   Which own'd the creature.
> Years he number'd scarce thirteen
>   When fates turn'd cruel,
> Yet three fill'd Zodiacs had he been
>   The stage's jewel;
> And did act, what now we moan.
>   Old men so duly,
> That the Parcœ thought him one
>   He played so truly."

The Shakespearian period had its grand Christmases, for

THE CHRISTMAS PLAYERS

at the Court of Queen Elizabeth included England's greatest dramatist, William Shakespeare; and the Queen not only took delight in witnessing Shakespeare's plays, but also admired the poet as a player. The histrionic ability of Shakespeare was by no means contemptible, though probably not such as to have transmitted his name to posterity had he confined himself exclusively to acting. Rowe informs us that "the tip-top of his performances was the ghost in his own *Hamlet*;" but Aubrey states that he "did act exceedingly well"; and Cheetle, a contemporary of the poet, who had seen him perform, assures us that he was "excellent in the quality he professed." An anecdote is preserved in connection with Shakespeare's playing before Queen Elizabeth. While he was taking the part of a king, in the presence of the Queen, Elizabeth rose, and, in crossing the stage, dropped her glove as she passed the poet. No notice was taken by him of the incident; and the Queen, desirous of finding out whether this was the result of inadvertence, or a determination to preserve the consistency of his part, moved again towards him, and again dropped her glove. Shakespeare then stooped down to pick it up, saying, in the character of the monarch whom he was playing—

"And though now bent on this high embassy,
Yet stoop we to take up our cousin's glove."

He then retired and presented the glove to the Queen, who was highly pleased with his courtly performance.

GRAND CHRISTMAS AT GRAY'S INN.

In 1594 there was a celebrated Christmas at Gray's Inn, of which an account was published in 1688 under the following title:—

"Gesta Grayorum: or the History of the High and Mighty Prince, Henry Prince of Purpoole, Arch-Duke of Stapulia and Bernardia, Duke of High and Nether Holborn, Marquis of St. Giles and Tottenham, Count Palatine of Bloomsbury and Clerkenwell, Great Lord of the Cantons of Islington, Kentish-Town, Paddington, and Knights-bridge, Knight of the most Heroical Order of the Helmet, and Sovereign of the same; Who Reigned and Died, A.D.1594. Together with a Masque, as it was presented (by his Highness's Command) for the entertainment of Q. Elizabeth; who, with the Nobles of both Courts, was present thereat. London, Printed for W. Canning, at his shop in the Temple-Cloysters, MDCLXXXVIII. Price one shilling." 4to nine sheets, dedicated "To the most honourable Matthew Smyth, Esq., Comptroller of the honourable society of the Inner Temple."

The Prince of Purpoole was Mr. Henry Helmes, a Norfolk gentleman, "who was thought to be accomplished with all good parts, fit for so great a dignity; and was also a very proper man of personage, and very active in dancing and revelling." His coffers were filled by voluntary contributors, amongst whom the lord treasurer, Sir William Cecil, sent him ten pounds, and a purse of rich needlework.

The performers were highly applauded by Queen Elizabeth, who expressed satisfaction in her own peculiar style. When the actors had performed their Masque, some of her Majesty's courtiers danced a measure, whereupon the Queen exclaimed: "What! shall we have bread and cheese after a banquet?" Finally the Prince and his Officers of State were honoured by kissing her fair hands, and receiving the most flattering commendations. The whole amusement terminated in fighting at barriers; the Earl of Essex, and others, challengers; the Earl of Cumberland and company defendants, "into which number," says the narrator, "our Prince was taken, and behaved himself so valiantly and skilfully therein, that he had the prize adjudged due unto him, which it pleased her Majesty to deliver him with her own hands; telling him, that it was not her gift, for if it had, it should have been better; but she gave it to him, as that prize which was due to his desert, and good behaviour in those exercises; and that hereafter he should be remembered with a better reward from herself. The prize was a jewel, set with seventeen diamonds and four rubies; in value accounted worth a hundred marks."

The following is the Gray's Inn list of performers, which included some gentlemen who were afterwards "distinguished members in the law."

[From "Gesta Grayorum," page 6.

"The order of the Prince of Purpoole's proceedings, with his officers and attendants at his honourable inthronization; which was likewise observed in all his solemn marches on grand days, and like occasions; which place every officer did duly attend, during the reign of his highness's government.

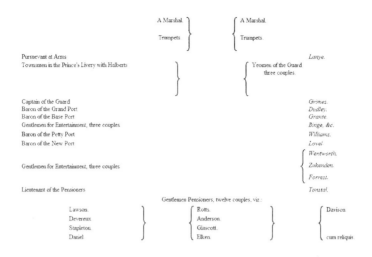

A Marshal.   A Marshal.

Trumpets   Trumpets.

Pursuevant at Arms   *Langa.*
Townsmen in the Prince's Livery with Halberts   Yeomen of the Guard three couples.

Captain of the Guard   *Grimes.*
Baron of the Grand Port   *Dudley.*
Baron of the Base Port   *Grante.*
Gentlemen for Entertainment, three couples   *Binge, &c.*
Baron of the Petty Port   *Williams.*
Baron of the New Port   *Lovel.*

                                         Wentworth.
Gentlemen for Entertainment, three couples   *Zukender.*
                                         Forrest.

Lieutenant of the Pensioners   *Tonstal.*

Gentlemen Pensioners, twelve couples, viz.:

Lawson.   Rotts.   Davison
Devereux   Anderson.
Stapleton   Glascott.
Daniel   Elken.   cum reliquis

Chief Ranger and Master of the Game	*Forrest.*
Master of the Revels	*Lambert.*
Master of the Revellers	*Tevery.*
Captain of the Pensioners	*Cooke.*
Sewer	*Archer.*
Carver	*Moseley.*
Another Sewer	*Drewery.*
Cup-bearer	*Painter.*
Groom-porter	*Bennet.*
Sheriff	*Leach.*
Clerk of the Council	*Jones.*
Clerk of the Parliament.	
Clerk of the Crown	*Downes.*
Orator	*Heke.*
Recorder	*Starkey.*
Solicitor	*Dunne.*
Serjeant	*Goldsmith.*
Speaker of the Parliament	*Bellen.*
Commissary	*Greenwood.*
Attorney	*Holt.*
Serjeant	*Hitchcombe.*
Master of the Requests	*Faldo.*
Chanplayersor of the Exchequer	*Kitts.*

Master of the Wards and Idiots	*Ellis.*
Reader	*Cobb.*
Lord Chief Baron of the Exchequer	*Briggs.*
Master of the Rolls	*Hetlen.*
Lord Chief Baron of the Common Pleas	*Damporte.*
Lord Chief Justice of the Princes Bench	*Crew.*
Master of the Ordnance	*Fitz-Williams.*
Lieutenant of the Tower	*Lloyd.*
Master of the Jewel-house	*Darlen.*
Treasurer of the House-hold	*Smith.*
Knight Marshal	*Bell.*
Master of the Ward-robe	*Conney.*
Comptroller of the House-hold	*Bouthe.*
Bishop of St. Giles's in the Fie	*Dandye.*
Steward of the House-hold	*Smith.*
Lord Warden of the four Ports	*Damporte.*
Secretary of State	*Jones.*
Lord Admiral	*Cecil (Richard).*
Lord Treasurer	*Morrey.*
Lord Great Chamberlain	*Southworth.*
Lord High Constable.	
Lord Privy Seal	*Knapolck.*
Lord Marshal	*Lamphew.*
Lord MarshalLord Chamberlain of the House-hold	*Markham.*
Lord High Steward	*Kempe.*
Lord Chancellor	*Johnson.*
Archbishop of St. Andrews in Holborn	*Bush.*
Serjeant at Arms, with the Mace	*Flemming.*
Gentleman-Usher	*Chevett.*
The Shield of Pegasus, for the Inner-Temple	*Scevington.*
Serjeant at Arms, with the Sword	*Glascott.*
Gentleman-Usher	*Paylor.*
The Shield of the Griffin, for Gray's-Inn	*Wickliffe.*
The King at Arms	*Perkinson.*
The great Shield of the Prince's Arms	*Cobley.*
The Prince of Purpoole	*Helmes.*
A Page of Honour	*Wandforde.*
Gentlemen of the Privy Chamber, six couples.	
A Page of Honour	*Butler (Roger).*

Vice-Chamberlain	*Butler (Thomas).*
Master of the Horse	*Fitz-Hugh.*
Yeomen of the Guard, three couples.	
Townsmen in Liveries.	

The Family and Followers."

CHRISTMAS'S LAMENTATION

is the subject of an old song preserved in the Roxburgh Collection of Ballads in the British Museum. The full title is: "Christmas's Lamentation for the losse of his acquaintance; showing how he is forst to leave the country and come to London." It appears to have been published at the end of the sixteenth or the beginning of the seventeenth century. The burden of the song is that Christmas "charity from the country is fled," and the first verse will sufficiently indicate the style of the writing:—

> Christmas is my name, far have I gone,
> Have I gone, have I gone, have I gone, without regard,
> Whereas great men by flocks there be flown,
> There be flown, there be flown, there be flown, to London-
>   ward;
> Where they in pomp and pleasure do waste
> That which Christmas was wonted to feast, Welladay!
> Houses where music was wont for to ring
> Nothing but bats and owlets do sing.
> Welladay! Welladay! Welladay! where should I stay?

OLD CHRISTMAS RETURNED

is the title of a lively Christmas ditty which is a kind of reply to the preceding ballad. It is preserved in the collection formed by Samuel Pepys, some time Secretary to the Admiralty, and author of the famous diary, and by him bequeathed to Magdalene College, Cambridge. The full title and first verse of the old song are as follows:—

"Old Christmas returned, or Hospitality revived; being a Looking-glass for Rich Misers, wherein they may see (if they be not blind) how much they are to blame for their penurious house-keeping, and likewise an encouragement to those noble-minded gentry, who lay out a great part of their estates in hospitality, relieving such persons as have need thereof:

'Who feasts the poor, a true reward shall find,
    Or helps the old, the feeble, lame, and blind.'"

"All you that to feasting and mirth are inclined,
Come, here is good news for to pleasure your mind;
Old Christmas is come for to keep open house,
He scorns to be guilty of starving a mouse;
Then come, boys, and welcome, for diet the chief,
Plum-pudding, goose, capon, minc'd pies, and roast beef."

Christmas-Keeping in the Country

was revived in accordance with the commands of Queen Elizabeth, who listened sympathetically to the "Lamentations" of her lowlier subjects. Their complaint was that the royal and public pageants at Christmastide allured to the metropolis many country gentlemen, who, neglecting the comforts of their dependents in the country at this season, dissipated in town part of their means for assisting them, and incapacitated themselves from continuing that hospitality for which the country had been so long noted. In order to check this practice, the gentlemen of Norfolk and Suffolk were commanded by Queen Elizabeth to depart from London before Christmas, and "to repair to their counties, and there to keep hospitality amongst their neighbours." The presence of the higher classes was needed among the country people to give that assistance which was quaintly recommended by Tusser in his "Hundreth good Points of Husbandrie":

"At Christmas be mery, and thanke God of all:
And feast thy pore neighbours, the great with the small.
Yea al the yere long have an eie to the poore:
And God shall sende luck to kepe open thy doore."

Henry Lord Berkeley, who had a seat in Warwickshire, appears to have set a good example in this respect to the noblemen of the period, for, according to Dugdale, "the greatest part of this lord's abydinge after his mother's death, happenynge in the sixth yeare of Queen Elizabeth, was at Callowdon, till his own death in the eleventh of Kinge James, from whence, once in two or three yeares, hee used in July to come to Berkeley." The historic house of Berkeley essentially belongs to Gloucestershire; but on the death of Edward VI., Henry Lord Berkeley,

With a good old fashion, when when Christmas was come,
To call in all his old neighbours with bagpipe and drum.

by descent from the Mowbrays and the Segraves, became possessed of the ancient Manor and castellated mansion of Caludon, near Coventry, where he lived in splendour, and kept a grand retinue, being profuse in his hospitalities at Christmas, as well as in his alms to the poor throughout the year. "As touchinge the Almes to the poore of 5 & six country p'ishes & villages hard adjoyninge to Callowdon were relieved, with each of them a neepe of holsome pottage, with a peece of beoffe or mutton therin, halfe a cheate loafe, & a kan of beere, besides the private Almes that dayly went out of his purse never without eight or ten shillings in single money of ijd iijd & groates, & besides his Maundy & Thursday before Ester day, wherein many poore men and women were clothed by the liberality of this lord and his first wife, whilest they lived; and besides twenty markes, or twenty pound, or more, which thrice each yeare, against the feaste of Christmas, Ester, and Whitsontide, was sent by this Lord to two or three of the chiefest Inhabitants of these villages, and of Gosford Street at Coventry, to bee distributed amongst the poore accordinge to their discretions. Such was the humanity of this Lord, that in tymes of Christmas and other festyvalls, when his neighbor townships were invited and feasted in his Hall, hee would, in the midst of their dynner, ryse from his owne, & goynge to each of their tables in his Hall, cheerfully bid them welcome. And his further order was, having guests of Honour or remarkable ranke that filled his owne table, to seate himselfe at the lower end; and when such guests filled but half his bord, & a meaner degree the rest of his table, then to seate himselfe the last of the first ranke, & the first of the later, which was about the midst of his large tables, neare the salt."

Another home of Christmas hospitality in the days of "Good Queen Bess" was Penshurst in Kent, the birthplace of the distinguished and chivalrous Sir Philip Sidney. "All who enjoyed the hospitality of Penshurst," says Mills's *History of Chivalry*, "were equal in consideration of the host; there were no odious distinctions of rank or fortune; 'the dishes did not grow coarser as they receded from the head of the table,' and no huge salt-cellar divided the noble from the ignoble guests." That hospitality was the honourable distinction of the Sidney family in general is also evident from Ben Jonson's lines on Penshurst:

> "Whose liberal board doth flow With all that hospitality
> doth know!
> Where comes no guest but is allow'd to eat,
> Without his fear, and of thy Lord's own meat
> Where the same beer and bread, and self-same wine,
> That is His Lordship's, shall be also mine."[57]

A reviewer of "The Sidneys of Penshurst," by Philip Sidney, says there is a tradition that the Black Prince and his Fair Maid of Kent once spent their Christmastide at Penshurst, whose banqueting hall, one of the finest in England, dates back to that age of chivalry. At Penshurst Spenser wrote part of his "Shepherd's Calendar," and Ben Jonson drank and rhymed and revelled in this stateliest of English manor houses.

CHRISTMAS IN THE HALL.

"A man might then behold,
    At Christmas, in each hall,
Good fires to curb the cold,
    And meat for great and small."

Queen Elizabeth died on March 23, 1603, after nominating James VI. of Scotland as her successor, and

THE ACCESSION OF KING JAMES,

as James I. of England, united the crowns of England and Scotland, which had been the aim of Mary Queen of Scots before her death.

49   Cassell's "History of England."
50   "Domestic Memoirs of the Royal Family."
51   "History of the English People."
52   "Progresses."
53   "English Plays."
54   Sir William Dugdale's "Origines Juridiciales."
55   "Progresses."
56   "History of Music," vol iii. p. 15.
57   Gifford's "Ben Jonson," vol. viii. p. 254.

CHAPTER VIII.

CHRISTMAS UNDER JAMES I.

(1603-1625.)

COURT MASQUES.

The Court entertainments of Christmastide in the reign of James the First consisted chiefly of the magnificent masques of Ben Jonson and others, who, by their training in the preceding reign, had acquired a mastery of the dramatic art. The company to which Shakespeare belonged (that of Lord Chamberlain's players) became the King's players on the accession of James, and several of Shakespeare's plays were produced at Court. But very early in this reign plays gave place to the more costly and elaborate entertainments called masques, but which were very different from the dumb-show masques of Elizabeth's reign, the masquerades of Henry the Eighth, and the low-buffoonery masques of earlier times. At the Court of James thousands of pounds were sometimes expended on the production of a single masque. To the aid of poetry, composed by poets of the first rank, came the most skilful musicians and the most ingenious machinists. Inigo Jones, who became architect to the Court in 1606, shared honours with Ben Jonson in the production of the Court masques, as did also Henry Lawes, the eminent musician. In some of the masques the devices of attire were the work of "Master Jones," as well as the invention and the architecture of the whole of the scenery. D'Israeli[58] says:— "That the moveable scenery of these masques formed as perfect a scenical illusion as any that our own age, with all its perfection and decoration, has attained to, will not be denied by those who have read the few masques that have been printed. They usually contrived a double division of the scene; one part was for some time concealed from the spectator, which produced surprise and variety. Thus in the Lord's Masque, at the marriage of the Palatine, the scene was divided into two parts from the roof to the floor; the lower part being first discovered, there appeared a wood in perspective, the innermost part being of "releeve or whole round," the rest painted. On the left a cave, and on the right a thicket from which issued Orpheus. At the back of the scene, at the sudden fall of a curtain, the upper part broke on the spectators, a heaven of clouds of all hues; the stars suddenly vanished, the clouds dispersed; an element of artificial fire played about the house of Prometheus—a bright and transparent cloud reaching from the heavens to the earth, whence the eight maskers descended with the music of a full song; and at the end of their descent the cloud broke in twain, and one part of it, as with a wind, was blown athwart the scene. While this cloud was vanishing, the wood, being the under part of the scene, was insensibly changing: a perspective view opened, with porticoes on each side, and female statues of silver, accompanied with ornaments of architecture, filled the end of the house of Prometheus, and seemed all of goldsmith's work. The women of Prometheus descended from their niches till the anger of Jupiter turned them again into statues. It is evident, too, that the size of the procenium accorded with the magnificence of the scene; for I find choruses described, 'and changeable conveyances of the song,' in manner of an echo, performed by more than forty different voices and instruments in various parts of the scene."

The masque, as Lord Bacon says, was composed for princes, and by princes it was played. The King and Queen, Prince Henry, and Prince Charles (afterwards Charles the First) all appeared in Court masques, as did also the nobility and gentry of the Court, foreign ambassadors, and other eminent personages.

In his notes to "The Masque of Queens," Ben Jonson refers several times to "the King's Majesty's book (our sovereign) of Demonology." The goat ridden was said to be often the devil himself, but "of the green cock, we have no other ground (to confess ingenuously) than a vulgar fable of a witch, that with a cock of that colour, and a bottom of blue thread, would transport herself through the air; and so escaped (at the time of her being brought to execution) from the hand of justice. It was a tale when I went to school."

That there was no lack of ability for carrying out the Court commands in regard to the Christmas entertainments of this period is evident from the company of eminent men who used to meet at the "Mermaid." "Sir Walter Raleigh," says Gifford,[59] "previously to his unfortunate engagement with the wretched Cobham and others, had instituted a meeting of *beaux esprits* at the Mermaid, a celebrated tavern in Friday Street. Of this club, which combined more talent and genius, perhaps, than ever met together before or since, Jonson was a member; and here, for many years, he regularly repaired with Shakespeare, Beaumont, Fletcher, Selden, Cotton, Carew, Martin, Donne, and many others, whose names, even at this distant period, call up a mingled feeling of reverence and respect." Here, in the full flow and confidence of friendship, the lively and interesting "wit-combats" took place between Shakespeare and Jonson; and hither, in probable allusion to them, Beaumont fondly lets his thoughts wander in his letter to Jonson from the country.

"What things have we seen,
Done at the Mermaid? heard words that have been,
So nimble, and so full of subtle flame,
As if that every one from whom they came,
Had meant to put his whole wit in a jest," &c.

Masques, however, were not the only Christmas diversions of royalty at this period, for James I. was very fond of hunting, and Nichols[60] says that, in 1604, the King kept

A ROYAL CHRISTMAS AT ROYSTON,

at his new hunting seat there, and "between the 18th of December and 22nd of January he there knighted Sir Richard Hussey, of Salop; Sir Edward Bushell, of Gloucestershire; Sir John Fenwick, of Northumberland; Sir John Huet, of London; Sir Robert Jermyn, of Suffolk; Sir Isaac Jermyn, of Suffolk; Sir John Rowse;

Sir Thomas Muschamp, of Surrey. Mr. Chamberlaine, in a letter to Mr. Winwood from London, December 18th, says: 'The King came back from Royston on Saturday; but so far from being weary or satisfyed with those sports, that presently after the holy-days he makes reckoning to be there againe, or, as some say, to go further towards Lincolnshire, to a place called *Ancaster Heath*.'"

In this letter Mr. Chamberlaine also refers to

Other Court Amusements of Christmastide,

for, proceeding, he says:—

"In the meantime here is great provision for Cockpit, to entertaine him at home, and of Masks and Revells against the marriage of Sir Philip Herbert and the Lady Susan Vere, which is to be celebrated on St. John's Day. The Queen hath likewise a great Mask in hand against Twelfth-tide, for which there was £3,000 delivered a month ago. Her brother, the Duke of Holst, is here still, procuring a levy of men to carry into Hungary. The Tragedy of 'Gowry,' with all the action and actors, hath been twice represented by the King's Players, with exceeding concourse of all sorts of people; but whether the matter or manner be not well handled, or that it be thought unfit that Princes should be played on the stage in their lifetime, I hear that some great Councellors are much displeased with it, and so 'tis thought shall be forbidden. And so wishing a merry Christmas and many a good year to you and Mrs. Winwood, I committ you to God. Yours, most assuredly, John Chamberlaine."

"On the 26th of January, Mr. Chamberlaine writes thus to Mr. Winwood: 'I doubt not but Dudley Carleton hath acquainted you with all their Christmas-games at Court, for he was a spectator of all the sports and shows. The King went to Royston two days after Twelfth-tide, where and thereabout he hath continued ever since, and finds such felicity in that hunting life, that he hath written to the Councill that it is the only means to maintain his health, which being the health and welfare of us all, he desires them to take the charge and burden of affairs, and foresee that he be not interrupted or *troubled with too much business*.'"

Campion's Masque in honour of Lord Hayes and his bride was presented before King James, at Whitehall, on Twelfth Night, 1606; and in reference to the Christmas festivities at Court the following year (1607), Mr. Chamberlaine, writing to Sir D. Carleton, on the 5th of January, says:

"The Masque goes forward at Court for Twelfth-day, though I doubt the New Room will be scant ready. All the Holidays there were Plays; but with so little concourse of strangers, that they say they wanted company. The King was very earnest to have one on Christmas-night; but the Lords told him it was not the fashion. Which answer pleased him not a whit; but he said, 'What do you tell me of the fashion? I will make it a fashion.' Yesterday he dined in the Presence in great pomp, with two rich cupboards of plate, the one gold, the other that of the House of Burgundy pawned to Queen Elizabeth by the States of Brabant, and hath seldom been seen abroad, being exceeding massy, fair, and sumptuous. I could learn no reason of this extraordinary bravery, but that he would show himself in glory to certain Scots that were never here before, as they say there be many lately come, and that the Court is full of new and strange faces. Yesterday there were to be shewn certain rare fire-works contrived by a Dane, two Dutchmen, and Sir Thomas Challoner, in concert."

On January 8th, another letter of Mr. Chamberlaine thus refers to gaming at Court: "On the Twelfth-eve there was great golden play at Court. No Gamester admitted that brought not £300 at least. Montgomery played the King's money, and won him £750, which he had for his labour. The Lord Montegle lost the Queen £400. Sir Robert Cary, for the Prince, £300; and the Earl Salisbury, £300; the Lord Buckhurst, £500; *et sic de cæteris*. So that I heard of no winner but the King and Sir Francis Wolley, who got above £800. The King went a hawking-journey yesterday to Theobalds and returns to-morrow.

"Above Westminster the Thames is quite frozen over; and the Archbishop came from Lambeth, on Twelfth-day, over the ice to Court. Many fanciful experiments are daily put in practice; as certain youths burnt a gallon of wine upon the ice, and made all the passengers partakers. But the best is, of an honest woman (they say) that had a great longing to encrease her family on the Thames" (Nichols's "Progresses").

dates from Christmas Day, 1607, when he knighted Robert Carr, or Ker, a young border Scot of the Kers of Fernihurst, the first of the favourites who ruled both the King and the kingdom. Carr had been some years in France, and being a handsome youth— "straight-limbed, well-formed, strong-shouldered, and smooth-faced"—he had been led to believe that if he cultivated his personal appearance and a courtliness of address, he was sure of making his fortune at the Court of James. "Accordingly he managed to appear as page to Lord Dingwall at a grand tilting match at Westminster, in 1606. According to chivalric usage it became his duty to present his lord's shield to his Majesty; but in manœuvring his horse on the occasion it fell and broke his leg. That fall was his rise. James was immediately struck with the beauty of the youth who lay disabled at his feet, and had him straightway carried into a house near Charing Cross, and sent his own surgeon to him... On Christmas Day, 1607, James knighted him and made him a gentleman of the bedchamber, so as to have him constantly about his person. Such was his favour that every one pressed around him to obtain their suits with the King. He received rich presents; the ladies courted his attention; the greatest lords did him the most obsequious and disgusting homage."[61] He afterwards formed that connection with Frances Howard, Countess of Essex, which resulted in her divorce from her husband, and, subsequently, on his marrying Lady Essex, the King made him Earl of Somerset, that the lady might not lose in rank. On the circumstances attending the murder of Sir Thomas Overbury being brought to light, the complicity of Somerset was thought to be involved in the ascertained guilt of his wife. In May, 1616, the Countess was convicted; a week later her husband shared her fate. After a long imprisonment Somerset was pardoned, and ended his life in obscurity.

In this reign the Court revels and shows of Christmas were imitated at the country seats of the nobility and gentry, and at the Colleges of Oxford and Cambridge. An account has been preserved of one of the most remarkable exhibitions of this kind, entitled—

It took place in the year 1607, at St. John's College, Oxford, and the authentic account was published from the original manuscript, in 1816, by Robert Tripbook, of 23, Old Bond Street, London: "To the President, Fellows, and Scholars of St. John Baptist College, in the University of Oxford, this curious Record of an ancient custom in their Society, is respectfully inscribed by the Publisher." Of the authenticity of this description the Publisher says "no doubt can possibly exist, it was written by an eye-witness of, and performer in, the sports; and is now printed, for the first time, from the original manuscript preserved in the College Library.

"From the Boy Bishop, the Christmas Prince may be supposed to derive his origin. Whilst the former was bearing sway in the ecclesiastical foundations, the latter was elected to celebrate the festivities of Christmas in the King's palace, at the seats of the nobility, at the universities, and in the Inns of Court. The custom prevailed till the ascendancy of the Puritans during the civil war; and some idea of the expense, and general support it received, may be formed from the account of the Gray's Inn Prince and an extract from one of the Strafford Papers. The latter is from a letter written by the Rev. G. Garrard to the Earl of Strafford, dated Jan. 8, 1635: 'The Middle Temple House have set up a prince, who carries himself in great state; one Mr. Vivian a Cornish gentleman, whose father Sir Francis Vivian was fined in the Star-Chamber about a castle he held in Cornwall, about three years since. He hath all his great officers attending him, lord keeper, lord treasurer, eight white staves at the least, captain of his pensioners, captain of his guard, two chaplains, who on Sunday last preached before him, and in the pulpit made three low legs to his excellency before they began, which is much laughed at. My lord chamberlain lent him two fair cloths of state, one hung up in the hall under which he dines, the other in his privy chamber; he is served on the knee, and all that come to see him kiss his hand on their knee. My lord of Salisbury hath sent him pole-axes for his pensioners. He sent to my lord of Holland, his justice in Eyre, for venison, which he willingly sends him; to the lord mayor and sheriffs of London for wine, all obey. Twelfth-day was a great day, going to the chapel many petitions were delivered him, which he gave to his masters of the requests.

He hath a favourite, whom with some others, gentlemen of great quality, he knighted at his return from church, and dined in great state; at the going out of the chambers into the garden, when he drank the King's health, the glass being at his mouth he let it fall, which much defaced his purple satten suit, for so he was clothed that day, having a cloak of the same down to his foot, for he mourns for his father who lately died. It cost this prince £2,000 out of his own purse. I hear of no other design, but that all this is done to make them fit to give the prince elector a royal entertainment with masks, dancings, and some other exercises of wit, in orations or arraignments, that day that they invite him.'

"The writer, or narrator, of the events connected with the Christmas Prince of St. John's was Griffin Higgs, who was descended of a respectable and opulent family in Gloucestershire, though he was himself born at Stoke Abbat, near Henley on Thames, in 1589. He was educated at St. John's, and thence, in 1611, elected fellow of Merton college, where he distinguished himself, in the execution of the procuratorial duties, as a man of great courage, though, says Wood, of little stature. In 1627 he was appointed chaplain to the Queen of Bohemia, by her brother Charles the First, and during his absence, in the performance of his duties, was created a doctor of divinity at Leyden by the learned Andrew Rivet. He returned, after a residence abroad of about twelve years, when he had the valuable rectory of Clive or Cliff, near Dover, and shortly after the deanery of Lichfield, conferred upon him. During the civil wars he was a sufferer for the royal cause, and, losing his preferment, retired to the place of his birth, where he died in the year 1659, and was buried in the chancel of the church of South Stoke.

"Thomas Tucker, the elected Prince, was born in London, in 1586, entered at St. John's in 1601, became fellow of that house and took holy orders. He afterwards had the vicarage of Pipping-burge, or Pemberge, in Kent, and the rectory of Portshead, near Bristol, and finally obtained the third stall in the cathedral church of Bristol, in which he was succeeded, August 25, 1660, by Richard Standfast."

The following explanation is given of "the apparently strange titles of the Prince of St. John's: 'The most magnificent and renowned Thomas, by the favour of Fortune, Prince of *Alba Fortunata*, Lord St. Johns, high Regent of the Hall, Duke of St.

Giles, Marquis of Magdalens, Landgrave of the Grove, County Palatine of the Cloisters, Chief Bailiff of the Beaumonts, High Ruler of Rome, Master of the Manor of Waltham, Governor of Gloucester Green, Sole Commander of all Tilts,' &c. The Prince of *Alba Fortunata* alludes, as may be readily conjectured, to the name of the founder, Sir Thomas *White*; St. John's, and the Hall, are equally clear; Magdalens is the parish in which a portion of the college stands, and a part of which belongs to the society; the Grove and the Cloisters are again parts of the home domain of the college; Beaumonts is the name of a portion of land belonging to the college, on which stands the ruin of the palace of Beaumonts, built about the year 1128 by King Henry the First; Rome is a piece of land so called, near to the end of the walk called *Non Ultra*, on the north side of Oxford. The manor of Waltham, or Walton, is situate in the north suburb of Oxford, and is the property of the college, as is a considerable portion of Gloucester-green, which though now better known as the site of an extensive bridewell, was in 1607 literally a meadow, and without any building more contiguous than Gloucester-hall, from which house it derived its name."

Then follows "A true and faithfull relation of the rising and fall of Thomas Tucker, Prince of *Alba Fortunata*, Lord St. Johns, &c., with all the occurrents which happened throughout his whole domination."

"It happened in the yeare of our Lord 1607, the 31 of October, beinge All Sayntes Eve, that at night a fier was made in the Hall of St. John Baptist's Colledge, in Oxon, accordinge to the custome and statuts of the same place, at which time the whole companye or most parte of the Students of the same house mette together to beginne their Christmas, of which some came to see sports, to witte the Seniors as well Graduates, as Under-graduates. Others to make sports, viz., Studentes of the seconde yeare, whom they call Poulderlings, others to make sporte with all, of this last sorte were they whome they call Fresh-menn, Punies of the first yeare, who are by no meanes admitted to be agents or behoulders of those sports, before themselves have been patient perfourmers of them. But (as it often falleth out) the Freshmen or patients, thinkinge the Poulderlings or Agentes too buysie and nimble, They them too dull and backwarde in theyr duety, the standers by findinge both of them too forwarde and violente, the sportes for that night for feare of tumultes weare broken upp, everye mann betakinge himself to his reste.

"The next night followinge, beinge the feast of All Sayntes, at nighte they mett agayne together; And whereas it was hoped a night's sleepe would have somewhat abated their rage, it contraryewise sett a greater edge on theyr furye, they havinge all this while but consulted how to gett more strength one agaynst another, and consequently to breed newe quarrells and contradictions, in so much that the strife and contentions of youthes and children had like to have sett Men together by the eares, to the utter annihilatinge of all Christmas sportes for the whole yeare followinge.

"Wherfore for the avoydinge both the one, and the other, some who studied the quiet of all, mentioned the choosinge of a Christmas Lord, or Prince of the Revells, who should have authorytie both to appoynt & moderate all such games, and pastimes as should ensue, & to punishe all offenders which should any way hinder or interrupte the free & quiet passage of any antient & allowed sporte.

"This motion (for that the person of a Prince or Lorde of the Revells had not been knowen amongst them for thirty yeares before, and so consequentlye the danger, charge and trouble of such jestinge was cleane forgotten) was presentlye allowed and greedilye apprehended of all; Wher upon 13 of the senior Under graduates (7 of the bodye of the House & 6 Comoners, Electors in such a case) withdrew themselves into the parlour, where after longe debatinge whether they should chouse a Graduate or an Under Graduate, thinkinge the former would not vouchsafe to undertake it at theyr appoyntmentes, the latter should not be upheld & backed as it was meete & necessary for such a place, they came forth rather to make triall what would be done, than to resolve what should be done. And therefore at their first entrance into the Hall meeting Sir Towse a younge man (as they thought) fitt for the choyse, they laid handes on him, and by maine strength liftinge him upp, *viva voce*, pronounced him Lord. But hee as stronglye refusinge the place as they violentlye thrust it upon him, shewing with all reasons why hee could by no meanes undergoe such a charge, they gott onlye this good by their first attempt, that they understood heer by how that the whole Colledge was rather willinge a Seniour Batchelour at least, if not a junior Master should be chosen in to the place rather than any Under graduate, because they would rather an earnest sporte than a scoffinge jest should be made of it. Wher fore the Electors returninge againe into the Parlour and shuttinge the dore close upon themselves begaune more seriously to consult of the matter, and findinge some unable, some unwillinge to take the place, at length they concluded to make the 2 assay but with more formalitie and deliberation; resolvinge, if they were not now seconded of all handes, to meddle no more with it. Wherfore, enteringe the second time in to the Hall they desired one of the 10 Seniors & one of the Deanes of the Colledge to hold the Scrutinye and the Vice-President to sitt by as overseer, who willingly harkeninge to their request, sate all 3 downe at the highe table: Then the Electors went up one by one in senioritye to give their voyce by writinge. In the meane time there was great expectation who should bee the Man. Some in the lower ende of the Hall, to make sporte, had theyr Names loudest in their mouthes whome they least thought of in their mindes, & whome they knew should come shortest of the place. At length all the voyces being given and, accordinge to custome, the Scrutinie at large being burned, the Vice-president with the rest stoode upp, and out of the abstract the Deane read distinctly in the hearinge of all present as followeth

"*Nominantur in hoc Scrutinio duo quorum*

{   1 Joanes Towse, *habet suffragia sex.*
{   2us Thomas Tucker, *habet suffragia septem.*

"These wordes were not out of his mouthe before a generall and loud crie was made of Tucker, Tucker, Vivat, Vivat, &ct. After which all the younger sorte rane forth of the Colledge crieinge the same in the streets; which Sir Tucker beinge then howsde not farr from the Colledge, over hearinge, kept himself close till the companye were past, and then, as soone and secretly as he could, gott him to his Chamber; where (after he had been longe sought for abroad in the Towne, and at home in the Colledge, haste and desire out runinge it self, and seekinge there last where it might first finde) he was in a manner surprised, and more by violence than any will of his owne, taken upp & with continuall & joyfull outcries, carried about the Hall, and so backe to his Chamber, as his owne request was, where for that night he rested, dismissinge the Company and desiringe some time to think of their loves and goodwill, and to consider of his owne charge and place.

"About 3 or 4 dayes after, on the 5 of November the Lord Elect with the Batchelours, and some of the Senior Under-graduates came into the Hall where every man beinge seated in his order, many speaches were made by diverse of diverse matters, some commendinge a monarchicall state of Governmente, and the sometimes suddayne necessitye of Dictators, others discommendinge both. Some again extollinge sportes & revells, others mainely disallowinge them, all of them drawinge some conclusion concerninge the like or dislike of the government newly begune, and like for a little space to continue amongst them. In the ende the Lord Elect himselfe, to conclude all, delivered his owne minde in manner followinge:—

"Quż beneficia (Viri Electores clarissimi) plus difficultatis atque, oneris apportant collacata, quâ debite administrata; poterunt honoris, cautè magis primo in limine credo excipienda quâ aut imensæ dignitatis expectatione appetenda auidè, aut boni incogniti cœco appetitu app'hendenda temere. Quorŭ in albo (Electores conscripti) cŭ semper dignitates istiusmodi serio retulerim, Vos (pace dicã vestrż diligentiż) non tam mihi videmini gratias debere expectare, qua ipse istud onus suscepturus videor promereri. Nâ illud demum gratijs excipitur beneficiŭ (pro temporŭ ratione loquor) quod nec sollicitudo vrget nec officiŭ—Infinitż autem adeo sunt anxietates, quż vel istam dominatus ανατύπωσιν circumcingunt, vt pauci velint ipsas cŭ dominatu lubentèr amplecti, nulli possint euitare, nulli sustinere. Nâ vbi veri imperij facies est reprżsentanda expectanda semper est aliqua curarŭ proportio. Veru cum dignitas Electoria, amicitia suffragatoria, populi applausus, ôniŭ consensus Democratiż tollendż causâ ad primatum euocauerint, lubens animi nostri strenuæ renuentis temperabo impetŭ, et sedulò impendà curam, vt Reip: (si vobis minus possim singulis) toti satisfaciâ. Hic ego non itâ existimo opportunŭ progressuŭ nostrorŭ aduersarijs curâ imperij promiscuam et indigestam collaudantibus respondere, aut status Monarchici necessitatç efferentibus assentari: Disceptationŭ vestrarŭ non accessi judex, accersor imperator; Amori vestro (Viri nobis ad prime chari) lubens tribuo gloriż nostrż ortŭ; progressŭ augustŭ atque, gloriosu a vobis ex officio vestro exigere, prżter amorç nostrum fore no arbitror. Tyraŭidem non profiteor, imperiŭ exercebo. Cujus fœliciores processus vt promoueantur, atque indies stabiliant æris magis quam oris debetis esse prodigi. Quarè primitias amoris, atque officij vestri statuo extemplo exigendas, nè aut ipse sinè authoritate imperare, aut imperium sinè gloriâ capessisse videar Πολιτείαν Atheniensem sequimur, cujus ad norman Ego ad munus regui jam suffectus, Mineruæ, Vulcano et Prometheo sacra cũ ludorum curatoribus pro moris vsu, primâ meâ in his sacris authoritate fieri curabo. Interim vero (Viri nostrâ authoritate adhuc majores) juxta prædictæ Reipublicæ jmaginç choragos, seu adjutores desidero, qui nô tantum ludis pržponantur, sed et liberalitate pro opũ ratione in Reipublicż impensas vtentes, ex żre publico pržmia partim proponant, partim de suo insumant, hoc nomine quod illorũ sint pržfecti. Quż alia vestri sunt officij moniti pržstabitis, quæ amoris, vltro (vti Spero) offeretis.

"This was counted sufficient for his private installmente, but with all it was thought necessary that some more publicke notice hereof should be given to the whole Universitie, with more solemnitie and better fashion; yet before they would venter to publish their private intendements, they were desirous to knowe what authoritie and jurisdiction would be graunted to them, what money allowed them towards the better going through with that they had begune. And not long after the whole company of the Batchelours sent 2 bills to the Masters fire, the one cravinge duety and alleageance, the other money and maintenance in manner & forme followinge:

"The coppye of a Bill sent by the Lord Elect, and the whole Company of the Batchelours to the Masters fire, cravinge their duety and alleageance.

"Not doubtinge of those ceremonious and outward duetyes which yourselves (for example sake) will performe, Wee *Thomas Tucker* with the rest of the Bacchelours are bold to entreat, but as *Thomas, Lord Elect*, with the rest of our Councell are ready to expect, that no Tutor or Officer whatsoever shall at any time, or upon any occasion, intermeddle, or partake with any scholler, or youth whatsoever, but leavinge all matters to the discretion of our selves, stand to those censures and judgementes which wee shall give of all offenders that are under our govermente in causes appertaininge to our government. All wayes promisinge a carefull readinesse to see schollerlike excercise performed, and orderly quietnesse mayntained in all sortes; This as Wee promise for our owne partes, so Wee would willingly desire that you should promise the performance of the rest of your partes, accordinge to that bountye & love which allready you have shewed us.

Yours,	Thomas Tucker
Joseph Fletcher	Thomas Downer
John Smith	Rouland Juxon
Richard Baylye	John Huckstepp
Richard Baylye	James Bearblocke
John Towse	John English

"'This Bill subscribed with all their handes was seene and allowed by all the Masters, who promised rather more than lesse than that which was demanded. But concerninge the other Bill for Subsidyes, it was answered that it was not in their power to grant it without the President, whose cominge home was every day expected: against which time it was provided, and delivered unto him; who together with the 10 Seniors, was loath to grant any thinge till they were certified what sportes should bee, of what quality & charge, that so they might the better proportion the one to the other, the meanes to the matter: They were allso willinge to knowe what particular Men would take upon them the care of furnishinge particular nightes. For they would by no meanes relye upon generall promises because they were not ignorant how that which concerneth all in generall is by no man in speciall regarded. Wherfore they beinge somewhat, although not fully, satisfied in their demaundes by some of the Masters, whom they seemed cheefly to trust with the whole businesse, the Bill was againe perused, and every man ceazed in manner and forme followinge:

"'The coppye of an auncient Act for taxes and subsidyes made in the raygne of our Predecessor of famous memorye, in this Parliament held in Aula Regni the vith of November 1577 and now for Our Self new ratified and published, anno regni j° November 7° 1607.

"'Because all lovinge & loyall Subjects doe owe not onely themselves, but allso their landes, livinges, goodes, and what soever they call theirs, to the good of the Commonwealth, and estate under which they peaceably enjoy all, It is further enacted that no man dissemble his estate, or hide his abilitye, but be willinge at all times to pay such duetyes, taxes, and subsidies, as shall be lawfully demaunded & thought reasonable without the hinderance of his owne estate, upon payne of forfettinge himself and his goodes whatsoever.'

[List of contributions amounting to 52li xiiis. vii

"Though the whole company had thus largely contributed towards the ensuinge sportes, yet it was found that when all thinges necessary should be layed toegether, a great sum of money would be wantinge, and therfor a course was thought upon of sendinge out privie Seales to able & willinge Gentlemen which had been sometimes Fellowes or commoners of the Colledge that it would please them to better the stocke, and out of their good will contribute somewhat towardes the Prince's Revells."

Then followed the form of the writ issued, "To our trustye and welbeloved Knight, or Esquire," &c. "Given under our privye Seale at our Pallace of St. John's in Oxen, the seventh of December in the first yeare of our rayne, 1607." Then follow "the names of those who were served with this writt, and who most willingly obeyed upon the receipt thereof," contributing altogether xvili xs 0. "Others were served and bragd of it, as though they had given, but sent nothing."

"For all these Subsidies at home, and helpes abroad, yet it was founde that in the ende there would rather be want (as indeed it happened) than any superfluitye, and therfore the Prince tooke order with the Bowsers to send out warrantes to all the Tenantes & other friendes of the Colledge, that they should send in extraordinary provision against every Feast, which accordingly was performed; some sendinge money, some wine, some venison, some other provision, every one accordinge to his abilitye.

"All thinges beinge thus sufficiently (as it was thought) provided for, the Councell table, with the Lord himself, mett together to nominate officers & to appoint the day of the Prince's publike installment which was agreed should be on St. Andrews Day at night; because at that time the Colledge allso was to chouse their new officers for the yeare followinge.

"Now for that they would not playnely and barely install him without any farther ceremonies, it was thought fitt that his whole ensuinge Regiment (for good lucke sake) should be consecrated to the *Deitie of Fortune*, as the sole Mistres and Patronesse of his estate, and therfore a schollerlike devise called *Ara Fortunæ* was provided for his installment; which was performed in manner & forme followinge:

ARA FORTUNÆ.

Inter-locutores.

Princeps.	Princeps.
Fortuna.	Stultus.
Tolmæa.	Rebellis Primus.
Thesaurarius.	—Secundus.
>Camerarius.	—Tertius.
Jurisconsultus.	—Quartus.
Philosophus.	Nuncius

* * * * *

[The Drama is not given on account of its length. And it will be remarked that, whenever asterisks are substituted, some portion of the MS. has been omitted.

"This showe by ourselves was not thought worthye of a stage or scaffoldes, and therfore after supper the tables were onlye sett together, which was not done with out great toyle & difficulty, by reason of the great multitude of people (which, by the default of the dorekeepers, and divers others, every man bringinge in his friends) had filled the Hall before wee thought of it. But for all this it began before 8 of clock, and was well liked by the whole audience, who, how unrulye so ever they meante to bee afterwardes, resolved I think at first with their good applause and quiet behaviour to drawe us on so farr, as wee should not bee able to returne backwardes without shame & discreditt. They gave us at the ende 4 severall & generall plaudites; at the 2 wherof the Canopie which hunge over the Altare of Fortune (as it had been frighted with the noise, or meante to signifie that 2 plaudites were as much as it deserved) suddenly fell downe; but it was cleanly supported by some of the standers by till the company was voyded, that none but our selves took notice of it.

"Some upon the sight of this Showe (for the better enoblinge of his person, and drawinge his pedigree even from the Godes because the Prince's name was Tucker, and the last Prince before him was Dr. Case) made this conceipt that *Casus et Fortuna genuerunt* Τυχερον *Principem Fortunatum*—so the one his father, and the other his mother.

"Another accident worthy observation (and which was allso then observed) was that the Foole carelesly sittinge downe at the Prince's feete brake his staff in the midst, whence wee could not but directly gather a verye ill omen, that the default and follye of some would bee the very breaknecke of our ensueing sports, which how it fell out, I leave to the censures of others; our selves (I am sure) were guilty to our selves of many weaknesses and faultes, the number wherof were increased by the crossinge untowardnesse, and backwardnesse of divers of the Prince's neerest followers, nay the Prince himself had some weaknesses which did much prejudice his state, wherof the chiefest weere his openesse, and familiaritye with all sortes, beinge unwillinge to displease eny, yet not able to please all. But to proceede:—On St. Thomas day at night the officers before elect were solemnly proclaimed by a Sergeant at armes, and an Herauld, the trumpetts soundinge beetwixt every title. This proclamation after it was read, was for a time hunge up in the Hall, that every man might the better understande the qualitie of his owne place, and they that were of lower, or no place, might learne what duety to performe to others.

"The manner wherof was as followeth:

"Whereas by the contagious poyson, and spreadinge malice of some ill disposed persons, hath been threatned not onelye the danger of subvertinge peaceable & orderlye proceedinges, but the allmost utter annihilatinge of auncient & laudable customes—It hath been thought convenient, or rather absolutely necessarye for the avoydinge of a most dangerous ensuinge Anarchie, a more settled order of goverment, for the better safetye of all well meaninge Subjects, and curbinge of discontented, headstronge persons, should bee established. And whereas through wante of good lawes by wise and discreet Magistrates to bee duely and truely executed, a giddye conceipt hath possest the mindes of manye turbulent spirites, of endueringe no superiour, hardly an equall, whereby the common-wealth might growe to bee a manye-headed monster—It hath been provided by the staide and mature deliberations of well-experienced governours and provident counsellours, that one whose highe deserts might answere his high advancement should bee sett over all to the rulinge and directinge of all—Therefore by these presentes bee it knowne unto all of what estate or condicion soever whome it shall concerne that Thomas Tucker, an honorable wise & learned Gentleman to the great comeforte of the weale-publique from hence-forth to be reputed, taken and obayed for the true, onely and undoubted Monarche of this revellinge Climate, whom the generall consent and joynte approbation of the whole Common-wealth hath invested and crowned with these honours and titles followinge:

"The most magnificent and renowned Thomas by the favour of Fortune, Prince of Alba Fortunata, Lord St. Johns, high Regent of the Hall, Duke of St. Giles, Marquesse of Magdalens, Landgrave of the Grove, County Palatine of the Cloisters, Chiefe Bailiffe of the Beaumonts, high Ruler of Rome, Maister of the Manor of Waltham, Governour of Gloster-greene, sole Commaunder of all Titles, Tourneaments, and Triumphes, Superintendent in all Solemnities whatsoever.

"Now because they whom the unknowne cares, & unweildie burdens of a sole regiment shall relie upon, neede extraordinary helpe in the more than ordinarye affaires, Hee hath as well for the better discharge & ease of those royall duetyes (as it were) which attend on his place, as for the avoidinge the odious & ingratefull suspition of a single dominion, and private Tyranye, selected and chosen unto himself a grave and learned assistance both for Councell and government, whom, and every of which, his princely will is, shall in their severall places & dignities bee both honoured and obeid, with no lesse respect and observance than if himself were there present in person. And that carelesse ignorance may bee no lawfull excuse for the breach of his will therin hee hath appointed their severall names and titles, with their subordinate officers and deputies to be signified & proclaimed to all his lovinge and leige Subjects, in manner followinge:

"The right gracious John Duke of Groveland, Earle de Bello-Monte, Baron Smith, chiefe Ranger of the Woods & Forests, great Master of the Prince's Game, hath for his subordinate officers—

Sir Frauncis Hudson, Keeper of the Parkes, & Warder of the Warrens.
Sir Thomas Grice, Forrester & Sargeaunt of the Woodhowse.

"The right honourable Rowland Lord Juxon, Lord Chauncelour, Keeper of the Great Seale, Signer of all publicke Charters, Allower of all Priviledges, hath for his subordinate officers.

Sir William Dickenson, Master of the Requests, & the Prince's Remembrancer.
Sir Owen Vertue, Clerke of the Signet, and Chafer of Waxe.

"The right honourable Thomas Lord Downer, Lord high Treasurer, Receaver General of all Rents, Revenues, Subsidies, belonginge by Nature, custome or accident to the Prince; the great Payemaster of all necessary charges appertayninge to the Court, hath for his subordinate Officers—

Sir John Williamson, Steward of the Household, Disburser for the Familye.
Sir Christopher Wren, Cofferer, and Clerke of the Exchequer.

"The right honourable Joseph Lord Fletcher, Lord high Admirall, great Commaunder of all the narrow seas, floods and passages; Surveyor of the Navye, Mayster of the Ordinance, hath for his subordinate Officers,

Sir Stephen Angier, Warden of the Cinque Ports, and Victualler of the Fleet.

Sir Anthony Steevens, Captayne of the Guard.

"The right honourable Richard Lord Baylie, Lord high Marshall,
President of all Titles, and Tourneaments, Commander in
all Triumphes, Suppressor of suddayne tumultes, Supervisor
of all games, and publique pastimes, hath for his subordinate
Officers,

Sir William Blagrove, Master of the Revells.
Sir John Hungerford, Knight Marshall, severe Commander of
the Wayes for the Prince's passage.

"The right honourable John Lord Towse, Lord high Chamberlayne,
Purveyor for the Prince's pallace, Overseer of all feasts and
banquets, furnisher of all Chambers, and Galleries, Examiner
of all private pastimes, hath for his subordinate Officers,

Sir Richard Swinerton   }   the Prince's Wards and
Sir William Cheyney   }   Squiers of his bodye.
Mr. Edward Cooper, Groome-Porter.

"The right honourable Richard Lord Holbrooke, Comptroller
Generall, Chiefe overseer of all Purseavants, Orderer of all
household Servaunts, hath for his subordinate officers,

Sir Thomas Stanley   } Sergeaunts at Armes &
Mr. John Alford   }   Gentlemen Ushers to the Prince
Mr. Brian Nailor, Master of the Robes of State, Keeper of the
Wardrobe, and Surveyor of Liveries.

"The right honourable James Lord Berbloke, principall Secretarye,
Lord privye Seale, designer of all Embasies, Drawer of
all Edicts and Letters, Scribe to the State, hath for his
subordinate Officers,

Sir Thomas Clarke, Master of the Roles, & Prothonotarye.
Mr. Marcheaumount Nedham, Clerke of the Councell-table.

"The right honourable John Lord English, Lord Chiefe Justice, Examiner of all causes Capitall; Sessor upon life and death, Judge of controversies criminall, hath for his subordinate Officers,

Sir John Alder, Attourney Generall, and the Prince's Solicitor.
Mr. John Sackevile, Baylife Erraunt.

"Now because good Governours without good laws, carefull Magistrates without wholesome Statutes are like dumb (though paynted) images, or unweapon'd soldiers—Hee of his absolute authoritye, conferred upon him in the late free election, doth ratifie and establish all such Decrees and Statutes, as Hee now findeth wisely and warely ordayned of his famous Predecessor; promisinge onely by a full and severe execution to put life in their dead remembrance, Adding moreover some few cautions to be observed in his ensuinge Triumphs."

These statutes were ratified and established by the Prince "at our Manor of Whites-Hall, December the 21st in the first of our Raygne."

"The same night the Prince, with the rest of his Councell meetinge at the high table in the Hall, a Bill was preferred by the Lord Treasurer for the advancement of Mr. Henery Swinarton to the Earldome of Cloyster-sheere, and the over-seeinge of the Princes great Librarye." After due consideration, "the Prince at length graunted the request, and his title was presently drawne by the Clerke of the Councell-table, and pronounced in manner followinge:

"The right honourable Henry Lord Swinarton, Earle of Cloister-Sheer, Barron of the Garden, chiefe Master of the Presse, and overseer of the Prince's great Librarye, hath for his subordinate Officers,

Mr. William Rippin, Surveyor of the Walkes.
Mr. Christopher Riley, Corrector of the Printe.

"From this time forward, and not before, the Prince was thought fully to be instal'd, and the forme of government fully established, in-so-much that none might or durst contradict anything which was appoynted by himself, or any of his officers.

"The Holy-dayes beinge now at hand, his privye-chamber was provided and furnisht, wherein a chayre of state was placed upon a carpett with a cloth of state hanged over it, newly made for the same purpose. On Christmas Day in the morninge he was attended on to prayers by the whole companye of the Bacchelours, and some others of his Gentlemen Ushers, bare before him. At dinner beinge sett downe in the Hall at the high table in the Vice-president's place (for the President himself was then allso present) he was served with 20 dishes to a messe, all which were brought in by Gentlemen of the Howse attired in his Guard's coats, ushered in by the Lord Comptroller, and other Officers of the Hall. The first messe was a Boar's Head, which was carried by the tallest and lustiest of all the Guard, before whom (as attendants) wente first, one attired in a horseman's coate, with a Boars-speare in his hande, next to him an other Huntsman in greene, with a bloody faucion drawne; next to him 2 Pages in tafatye sarcenet, each of them with a messe of mustard; next to whome came hee that carried the Boares-head crost with a greene silk scarfe, by which hunge the empty scabbard of the faulcion which was carried before him. As they entered the Hall, he sang this Christmas Caroll, the three last verses of everie staffe beinge repeated after him by the whole companye:

> 1. The Boare is dead,
>   Loe, here is his head,
>   What man could have done more
>   Than his head off to strike,
>   Meleager like,
>   And bringe it as I doe before?

> 2. He livinge spoyled
>   Where good men toyled,
>   Which made kinde Ceres sorrye;
>   But now dead and drawne,
>   Is very good brawne,
>   And wee have brought it for you.

3. Then sett downe the Swineyard,
    The foe to the Vineyard,
      Lett Bacchus crowne his fall,
    Lett this Boare's-head and mustard
    Stand for Pigg, Goose, and Custard,
      And so you are wellcome all.

"At this time, as on all other Holy-dayes, the Princes allowed Musitions (which were sent for from Readinge, because our owne Town Musick had given us the slipp, as they use to doe at that time when we had most need of them) played all dinner time, and allso at supper. The Prince as ofte as hee satt in the Hall was attended on by a Commoner and Scholler of the Colledge in tafaty sarcenett. After supper there was a private Showe performed in the manner of an Interlude, contayninge the order of the Saturnalls, and shewinge the first cause of Christmas-candles, and in the ende there was an application made to the Day and Nativitie of Christ, all which was performed in manner followinge:

SATURNALIA.

HERCULES
CURIUS
DOULUS

* * * * *

"This shew was very well liked of our selves, and the better: first, because itt was the voluntary service of a younge youth; nexte, because there were no strangers to trouble us.

"St. Steevens day was past over in silence, and so had St. John's day also; butt that some of the Prince's honest neighbours of St. Giles's presented him with a maske, or morris, which though it were but rudely performed, yet itt being so freely and lovingly profered, it could not but bee as lovingly received.

"The same nighte, the twelve daies were suddenly, and as it were extempore, brought in, to offer their service to the Prince, the holy-daies speaking Latine, and the working-daies English, the transition was this:

Yee see these working-daies they weare no satten,
And I assure you they can speake no Latten;
But if you please to stay a-while,
Some shepheard for them will change the style.

"After some few daunces the Prince, not much liking the sporte (for that most of them were out both in their speeches and measures, having but thought of this devise some few houres before) rose, and lefte the hall, after whose departure, an honest fellow to breake of the sportes for that night, and to void the company made suddenly this Epilogue:

These daunces were perform'd of yore
By many worthy Elfes,
Now if you will have any more
Pray shake your heeles your selves.

"The next day being Innocents-day, it was expected, and partly determined by our selves, that the Tragedy of *Philomela* should have been publickly acted, which (as wee thought) would well have fitted the day, by reason of the murder of Innocent Itis. But the carpenters being no way ready with the stage, or scaffolds (whereof notwithstanding some were made before Christmas), wee were constrained to deferre it till the nexte day, which was the 29th of December.

PHILOMELA.

TEREUS, REX THRACIÆ.
PROGNE, REGINA, UXOR TEREI,
EUGENES, A CONSILIJS TEREI.
TRES SOCII TEREI A CLASSE,
ANCILLA PROGNES.
PHILOMELA, SOROR PROGNES
ITIS, FILIUS PRONGES ET TEREI
ANCILLA PHILOMELÆ.
FAUSTULUS, PASTOR REGIUS.
FAUSTULA, PASTORIS FILIA.

CHORUS.
Terra
Mare.

* * * * *

"The whole play was wel acted and wel liked.

"New-yeare's eve was wholly spent in preparation for the Prince's triumphs, so that nothing was done or expected that night.

"Next day in the morning (beeing New-yeare's-day) the Prince sent Mr. Richard Swinnerton, one of the Squires of his body to Mr. President with a paire of gloves, charging him to say nothing but these two verses:

The Prince and his Councell, in signe of their loves,

Present you, their President, with these paire of gloves.

"There was some what else written in the paper which covered them, but what it is uncertaine.

"At night were celebrated the Prince's triumphs, at which time onely and never before nor after he was carryed in full state from his pallace to the hall, where in the sight of the whole University a supplication was presented unto him by Time and seconded with a shew called *Times Complaint*. It was performed in manner and forme following:

TIME'S COMPLAINT.

Time.
Veritas, the Daughter of Time.
Opinion   }   Seducers of Veritas.
Error   }
Studioso, a Scholler.
Manco, a lame Souldiour.
Clinias, a poore Country-man.
Humphry Swallow, a drunken Cob
Goodwife Spiggot, an Ale-wife.
Philonices, a rangling Lawyer.
Seruus Philonices.
Bellicoso, a Casheere Corporall.

"Worthelie heere wee bring you Time's Complaint
Whom we have most just cause for to complaine of,
For hee hath lent us such a little space
That what wee doe wants much of its true grace.
Yet let your wonted love that kindelie take,
Which we could wish were better for your sake.

EnterTIME with the Musicians to place them

Time. O wellsaid, wellsaid; wellcome, wellcome, faith!
It doth mee good to see I have some friends.
Come, true observers of due time, come on:
A fitt of musicke, but keepe time, keepe time
In your remembrance still, or else you jarre:
These for my sake too much neglected are.
The world termes them beggars, fidling roagues,
But come my fidling friends, I like you well,
And for my sake I hope this company,
Naie more the Prince himselfe, will like your tunes.
Here take your place and shew your greatest skill,
All now is well that is not verie ill.

TIME expecting the comming of the Prince (to whom hee preferreth a petition) placeth himselfe on the stage till the traine bee past.

This waie hee comes, here will I place my selfe,
They saie hee is an honourable Prince,
Respectfull, curteous, liberall, and learn'd:
If hee bee soe hee will not choose but heare mee.
Poore aged Time was never so abused,
If not for my sake, yet for his owne good,
Hee will read over my petition.
Oft hath the like beene drawne and given up
To his nobilitie; But carelesse they
In theire deepe pockets swallow good men's praiers.
This his owne hand shall have, or I will keepe it:—
But here they come, stand close and viewe the traine.

Enter first six Knighte Marshalls men in suitable liveries with links and truncheons two by two.

Next the Knighte Marshall alone in armour and bases with a truncheon.

Then fower other of his men as before.

After these fower Knightes in rich apparell with hats and feathers, rapiers and daggers, bootes and spurres, everie one his Lackie attending on him with torch-light, all two by two.

After these the Master of the Requests, the Master of the Robes in vaste velvet gownes, with Lackies and torches before them.

After these fower Barons in velvet cloakes, likewise attended with Lackies and torches.

After these an Herald at Armes bare, with two Lackies attendant bearing torches.

After these six of the privie Counsell in Schollars gownes and civill hoods, everie one attended on by a Footman bearing on his jacket both behind and before his Lord's armes according to his office (as it is before mentioned) with torches alsoe in theire hands.

After those two Sergeants at armes, with great Maces, and two Squiers before them with torches, all bare.

After these two Hench-men, the one with a sword, the other with a scepter, likewise attended by two Squiers with torch lights, all bare.

After these the Prince himselfe in a scholler's gowne and civill hood, with a coronett of laurell about his hat, attended on by fower footmen in suitable liveries with torches.

After these the Captaine of the guard alone in hose and dublett, hatt and feather, etc., and following him, twenty of the guard in suitable guards' coats and halberds in their hands, and lightes intermingled here and there.

"When this traine first entered out of the Prince's palace there was a volye of shotte to the number of fiftie or three-score gunnes, and once againe as it passed through the quadrangle, and the third time when the Prince was readie to enter uppon the stage in the hall, after which third peale ended, the nobilitie having past along some parte of the stage, the rest of the traine disposed in places provided for them, and the Prince himselfe newlie entered, the showe went forward.

* * * * *

"It hath beene observed if they which performe much in these kinde of sportes must needs doe something amisse, or at the least such is the danger and trouble of them, that something in the doing will miscarry, and so be taken amisse, and such was our fortune at this time; for the Prologue (to the great prejudice of that which followed) was most shamefully out, and having but halfe a verse to say, so that by the very sense the audience was able to prompt him in that which followed, yet hee could not goe forward, but after long stay and silence, was compelled abruptly to leave the stage, whereupon beeing to play another part, hee was so dasht, that hee did nothing well that night.

"After him Good-wife Spiggot, comming forth before her time, was most miserably at a non plus & made others so also, whilst her selfe staulked in the middest like a great Harry-Lion (as it pleased the audience to terme it), either saying nothing at all, or nothing to the purpose.

"The drunken-man, which in the repetitions had much pleased and done very well, was now so ambitious of his action, that he would needs make his part much longer than it was, and stood so long upon it all, that he grew most tedious, whereuppon it was well observed and said by one that

> —'twas pitty there should bee
> In any pleasing thing satiety.

"To make up the messe of absurdities the company had so fil'd the stage, that there was no roome to doe any thing well, to bee sure many thinges were mistaken and therefore could not but bee very distastfull, for it was thought that particular men were aymed at, and disciphered by the drunken-man, and Justice Bryar, though it was fully knowne to our-selves that the author had no such purpose.

"In fine, expectation the devourer of all good endeavours had swallowed more in the very name and title of the interlude than was either provided or intended in the whole matter, for wee onely proposed to our selves a shew, but the towne expected a perfect and absolute play, so that all things mett to make us unhappy that night, and had not Time him selfe (whose lines and actions were thought good) somewhat pleased them, they would never have endured us without hissing, howsoever in the end they gave us two or three cold plaudites, though they departed no way satisfyed, unlesse it were in the shew about the quadrangle, wherein the Prince was carryd to his chamber in the same state that hee came from thence in the beginning (as is above mentioned), the whole company of actors beeing added to his traine who immediately followed him before the guard in this order:

First, Time alone, attended, with two pages and lightes.

Next, Veritas alone, likewise attended.

Then Error and Opinion, which all the way they went pull'd Veritas by the sleeve, one by one and the other by the other, but shee would not harken to them.

After these came Studioso and Philonices, both pleading the case, one upon his ringers and the other with both his hands.

Then came Manco, the lame souldiour and Philonices his man; the souldiour haulting without his cruch, the other beating him with the cruch for counterfeyting.

After these came Clinias and Bellicoso houlding the halter betwixt them, which Bellicoso had found in Clinias his pocket.

Last after these came Humphry Swallow and good wife Spiggot, hee reeling uppon her, she pulling and hayling him for the money he ought her.

After these came the guard as before, and so the Prince in full state was conveyed to his pallace.

"Here wee were all so discouraged that wee could have found in our heartes to have gone no farther. But then consulting with our selves wee thought it no way fitt to leave when thinges were at the worst, and therefore resolved by more industry and better care of those things which should follow, to sue out a fine of recovery for our credites. Whereuppon the comedy which was already a foote and appointed to bee done on 12 day, was revewed and corrected by the best judgments in the house, & a Chorus by their direction inserted, to excuse former faults, all which was a cause that Twelfe eve & Twelfe day past away in silence, because the comedy beeing wholy altered could not bee so soone acted, neyther could any other thing bee so suddenly provided to furnish those nights.

"Heere the Lord-treasurer made a complaint to the King and the rest of his councell that his treasure was poore and almost exhausted, so that without a fresh supply or new subsidy nothing more could bee done. And that this might not seem an idle complaint, a bill of some of the particulars and chiefe expences was exhibited, wherein it might appeare how costly the presedent revels had beene."

The "Bill of Expences" amounted to lxiiijli vs od.

"This bill beeing seene and allowed, they begane to cast about for more money, whereuppon a new privy seale was drawn in Latin." "Those which were served with this writte and obey'd" contributed a total sum of 5li.

"This beeing not as yet sufficient there was a new subsedy levyed by the Junior Masters and the rest of the Colledge to the summe of Six Poundes three shillings, whereuppon finding themselves againe before hand, and resolving to save nothing for a deare yeare, they proceeded to new expences and new troubles.

"The Suneday after, beeing the last day of the Vacation and tenth day of the moneth, two shewes were privately performed in the Lodging, the one presently after dinner called *Somnium Fundatoris*, viz., the tradition that wee have concearning the three trees that wee have in the President his garden. This interlude by the reason of the death of him that made it, not long after was lost, and so could not bee heere inserted; but it was very well liked, and so wel deserved, for that it was both wel penned and well acted.

"Now because before were divers youths whose voyces or personages would not suffer them to act any thing in publicke, yet withall it was thought fitt, that in so publicke a buisnes every one should doe some thing, therefore a mocke play was provided called *The 7 Dayes of the Weeke*, which was to be performed by them which could do nothing in earnest, and, that they should bee sure to spoyle nothing, every man's part was sorted to his person, and it was resolved that the worse it was done, the better it would be liked, and so it fell out; for the same day after supper it was presented by one who bore the name of the Clerke of St. Gyleses, and acted privately in the lodging in manner and forme following:

THE SEVEN DAYES OF THE WEEKE.

Interloqutores.

The Clerke of St. Gyleses.
Mooneday.
Tuseday.
Wenesday.
Thurseday.
Frieday.
Satterday.
Suneday.
Night.

CHORUS.

A Woman
A Paire of Snuffers.

Enter the Clerke with all his Acteurs.

PROLOGUE

Clerke.

"I am the poore, though not unlettered, Clerke,
And these your subjects of St. Gyles his parishe,
Who in this officious season would not sharke
But thought to greet your highnesse with a morrice,
Which since my riper judgement thought not fitt,
They have layd down their wisedomes to my witt.

And that you might perceive (though seeminge rude)
Wee savour somewhat of the Academie,
Wee had adventur'd on an enterlude
But then of actors wee did lacke a manye;
Therefore we clipt our play into a showe,
Yet bigg enough to speake more than wee knowe.

The subject of it was not farr to seeke
Fine witts worke mickle matter out of nifle:
Nam'd it I have *The Seven Dayes of the Weeke*,
Which though perchaunce grave heads may judge a trifle,
Yet if their action answere but my penninge,
You shall heare that, that will deserve a hemminge.

To tell the argument, were to forstalle
And sour the licquour of our sweete conceate;
Here are good fellowes that will tell you all
When wee begin once, you shall quickely ha'te,
Which if your grace will grace with your attention,
You shall soone sounde the depth of our invention."

[Then follows the mock play in seven Acts.

"Nothing, throughout the whole yeare, was better liked and more pleasant than this shewe, in so much that, although it were more privately done before our selves onely or some few friends, yet the report of it went about all the towne, till it came to the Vice-chauncellours and L. Clifford's eares, who were very desyrous to see it acted againe, and so it was as heereafter shal bee specifyed.

"The next day beeing Munday the 11 of January the terme should have begun in the house, but because of the extreame cold and froast which had now continued full six weekes and better without any intermission, as also by reason the hall was still pestered with the stage and scaffolds which were suffered to stand still in expectation of the Comedy, therefore it was agreed by the President and the officers that the terme should bee prorogued for 7 dayes longer in which time it was agreed the Comedy should bee publickely acted on Friday, the 15th day of January.

"But heere the President and some of the Seniors in abundance of care were affrayd to put any thing againe to the publicke view of the University, because their last paines at *The Complaint of Time* had so ill thriving. Besides the season was so severe and tempestuous with wind and snow, which had continued some dayes without ceasing, and the complaint of the poore was so grievious for want of wood and meate, which by this time were growne very scant and deere, that they urged it was a time rather to lament and weepe than make sports in, whereupon a streight inhibition was sent out from the officers, that no man should thinke of playing that night or any time after, till the weather should breake up and bee more temperate, for they thought it no way fitt publickly to revell at a time of such generall wo and calamity.

"But yet because all thinges were in a readinesse and the expectation of the whole towne was set uppon that night, the younger men of the Colledge went forward with their buisnes, intending to take no notice of what the officers had aggreed uppon, wherefore some of the officers were fayne to come in person to forbid the worke-men, and to undo some things which were already done, to the great griefe and discouragement of all the youth, who, though the weather was extreame cold, were themselves most hotte uppon the matter in hand, resolving now or never to recover their losse credit.

"And, as though the heavens had favoured their designes, so it happened that about noone the weather brake up and it begann to thaw, whereuppon the President was agayne importun'd by the Prince himselfe and his councell for the performance of the Comedy that night; who (seeing they were all so earnest) did not so much graunt, as not deny them, their request, whereuppon they begann againe to sett forward the buisnes, and what they wanted in time they made up by their willingnesse and paynes, so that for all these crosses they begann the play before 7 a clocke and performed it in manner following:

PHILOMATHES.

INTERLOQUTORES.

CHORUS.

JANUS.

TEMPUS.

| Motus. | Locus. |
| Quies. | Vacuum. |

Philomathes.	Sophia.
Chrysophilos, Senex Avarus.	Antarchia.
Phantasta, Stolidus Generosus.	Anthadia.
Phantasta, Stolidus Generosus.	Anthadia.
Αφρόνιος, Filius Chrysophili.	Anæa, Mulier Inepta.

Chrestophilos, Socius Philomathis.
Crito, Senex, Pater Sophiæ.
Critonis Seruus.
Cerdoos, Seruus Chrysophili.
Petinus, Seruus Phantastæ.

* * * * *

"This play was very well acted, but especially the Chorus, the stage was never more free, the audience never more quiett and contented, so that they went away many of them crieing—*Abundè satisfactum est!* itt was so well liked and applauded of all that saw itt.

"Here the stage & scaffold were pul'd downe which had stood from Cristmas, and it was resolved that upon the chaunge of the weather, the terme should begin on the Munday following.

"But in the meane time on Sunday nighte, being the Seventeenth of January, the Vice-chancelor, and the L. Clifford, with many other Doctors and Gentlemen were invited to supper in the President's lodging, where after supper they were entertained with a shew before mentioned, to witt, *The Seven Dayes in the Weeke*, to which, by this time, there was somewhat added, but not much: all was most kindly accepted, and the nighte was spent in great mirth. For the straungenes of the matter, and rarity of the fashion of their action pleased above expectation.

"At the end of this shew for the more rarity, there was one brought in my Lord's Stockes with this speech made uppon itt:

"'My Lord, I which am the lowest, am now become the lowdest, though (I hope) not the lewdest of your Lordshippe's servauntes. And though I come *pridie Calendas*, before I am cald, yet (I hope) my audacity shall have audience, and my faithfulnes favor. I am your Lordshippe's Elephaunt and heere is your castell, so that where other Lords are brought to their castells, heere your castell is brought to you. *Est locus in carcere*, there is a locke upon your Lordshippe's castell, which was committed unto my trust, how faithfull I have been therein they can tell who have taken an exact measure of my office by the foote: the matter of which your castell is builded is so precious, that there is none amongst company but is contented to wear of it within his buttons, the end for which it was builded is very commendable, that they may bee kepte in order with wood, which otherwise would not bee kepte in order, heere is *fons latus pedibus tribus*, a fountaine to wash three mens legs, that they which have bene *aurium tenus*, over shoes, heere may be *crurum tenus* over bootes too, This your Lordshippe's oracle or Tripos, out of which malefactors tell the truth and foretell of their amendment. Nay, I wil bee bould to compare it to your Lordshippe's braine, for what is there designed is heere executed. In these sells or ventricles are fancy, understanding, and memory. For such as your Lordshippe doth not fancy are put in the first hole, such as were dull and without understanding were put in the second hole, but such as your Lordshippe threatned (remember this) or I'le remember you, were put in the last and lowest dungeon, *cum nemini obtrudi potest itur ad me*. When they cannot bee ruled otherwise they are brought unto mee, and my entertainment is *strato discumbitur ostro*, they straite sett downe att this oister table, where they are fast and doe fast, ffor *vinitur exiguo melius*, they make small meales, till the flames of clemency doe mitigate the Salamanders of your Lordshippe's severity. Now, my Lord, since I have told you what I am, I will bee bould to tell you what you may bee—You are mortall—Ergo you must die, the three sisters will not spare you, though you were their owne brother, and therefore while you have your good witts about you, *fac quid vobis*, make your will, that wee may know amongst so many well deserving men, that doe lay claime to this your castell, to whome as rightfull heire itt shall lawfully descend, that so all controversies being ended, before your Lordshippe's deceasse, hereafter your bones may ly, and wee your subjects live, in all rest and quietnes.

"'Dixi.'

"To make an end of this nighte's sporte, all departed merry and very well pleased, the actors were much commended, and the terme for their sakes prorogued one day longer.

"On the Thursday following the Prince was solemnly invited by the Canons of Christchurch to a comedy called *Yuletide*, where many thinges were either ill ment by them, or ill taken by us, but wee had very good reason to think the former, both for that the whole towne thought so, and the whole play was a medley of Christmas sportes, by which occasion Christmas Lords were much jested at, and our Prince was soe placed that many thinges were acted upon him, but yet, Mr. Deane himselfe, then vice-chancelor, very kindly sent for the Prince and some others of our howse, and laboured to satisfie us, protesting that no such thing was mente, as was reported, whereupon wee went away contented, and forebore the speaking of many things which otherwise were afterwards intended, for aunswering of them in their owne kind.

"On Candlemas nighte it was thoughte by our selves, and reported in the towne, that the Prince should resigne his place, but nothing being in readines for that purpose itt was deferred, but yet, least nothing should bee done, there was a Vigilate (as they terme it) a watching nighte procured by the Prince and his Counsell, and graunted by the officers of the Colledge, which was performed in manner following.

"THE VIGILATE.

"First, about eighte of the Clocke (for then itt was to begin, and to continue till fowre in the morning) the Colledge gates were shutt, and all the students summon'd by the sounding of a Trumpett three times, to make their personall appearance in the greate Hall, where after they were all come together, that the Prince's pleasure might bee the better knowne, this proclamation was publikely pronounced by a Serjeant att Armes, in the hearing of them all.

"The high and mighty Thomas by the favour of Fortune Prince of Alba Fortunata, Lord St. Johns, High Regent of the Hall, &c. To all Presidents, Vice Presidents, Officers, Readers, Masters, Batchelors, Felowes, Schollers, Commoners, Under-commoners, Servaunts, Scruitors, sendeth greeting.

Whereas of late by the turbulent spirits of seditious minded persons hath bene buzzed into the eares of many of our loving and liege subjectes a fearefull and dangerous report of our sudden downefall, which according to their libelling speeches should att this nighte fall upon us—We have thought it necessary not so much for our owne feares which are none at all, as for satisfieing and strengthening our welmeaning friends in their love and duty, to publish and by these presents to all our loyal subjects of what state and condicion soever, that they make their personall appearance to the setting and furnishing of a most strong guarde and carefull watch as well for their security as the safety of our owne royall person, & the whole Common-wealth; In the which generall watch for the better comfort and ease of all men, our selfe, with our honourable privy Counsell, and the rest of our Nobility, intend to bee personally present.

"But because wee are no way minded to oppresse any man above his power, on our princely bounty, wee give licence to such as (for age or infirmity) are not able to perform that duty, to forfaite for their absence, yf they plead age ijs. vid.; if infirmity, xiid., towards the furnishing of his Highnes with a tall and sufficient watchman.

"Now because that which wee have wisely thought, and for our peace and safety, may not proove the cause of new troubles and dissentions, wee have thought good to adjoine some few cautions, in way of admonitions to bee observed.

"First, for that the disorders of an unruly and mutinous watch doe often open as it were the gate of danger and outrage, our princely will and pleasure is, that each man keepe his station with out murmuring, performing cheerefully all such offices and duties, as shal bee lawfully enjoin'd by us, or our offices, upon paine of forfeiting ijs. vid., as for age.

"Secondly, because sloth is a kind of disease in a well-ordered Common-wealth wee further charge and command by the vertue of our absolute authority, that no man bee found winking, or pincking, or nodding, much lesse snorting, upon paine of forfaiting twelve pence, as for infirmity.

"Thirdly, for the avoiding of a sudden dearth, or lingring famine which may ensue and justly follow the free and undoubted liberty of a riotous and luxurious time, yt is by us thought necessary that no man should in hugger mugger eate or drincke more than is publickly seene and allowed by the face of the body civill and politicke, upon paine of paieing twise, for such is in a manner stolen provision, and the second paiement to bee arbitrary.

"Given att our Mannor of Whites-hall, the seacond of February, and in the first of our Raigne.

"This proclamation being read and set up in the great hall, the Prince called for his officers and servants about him, charging every man carefully to execute his office. First the steward and buttler (who for their auncient fidelity kept their places according as they had long before beene appointed by the Colledge) were commaunded to bring their bookes, and by them to call up all the howse, whereupon (every one beeing first charged to aunswere to his name) it presently appeared who were present and who were absent.

"After this the Master of the Revels and the Knight Marshall were willed to appoint severall sportes that no man might bee seene idle upon payne of the Prince's high displeasure whereupon presently some went to cardes, some to dice, some to dauncing, every one to some thing.

"Not long after, for more variety sake, there was brought in a maske; the devise was sudden and extempore, videl: a little page attired in his long coats, with these six verses which were spoke as soone as he entered the hall.

"These are six carpet knights, and I one page
Can easily bring in six that bee of age,
They come to visite this your highnes court,
And if they can, to make your honour sport.
Nay, this is all, for I have seene the day
A richer maske had not so much to say.

"After these maskers had finished the measures, and some few other daunces, the said page waved them forth with his wan, and spake these two verses:

"There are three they say would shew you an anticke,
But when you see them, you'll thinke them franticke.

"Then there came in three in an anticke which were well attyred for that purpose, and daunced well to the great delite of the beholders.

"After these had stollen away one by one, as the manner is, it pleased the Prince to aske what was a clocke, it beeing aunswered almost twelve hee presently called in for supper. But first the bill of those which were before noted to bee absent was called, to see whether any of them would yet appeare, and the Prince would deale favourably with them. It was also examined whether any of those which were present before were now gon to bed, and accordingly authority was given by the Prince to the marshalls of the hall and other officers to search the chambers for sleepers, and where they made aunswere to aske the reason of their slothfull neglect or wilfull contempt of the Prince's commands, and if they pleaded either infirmity or age to take their fine, and so quietly to depart, first causing them faithfull to give their words that they harboured no other idle or suspicious parsons. But if they knoct at any of the chambers of those that were absent and nobody would answer, then they had full authority to breake open the dores and to make a privy search, and if they found any abed they tooke them as they were in their shirts and carryed them downe in state to the hall after this manner:—

"First went the marshals with lights to make room.

Then came one squire carrying the goune of him whom they brought and another that carryed his hatt & band.

Then came two other squires whereof one carryed his dublet the other his breeches.

Then came two with lights.

Next came he that was in his shirt carryed by two in a chaire and covered with a blanket.

Last behind came one squire more that carryed his shoes & stockings.

"All these beeing entered the hall, the squires made their attendance about him, with great observance, every one reaching him his apparrell as it pleased him to call for it, and then also helping him on with it. And this was the punishment of those that were found a bed.

"Others which were found up in their chambers & would not answer were violently brought downe with bills and staves as malefactors and by the Knight Marshals appointment were committed close prisoners to the Prince's castle, videl. the stocks, which were placed upon a table to that purpose, that those which were punished might bee seene to the terrour of others.

"By this time supper was ready and the sewer called to the dresser whereupon the buttery bell was presently rung, as it uses to bee at other ordinary meales, besides a trumpet was sounded at the kitchen hatch to call the wayters together.

"After the first messe was served in, the Prince with the rest of his councell satt downe, then all the rest of the howse in seniority.

"Towardes the end of supper two gentlemen of the second table fell out, wee could never distinctly know about what, it was verely supposed themselves scarsly knew, but from wordes they fell suddenly to blowes, and ere any man was aware, one of them had stabbed the other into the arme with his knife to the great prejudice of the mirth, which should or would have followed that night. But the offender was presently apprehended (and though a gentleman of some worth) put into my Lord's stocks, where hee lay most part of that night with shame and blame enough. And yet for all that punishment the next day he was convented before the officers of the Colledge, and there agayne more grievously punished; for the fault was much agravated by the circumstances of the time, place and person that was hurt, who was a very worshipfull knight's sonne and heyre.

"After this the Prince with some of the better sort of the howse beeing much disconted with the mischaunce that had happened, retyred themselves into the president lodging, where privatly they made themselves merry, with a wassall called the five bells of Magdalen Church, because it was an auncient note of those bells, that they were almost never silent. This shew for the better grace of the night was performed by some of the Masters and officers themselves in manner following:

"Your kind acceptance of the late devise
Presented by St. Gyles's clerke, my neighbour,
Hath hartned mee to furnish in a trice
This nights up sitting with a two houres labour:
  For any thing I hope, though ne're so naghty
  Wil be accepted in a Vigilate.
I have observed as your sportes did passe all
(A fault of mine to bee too curious)
The twelfe night slipt away without a wassall,
A great defect, to custome most injurious:
  Which I to mend have done my best endeavour
  To bring it in, for better late than never.

And more, for our more tuneable proceeding,
I have ta'ne downe the five bells in our towre,
Which will performe it, if you give them heeding,
Most musically, though they ring an houre.——
  Now I go in to oyle my bells and pruin them,
  When I come downe Ile bring them downe & tune
  them.
Exit.

"After a while he returned with five others presenting his five bells, and tyed with five bell-ropes, which after he had pulled one by one, they all began a peale, and sang in Latin as followeth:—

   "Jam sumus lætis dapibus repleti,
   Copiam vobis ferimus fluentem,
   Gaudium vobis canimus jocose
        Vivite læti.

   Te deum dicunt (venerande Bacche)
   Te deum dicunt (reverenda mater)
   Vos graves vobis removete luctus:
        Vivite læti.

   Dat Ceres vires, hominumque firmat
   Corpora, et Bacchus pater ille vini

Liberat curis animos molestis:
              Vivite læti.

Ne dolor vestros animos fatiget,
Vos jubet læta hæc removere curas
Turba, lætari feriæque suadent
              Vivite læti.

En Ceres lætæ segetis creatrix,
Et pater vini placidique somni
Pocula hæc vobis hilares ministrant
              Sume   {monarcha
                        {magister.

Bibunt omnes ordine dum, actores hæc ultima carmina sæpius repetunt; max singuli toti conventui sic ordine gratulantur.

Tenor.   Reddere fælicem si quemquam copia possit
             Copia fælicis nomen habere jubet,
             Copia læte jubet tristes depellere curas,
             Copia quam cingit Bacchus et alma Ceres.

Counter. Copia quam cingit Bacchus et alma Ceres.

Tenor.   Cujus non animum dulcia vina juvant?
             Dulcia vina juvant dulcem dant vina soporem,
             Magnificas ornant dulcia vina dapes.

Meane.   Frugibus alma Ceres mortalia pectora nutrit,
             Exornant campurn frugibus alma Ceres.
             Si cuiquam desint Cerelia dona, nec illi
             Lenæi patris munera grata placent.

             Nec vobis Cereris nec Bacchi munera desint,
             Annuat et votis Jupiter ipse meis.

Treble.   Copia cum Baccho gaudia læta canunt
             Copia cum Baccho gaudia læta canunt
                        Mox omnes cantantes Exeunt.
             Gaudium lætum canimus, canemus

Hoc idem semper, nec enim dolere
Jam licet, lætae feriæ hic aguntur
Vivite læti.

Sæpius nobis reriæ revertant,
Sæpius vinum liceat potare,
Sæpius vobis hilares cánamus
Vivite læti.

"This then was suddenly and extempore clapt together for want of a better, but notwithstanding was as willingly and chearefully receaved as it was proferd.

"By this time it was foure a clocke and liberty was given to every one to goe to bed or stay up as long as they pleased. The Prince with his councell brake up their watch, so did most of the Masters of the house, but the younger sort stayed up till prayers time, and durst not goe to bed for feare of one another. For some, after they had licence to depart, were fetch out of their beds by their fellowes, and not suffered to put on their clothes till they came into the hall. And thus the day came and made an end of the night's sport.

"On the sixt of February, beeing egge Satterday, it pleased some gentlemen schollers in the towne to make a dauncing night of it. They had provided many new and curious daunces for the maske of Penelope's Woers, but the yeare beeing far spent and Lent drawing on and many other thinges to bee performed, the Prince was not able to bestow that state upon them which their love & skill deserved. But their good will was very kindely received by the Prince in this night's private travels. They had some apparell suddenly provided for them, and these few Latin verses for their induction:

"Isti fuere credo Penelopes proci
Quos justa forsan ira Telemachi domo
Expulit Ulyssis.

"After all this sport was ended the Prince entertayned them very royally with good store of wine and a banquet, where they were very merry and well pleased all that night.

"Against the next Tuesday following, beeing Shrovetuesday, the great stage was againe set up and the scaffolds built about the hall for the Prince's resignation, which was performed that night with great state and solemnity in manner and forme following:

IRA SEU TUMULUS FORTUNE.
INTERLOCUTORES.

Princeps.
Admiralius.
Thesaurarius.
Comptrollarius.
Cancellarius.
Justitiarius.
Marescallus.
Camerarius.
Camerarius.

Philosophus.	Juridicus.
Cynicus.	Magister Ludorem.
Momus.	Anteambulo Primus.
Polycrates.	Anteambulo Secundus.
Philadelphus.	Stultus.

CHORUS.

Minerva	Fortuna.
Euphemia	Tolmæa.

* * * * *

"Many straungers of all sorts were invited to this shew, and many more came together, for the name's sake only of a resignacon, to see the manner and solemnity of it, for that it was reported (and truly) that there was nothing els to bee done or seene beside the resignacon and no man thought so much could have beene said of so little matter.

"The stage was never so oppressed with company, insomuch that it was verely thought it could not bee performed that night for want of roome; but the audience was so favourable as to stand as close and yeeld as much backe as was possible; so that for all tumults it began about 7 a clocke, and was very well liked of all.

"Only some few, more upon their owne guilty suspicion than our plaine intention, thinking themselves toucht at that verse of *Momus*:

"Dixi et quem dederat cursum fortuna peregi,

laboured to raise an hissing, but it was soon smothered, and the whole company in the end gave us good applause and departed very well pleased.

"After the shew was ended, the sometimes Lord was carried in state to his owne private chamber after this manner:

First went two Squires with lights.

Next Euphemia and Tolmæa.

Then 2 other Squires with lightes.

Next Minerva and Fortuna.

Then came 4 other Squires with lightes, and in the midst of them 4 schollers bearing on their shoulders a tombe or sepulcher adorned with scutchions and little flagges, wherein all the Prince's honours had bene buried before.

After this came the Prince alone in his schollers gowne and hood as the chiefe mourner.

Then all the rest of his Counsell and company likewise in blacke gownes and hoodes, like mourners, two by two.

"All these were said to goe to the Temple of Minerva there to consecrate and erecte the sepulcher, and this state was very well liked of all that saw itt.

"Heere wee thought to have made an end of all, and to have puld downe the scaffolds and stage, but then many said that so much preparacon was too much for so small a show. Besides there was an English Tragedy almost ready, which they were very earnest should bee performed, but many arguments were alledged against it: first, for the time, because it was neere Lent, and consequently a season unfitt for plaies—Secondly, the stile for that itt was English, a language unfitt for the Universitie, especially to end so much late sporte with all—Thirdly, the suspicon of some did more hinder it than all the rest, for that it was thought that some particulars were aimed att in the Chorus, which must needs bee distastfull—Lastly, the ill lucke, which wee had before with English, made many very loth to have any thing done againe in that straine.

"But these objections being aunswered all well as might bee, and faithfull promise being made and taken that if any word were thought personall, it should be presently put out, the stage was suffered to stand, and the scaffolds somewhat enlarged against the Saturday following. Att which time such a concourse of people from all places, and of all sorts came together presently after dinner, that itt was thought impossible any thing should have beene done that night for tumults. Yet in the beginning such order and care was taken (every one being willing att the last cast to helpe towardes the making a good end,) that the stage was kept voide of all company, and the scaffoldes were reserved for straungers and men sorte, better than ever they were before, so that it began very peaceably somewhat before six a clocke, and was performed in manner following:

PERIANDER.

CHORUS

The Master of the Revels.	Detraction.
The Master of the Revels Boy.	Resolution.
Ingenuity a Doctor of Physicke.	

INTERLOCUTORES.

Periander, Tyrannus Corinthi.
Cypsilus, Hæres Periandri, Stultus.
Lycophron Frater Cypsili.
Neotinos, Puer, Satelles Lycoph.

Lysimachos }	Nobiles et a Consilijs Periandri.
Aristhæus }	
Philarches }	
Eriterus }	Juuenes Nobiles in Aulâ Periandri.
Symphilus }	

Cratæa Mater Periandri.

Melissa Uxor Periandri.

Melissæ Umbra.

Eugenia Filia Periandri.

Pronæa   }   Duæ Meritriculæ Periandri.

Zona   }

Larissæa Soror Philarchis.

Europe Aristhæi Filia.

Fæminæ Quatuor Corinthiæ cum 4 or Pueris Inseruientibus.

Arion Celebris Musicus.

Nantæ Quatuor.

Cines Duo Togati.

Vigiles Duo.

Calistus   }   Satellites Periandri.

Stratocles }

Borius   }

Tres Aut 4 or Alij Satellites.

Epilogus.

* * * * *

"EPILOGUE.

"Gentlemen, welcome! our great promises
Wee would make upp, your selves must needs confesse,
But our small timbred actors, narrow roome,
Necessity of thrifte make all short come
Of our first apprehensions; wee must keepe
Our auntient customes though wee after creepe.
But wee forgett times limitts, Nowe tis Lente—
Old store this weeke may lawfully be spente
Our former shewes were giv'n to our cal'd Lorde,
This, and att his request, for you was storde.
    By many hands was Periander slaine,
    Your gentler hands will give him live againe.

FINIS.

"A certain gentlewoman, upon the hearing of these two last verses, made two other verses, and in way of an aunswer sent them to the Prince, who having first plaied Periander afterwards himselfe also pronounced the Epilogue.

"The verses were these

> If that my hand or hart him life could give,
> By hand and hart should Periander live.

"But it is almost incredible to thinke how well this Tragedy was performed of all parties, and how well liked of the whole, which (as many of them as were within the hall) were very quiet and attentive. But those that were without and could not get in made such an hideous noice, and raised such a tumult with breaking of windows all about the colledge, throwinge of stones into the hall and such like ryott, that the officers of the coll: (beeing first dar'd to appeare) were faine to rush forth in the beginning of the play, with about a dozen whiflers well armed and swords drawne, whereat the whole company (which were gathered together before the chapell doore to try whether they could breake it open) seeing them come behind them out of the lodging, presently gave backe, and ranne away though itt was thought they were not so few as 4 or 500.

"The officers gave some faire words and some fowle as they saw occasion, the whiflers were very heedfull to marke who were the ringleaders of the rest, and having some notice given of them by some of our friendes, they took some of them and committed them to the Porter's lodge, where they lay close prisoners till the play was done, and then they were brought forth and punished, and so sente home.

"After this all was quiet only some were so thrust in the hall, that they were carried forth for dead but soone recovered, when they came into the aire.

"The Chorus of this Tragedy much pleased for the rarity of it. *Detraction* beeing taken from among the company, where hee had liked to have been beaten for his sawsines (as it was supposed) for nobody at first toke him for an actor. The chiefest in the hall commaunded that notice should be taken of him, that hee might afterwards bee punished for his boldnes;—but as soone as it at once appeared that he was an actor, their disdaine and anger turned to much pleasure and content.

"All were so pleased att the whole course of this play, that there were at least eight generall plaudites given in the midst of it in divers places and to divers persons.

"In the end, they clapped their hands so long, that they went forth of the colledge clapping.

"But in the midst of all this good liking wee were neere two mischaunces, the one from Lycophron who lost a faire gold ring from his finger, which notwithstanding all the hurleburly in the end of the play, was soone found againe; the other from Periander, who, going to kill his daughter Eugenia, did not so couch his dagger within his hand, but that hee prickt her through all her attire, but (as God would have it) it was onely a scratch and so it passed.

THE CONCLUSION.

"Many other thinges were in this yeare intended which neither were nor could be performed. As the maske of Penelope's Wooer, with the State of Telemachus, with a Controversie of Jrus and his ragged Company, whereof a great parte was made. The devise of the Embassage from Lubber-land, whereof also a parte was made. The Creation of White Knights of the order of Aristotle's Well, which should bee sworne to defend Aristotle against all authors, water against wine, footemen against horsemen, and many more such like injunctions. A lottery for those of the colledge or straungers as itt pleased them to draw, not for matters of wealth, but only of mirth and witt. The triumph of all the founders of the colledges in Oxford, a devise much thought on, but it required more invention, more cost than the time would affoord. The holding of a court leet and baron for the Prince, wherein there should have beene leasses drawne, copies taken, surrenders made, all which were not so much neglected as prevented by the shortnes of time and want of money, better wits and richer daies may hereafter make upp which was then lefte unperfect.

"Here some letters might be inserted, and other gratulatory messages from divers friends to the Prince, but it is high time to make an end of this tedious and fruitelesse relation, unlesse the knowledge of trouble and vanity bee fruitefull.

"Wee intended in these exercises the practise and audacity of our youth, the credit and good name of our colledge, the love and favor of the University; but instead of all these (so easie a thing it is to be deceived in a good meaning) wee met with peevishnesse at home, perversnes abroad, contradictions everywhere; some never thought themselves entreated enough to their owne good and creditt; others thought themselves able to doe nothing if they could not thwarte and hinder something; most stood by and gave aime, willing to see much and doe nothing, nay perchaunce they were ready to procure most trouble, which would bee sure to yield least helpe. And yet wee may not so much grudge at faults at home as wee may justly complaine of hard measure abroad; for instead of the love and favour of the Universitie, wee found our selves (wee will say justly) taxed for any the least error (though ingenious spirits would have pardoned many things, where all things were intended for their owne pleasure) but most unjustly censured, and envied for that which was done (wee dare say) indifferently well: so that, in a word, wee paide deere for trouble, and in a manner hired and sent for men to doe us wrong.

"Let others herafter take heed how they attempte the like, unlesse they find better meanes at home, and better mindes abroad. And yet wee cannot complaine of all, some ment well and said well, and those tooke good will for good paiment, good endevors for good performaunce, and such (in this kind) shall deserve a private favour, when other shal bee denied a common benefitt.

"Seria vix recte agnoscit, qui ludicra nescit.

"FINIS"

CHRISTMAS TOURNAMENTS.

During the reign of James the First there was a revival of chivalric exercises, especially in connection with the training of the young Prince Henry. Almost as soon as he could wield a lance and manage his horse when clothed in complete armour, he insisted on taking his place at the lists; and from this time no great tournament took place in England in which his Royal Highness did not take part. The most important of these exhibitions was which took place on Twelfth Night, 1610, at the palace of Whitehall, in the presence of King James I. and his queen, and a brilliant assemblage of lords, ladies, and gentlemen, among whom were several foreign ambassadors, when the heir-apparent, Prince Henry, was in the 16th year of his age, and therefore arrived at the period for claiming the principality of Wales and the duchy of Cornwall. It was granted to him by the king and the High Court of Parliament, and the 4th of June following appointed for his investiture: "the Christmas before which," Sir Charles Cornwallis says, "his highnesse, not onely for his owne recreation, but also that the world might know what a brave prince they were likely to enjoy, under the name of Meliades, lord of the isles, (an ancient title due to the first born of Scotland,) did, in his name, by some appointed for the same purpose, strangely attired, accompanied with drummes and trumpets, in the presence, before the king and queene, and in the presence of the whole Court, deliver a challenge to all knights of Great Britaine." The challenge was to this effect, "That Meliades, their noble master, burning with an earnest desire to trie the valour of his young yeares in foraigne countryes, and to know where vertue triumphed most, had sent them abroad to espy the same, who, after their long travailes in all countreys, and returne," had nowhere discovered it, "save in the fortunate isle of Great Britaine: which ministring matter of exceeding joy to their young Meliades, who (as they said) could lineally derive his pedigree from the famous knights of this isle, was the cause that he had now sent to present the first fruits of his chivalrie at his majesties' feete: then after returning with a short speech to her majestie, next to the earles, lords, and knights, excusing their lord in this their so sudden and short warning, and, lastly, to the ladies; they, after humble delivery of their chartle concerning time, place, conditions, number of weapons and assailants, tooke their leave, departing solemnly as they entered."

Then preparations began to be made for this great fight, and each was happy who found himself admitted for a defendant, much more an assailant. "At last to encounter his highness, six assailants, and fifty-eight defendants, consisting of earles, barons, knights, and esquires, were appointed and chosen; eight defendants to one assailant, every assailant being to fight by turnes eight several times fighting, two every time with push and pike of sword, twelve strokes at a time; after which, the barre for separation was to be let downe until a fresh onset." The summons ran in these words:

"To our verie loving good ffreind sir Gilbert Loughton, knight, geave theis with speed:

"After our hartie commendacions unto you. The prince, his highnes, hath commanded us to signifie to you that whereas he doth intend to make a challenge in his owne person at the Barriers, with six other assistants, to bee performed some tyme this Christmas; and that he hath made choice of you for one of the defendants (whereof wee have comandement to give you knowledge), that theruppon you may so repaire hither to prepare yourselfe, as you may bee fitt to attend him. Hereunto expecting your speedie answer wee rest, from Whitehall this 25th of December, 1609. Your very loving friends,

NOTTINGHAM.   T. SUFFOLKE.   E. WORCESTER.

On New Year's Day, 1610, or the day after, the Prince's challenge was proclaimed at court, and "his highnesse, in his own lodging, in the Christmas, did feast the earles, barons, and knights, assailants and defendants, until the great Twelfth appointed night, on which this great fight was to be performed."

On the 6th of January, in the evening, "the barriers" were held at the palace of Whitehall, in the presence of the king and queen, the ambassadors of Spain and Venice, and the peers and ladies of the land, with a multitude of others assembled in the banquetting-house: at the upper end whereof was the king's chair of state, and on the right a sumptuous pavilion for the prince and his associates, whence, "with great bravery and ingenious devices, they descended into the middell of the roome, and there the prince performed his first feates of armes, that is to say, at *Barriers*, against all commers, being assisted onlie with six others, viz., the duke of Lenox, the earle of Arundell, the earle of Southampton, the lord Hay, sir Thomas Somerset, and sir Richard Preston, who was shortly afterwards created lord Dingwell."

To answer these challengers came fifty-six earles, barons, knights, and esquiers. They were at "the lower end of the roome, where was erected a very delicat and pleasant place, where in privat manner they and their traine remained, which was so very great that no man imagined that the place could have concealed halfe so many." Thence they issued in comely order, "to the middell of the roome, where sate the king and the queene, and the court, to behold the barriers, with the several showes and devices of each combatant." Every challenger fought with eight several defendants two several combats at two several weapons, viz. at push of pike, and with single sword. "The prince performed this challenge with wonderous skill and courage, to the great joy and admiration of the beholders," he "not being full sixteene yeeres of age until the 19th of February." These feats, and other "triumphant shewes," began before ten o'clock at night, and continued until three o'clock in the morning, "being Sonday." The speeches at "the barriers" were written by Ben Jonson. The next day (Sunday) the prince rode in great pomp to convoy the king to St. James', whither he had invited him and all the court to supper, the queen alone being absent; and then the prince bestowed prizes to the three combatants best deserving; namely, the Earl of Montgomery, Sir Thomas Darey (son of Lord Darey), and Sir Robert Gourdon. Thus ended the Twelftide court festivities in 1610.

During the early years of James's reign tournaments divided with masques the favour of the Court; and, as we have just seen when Prince Henry reached his sixteenth year, he put himself forth in a more heroic manner than usual with princes of his time to engage in "feats of armes" and chivalric exercises; but after his death (1612) these sports fell quite out of fashion, and George Wither, a poet of the period, expresses, in the person of Britannia, the feelings of the nation:—

> "Alas! who now shall grace my tournaments,
> Or honour me with deeds of chivalry?
> What shall become of all my merriments,
> My ceremonies, shows of heraldry,
> And other rites?"

Religious matters received a good deal of attention from James I. in the later years of his reign, and his Majesty's proposals raised the question of the observance of

THE CHRISTMAS FESTIVAL IN SCOTLAND.

In 1617 the King made a journey to Scotland with the object of establishing the English Church in all its forms and authority as the State Church of Scotland for ever. One of the famous Five Articles in which the King set forth his will proposed "That the festivals of Christmas, Good Friday, Easter, Ascension Day, and Whit Sunday, should be observed in Scotland just as in England." The Articles were received with unequivocal marks of displeasure, many of the churches refusing to obey the royal command, and the revival of the festival of Christmas was denounced as the return of the ancient Saturnalia. Three years later the King obtained an Act of Parliament enforcing the Articles on the repugnant spirit of the people. "Dr. Laud, whose name we now meet for the first time, afterwards to become so notorious, even urged James to go further lengths; but his fatal advice was destined to act with more force on the next generation."[63]

The King returned to London very much displeased with the religious views of his Scotch subjects, and his sourness seems to have manifested itself even at Christmastide, for on December 20th of this year Mr. Chamberlaine thus wrote to Sir Dudley Carleton: "The King hath been at Theobald's ever since Wednesday, and came to town this day. I am sorry to hear that he grows every day more froward, and with such a kind of morosity, that doth either argue a great discontent in mind, or a distemper of humours in his body. Yet he is never so out of tune but the very sight of my Lord of Buckingham doth settle and quiet all."[64] So soothed and softened was the King by "my Lord of Buckingham" that Mr. Chamberlaine, writing again on the 3rd of January, says that on New Year's Day the earl was created "Marquis of Buckingham, a dignity the King hath not bestowed since his coming to this crown." And, says the same writer, "This night was the Lord Marquiss's [Buckingham's] great

FEAST, WHERE WERE THE KING AND PRINCE,

with Lords and Ladies *sans nombre*. You may guess at the rest of the cheer by this scantling, that there were said to be seventeen dozen of pheasants, and twelve partridges in a dish throughout; which methinks was rather spoil than largess; yet for all the plenty of presents, the supper cost £600. Sir Thomas Edmondes undertook the providing and managing of all, so that it was much after the French. The King was exceedingly pleased, and could not be satisfied with commending the meat and the Master; and yet some stick not to say, that young Sir Henry Mildmay, a son of George Brooke, that was executed at Winchester, and a son of Sir William Monson's, begins to come into consideration."

THE FAILING HEALTH OF THE KING

interfered somewhat with the celebration of the subsequent Royal Christmases of this reign; and Nichols, referring to the Court celebrations of Twelfth Day, 1620-1, says:

"'On Twelfth Day the King went to Chappel, but they had much ado to support him. He offered gold, frankincence, and myrrhe, and touched 80 of the evil.'[65] In the evening 'the French Ambassador and his choise followers were brought to court by the Earle of Warwick to be present at a Maske; he seated as before with the King, the better sort of the other on a fourme behind the

Lords, the Lord Treasurer onely and the Marquesse of Hamilton sitting at the upper end of it, and all the rest in a box, and in the best places of the scaffolds on the right hand of his Majesty. No other Ambassadors were at that time present or invited.'"

As to

THE CHRISTMAS FESTIVITIES

of the next year (1621-2) Nichols[66] says Mr. Meade wrote thus to Sir Martin Stuteville:—

"'The Lieutenant of Middle Temple played a game this Christmas-time, whereat his Majesty was highly displeased. He made choise of some thirty of the civillest and best-fashioned gentlemen of the House to sup with him; and, being at supper, took a cup of wine in one hand, and held his sword drawn in the other, and so began a health to the distressed Lady Elizabeth [the Queen of Bohemia , and having drunk, kissed his sword, and laying ' his hand upon it, took an oath to live and die in her service; then delivered the cup and sword to the next, and so the health and ceremonie went round.

"'The Gentlemen of Graye's Inne, to make an end of Christmas on Twelfe-night, in the dead time of the night, shot off all the chambers they had borrowed from the Tower, being as many as filled four carts. The King, awakened with this noise, started out of his bed, and cryed, "Treason, treason," &c., and that the Cittie was in an uprore, in such sort (as it is told) that the whole court was raised and almost in armes, the Earle of Arundell running to the Bed-chamber with his sword drawne as to rescue the King's person.'"

In this reign many accomplished writers assisted in the Christmas festivities. Professor Henry Morley[67] mentions that in December, 1623, the name of Philip Massinger, poet and dramatist, first appeared in the office book of the Master of the Revells, when his "Bondman" was acted, and the play was first printed in 1624.

King James I. died at Theobald's, Herts, on the 27th March, 1625, and was buried in Westminster Abbey.

The remarkable fact that Bishop Andrewes preached seventeen sermons on the Nativity before James I. gives an unusual interest to the Christmas Day services of this reign. Nichols makes the following references to them:—

1605. "On Christmas Day the King attended Divine Service at Whitehall, where Dr Lancelot Andrews, then recently promoted to the Bishoprick of Chichester, preached before his Majesty, on the Epistle of St. Paul to the Hebrews, ii. 16."

1606. "On Christmas Day, the King attended Divine Service at Whitehall, where Bishop Andrews, now decidedly the King's favourite Preacher, discoursed on Esaias ix. 6."

1607. "On Thursday, being Christmas Day, the King attended Divine Service at Whitehall, and there heard Bishop Andrews preach on 1 Tim. iii. 16."

1609. "Monday, December 25, being Christmas Day, the King attended Divine Service at Whitehall, and there heard the Bishop of Ely, Dr. Andrews, on Galat. iv. 4, 5." In a note Nichols says: "This sermon was much admired by the King. This was probably the reason that it was printed in 1610, together with that the Bishop preached on the same occasion in that year, under the following title: 'Two Sermons preached before the King's Majestie at Whitehall; of the Birth of Christ; the one on Christmas Day, anno 1609, the other on Christmas Day last, anno 1610. By the Bishop of Elie, his Majestie's Almoner. Imprinted at London by Robert Barker, Printer to the King's most excellent Majestie, anno 1610.'"

1610. "On Tuesday, the 25th December, Christmas Day, the King attended Divine Service at Whitehall, where Bishop Andrews preached on Luke ii. 9, 10."

1611. "On Christmas Day the King attended Divine Service at Whitehall, and Bishop Andrews preached on John. i. 14."

1612. "On Friday, 25th December, Christmas Day was kept as usual at Whitehall; where the King attended Divine Service, and Bishop Andrews (as usual) preached."

1613. "Saturday, 25th December, being Christmas Day, was kept with the usual solemnities; the King attended Divine service at Whitehall, and Bishop Andrews preached."

1614. "His Majesty returned to keep Christmas Day, as was customary, at Whitehall. Bishop Andrews addressed him from the pulpit as usual."

1615. "'On Christmas Day, the King, being sorely troubled with the gout, was not able to go to Divine service; but heard a sermon in private, and took the Sacrament.' The Preacher was, as usual, Bishop Andrews."

1616. "On Christmas Day, Thomas, Earl of Arundel, who was educated from his youth in the Popish Religion, and had lately travelled all over Italy detesting the abuses of the Papists, embraced the Protestant religion, and received the Sacrament in the King's Chapel at Whitehall, where Bishop Andrews preached, as was customary, a sermon suited to the Festival of the Nativity."

1618. "On the 25th [December , Bishop Andrews resumed his post as preacher on Christmas Day, before the King at Whitehall. His text was from Luke ii. 12, 13."

1619. "Christmas was kept by the King at Whitehall, as had ever been his practice; and Bishop Andrews preached then before him, on Saturday, the 25th."

1620. "During the month of December, before the King left the country, he knighted at Newmarket, Sir Francis Michell, afterward degraded in June 1621; and at Theobalds, Sir Gilbert Cornwall. On the 23rd, his Majestie 'came to Westminster, but went not to Chappel, being prevented by the gout.' On Monday, the 25th, however, being Christmas Day, Bishop Andrews preached before him at Whitehall, on Matt. ii. 1, 2; and during Christmas, Sir Clement Cotterell and Sir Henry Carvell were there knighted."

1622. "On the 25th [December Bishop Andrews resumed his Christmas station in the pulpit at Whitehall, and thence preached to the King and his Court on the same text as he had adopted on the same occasion two years before, Matt. ii. 1, 2."

1623. "The King kept inviolate his old custom of being at Whitehall on Christmas Day, and hearing there a sermon from Bishop Andrews, who this year preached on Ephes. i. 10."

1624. "On Saturday, the 25th of December, Bishop Andrews preached before his Majesty at Whitehall, on Psalm ii. 7, it being at least the seventeenth, as it was the last, Christmas Day on which King James heard that favourite preacher."

The unique series of "Seventeen Sermons on the Nativity, preached before King James I. at Whitehall, by the Right Honourable and Reverend Father in God, Lancelot Andrewes, sometime Lord Bishop of Winchester," were preserved to posterity by an order of Charles I., who, after Bishop Andrewes's death, commanded Bishops Laud and Buckeridge to collect and publish his sermons. This series of sermons on the Nativity have recently been reprinted in "The Ancient and Modern Library of Theological Literature," and the editor, after referring to the ability and integrity of Bishop Andrewes, says: "An interest apart from that which must be created by his genius, learning, and character, belongs to him as the exponent of the mind and practice of the English Church in the years that intervened between the Reformation and the Revolution."

THE POPULAR AMUSEMENTS OF CHRISTMASTIDE

at this period are thus enumerated by Robert Burton in his "Anatomy of Melancholy," published in 1621:—

"The ordinary recreations which we have in winter are cards, tables and dice, shovelboard, chess-play, the philosopher's game, small trunks, billiards, music, masks, singing, dancing, ule games, catches, purposes, questions; merry tales of errant knights, kings, queens, lovers, lords, ladies, giants, dwarfs, thieves, fairies, goblins, friars, witches, and the rest."

The following curious cut is from the title-page of the amusing story of the great "Giant Gargantua" of this period:—

The legends of Arthur and the Knights of the Round Table, Bevis of Southampton, Guy of Warwick, Adam Bell, and Clymme of Clough, were favourites among the lovers of romance; but the people of this age, being very superstitious, were very fond of stories about ghosts and goblins, believing them to be founded on fact, and also attributing feats performed by conjurors and jugglers to supernatural agency. The King himself was equally superstitious, for Strutt in describing the tricks of jugglers says: "Our learned monarch, James I., was perfectly convinced that these, and other inferior feats exhibited by the tregetours, could only be performed by the agency of the devil, 'who,' says he, 'will learne them many juglarie tricks, at cardes and dice, to deceive men's senses thereby, and such innumerable false practiques, which are proved by over-many in this age.'"[68]

Looking back to the ancient superstitions about ghosts and fairies, Dryden, the poet, has some lines which may fitly close this chapter:—

> "I speak of ancient times, for now the swain
> Returning late may pass the woods in vain,
> And never hope to see the mighty train;
> In vain the dairy now with mint is dressed,
> The dairy-maid expects no fairy guest,

To skim the bowls and after pay the feast.
She sighs and shakes her empty shoes in vain,
No silver penny to reward her pain:
For priests, with prayers and other godly gear,
Have made the merry goblins disappear."

58   "Curiosities of Literature."
59   "Memoirs of Ben Jonson."
60   "Progresses of King James the First."
61   Cassell's "History of England."
62   This portion is inserted to introduce *the Prince's Triumph*, as they are termed.
63   Cassell's "History of England."
64   Nichols's "Progresses."
65   "Camden's Annals."
66   "Progresses."
67   "Library of English Literature."
68   "Dæmonologie," by King James I.

CHAPTER IX.

CHRISTMAS UNDER CHARLES I. AND THE COMMONWEALTH.

(1625-1660.)

was the second son of James I. and of Anne, daughter of Frederick III., King of Denmark, and he came to the throne on the death of his father in March 1625. As Prince Charles he had taken part in the Court entertainments of Christmastide, and had particularly distinguished himself in Ben Jonson's masque, "The Vision of Delight." These magnificent Christmas masques were continued after Charles's accession to the throne until the troubles of his reign stopped them. Gifford[69] mentions that Jonson's "Masque of Owls" was presented at Kenilworth Castle, "By the Ghost of Captain Cox mounted on his Hobby-horse, in 1626":—

"*Enter* Captain Cox, *on his Hobby-horse.*

Room! room! for my horse will wince,
If he come within so many yards of a prince;
And though he have not on his wings,
He will do strange things,
He is the Pegasus that uses
To wait on Warwick Muses;
And on gaudy-days he paces

Before the Coventry Graces;
For to tell you true, and in rhyme,
He was foal'd in Queen Elizabeth's time,
When the great Earl of Lester
In this castle did feast her."

THE HOBBY-HORSE.

Jonson's "The Fortunate Isles, and Their Union," a masque designed for the Court, was presented on Twelfth Night, 1626; and "Love's Triumph through Callipolis" (a masque invented by Ben Jonson and Inigo Jones) was presented at Court in 1630.

The Lord of Misrule

also made merry at Christmas at this period; but it sometimes happened that when he went forth with his band of merry men, they got into trouble. An instance of this, which occurred in 1627, is recorded in one of Meade's letters to Sir Martin Stuteville. The letter is worth reprinting as an illustration of the manners of the age, and as relating to what was probably the last Lord of Misrule elected by the barristers. Meade writes:—"On Saturday the Templars chose one Mr. Palmer their Lord of Misrule, who, on Twelfth-eve, late in the night, sent out to gather up his rents at five shillings a house in Ram-alley and Fleet Street. At every door they came to they winded the Temple-horn, and if at the second blast or summons they within opened not the door, then the Lord of Misrule cried out, 'Give fire, gunner!' His gunner was a robustious Vulcan, and the gun or petard itself was a huge overgrown smith's hammer. This being complained of to my Lord Mayor, he said he would be with them about eleven o'clock on Sunday night last; willing that all that ward should attend him with their halberds, and that himself, besides those that came out of his house, should bring the watches along with him. His lordship, thus attended, advanced as high as Ram-alley in martial equipage: when forth came the Lord of Misrule, attended by his gallants, out of the Temple-gate, with their swords all armed *in cuerpo*. A halberdier bade the Lord of Misrule come to my Lord Mayor. He answered, No! let the Lord Mayor come to me! At length they agreed to meet halfway: and, as the interview of rival princes is never without danger of some ill accident, so it happened in this: for first, Mr. Palmer being quarrelled with for not pulling off his hat to my Lord Mayor, and giving cross answers, the halberds began to fly about his ears, and he and his company to brandish their swords. At last being beaten to the ground, and the Lord of Misrule sore wounded, they were fain to yield to the longer and more numerous weapon. My Lord Mayor taking Mr. Palmer by the shoulder, led him to the Compter, and thrust him in at the prison-gate with a kind of indignation; and so, notwithstanding his hurts, he was forced to lie among the common prisoners for two nights. On Tuesday the King's attorney became a suitor to my Lord Mayor for their liberty: which his lordship granted, upon condition that they should repay the gathered rents, and do reparations upon broken doors. Thus the game ended. Mr. Attorney-General, being of the same house, fetched them in his own coach, and carried them to the court, where the King himself reconciled my Lord Mayor and them together with joining all hands; the gentlemen of the Temple being this Shrovetide to present a Mask to their majesties, over and besides the King's own great Mask, to be performed at the Banquetting-house by an hundred actors."

We get other glances at

through contemporary writers of the period. Nicholas Breton,[70] writing in merry mood, says: "It is now Christmas, and not a cup of drink must pass without a carol; the beasts, fowl, and fish come to a general execution, and the corn is ground to dust for the bakehouse and the pastry: cards and dice purge many a purse, and the youth show their agility in shoeing of the wild mare: now, good cheer, and welcome, and God be with you, and I thank you:—and against the New Year provide for the presents:—The Lord of Misrule is no mean man for his time, and the guests of the high table must lack no wine: the lusty bloods must look about them like men, and piping and dancing puts away much melancholy: stolen venison is sweet, and a fat coney is worth money: pit-falls are now set for small birds, and a woodcock hangs himself in a gin: a good fire heats all the house, and a full alms-basket makes the beggar's prayers:—the maskers and the mummers make the merry sport, but if they lose their money their drum goes dead: swearers and swaggerers are sent away to the ale-house, and unruly wenches go in danger of judgment; musicians now make their instruments speak out, and a good song is worth the hearing. In sum it is a holy time, a duty in Christians for the remembrance of Christ and custom among friends for the maintenance of good fellowship. In brief I thus conclude it: I hold it a memory of the Heaven's love and the world's peace, the mirth of the honest, and the meeting of the friendly. Farewell."

In 1633, William Prynne, a Puritan lawyer, published his "Histriomastix," against plays, masques, balls, the decking of houses with evergreens at Christmas, &c., for which he was committed to the Tower, prosecuted in the Star Chamber, and sentenced to pay a fine to the King of £5,000, to be expelled from the University of Oxford, from the Society of Lincoln's Inn, and from his profession of the law; to stand twice in the pillory, each time losing an ear; to have his book burnt before his face by the hangman; and to suffer perpetual imprisonment: a most barbarous sentence, which Green[71] says, "showed the hard cruelty of the Primate."

Milton's masque of "Comus" was produced the following year (1634) for performance at Ludlow Castle, in Shropshire, which was the seat of government for the Principality of Wales, the Earl of Bridgewater being then the Lord President, and having a jurisdiction and military command that comprised the English counties of Gloucester, Worcester, Hereford and Shropshire. Ludlow Castle was to the Lord President of Wales of that period what Dublin Castle is to the Lord Lieutenant of Ireland in the present day; and, as hospitality was one of the duties of the Lord President's office, the Earl and Countess of Bridgewater gave a grand entertainment to the country people, in which the masque of "Comus" was an important feature. The music was composed by the eminent musician Henry Lawes, and the masque was adapted for performance by the family of the earl and countess, who then had ten children—eight daughters and two sons.

It is quite refreshing to think of the author of "Paradise Lost," with his friend Lawes, the musician, among the country dancers, listening to the song of the attendant spirit:—

> Back, shepherds, back; enough your play
> Till next sun-shine holiday:
> Here be, without duck or nod,
> Other trippings to be trod
> Of lighter toes, and such court guise
> As Mercury did first devise
> With the mincing Dryades,
> On the lawns, and on the leas."

"But Milton was a courtier when he wrote the Masque at Ludlow Castle," says Charles Lamb, "and still more of a courtier when he composed the 'Arcades'" (a masque, or entertainment presented to the Countess Dowager of Derby, at Harefield, by some noble persons of her family). "When the national struggle was to begin, he becomingly cast these varieties behind him."

From "Archæologia" (vol. xviii. p. 335), we learn that "Richard Evelyn, Esq., High Sheriff of Surrey and Sussex in 1634, held a splendid Christmas at his mansion at Wotton, having a regular Lord of Misrule for the occasion: and it appears it was then the custom for the neighbours to send presents of eatables to provide for the great consumption consequent upon such entertainments. The following is a list of those sent on this occasion: two sides of venison, two half brawns, three pigs, ninety capons, five geese, six turkeys, four rabbits, eight partridges, two pullets, five sugar loaves, half a pound of nutmeg, one basket of apples, two baskets of pears."

Hone[72] states that "in the ninth year of King Charles I. the four Inns of Court provided a Christmas mask, which cost £2,400, and the King invited a hundred and twenty gentlemen of the four Inns to a mask at Whitehall on Shrove Tuesday following." And Sandys says that on the 13th December, 1637, a warrant under Privy Seal was issued to George Kirke, for £150 to provide masking apparel for the King; and on the 1st of the same month Edmund Taverner had a warrant for £1,400 towards the charge of a mask to be presented at Whitehall the next Twelfth Night. A similar sum for a similar purpose was granted to Michael Oldisworth on the 3rd of January, 1639.

In connection with the entertainments at the Inns of Court, Sandys mentions that by an order, 17th November, 4th Charles I., all playing at dice, cards, or otherwise was forbidden at Gray's Inn, except during the 20 days in Christmas.

As indicating the prolongation of the Christmas revels at this period, it is recorded that in February, 1633, there was a celebrated masque, called "The Triumph of Peace," presented jointly by the two Temples, Lincoln's Inn and Gray's Inn, which cost the Societies about £20,000. Evelyn, in his "Memoirs," relates, that on the 15th December, 1641, he was elected one of the Comptrollers of the Middle Temple revellers, "as the custom of ye young students and gentlemen was, the Christmas being kept this yeare with greate solemnity"; but he got excused.

An order still existed directing the nobility and gentry who had mansions in the country "to repair to them to keep hospitality meet to their degrees;" for a note in Collier's History states that Sir J. Astley, on the 20th of March, 1637, in consequence of ill-health, obtained a license to reside in London, or where he pleased, at Christmas, or any other times; which proves such license to have been requisite.

At this period noblemen and gentlemen lived like petty princes, and in the arrangement of their households copied their sovereign, having officers of the same import, and even heralds wearing their coat of arms at Christmas, and other solemn feasts, crying largesse thrice at the proper times. They feasted in their halls where many of the Christmas sports were performed. When coals were introduced the hearth was commonly in the middle, whence, according to Aubrey, is the saying, "Round about our coal-fire." Christmas was considered as the commemoration of a holy festival, to be observed with cheerfulness as well as devotion. The comforts and personal gratification of their dependants were provided for by the landlords, their merriment encouraged, and their sports joined. The working man looked forward to Christmas as the time which repaid his former toils; and gratitude for worldly comforts then received caused him to reflect on the eternal blessings bestowed on mankind by the event then commemorated.

SERVANTS' CHRISTMAS FEAST.

Of all our English poets, Robert Herrick, a writer of the seventeenth century, has left us the most complete contemporary picture of the Christmas season. He was born in Cheapside, London, and received his early education, it is supposed, at Westminster School, whence he removed to Cambridge, and after taking his M.A. degree in 1620, left Cambridge. He afterwards spent some years in London in familiar intercourse with the wits and writers of the age, enjoying those "lyric feasts" which are celebrated in his "Ode to Ben Jonson":—

"Ah Ben!
Say how or when
Shall we, thy guests
Meet at those lyric feasts
Made at the Sun,
The Dog, the Triple Tun;
Where we such clusters had
As made us nobly wild, not mad?
And yet each verse of thine
Outdid the meat, outdid the frolic wine.

In 1629 he accepted the living of Dean Prior, in Devonshire, where he lived as a bachelor Vicar, being ejected by the Long Parliament, returning on the Restoration under Charles the Second, and dying at length at the age of eighty-four. He was buried in the Church at Dean Prior, where a memorial tablet has latterly been erected to his memory. And it is fitting that he should die and be buried in the quiet Devonshire hamlet from which he drew so much of his happiest inspiration, and which will always be associated now with the endless charm of the "Hesperides."

In "A New Year's Gift, sent to Sir Simeon Steward," included in his "Hesperides," Herrick refers to the Christmas sports of the time, and says:—

"No new device or late-found trick

* * * * *

We send you; but here a jolly
Verse crowned with ivy and with holly;
That tells of winter's tales and mirth,
That milk-maids make about the hearth,
Of Christmas sports, the Wassail bowl,
That's tossed up after Fox-i'-th'-hole;
Of Blind-man's-buff, and of the care
That young men have to shoe the Mare;
Of Twelfth-tide cake, of peas and beans,
Wherewith ye make those merry scenes,

When as ye choose your king and queen,
And cry out, 'Hey for our town green.'
Of ash-heaps in the which ye use
Husbands and wives by streaks to choose:
Of crackling laurel, which fore-sounds
A plenteous harvest to your grounds;
Of these, and such like things, for shift,
We send instead of New-year's gift.
Read then, and when your faces shine
With bucksome meat and cap'ring wine,
Remember us in cups full crowned,
And let our city's health go round,
Quite through the young maids and the men,
To the ninth number, if not ten,
Until the firèd chestnuts leap
For joy to see the fruits ye reap,
From the plump chalice and the cup
That tempts till it be tossèd up.
Then as ye sit about your embers,
Call not to mind those fled Decembers;
But think on these, that are t' appear,
As daughters to the instant year;
Sit crowned with rose-buds and carouse,
Till *Liber Pater* twirls the house
About your ears, and lay upon
The year, your cares, that's fled and gone.
And let the russet swains the plough
And harrow hang up resting now;
And to the bagpipe all address
Till sleep takes place of weariness.
And thus, throughout, with Christmas plays,
Frolic the full twelve holy-days."

SIR ISAAC NEWTON'S BIRTH, ON CHRISTMAS DAY,

at Woolsthorpe, Lincolnshire, was the most important Christmas
event of the memorable year which saw the outbreak of the Civil
War (1642). In the year of the Restoration he entered Cambridge,
where the teaching of Isaac Barrow quickened his genius for

mathematics, and from the time he left College his life became a series of wonderful physical discoveries. As early as 1666, he discovered the law of gravitation, but it was not till the eve of the Revolution that his "Principia" revealed to the world his new theory of the universe.

"A Christmas Carol," by George Wither, a well-known poet of this period, contains many allusions to the customs of Christmastide:—

> So, now is come our joyful'st feast;
>   Let every man be jolly;
> Each room with ivy leaves is drest,
>   And every post with holly.
> Though some churls at our mirth repine,
> Round your foreheads garlands twine;
> Drown sorrow in a cup of wine,
>   And let us all be merry.
>
> Now all our neighbours' chimneys smoke,
>   And Christmas blocks are burning;
> Their ovens they with baked meats choke,
>   And all their spits are turning.
> Without the door let sorrow lie;
> And if for cold it hap to die,
> We'll bury 't in a Christmas pie,
>   And ever more be merry.
>
> Now every lad is wondrous trim,
>   And no man minds his labour;
> Our lasses have provided them
>   A bag-pipe and a tabour;
> Young men and maids, and girls and boys,
> Give life to one another's joys;
> And you anon shall by their noise
>   Perceive that they are merry.
>
> Rank misers now do sparing shun;
>   Their hall of music soundeth;

And dogs thence with whole shoulders run,
　　So all things there aboundeth.
The country folks themselves advance
With crowdy-muttons[73] out of France;
And Jack shall pipe, and Jill shall dance,
　　And all the town be merry.

Ned Squash hath fetched his bands from pawn,
　　And all his best apparel;
Brisk Nell hath bought a ruff of lawn
　　With droppings of the barrel;
And those that hardly all the year
Had bread to eat, or rags to wear,
Will have both clothes and dainty fare,
　　And all the day be merry.

Now poor men to the justices
　　With capons make their errants;
And if they hap to fail of these;
　　They plague them with their warrants;
But now they feed them with good cheer.
And what they want they take in beer;
For Christmas comes but once a year,
　　And then they shall be merry.

Good farmers in the country nurse
　　The poor that else were undone;
Some landlords spend their money worse,
　　On lust and pride at London.
There the roys'ters they do play,
Drab and dice their lands away,
Which may be ours another day;
　　And therefore let's be merry.

The client now his suit forbears,
　　The prisoner's heart is eased:
The debtor drinks away his cares,
　　And for the time is pleased.
Though other purses be more fat,
Why should we pine or grieve at that?

Hang sorrow! care will kill a cat,
    And therefore let's be merry.

Hark! how the wags abroad do call
    Each other forth to rambling:
Anon you'll see them in the hall
    For nuts and apples scrambling.
Hark! how the roofs with laughter sound!
Anon they'll think the house goes round,
For they the cellar's depth have found,
    And there they will be merry.

The wenches with their wassail bowls
    About the streets are singing;
The boys are come to catch the owls,
    The wild mare in is bringing.
Our kitchen-boy hath broke his box,[74]
And to the dealing of the ox
Our honest neighbours come by flocks,
    And here they will be merry.

Now kings and queens poor sheep cotes have,
    And mate with everybody;
The honest now may play the knave,
    And wise men play the noddy.
Some youths will now a mumming go,
Some others play at Rowland-ho
And twenty other gambols mo,
    Because they will be merry.

Then wherefore in these merry days
    Should we, I pray, be duller?
No, let us sing some roundelays,
    To make our mirth the fuller.
And, whilst thus inspired we sing,
Let all the streets with echoes ring,
Woods and hills, and everything,
    Bear witness we are merry.

the overthrow of the monarchy, and the changes resulting therefrom at Christmastide are alluded to in "The Complaint of Christmas, written after Twelftide, and printed before Candlemas, 1646," by old John Taylor, the Water Poet, who says: "All the liberty and harmless sports, the merry gambols, dances and friscols, with which the toiling ploughman and labourer once a year were wont to be recreated, and their spirits and hopes revived for a whole twelvemonth, are now extinct and put out of use, in such a fashion as if they never had been. Thus are the merry lords of bad rule at Westminster; nay, more, their madness hath extended itself to the very vegetables; senseless trees, herbs, and weeds, are in a profane estimation amongst them—holly, ivy, mistletoe, rosemary, bays, are accounted ungodly branches of superstition for your entertainment. And to roast a sirloin of beef, to touch a collar of brawn, to take a pie, to put a plum in the pottage pot, to burn a great candle, or to lay one block the more in the fire for your sake, Master Christmas, is enough to make a man to be suspected and taken for a Christian, for which he shall be apprehended for committing high Parliament Treason and mighty malignancy against the general Council of the Directorian private Presbyterian Conventicle."

With the success of the Parliamentarians, certain changes came in the ruling manners of the age; but

THE ATTEMPT TO ABOLISH CHRISTMAS DAY

was, of course, a signal failure. The event commemorated made it impossible for the commemoration to cease. Men may differ as to the mode of celebration, but the Christ must and will be celebrated.

"In 1642," says Sandys, "the first ordinances were issued to suppress the performance of plays, and hesitation was expressed as to the manner of keeping Christmas. Some shops in London were even opened on Christmas Day, 1643, part of the people being fearful of a Popish observance of the day. The Puritans gradually prevailed, and in 1647 some parish officers were committed for permitting ministers to preach upon Christmas Day, and for adorning the church. On the 3rd of June in the same year, it was ordained by the Lords and Commons in Parliament that the feast of the Nativity of Christ, with other holidays, should be no longer observed, and that all scholars, apprentices, and other servants, with the leave and approbation of their masters, should have such relaxation from labour on the second Tuesday in every month as they used to have from such festivals and holy days; and in Canterbury, on the 22nd of December following, the crier went round by direction of the Mayor, and proclaimed that Christmas Day and all other superstitious festivals should be put down, and a market kept upon that day."

In describing "The First Christmas under the Puritan Directory," the *Saturday Review* (December 27, 1884) says:—"It must have been taken as a piece of good luck by the Parliamentary and Puritanical masters of England, or, as they would have said, as 'a providence,' that the Christmas Day of 1645 fell upon a week-day. It was the first Christmas Day after the legislative abolition of the Anglican Prayer-book and the establishment of 'the Directory' in its stead; and, if it had fallen upon a Sunday, the Churches must have been opened. A 'Sabbath' could not be ignored, even though it chanced to be the 25th of December. There can be small doubt that, if the Presbyterian and Independent preachers who held all the English parishes subject to the Parliament had been obliged to go into the pulpits on the 25th of December 1645, they would again have irritated the masses of the people by ferociously 'improving the occasion.' The Parliament had not the courage to repeat the brutal experiment of the previous year. It was easy to abolish the feast by an ordinance; but it was risky to insist by an ordinance that the English people and English families should keep the dearest and most sacred of their festivals as a fast. The rulers knew that such an ordinance would not be obeyed. They resolved simply to ignore the day, or treat it as any ordinary Thursday. Doubtless many of the members kept up some sort of celebration of the old family festival in their own private houses. But the legislators marched solemnly to the Lower House, and the 'divines' marched as solemnly to the Assembly in the Jerusalem Chamber, affecting to take no notice of the unusual aspect of the shops and streets, which everywhere bore witness to the fact that there was a deep and fundamental estrangement between 'the State' and 'the people,' and that the people were actually keeping the festival which the 'Synod' had declared to be profane and superstitious, and which the Parliament to please the Scots, the Nonconformists, and the Sectaries, had abolished by law. 'Notwithstanding the Ordinance,' wrote a Member of the House of Commons, the Erastian Whitelock, in his 'Memorials,' 'yet generally this day, in London, the shops were shut and the day observed.' The Christmas number of the *Mercurius Academicus* (December 25 to 31, 1645), states that General Browne, who was a Presbyterian zealot, 'proclaimed' the abolition of Christmas Day at Abingdon, and 'sent out his warrants for men to work on that day especially.'... The Parliamentary newspaper, *The Weekly Account*, (LIII. week, 1645), has the bald record: 'Thursday, Decemb. 25. The Commons sate in a Grand Committee concerning the privileges of members of their House.' The news in the Tuesday paper, *The Kingdome's Weekly Intelligencer* (No. 152), is equally thin: 'Thursday, Decemb. 25, vulgarly known by the name of Christmas Day, both Houses sate. The House of Commons more especially debated some things in reference to the privileges of that House, and made some orders therein.'... The Presbyterian and Independent divines spent Christmas Day in the 'Synod' of Westminster. December the 25th, 1645, was entered in their minutes as 'Session 561.'... The City newspaper of that period, *Mercurius Civicus, or London's Intelligencer*, in what we may call its Christmas number (No. 135, December 18 to December 24, 1645), printed an article explaining to the citizens of London the absurdity, if not the impiety, of keeping Christmas Day. Every good citizen was expected to open his shop as usual on the coming Thursday, and compel his apprentices to keep behind the counter. The City newspaper stated, that it was more probable that the Saviour was born in September than in December, and quotes 'a late reverend minister's opinion, that God did conceale the time when Christ was borne, upon the same reason that He tooke away the body of Moses, that they might not put an holinesse upon that day.' If the apprentices want a holiday, 'let them keep the fift of November, and other dayes of that nature, or the late great mercy of God in the taking of Hereford, which deserves an especiall day of thanksgiving.' The mass of the English folk meanwhile protested by all such ways as were open to them against the outlandish new religion which was being invented for them. The *Mercuricus Civicus* complained that, 'Many people in these times are too much addicted to the superstitious observance of this day, December 25th, and other saints days, as they are called.' It was asked in a 'Hue and Cry after Christmas,' published anonymously at the end of the year 1645, 'Where may Christmas be found?' The answer is, 'In the corner of a translator's shop, where the cobbler was wont so merrily to chant his carols.' *The Moderate Intelligencer*, which devoted itself to 'impartially communicating martiall affaires,' in its forty-third number (December 25, 1645, to January 1, 1646), expressed itself as scandalized at the zeal with which the English people, in spite of Parliament and the Assembly, had kept their Christmas. Social phenomena lay beyond the usual ken of the military chroniclers; but 'we shall only observe,' they wrote, 'the loathnesse of the People to part with it, which certainly argues a greater adoration than should have been. Hardly forty shops were open within the lines upon that day. The State hath done well to null it out of this respect, as Moses did the Brazen Serpent.' The Scriptural knowledge of the Puritan military newsmen was curiously at fault; they evidently confounded Moses with Hezekiah, unless they substituted the lawgiver for the king, because they thought it unwise to represent the King as the foe of idolatry. The traditional scorn of the Pharisee for the common people which know not the law comes out in the ironical passage with which the 'martiall' organ concludes its reference to the distressing social symptom; 'Sure if there were an ordinance for recreation and labour upon the Lord's Day, or Sabbath (like the prelatical Book of Sports), these would want no observers. Unwillingness to obey, in a multitude, argues generally the goodnesse of a law, readinesse the contrary, especially in those laws which have anything of religion in them.' Hence the puritanical tyrants thought the observation of Christmas Day should be visited in future years with more severe penalties. A few days after Christmas a pamphlet was issued under the title of 'The Arraignment, Conviction, and Imprisonment of Christmas.' A letter from a 'Malignant scholar' in Oxford, where Christmas had been observed as usual, to 'a Malignant lady in London,' had contained the promise or threat, according to the pamphleteer, that the King would shortly appear in London, and restore to his poor people their old social and religious liberties. 'We shall soon be in London, and have all things as they were wont.' There was small chance, six months after

Naseby, of the fulfilment of the prediction. The puritanical pamphleteer, however, owns that it would be welcome to 'every 'prentice boy,' because the return of the King would have meant the return of a free Christmas, which he sorely missed. 'All popish, prelatical, Jesuitical, ignorant, Judaical, and superstitious persons,' said he, 'ask after the old, old, old, very old grey-bearded gentleman called Christmas, who was wont to be a very familiar ghest (*sic*). Whoever finds him again shall be rewarded with a benediction from the Pope, a hundred oaths from the Cavaliers, forty kisses from the wanton wenches, and be made pursuivant to the next Archbishop.' 'The poor,' he added, 'are sorry for it. They go to every door a-begging, as they were wont to do, 'Good Mistress, somewhat against this good time.' Instead of going to the alehouse to be drunke, they are fain to work all the holy dayes.' Again, 'The schollars come into the hall, where their hungry stomacks had thought to have found good brawne and Christmas pie, roast-beef and plum-porridge. But no such matter. Away, ye profane! These are superstitious meats; your stomacks must be fed with sound doctrine.'"

In the *National Magazine* (1857), Dr. Doran, on "The Ups and Downs of Christmas," remarks upon the stout resistance given by the citizens of London to the order of the Puritan Parliament, that shops should be opened and churches closed on Christmas Day. "We may have a sermon on any other day," said the London apprentices, who did not always go to hear it, "why should we be deprived on this day?" "It is no longer lawful for the day to be kept," was the reply. "Nay," exclaimed the sharp-witted fellows, "you keep it yourselves by thus distinguishing it by desecration." "They declared," says Dr. Doran, "they would go to church; numerous preachers promised to be ready for them with prayer and lecture; and the porters of Cornhill swore they would dress up their conduit with holly, if it were only to prove that in that orthodox and heavily-enduring body there was some respect yet left for Christianity and hard drinking—for the raising of the holly was ever accompanied by the lifting of tankards.

"Nor was the gallant Christmas spirit less lively in the country than in the capital. At Oxford there was a world of skull-breaking; and at Ipswich the festival was celebrated by some loss of life. Canterbury especially distinguished itself by its violent opposition to the municipal order to be mirthless. There was a combat there, which was most rudely maintained, and in which the mayor got pummelled until he was as senseless as a pocket of hops. The mob mauled him terribly, broke all his windows, as well as his bones, and, as we are told, 'burnt the stoupes at the coming in of his door.' So serious was the riot, so complete the popular victory, and so jubilant the exultation, that thousands of the never-conquered men of Kent and Kentish men met in Canterbury, and passed a solemn resolution that if they could not have their Christmas Day, they were determined to have the King on his throne again."

Of the Canterbury riot an account is given in a rare tract, published in 1647 (preserved in the British Museum), and entitled—

"The Declaration of many thousands of the city of Canterbury, or county of Kent. Concerning the late tumult in the city of Canterbury, provokt by the Mayor's violent proceedings against those who desired to continue the celebration of the Feast of Christ's Nativity, 1,500 years and upwards maintained in the Church. Together with their Resolutions for the restitution of His Majestie to his Crown and dignity, whereby Religion may be restored to its ancient splendour, and the known Laws of this Kingdom maintained. As also their desires to all His Majesties loyall subjects within his Dominions, for their concurrence and assistance in this so good and pious a work."

The resolutions of the Canterbury citizens were not couched in the choicest terms, for the tract states that the two Houses of Parliament "have sate above seven years to hatch Cocatrices and Vipers, they have filled the kingdom with Serpents, bloodthirsty Souldiers, extorting Committees, Sequestrators, Excisemen; all the Rogues and scumme of the kingdom have they set on work to torment and vex the people, to rob them, and to eat the bread out of their mouthes; they have raised a causelesse and unnaturall Warre against their own Soveraigne Lord and King, a most pious Christian Prince, contrary to their allegiance and duty, and have shed innocent blood in this Land. Religion is onely talkt of, nothing done; they have put down what is good," &c., &c. And further on the tract says:—"The cause of this so sudden a posture of defence which we have put our selves into was the violent proceedings of the Mayor of this city of Canterbury and his uncivill carriage in persuance of some petty order of the House of Commons for hindering the celebration of Christ's Nativity so long continued in the Church of God. That which we so much desired that day was but a Sermon, which any other day of the weeke was tollerable by the orders and practise of the two Houses and all their adherents, but that day (because it was Christ's birth day) we must have none; that which is good all the yeer long, yet is this day superstitious. The Mayor causing some of us to be beaten contrary to his oath and office, who ought to preserve the peace, and to that purpose chiefly is the sword of justice put into his hands, and wrongfully imprisoned divers of us, because we did assemble ourselves to hear the Word of God, which he was pleased to interpret a Ryot; yet we were unarmed, behaved ourselves civilly, intended no such tumult as afterwards we were forc'd unto; but at last, seeing the manifest wrong done to our children, servants, and neighbours, by beating, wounding, and imprisoning them, and to release them that were imprisoned, and did call unto our assistance our brethren of the county of Kent, who very readily came in to us, as have associated themselves to us in this our just and lawfull defence, and do concurre with us in this our Remonstrance concerning the King Majestie, and the settlement of the peace in this Kingdome." And the tract afterwards expresses the desire that "all his Majesties loyall subjects within his Dominions" will "readily and cheerfully concurre and assist in this so good and pious a work."

Among the single sheets in the British Museum is an order of Parliament, dated the 24th of December, 1652, directing,

"That no observation shall be had of the five and twentieth day of December, commonly called Christmas Day; nor any solemnity used or exercised in churches upon that day in respect thereof."

Referring to the celebration of Christmas Day in 1657, Evelyn says:—

"I went to London with my wife to celebrate Christmas Day, Mr. Gunning preaching in Exeter Chapel, on Micah vii. 2. Sermon ended; as he was giving us the Holy Sacrament the chapel was surrounded with soldiers, and all the communicants and assembly surprised and kept prisoners by them, some in the house, others carried away. It fell to my share to be confined to a room in the house, where yet I was permitted to dine with the master of it, the Countess of Dorset, Lady Hatton, and some others of quality who invited me. In the afternoon came Colonel Whalley, Goffe, and others from Whitehall to examine us one by one; some they committed to the Marshal, some to prison. When I came before them they took my name and abode, examined me why, contrary to the ordinance made that none should any longer observe the superstitious time of the Nativity (as esteemed by them), I durst offend, and particularly be at Common Prayers, which they told me was but the mass in English, and particularly pray for Charles Stuart, for which we had no Scripture. I told them we did not pray for Charles Stuart, but for all Christian kings, princes, and governors. They replied, in so doing we prayed for the King of Spain too, who was their enemy and a Papist; with other frivolous and ensnaring questions and much threatening, and, finding no colour to detain me, they dismissed me with much pity of my ignorance. These were men of high flight and above ordinances, and spake spiteful things of our Lord's Nativity. As we went up to receive the sacrament the miscreants held their muskets against us, as if they would have shot us at the altar, but yet suffering us to finish the office of communion, as perhaps not having instructions what to do in case they found us in that action; so I got home late the next day, blessed be God!"

Notwithstanding the adverse acts of the Puritans, however, and the suppression of Christmas observances in high places, the old customs and festivities were still observed in different parts of the country, though with less ostentation than formerly; and various publications appeared which plainly showed that the popular sentiments were in favour of the festivities. The motto of No. 37 of *Mercurius Democritus*, from December 22, 1652, begins:

> "Old Christmas now is come to town
>   Though few do him regard,
> He laughs to see them going down
>   That have put down his Lord."

In "The Vindication of Father Christmas," 1653, a mock complaint in the character of Father Christmas, he laments the treatment he had received for the last twelve years, and that he was even then but coolly received. "But welcome, or not welcome, I am come," he says, and then states that his "best and freest welcome was with some kinde of country farmers in Devonshire," thus describing his entertainment among them:—"After dinner we arose from the boord, and sate by the fire, where the harth was imbrodered all over with roasted apples, piping hot, expecting a bole of ale for a cooler, which immediately was transformed into warm lamb wool. After which we discoursed merily, without either prophaneness or obscenity; some went to cards; others sung carols and pleasant songs (suitable to the times), and then the poor laboring Hinds, and maid-servants, with the plow-boys, went nimbly to dancing; the poor toyling wretches being glad of my company, because they had little or no sport at all till I came amongst them; and therefore they skipped and leaped for joy, singing a carol to the tune of hey,

> "Let's dance and sing, and make good chear,
>   For Christmas comes but once a year:
> Draw hogsheads dry, let flagons fly,
>   For now the bells shall ring;
> Whilst we endeavour to make good
>   The title 'gainst a King.

"Thus at active games, and gambols of hot cockles, shooing the wild mare, and the like harmless sports, some part of the tedious night was spent."

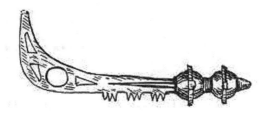

THE NATIONAL TROUBLES

were not brought to an end by the execution of Charles I. on the 30th of January, 1649. In addition to the rioting caused by the attempt to abolish the festival of Christmas by law, the Lord Protector (Oliver Cromwell) had to struggle against discontented republicans and also against fresh outbreaks of the Royalists; and, although able to carry on the Protectorate to the end of his own life, Cromwell was unable to secure a strong successor. He died on September 3, 1658, having on his deathbed nominated his son Richard to succeed him. Richard Cromwell was accepted in England and by the European Powers, and carried himself discreetly in his new position. A Parliament was assembled on January 17, 1659, which recognised the new Protector, but the republican minority, headed by Vane and Haselrig, united with the officers of the army, headed by Lambert, Fleetwood, and Desborough, to force him to dissolve Parliament (April 22, 1659). The Protector's supporters urged him to meet force by force, but he replied, "I will not have a drop of blood spilt for the preservation of my greatness, which is a burden to me." He signed a formal abdication (May, 1659), in return for which the restored Rump undertook the discharge of his debts. After the Restoration Richard Cromwell fled to the Continent, where he remained for many years, returning to England in 1680. A portion of his property was afterwards restored to him. He died at Cheshunt, Hertfordshire, in 1712.

On Richard Cromwell declining to uphold the Protectorate by force of arms, the only hope of establishing a settled form of government and of saving the country from a military despotism seemed to be in the restoration of the monarchy; therefore, chiefly through the instrumentality of General Monk, Charles, the son of Charles I. and Henrietta Maria, was invited to return to England. He at once responded, and entered London in triumph as Charles II., on May 29, 1660, having previously signed the declaration of Breda. By this declaration the King granted a free and general pardon to all "who within forty days after the publishing hereof shall lay hold upon this our grace and favour, and shall by any public act declare their doing so," except such as the Parliament of both houses should except.

69   "Works of Ben Jonson."
70   "Fantasticks," 1626.
71   "History of the English People."
72   "Year Book."
73   Fiddlers.
74   An allusion to the Christmas money-box, made of earthenware which required
       to be broken to obtain possession of the money it held.

CHAPTER X.

CHRISTMAS FROM THE RESTORATION TO THE DEATH OF GEORGE II.

(1660-1760.)

The Restoration of the Monarchy

under Charles II., sometimes styled the "Merry Monarch," was an occasion of great rejoicing, and the spirit in which the so-long-fugitive Prince, who once eluded his pursuers by hiding in an oak, was now welcomed as "Charles our King" by "the roaring, ranting" portion of the populace is set forth in the following ballad, written for the first Christmas after the Restoration, printed in London, the same year, and now copied from a collection of illustrated broadsides preserved in the Library of the British Museum:—

MERRY BOYS OF CHRISTMAS,

OR

THE MILK-MAID'S NEW YEAR'S GIFT.

When Lads and Lasses take delight,
    together for to be;
They pass away the Winter night,
    and live most merrily.

To the tune of, *Hey boys up go we.*

Come, come my roaring ranting boys
    lets never be cast down,
We'l never mind the female toys,
    but Loyal be to th' Crown:
We'l never break our hearts with care,
    nor be cast down with fear,
Our bellys then let us prepare
    to drink some Christmas Beer.
    to drink some Christmas Beer.
Then here's a health to Charles our King,
    throughout the world admir'd,
Let us his great applauses sing,
    that we so much desir'd,
And wisht amongst us for to reign,
    when Oliver rul'd here,
But since he's home return'd again,
    come fill some Christmas Beer.
These holidays we'l briskly drink,
    all mirth we will devise,
No Treason we will speak or think,
    then bring us brave minc'd pies
Roast Beef and brave Plum porridge,
    our Loyal hearts to chear,
Then prithee make no more ado,
    but bring us Christmas Beer.

THE HACKIN.

[In these Times all the Spits were sparkling the *Hackin* must be boiled by Daybreak or else two young Men took the Maiden by the Arms and run her round the Market Place till she was ashamed of her laziness.—*Round about our Coal Fire or Christmas Entertainments* published in 1740.

Many of the popular songs of this period complain of the decline of the Christmas celebrations during the time of the Commonwealth, and some of them contrast the present with former celebrations. In a ballad called "The Old and Young Courtier," printed in 1670, comparing the times of Queen Elizabeth with those of her successors, the fifth and twelfth verses contain the following parallel respecting Christmas—

V

"With a good old fashion, when Christmasse was come,
To call in all his old neighbours with bagpipe and drum,
With good chear enough to furnish every old room,
And old liquor, able to make a cat speak, and man dumb
     Like an old Courtier of the Queen's,
     And the Queen's old Courtier"

"With a new fashion, when Christmas is drawing on,
On a new journey to London straight we all must begone,
And leave none to keep house, but our new porter John,
Who relieves the poor with a thump on the back with a
stone,
    Like a young courtier of the King's,
    And the King's young courtier"   (*Percy's Reliques*)

Another called "Time's Alteration, or, the Old Man's Rehearsal, what brave dayes he knew a great while agone, when his old cap was new," says—

"A man might then behold,
    At Christmas, in each hall,
Good fires to curb the cold
    And meat for great and small;
The neighbours were friendly bidden,
    And all had welcome true,
The poor from the gates were not chidden,
    When this old cap was new

Black jacks to every man
    Were filled with wine and beer,
No pewter pot nor can
    In those days did appear
Good cheer in a nobleman's house
    Was counted a seemly shew,
We wanted no brawn nor souse,
    When this old cap was new."   (*Evans's Ballads*)

Referring to the Restoration of the monarchy, and contrasting it with the Protectorate period, *Poor Robin's Almanack*, 1685, says—

"Now thanks to God for Charles' return,
Whose absence made old Christmas mourn,
For then we scarcely did it know,
Whether it Christmas were or no

* * * * *

To feast the poor was counted sin,
When treason that great praise did win
May we ne'er see the like again,
The roguish Rump should o'er us reign."

After the Restoration an effort was made to revive the Christmas entertainments of the Court at Whitehall, but they do not appear to have recovered their former splendour. The habits of Charles the Second were of too sensual a nature to induce him to interest himself in such pursuits; besides which the manners of the country had been changed during the sway of the Puritans. Pepys states that Charles II. visited Lincoln's Inn to see the Christmas revels of 1661, "there being, according to an old custom, a Prince and all his nobles, and other matters of sport and charge." And the diary of the Rev. John Ward, vicar of Stratford-upon-Avon, extending from 1648 to 1679, states: "The Duke of Norfolk expended £20,000 in keeping Christmas. Charles II. gave over keeping that festival on this account; his munificence gave great offence at Court." Sandys mentions that a pastoral called *Calisto*, written by Crowne, was acted by the daughters of the Duke of York and the young nobility. About the same time the Lady Anne, afterwards Queen, acted the part of Semandra in Lee's "Mithridates." Betterton and his wife instructed the performers, in remembrance of which, when Anne came to the throne, she gave the latter a pension of £100 a year.

The Inns of Court also had their Christmas feasts; but the conduct of them was evidently not so much coveted as in former times, for there is an entry in the records of Gray's Inn on November 3, 1682, "That Mr. Richard Gipps, on his promise to perform the office of Master of the Revels, this and the next Term, be called to the Bar of Grace," *i.e.*, without payment of the usual fees: thus holding out a reward for his services, instead of allowing him, as in former times, to spend a large portion of his private fortune unrequited, except by the honour of the temporary office.

Among the principal of the royal amusements in the time of Charles the Second were horse-racing and theatrical performances. The King kept an establishment at Newmarket, where, according to Strutt, "he entered horses and ran them in his name." And the author of some doggerel verses, referring to Burford Downs, says:—

"Next for the glory of the place,
Here has been rode many a race,—
King Charles the Second I saw here;
But I've forgotten in what year."

CHRISTMAS AT SEA IN 1675.

The Rev. Henry Teonge, chaplain of an English ship of war, gives in his diary a description of the manner in which the Christmas was spent on board, in 1675:—"Dec. 25, 1675.—Crismas day wee keepe thus. At 4 in the morning our trumpeters all doe flatt their trumpetts, and begin at our Captain's cabin, and thence to all the officers' and gentlemen's cabins; playing a levite at each cabine door, and bidding good morrow, wishing a merry Crismas. After they goe to their station, viz., on the poope, and sound 3 levitts in honour of the morning. At 10 wee goe to prayers and sermon; text, Zacc. ix. 9. Our Captaine had all his officers and gentlemen to dinner with him, where wee had excellent good fayre: a ribb of beife, plumb-puddings, minct pyes, &c. and plenty of good wines of severall sorts; dranke healths to the King, to our wives and friends, and ended the day with much civill myrth."

CHRISTMAS-KEEPING IN THE COUNTRY,

at this period, is referred to by different writers.

Among the Garrick Plays in the British Museum is "*The Christmas Ordinary, a Private Show,* wherein is expressed the jovial

Freedom of that Festival: as it was acted at a Gentleman's House among other Revels. By W. R., Master of Arts, 4 to. London, 1682."

The Memoirs of the hospitable Sir John Reresby (Camden Society) contain references to the Christmas festivities at Thrybergh. In 1682, there assembled on Christmas Eve nineteen of the poorer tenants from Denby and Hooton; on Christmas Day twenty-six of the poorer tenants from Thrybergh, Brinsford, and Mexborough; on St. Stephen's Day farmers and better sort of tenants to the number of fifty-four; on St. John's-day forty five of the chief tenants; on the 30th of December eighteen gentlemen of the neighbourhood with their wives; on the 1st of January sixteen gentlemen; on the 4th twelve of the neighbouring clergymen; and on the 6th seven gentlemen and tradesmen. Among the guests who lodged at the house were "Mr. Rigden, merchant of York, and his wife, a handsome woman," and "Mr. Belton, an ingenious clergyman, but too much a good fellow." How the "ingenious clergyman" became "too much of a good fellow" may be easily guessed from Sir John's further observation that "*the expense of liquor, both of wine & others, was considerable*, as of other provisions, and my friends appeared well satisfied." In 1684, writes Sir John, "I returned to Thrybergh, by God's mercy, in safety, to keep Christmas amongst my neighbours and tenants. I had more company this Christmas than heretofore. The four first days of the new year all my tenants of Thrybergh, Brinsford, Denby, Mexborough, Hooton Roberts, and Rotterham dined with me; the rest of the time some four-score of gentlemen and yeomen with their wives were invited, besides some that came from York; so that all the beds in the house and most in the town were taken up. There were seldom less than four-score, counting all sorts of people, that dined in the house every day, and some days many more. On New Year's-day chiefly there dined above three hundred, so that whole sheep were roasted and served up to feed them. For music I had four violins, besides bagpipes, drums, and trumpets."

At Houghton Chapel, Nottinghamshire, says an old writer, "the good Sir William Hollis kept his house in great splendour and hospitality. He began Christmas at All Hallowtide, and continued it till Candlemas, during which time any man was permitted to stay three days without being asked who he was, or from whence he came." This generous knight had many guests who rejoiced in the couplet:—

> "If I ask'not my guest whence and whither his way,
> 'Tis because I would have him here with me to stay."

It is no part of our purpose to enter into details of the events which led up to the Revolution. Suffice it to say, that during the reign of Charles II. began the great struggle between the King and the people, but Charles steadily refused to alter the succession by excluding his brother James. He died on the 6th of February, 1685, and

JAMES II. CAME TO THE THRONE

in the midst of an unsettled state of affairs. James made a bold, but unsuccessful, attempt to restore the power of Romanism in England, and, ultimately, consulted his own safety by fleeing to France, landing at Ambleteuse, in Brittany, on Christmas Day, 1688,

THE CHRISTMAS OF THE REVOLUTION.

The flight of James put an end to the struggle between Crown and people, and the offering of the Crown, with constitutional limitations, to William, Prince of Orange, and his wife Mary, daughter of King James II. and granddaughter of King Charles I. of England, speedily followed.

WILLIAM AND MARY

accepted the invitation of the English people, and began their reign on February 13, 1689. They both took an interest in the sports and pastimes of the people. Strutt says William patronised horse-racing, "and established an academy for riding; and his queen not only continued the bounty of her predecessors, but added several plates to the former donations." The death of Queen Mary, from small-pox, on the 28th of December, 1694, cast a gloom over the

Christmas festivities, and left King William almost heart-broken at her loss. As to

THE CHRISTMAS FESTIVITIES

Brand says that in "Batt upon Batt," a Poem by a Person of Quality (1694), speaking of Batt's carving knives and other implements, the author asks:—

"Without their help, who can good Christmas keep?
Our teeth would chatter and our eyes would weep;
Hunger and dullness would invade our feasts,
Did not Batt find us arms against such guests.
He is the cunning engineer, whose skill
Makes fools to carve the goose, and shape the quill:
Fancy and wit unto our meals supplies:
Carols, and not minc'd-meat, make Christmas pies.
'Tis mirth, not dishes, sets a table off;
Brutes and Phanaticks eat, and never laugh.

* * * * *

When *brawn, with powdred wig*, comes swaggering in,
And mighty serjeant ushers in the Chine,
What ought a wise man first to think upon?
Have I my Tools? if not, I am undone:
For 'tis a law concerns both saint and sinner,
He that hath no knife must have no dinner.
So he falls on; pig, goose, and capon, feel
The goodness of his stomach and Batt's steel.
In such fierce frays, alas! there no remorse is;
All flesh is grass, which makes men feed like horses:
But when the battle's done, *off goes the hat*,
And each man sheaths, with God-a-mercy Batt.'"

"Batt upon Batt" also gives the following account of the Christmas Gambols in 1694:—

"O mortal man! is eating all you do
At Christ-Tide? or the making Sing-songs? No:
Our Batt can *dance*, play at *high Jinks with Dice*,

At any primitive, orthodoxal Vice.
Shooing the wild Mare, tumbling the young Wenches,
Drinking all Night, and sleeping on the Benches.
Shew me a man can *shuffle fair and cut,*
Yet always *have three Trays in hand at Putt.*
Shew me a man can *turn up Noddy* still,
And *deal himself three Fives too* when he will:
Conclude with *one and thirty, and a Pair,*
Never fail *Ten in stock,* and yet play fair,
If Batt be not that Wight, I lose my aim."

Another enumeration of the festive sports of this season occurs (says Brand) in a poem entitled Christmas—

"Young Men and Maidens, now
At *Feed the Dove* (with laurel leaf in mouth)
Or *Blindman's Buff,* or *Hunt the Slipper* play,
Replete with glee. Some, haply, *Cards* adopt;
Of it to *Forfeits* they the Sport confine,
The happy Folk, adjacent to the fire,
Their Stations take; excepting one alone.
(Sometimes the social Mistress of the house)
Who sits within the centre of the room,
To cry the pawns; much is the laughter, now,
Of such as can't the Christmas Catch repeat,
And who, perchance, are sentenc'd to salute
The jetty beauties of the chimney black,
Or Lady's shoe: others, more lucky far,
By hap or favour, meet a sweeter doom,
And on each fair-one's lovely lips imprint
The ardent kiss."

Poor Robin's Almanack (1695) thus rejoices at the return of the festival:—

"Now thrice welcome, Christmas,
    Which brings us good cheer,
Minc'd-pies and plumb-porridge,
    Good ale and strong beer;
With pig, goose, and capon,

286

The best that may be,
So well doth the weather
    And our stomachs agree.

Observe how the chimneys
    Do smoak all about,
The cooks are providing
    For dinner, no doubt;
But those on whose tables
    No victuals appear,
O may they keep Lent
    All the rest of the year!

With holly and ivy
    So green and so gay;
We deck up our houses
    As fresh as the day,
With bays and rosemary,
    And laurel compleat,
And every one now
    Is a king in conceit.

* * * * *

But as for curmudgeons,
    Who will not be free,
I wish they may die
    On the three-legged tree."

At Christmastide, 1696, an Act of Attainder was passed against Sir John Fenwick, one of the most ardent of the Jacobite conspirators who took part in the plot to assassinate the King. He was executed on Tower Hill, January 28, 1697. This was the last instance in English history in which a person was attainted by Act of Parliament, and Hallam's opinion of this Act of Attainder is that "it did not, like some acts of attainder, inflict a punishment beyond the offence, but supplied the deficiency of legal evidence."

Peter the Great, of Russia, kept the Christmas of 1697 in England, residing at Sayes Court, a house of the celebrated John Evelyn, close to Deptford Dockyard.

CHRISTMAS, 1701.

[From *Poor Robin's Almanack*.

Now enter Christmas like a man,
Armed with spit and dripping-pan,
Attended with pasty, plum-pie,
Puddings, plum-porridge, furmity;
With beef, pork, mutton of each sort
More than my pen can make report;
Pig, swan, goose, rabbits, partridge, teal,
With legs and loins and breasts of veal:
But above all the minced pies
Must mention'd be in any wise,
Or else my Muse were much to blame,
Since they from Christmas take their name.
With these, or any one of these,
A man may dine well if he please;
Yet this must well be understood,—
Though one of these be singly good,
Yet more the merrier is the best
As well of dishes as of guest.

　　But the times are grown so bad
Scarce one dish for the poor is had;
Good housekeeping is laid aside,
And all is spent to maintain pride;
Good works are counted popish, and
Small charity is in the land.
A man may sooner (truth I tell ye)
Break his own neck than fill his belly.

Good God amend what is amiss
And send a remedy to this,
That Christmas day again may rise
And we enjoy our Christmas pies.

The Christmas customs of this period are thus referred to by the "Bellman, on Christmas Eve":—

"This night (you may my Almanack believe)
Is the return of famous Christmas Eve:
Ye virgins then your cleanly rooms prepare,
And let the windows bays and laurels wear;
Your *Rosemary* preserve to dress your *Beef*,
Not forget me, which I advise in chief."

CHRISTMAS, AT HADDON HALL,

was magnificently kept in the early part of the eighteenth century. The amount of good cheer that was required for the table may be readily imagined from the magnitude of the culinary furniture in the kitchen—two vast fireplaces, with irons for sustaining a surprising number of spits, and several enormous chopping-blocks—which survived to the nineteenth century. John, the ninth Earl and first Duke of Rutland (created Marquis of Granby and Duke of Rutland in 1703), revived in the ancient spirit the hospitality of Christmastide. He kept sevenscore servants, and his twelve days' feasts at Christmas recalled the bountiful celebrations of the "King of the Peak," Sir George Vernon—the last male heir of the Vernon family in Derbyshire who inherited the manor of Haddon, and who died in the seventh year of Queen Elizabeth's reign. "The King of the Peak" was the father of the charming Dorothy Vernon, the fair heiress, whose romantic elopement is thus depicted in "Picturesque Europe":—"In the fullness of time Dorothy loved, but her father did not approve. She determined to elope; and now we must fill, in fancy, the Long Gallery with the splendour of a revel and the stately joy of a great ball in the time of Elizabeth. In the midst of the noise and excitement the fair young daughter of the house steals unobserved away. She issues from *her* door, and her light feet fly with tremulous speed along the darkling Terrace, flecked with light from the blazing ball-room, till they reach a postern in the wall, which opens upon the void of the night outside dancing Haddon. At that postern some one is waiting eagerly for her; waiting with swift horses. That some one is young Sir John Manners, second son of the House of Rutland, and her own true love. The anxious lovers mount, and ride rapidly and silently away; and so Dorothy Vernon transfers Haddon to the owners of Belvoir; and the boar's head of Vernon becomes mingled, at Haddon, with the peacock of Manners. We fancy with sympathetic pleasure that night-ride and the hurried marriage; and— forgetting that the thing happened 'ages long agone'—we wish, with full hearts, all happiness to the dear and charming Dorothy!"

From the boar's head of Vernon and the peacock of Manners, thought passes quite naturally to the boar's head and peacock, which were principal items of Christmas fare in the olden time.

In her "Collected Writings," Janetta, Duchess of Rutland, gives an interesting account of a revival of some of the ancient glories of Haddon:

"In the winter of 1872 the late Duke entertained the Prince and Princess of Wales in the banqueting hall at luncheon, when the boar's head and peacock in pride were carried in, and formed part of the fare, as in olden days: while once more musicians filled the minstrels' gallery, great logs blazed in the huge fireplace, and scarlet hangings were spread over the walls."

On the 20th of February, 1702, King William III. fell from his horse, breaking his collar-bone and sustaining other serious injuries, which terminated fatally on Sunday, the 8th of March. He was succeeded by Queen Anne, who was the second daughter of King James II., and the last of the Stuart sovereigns.

QUEEN ANNE KEPT A ROYAL CHRISTMAS

at Windsor, in 1703, and entertained the new King of Spain, who arrived at Spithead on the 26th of December. "The Queen dispatched the Dukes of Somerset and Marlborough to conduct him to Windsor, and Prince George met him on the way at Petworth, the seat of the Duke of Somerset, and conducted him to Windsor on the 29th. The King was entertained in great state for three days at Windsor, during which time he was politic enough to ingratiate himself with the Duchess of Marlborough. When the Duchess presented the basin and napkin after supper to the Queen for her to wash her hands, the King gallantly took the napkin and held it himself, and on returning it to the Queen's great favourite, he presented her with a superb diamond ring. After three days the King returned to Portsmouth, and on the 4th of January, 1704, he embarked on board the fleet commanded by Sir George Rooke, for Portugal, accompanied by a body of land forces under the Duke of Schomberg. The voyage was, however, a most stormy one, and when the fleet had nearly reached Cape Finisterre, it was compelled to put back to Spithead, where it remained till the middle of February. His next attempt was more successful, and he landed in Lisbon amid much popular demonstration, though the court itself was sunk in sorrow by the death of the Infanta, whom he went to marry."[75]

At the Christmas festivities the following year (1704) there were great rejoicings over the return home of the Duke of Marlborough from the continental wars. "He arrived in England in the middle of December, carrying with him Marshal Tallard and the rest of the distinguished officers, with the standards and other trophies of his victories. He was received with acclaim by all classes, except a few Ultra Tories, who threatened to impeach him for his rash march to the Danube. As Parliament had assembled, Marlborough took his seat in the House of Peers the day after his arrival, where he was complimented on his magnificent success by the Lord Keeper. This was followed by a deputation with a vote of thanks from the Commons, and by similar honours from the City. But perhaps the most palpable triumph of Marlborough was the transferring of the military trophies which he had taken from the Tower, where they were first deposited, to Westminster Hall. This was done by each soldier carrying a standard or other trophy, amid the thunders of artillery and the hurrahs of the people; such a spectacle never having been witnessed since the days of the Spanish Armada. The Royal Manor of Woodstock was granted him, and Blenheim Mansion erected at the cost of the nation."

CHRISTMAS-KEEPING IN THE COUNTRY.

The country squire of three hundred a year, an independent gentleman in the reign of Queen Anne, is described as having "never played at cards but at Christmas, when the family pack was produced from the mantle-piece." "His chief drink the year round was generally ale, except at this season, the 5th of November, or some gala days, when he would make a bowl of strong brandy punch, garnished with a toast and nutmeg. In the corner of his hall, by the fireside, stood a large wooden two-armed chair, with a cushion, and within the chimney corner were a couple of seats.

Here, at Christmas, he entertained his tenants, assembled round a glowing fire, made of the roots of trees, and other great logs, and told and heard the traditionary tales of the village, respecting ghosts and witches, till fear made them afraid to move. In the meantime the jorum of ale was in continual circulation."[76]

> "This is Yuletide! Bring the holly boughs,
>   Deck the old mansion with its berries red;
> Bring in the mistletoe, that lover's vows
>   Be sweetly sealed the while it hangs o'erhead.
> Pile on the logs, fresh gathered from the wood,
>   And let the firelight dance upon the walls,
> The while we tell the stories of the good,
>   The brave, the noble, that the past recalls."[77]

Many interesting tales respecting the manners and customs of the eighteenth century are given by Steele and Addison in their well-known series of papers entitled the *Spectator*. Charity and hospitality are conspicuous traits of the typical country gentleman of the period, Sir Roger de Coverley. "Sir Roger," says the *Spectator*, "after the laudable custom of his ancestors, always keeps open house at Christmas. I learned from him, that he had killed eight fat hogs for this season; that he had dealt about his chines very liberally amongst his neighbours; and that in particular he had sent a string of hog's puddings with a pack of cards to every poor family in the parish. 'I have often thought,' says Sir Roger, 'it happens well that Christmas should fall out in the middle of winter. It is the most dead uncomfortable time of the year, when the poor people would suffer very much from their poverty and cold, if they had not good cheer, warm fires, and Christmas gambols to support them. I love to rejoice their poor hearts at this season, and to see the whole village merry in my great hall. I allow a double quantity of malt to my small beer, and set it running for twelve days to every one that calls for it. I have always a piece of cold beef and a mince-pie upon the table, and am wonderfully pleased to see my tenants pass away a whole evening in playing their innocent tricks, and smutting one another. Our friend Will Wimble is as merry as any of them, and shows a thousand roguish tricks upon these occasions."

Puppet-shows and other scenic exhibitions with moving figures were among the Christmas amusements in the reign of Queen Anne. Strutt quotes a description of such an exhibition "by the manager of a show exhibited at the great house in the Strand, over against the Globe Tavern, near Hungerford Market; the best places at one shilling and the others at sixpence each: 'To be seen, the greatest Piece of Curiosity that ever arrived in England, being made by a famous engineer from the camp before Lisle, who, with great labour and industry, has collected into a moving picture the following figures: first, it doth represent the confederate camp, and the army lying intrenched before the town; secondly, the convoys and the mules with Prince Eugene's baggage; thirdly, the English forces commanded by the Duke of Marlborough; likewise, several vessels laden with provisions for the army, which are so artificially done as to seem to drive the water before them. The city and the citadel are very fine, with all its outworks, ravelins, horn-works, counter-scarps, half-moons, and palisades; the French horse marching out at one gate, and the confederate army marching in at the other; the prince's travelling coach with two generals in it, one saluting the company as it passes by; then a trumpeter sounds a call as he rides, at the noise whereof a sleeping sentinel starts, and lifts up his head, but, not being espied, lies down to sleep again; beside abundance more admirable curiosities too tedious to be inserted here.' He then modestly adds, 'In short, the whole piece is so contrived by art that it seems to be life and nature.'"

A DRUID PRIESTESS BEARING MISTLETOE.

Tumbling and feats of agility were also fashionable during the Christmas festival at this period, for in one of the *Tatlers* (No. 115, dated January 3, 1709) the following passage occurs: "I went on Friday last to the Opera, and was surprised to find a thin house at so noble an entertainment, 'till I heard that the tumbler was not to make his appearance that night." The sword-dance—dancing "among the points of swords and spears with most wonderful agility, and even with the most elegant and graceful motions"— rope-dancing, feats of balancing, leaping and vaulting, tricks by horses and other animals, and bull-baiting and bear-baiting were also among the public amusements. And *Hot Cockles* was one of the favourite indoor amusements of Christmastide. Strutt, in his "Sports and Pastimes," says, *Hot Cockles* is from the French *hautes-coquilles*, "a play in which one kneels, and covering his eyes, lays his head in another's lap and guesses who struck him." John Gay, a poet of the time, thus pleasantly writes of the game:—

"As at Hot Cockles once I laid me down,
And felt the weighty hand of many a clown,
Buxoma gave a gentle tap, and I
Quick rose, and read soft mischief in her eye."

On the death of Queen Anne (August 11, 1714) Prince George Louis of Hanover was proclaimed King of England as

GEORGE THE FIRST.

There was little change in the Christmas festivities in this reign, for, as Mr. Thackeray says in his lively sketch of George I.: "He was a moderate ruler of England. His aim was to leave it to itself as much as possible, and to live out of it as much as he could. His heart was in Hanover." The most important addition to the plays of the period was

THE CHRISTMAS PANTOMIME.

In his "English Plays," Professor Henry Morley thus records the introduction of the modern English pantomime, which has since been the great show of Christmastide:—

A NEST OF FOOLS.

"The theatre in Lincoln's Inn Fields, which Christopher Rich had been restoring, his son, John Rich, was allowed to open on the 18th of December, 1714. John Rich was a clever mimic, and after a year or two he found it to his advantage to compete with the actors in a fashion of his own. He was the inventor of the modern English form of pantomime, with a serious part that he took from Ovid's Metamorphosis or any fabulous history, and a comic addition of the courtship of harlequin and columbine, with surprising tricks and transformations. He introduced the old Italian characters of pantomime under changed conditions, and beginning with 'Harlequin Sorcerer' in 1717, continued to produce these entertainments until a year before his death in 1761. They have since been retained as Christmas shows upon the English stage."

In a note to "The Dunciad," Pope complains of "the extravagancies introduced on the stage, and frequented by persons of the first quality in England to the twentieth and thirtieth time," and states that "*all* the extravagances" in the following lines of the poem actually appeared on the stage:—

> "See now, what Dulness and her sons admire!
> See what the charms, that smite the simple heart
> Not touch'd by nature, and not reach'd by art.
> His never-blushing head he turn'd aside,
> (Not half so pleased when Goodman prophesied)
> And look'd, and saw a sable Sorcerer rise,
> Swift to whose hand a winged volume flies:
> All sudden, gorgons hiss, and dragons glare,
> And ten-horn'd fiends and giants rush to war.
> Hell rises, Heaven descends, and dance on earth:
> Gods, imps, and monsters, music, rage, and mirth,
> A fire, a jig, a battle, and a ball,
> Till one wide conflagration swallows all.
>
> Thence a new world, to nature's laws unknown,
> Breaks out refulgent, with a heaven its own:
> Another Cynthia her new journey runs,
> And other planets circle other suns.
> The forests dance, the rivers upward rise,
> Whales sport in woods, and dolphins in the skies;
> And last, to give the whole creation grace,
> Lo! one vast egg produces human race."

David Garrick, the eminent actor, wrote in a similar strain, finding it hard to hold his own against the patrons of the pantomime:—

"They in the drama find no joys,
But doat on mimicry and toys.
Thus, when a dance is in my bill,
Nobility my boxes fill;
Or send three days before the time,
To crowd a new-made pantomime."

"OLD MERRY PLENTIFUL CHRISTMAS,"

at this period, is sketched by a writer in *Poor Robin's Almanack*, for 1723, thus:—"Now comes on old merry plentiful Christmas. The Husbandman lays his great Log behind the fire, and with a few of his neighbours, over a good fire, taps his Christmas beer, cuts his Christmas cheese, and sets forward for a merry Christmas. The Landlord (for we hope there are yet some generous ones left) invites his Tenants and Labourers, and with a good Sirloin of Roast Beef, and a few pitchers of nappy ale or beer, he wisheth them all a merry Christmas. The beggar begs his bread, sells some of it for money to buy drink, and without fear of being arrested, or call'd upon for parish duties, has as merry a Christmas as any of them all."

THE MASK DANCE.

So the people made merry at Christmas throughout the reign of George I., who died on June 10, 1727, and was succeeded by his son,

GEORGE THE SECOND.

In this reign the customs of Christmas were kept up with unabated heartiness, and liberality to the poor was not forgotten. The customary distributions of creature comforts on Christmas Eve were continued, and, in some instances, provision for the maintenance of them was made in the wills of worthy parishioners. An instance of this kind is recorded in Devonshire. "It appears, from a statement of charities in an old book, that John Martyn, by will, 28th of November, 1729, gave to the churchwardens and overseers of the poor of the parish of St. Mary Major, Exeter, twenty pounds, to be put out at interest, and the profits thereof to be laid out every Christmas Eve in twenty pieces of beef, to be distributed to twenty poor people of the parish, such as had no relief on that day, for ever."[78]

That

CHRISTMAS HOUSEKEEPING IN LONDON,

at this period, was excellent, both as to quantity and quality, is evident, from a contribution made to *Read's Weekly Journal*, of Saturday, January 9, 1731, by Mr. Thomas North, who thus describes the Christmas entertainment and good cheer he met with in London at the house of a friend: "It was the house of an eminent and worthy merchant, and tho', sir, I have been accustomed in my own country to what may very well be called good housekeeping, yet I assure you I should have taken this dinner to have been provided for a whole parish, rather than for about a dozen gentlemen: 'Tis impossible for me to give you half our bill of fare, so you must be content to know that we had turkies, geese, capons, puddings of a dozen sorts more than I had ever seen in my life, besides brawn, roast beef, and many things of which I know not the names, minc'd pyes in abundance, and a thing they call plumb pottage, which may be good for ought I know, though it seems to me to have 50 different tastes. Our wines were of the best, as were all the rest of our liquors; in short, the God of plenty seemed to reign here, and to make everything perfect, our company was polite and every way agreeable; nothing but mirth and loyal healths went round. If a stranger were to have made an estimate of London from this place, he would imagine it not only the most rich but the most happy city in the world."

Another interesting item of this period is the following—

CURIOUS CHRISTMAS ADVERTISEMENT,

which has been cut from some publication and (by the late Mr. Joseph Haslewood) inserted between pages 358 and 359 of the British Museum large paper copy of Brand's "Antiquities," and dated December, 1739:—

"This day is published, Price 6d.

"THE TRIAL OF OLD FATHER CHRISTMAS for encouraging his Majesty's subjects in Idleness, Drunkenness, Gaming, Rioting, and all manner of Extravagance and Debauchery, at the Assizes held in the city of Profusion before the Lord Chief Justice Churchman, Mr. Justice Feast, Mr. Justice Gambol, and several other his Majesty's Justices of Oyer and Terminer, and Gaol-Delivery.

"To which is added a Diary found in the Pocket of Old Father Christmas, with Directions to all Lovers of him how to welcome their neighbours; likewise the Judge's sentence and Opinion how Christmas ought to be kept; and further Witty Tales and Merry Stories designed for Christmas Evenings Diversion, when round about our Coal Fire.

BY JOSIAH KING,

Printer for T. Cooper, at the Globe in Pater-noster Row; and sold by the Pamphlet-shops of London and Westminster."

Now we come to a quaintly interesting account of

CHRISTMAS ENTERTAINMENT IN THE OLDEN TIME.

The manner of observing the Christmas festival in the time of George the Second is described in an amusing little book entitled

"Round about our Coal Fire, or Christmas Entertainments," published in 1740, and "illustrated with many diverting cuts." We quote the following extracts:—

PROLOGUE

I.

"O you merry, merry souls,
    Christmas is a coming,
We shall have flowing Bowls,
    Dancing, piping, drumming.

II.

"Delicate minced Pies,
    To feast every Virgin,
Capon and Goose likewise,
    Brawn and a dish of Sturgeon.

III.

"Then for your Christmas Box,
    Sweet Plumb-cakes and money,
Delicate Holland Smocks,
    Kisses sweet as Honey.

IV.

"Hey for the Christmas Ball,
    Where we shall be jolly,
Jigging short and tall,
    Kate, Dick, Ralph, and Molly.

V.

"Then to the Hop we'll go,
    Where we'll jig and caper,
Maidens all-a-row,
    Will shall pay the Scraper.

"Hodge shall dance with Prue,
    Keeping Time with Kisses
We'll have a jovial Crew,
    Of sweet smirking Misses.

THE CHRISTMAS MUMMERS.

"First acknowledging the sacredness of the Holy Time of *Christmas*, I proceed to set forth the Rejoicings which are generally made at that great Festival.

"You must understand, good People, that the manner of celebrating this great Course of Holydays is vastly different now to what it was in former days: There was once upon a time Hospitality in the land; an *English* gentleman at the opening of the great Day, had all his Tenants and Neighbours enter'd his Hall by Day-break, the strong Beer was broach'd, and the Black Jacks went plentifully about with Toast, Sugar, Nutmeg, and good Cheshire Cheese; the Rooms were embower'd with Holly, Ivy, Cypress, Bays, Laurel, and Missleto, and a bouncing *Christmas* Log in the Chimney glowing like the cheeks of a country Milk-maid; then was the pewter as bright as *Clarinda*, and every bit of Brass as polished as the most refined Gentleman; the Servants were then running here and there, with merry Hearts and jolly Countenances; every one was busy welcoming of Guests, and look'd as smug as new-lick'd Puppies; the Lasses as blithe and buxom as the maids in good Queen *Bess's* Days, when they eat Sir-Loins of Roast Beef for Breakfast; *Peg* would scuttle about to make a Toast for *John*, while *Tom* run *harum scarum* to draw a Jug of Ale for *Margery*. Gaffer *Spriggins* was bid thrice welcome by the 'Squire, and Gooddy *Goose* did not fail of a smacking Buss from his Worship while his Son and Heir did the Honours of the House: in a word, the Spirit of Generosity ran thro' the whole House.

"In these Times all the Spits were sparkling, the *Hackin* must be boiled by Day-break, or else two young Men took the Maiden by the Arms, and run her round the Market-place, till she was ashamed of her Laziness. And what was worse than this, she must not play with the Young Fellows that Day, but stand Neuter, like a Girl doing penance in a Winding-sheet at a Church-door.

"But now let us enquire a little farther, to arrive at the Sense of the Thing; this great Festival was in former Times kept with so much Freedom and Openness of Heart, that every one in the Country where a Gentleman resided, possessed at least a Day of Pleasure in the *Christmas* Holydays; the Tables were all spread from the first to the last, the Sir-Loyns of Beef, the Minc'd-Pies, the Plumb-Porridge, the Capons, Turkeys, Geese, and Plumb-Puddings, were all brought upon the board; and all those who had sharp stomachs and sharp Knives eat heartily and were welcome, which gave rise to the Proverb—

Merry in the Hall, when Beards wag all".

"There were then Turnspits employed, who by the time Dinner was over, would look as black and as greasy as a Welch Porridge-pot, but the Jacks have since turned them all out of Doors. The Geese which used to be fatted for the honest Neighbours, have been of late sent to *London*, and the Quills made into Pens to convey away the Landlord's Estate; the Sheep are drove away to raise Money to answer the Loss of a Game at Dice or Cards, and their Skins made into Parchment for Deeds and Indentures; nay even the poor innocent Bee, who used to pay its Tribute to the Lord once a Year at least in good Metheglin, for the Entertainment of the Guests, and its Wax converted into beneficial Plaisters for sick Neighbours, is now used for the sealing of Deeds to his Disadvantage.

"But give me the Man *who has a good Heart*, and has Spirit enough to keep up the Old way of Hospitality, feeds his People till they are as plump as Partridges, and as fat as Porpoises that every Servant may appear as jolly as the late Bishop of *Winchester's* Porter at *Chelsea*.

"The News-Papers however inform us, that the Spirit of Hospitality has not quite forsaken us; for three or four of them tell us, that several of the Gentry are gone down to their respective Seats in the Country, in order to keep their *Christmas* in the Old Way, and entertain their Tenants and Trades-folks as their Ancestors used to do and I wish them a merry *Christmas* accordingly. I must also take notice to the stingy Tribe, that if they don't at least make their Tenants or Tradesmen drink when they come to see them in the Christmas Holydays, they have Liberty of retaliating which is a Law of very ancient Date.

"A merry Gentleman of my Acquaintance desires I will insert, that the old Folks in Days of yore kept open House at *Christmas* out of Interest; for then, says he, they receive the greatest Part of their Rent in Kind; such as Wheat, Barley or Malt, Oxen, Calves, Sheep, Swine, Turkeys, Capon, Geese, and such like; and they not having Room enough to preserve their Grain, or Fodder enough to preserve their Cattle or Poultry, nor Markets to sell off the Overplus, they were obliged to use them in their own Houses; and by treating the People of the Country, gained Credit amongst them, and riveted the Minds and Goodwill of their Neighbours so firmly in them, that no one durst venture to oppose them. The 'Squire's Will was done whatever came on it; for if he happened to ask a Neighbour what it was a Clock, they returned with a low Scrape, it is what your Worship pleases.

"The Dancing and Singing of the Benchers in the great Inns of Court in *Christmas*, is in some sort founded upon Interest; for they hold, as I am informed, some Priviledge by Dancing about the Fire in the middle of their Hall, and singing the Song of *Round about our Coal Fire*, &c.

"This time of year being cold and frosty generally speaking, or when Jack-Frost commonly takes us by the Nose, the Diversions are within Doors, either in Exercise or by the Fire-side.

"Country-Dancing is one of the chief Exercises...

"Then comes Mumming or Masquerading, when the 'Squire's Wardrobe is ransacked for Dresses of all Kinds, and the coal-hole searched around, or corks burnt to black the Faces of the Fair, or make Deputy-Mustaches, and every one in the Family except the 'Squire himself must be transformed from what they were...

"Or else there is a Match at *Blind-Man's-Buff*, and then it is lawful to set anything in the way for Folks to tumble over...

"As for *Puss in the Corner*, that is a very harmless Sport, and one may romp at it as much as one will...

"The next game to this is *Questions and Commands*, when the Commander may oblige his Subject to answer any lawful Question, and make the same obey him instantly, under the penalty of being smutted, or paying such Forfeit as may be laid on the Aggressor; but the Forfeits being generally fixed at some certain Price, as a Shilling, Half a Crown, &c., so every one knowing what to do if they should be too stubborn to submit, make themselves easy at discretion.

"As for the Game of *Hoop and Hide*, the Parties have the Liberty of hiding where they will, in any part of the House; and if they happen to be caught, the Dispute ends in Kissing, &c.

"Most of the other Diversions are Cards and Dice, but they are seldom set on foot, unless a Lawyer is at hand, to breed some dispute for him to decide, or at least have some Party in.

"And now I come to another Entertainment frequently used, which is of the Story-telling Order, *viz*: of Hobgoblins, Witches, Conjurers, Ghosts, Fairies, and such like common Disturbers."

At this period

DAVID GARRICK'S CHRISTMAS ACTING

won him great applause. At Christmas, 1741, he brought out at Goodman's Fields a Christmas Farce, written by himself, entitled "The Lying Valet," wherein the great actor took the part of "Sharp." It was thought the most diverting farce ever performed. "There was a general roar from beginning to end. So great was his versatility that people were not able to determine whether he was best in tragedy or comedy." On his benefit, when his real name was placed on the bills for the first time, there was an immense gathering, and the applause was quite extraordinary.

The Christmas festivities of 1745 were marred by the

DISTURBANCES OF THE JACOBITES,

under the romantic "Prince Charlie," whose attempted invasion of England speedily collapsed.

Pointer, in his *Oxoniensis Academia* (1749) refers to

AN OLD CHRISTMAS CUSTOM

of this period. He states that at Merton College, Oxford, the Fellows meet together in the Hall, on Christmas Eve, to sing a Psalm and drink a grace-cup to one another (called *Poculum Charitatis*), wishing one another health and happiness.

The Christmas of 1752 was

THE FIRST CHRISTMAS UNDER THE "NEW STYLE,"

and many refused to observe the festival eleven days earlier than usual, but insisted on keeping "Old Christmas Day." Why should they be robbed of eleven days by a new Act of Parliament? It was of no use to tell them that it had been discovered that the fractional few minutes which are tailed on to the days and hours which make up the year had, by neglect through many centuries, brought us into a wrong condition, and that to set us right it would be necessary to give credit for eleven days which nobody was conscious of having enjoyed. The law, however, had said that it should be so. Accordingly, the day after the 2nd of September, 1752, was called the 14th, to the great indignation of thousands, who reckoned that they had thus been cut off from nearly a fortnight of life which honestly belonged to them. These persons sturdily refused to acknowledge the Christmas Eve and Day of the new calendar. They averred that the true festival was that which now began on the 5th of January *next year*. They would go to church, they said, on no other day; nor eat mince-pies nor drink punch but in reference to this one day. The clergy had a hard time of it with these recusants. It will be well, therefore, to quote one singular example to show how this recusancy was encountered. It is from a collection of pamphlet-sermons preserved by George III., none of which, however, have anything curious or particularly meritorious about them save this one, which was preached on Friday, January 5, 1753, "Old Christmas Day." Mr. Francis Blackburne, "one of the candid disquisitors," opened his church on that day, which was crowded by a congregation anxious to see the day celebrated as that of the anniversary of the Nativity. The service for Christmas Day, however, was not used. "I will answer your expectations so far," said the preacher in his sermon, "as to give you a *sermon on the day*; and the rather because I perceive you are disappointed of *something else* that you expected." The purport of the discourse is to show that the change of style was desirable, and that it having been effected by Act of Parliament, with the sanction of the King, there was nothing for it but acquiescence. "For," says the preacher, "had I, to oblige you, disobeyed this Act of Parliament, it is very probable I might have lost my benefice, which, you know, is all the subsistence I have in the world; and I should have been rightly served; for who am I that I should fly in the face of his Majesty and the Parliament? These things are left to be ordered by the higher powers; and in any such case as that, I hope not to think myself wiser than the King, the whole nobility, and principal gentry of Great Britain"!!

The peasants of Buckinghamshire, however, pitched upon a very pretty method to settle the question of Christmas, left so meekly by Mr. Blackburne to the King, nobility, and most of the gentry. They bethought themselves of a blackthorn near one of their villages; and this thorn was for the nonce declared to be the growth of a slip from the Christmas-flowering thorn at Glastonbury. If the Buckinghamshire thorn, so argued the peasants, will only blossom in the night of the 24th of December, we will go to church next day, and allow that the Christmas by Act of Parliament is the true Christmas; but no blossom no feast, and there shall be no revel till the eve of old Christmas Day. They watched the thorn and drank to its budding; but as it produced no promise of a flower by the morning, they turned to go homewards as best they might, perfectly satisfied with the success of the experiment. Some were interrupted in their way by their respective "vicars," who took them by the arm and would fain have persuaded them to go to church. They argued the question by field, stile, and church-gate; but not a Bucks peasant would consent to enter a pew till the parson had promised to preach a sermon to, and smoke a pipe with, them on the only Christmas Day they chose to acknowledge.

Now, however, this old prejudice has been conquered, and the "new style" has maintained its ground. It has even done more, for its authors have so arranged the years and leap years that a confusion in the time of Christmas or any other festival is not likely to occur again.

75   Cassell's "History of England."
76   Grose.
77   Herbert H. Adams.
78   "Old English Customs and Charities," 1842.

CHAPTER XI.

MODERN CHRISTMASES AT HOME.

THE WAITS.

KING GEORGE THE THIRD

came to the throne on the death of his grandfather, George II. (October 25, 1760), and the first Christmas of his reign "was a high festival at Court, when his Majesty, preceded by heralds, pursuivants, &c., went with their usual state to the Chapel Royal, and heard a sermon preached by his Grace the Archbishop of York; and it being a collar day, the Knights of the Garter, Thistle and Bath, appeared in the collars of their respective orders. After the

sermon was over, his Majesty, Prince Edward and Princess Augusta
went into the Chapel Royal, and received the sacrament from the
hands of the Bishop of Durham; and the King offered the byzant,
or wedge of gold, in a purse, for the benefit of the poor, and the
royal family all made offerings. His Majesty afterwards dined with
his royal mother at Leicester House, and in the evening returned to
St. James's."[79]

At this period

THE FAVOURITE CHRISTMAS DIVERSION

was card-playing. The King himself spent a great deal of his time
in playing at cards with the ladies and gentlemen of his court. In
doing so, however, he was but following the example of George II.,
of whom the biographer already quoted (Mr. Huish) says:—

"After the death of Queen Caroline, the King was very fond
of a game at cards with the Countess of Pembroke, Albemarle, and
other distinguished ladies. His attachment to cards was transferred
to his attachment for the ladies, and it was said that what he gained
by the one he lost by the other." Cards were very much resorted
to at the family parties and other social gatherings held during the
twelve days of Christmas. Hone makes various allusions to card-
playing at Christmastide, and Washington Irving, in his "Life of
Oliver Goldsmith," pictures the poet "keeping the card-table in
an uproar." Mrs. Bunbury invited Goldsmith down to Barton to
pass the Christmas holidays. Irving regrets "that we have no record
of this Christmas visit to Barton; that the poet had no Boswell to
follow at his heels, and take notes of all his sayings and doings. We
can only picture him in our minds, casting off all care; enacting the
Lord of Misrule; presiding at the Christmas revels; providing all
kinds of merriment; keeping the card-table in an uproar, and finally
opening the ball on the first day of the year in his spring-velvet suit,
with the Jessamy Bride for a partner."

From the reprint additions made in the British Museum
large paper copy of Brand's "Antiquities," by the late Mr. Joseph
Haslewood, and dated January, 1779, we quote the following verses
descriptive of the concluding portion of the Christmas festivities
at this period:—

Now the jovial girls and boys,
    Struggling for the cake and plumbs,
Testify their eager joys,
    And lick their fingers and their thumbs.

Statesmen like, they struggle still,
    Scarcely hands kept out of dishes,
And yet, when they have had their fill,
    Still anxious for the loaves and fishes.

Kings and Queens, in petty state,
    Now their sovereign will declare,
But other sovereigns' plans they hate,
    Full fond of peace—detesting war.

One moral from this tale appears,
    Worth notice when a world's at stake;
That all our hopes and all our fears,
    Are but a *struggling for the* Cake.

Other particulars of the

POPULAR CHRISTMAS FESTIVITIES

in the latter part of the eighteenth century are gleaned from contemporary writers:—

"At Ripon, on Christmas Eve, the grocers, send each of their customers a pound or half of currants and raisins to make a Christmas pudding. The chandlers also send large mould candles, and the coopers logs of wood, generally called **Yule clogs**, which are always used on Christmas Eve; but should it be so large as not to be all burnt that night, which is frequently the case, the remains are kept till old Christmas Eve."[80]

In Sinclair's Account of Scotland, parish of Kirkden, county of Angus (1792), Christmas is said to be held as a great festival in the neighbourhood. "The servant is free from his master, and goes about visiting his friends and acquaintance.

The poorest must have beef or mutton on the table, and what they call a dinner with their friends. Many amuse themselves with various diversions, particularly with shooting for prizes, called here *wad-shooting*; and many do but little business all the Christmas week; the evening of almost every day being spent in amusement." And in the account of Keith, in Banffshire, the inhabitants are said to "have no pastimes or holidays, except dancing on Christmas and New Year's Day."

Boyhood's Christmas Breaking-up is thus described in a poem entitled "Christmas" (Bristol, 1795):—

> "A school there was, within a well-known town,
> (Bridgwater call'd), in which the boys were wont,
> At *breaking-up* for Christmas' lov'd recess,
> To meet the master, on the happy morn,
> At early hour; the custom, too, prevail'd,
> That he who first the seminary reach'd
> Should, instantly, perambulate the streets
> With sounding horn, to rouse his fellows up;
> And, as a compensation for his care,
> His flourish'd copies, and his chapter-task,
> Before the rest, he from the master had.
> For many days, ere breaking-up commenced,
> Much was the clamour, 'mongst the beardless crowd,
> Who first would dare his well-warm'd bed forego,
> And, round the town, with horn of ox equipp'd,
> His schoolmates call. Great emulation glow'd
> In all their breasts; but, when the morning came,
> Straightway was heard, resounding through the streets,
> The pleasing blast (more welcome far, to them,
> Than is, to sportsmen, the delightful cry
> Of hounds on chase), which soon together brought
> A tribe of boys, who, thund'ring at the doors
> Of those, their fellows, sunk in Somnus' arms,
> Great hubbub made, and much the town alarm'd.
> At length the gladsome, congregated throng,
> Toward the school their willing progress bent,
> With loud huzzas, and, crowded round the desk,
> Where sat the master busy at his books,
> In reg'lar order, each receiv'd his own,

The youngsters then, enfranchised from the school,
Their fav'rite sports pursued."

A writer in the *Gentleman's Magazine* for February, 1795, gives the following account of a Christmas Eve custom at the house of Sir—Holt, Bart., of Aston, near Birmingham:

"As soon as supper is over, a table is set in the hall. On it is placed a brown loaf, with twenty silver threepences stuck on the top of it, a tankard of ale, with pipes and tobacco; and the two oldest servants have chairs behind it, to sit as judges if they please. The steward brings the servants, both men and women, by one at a time, covered with a winnow-sheet, and lays their right hand on the loaf, exposing no other part of the body. The oldest of the two judges guesses at the person, by naming a name, then the younger judge, and lastly the oldest again. If they hit upon the right name, the steward leads the person back again; but, if they do not, he takes off the winnow-sheet, and the person receives a threepence, makes a low obeisance to the judges, but speaks not a word. When the second servant was brought, the younger judge guessed first and third; and this they did alternately, till all the money was given away. Whatever servant had not slept in the house the preceding night forfeited his right to the money. No account is given of the origin of this strange custom, but it has been practised ever since the family lived there. When the money is gone, the servants have full liberty to drink, dance, sing, and go to bed when they please."

Brand quotes the foregoing paragraph and asks: "Can this be what Aubrey calls the sport of 'Cob-loaf stealing'?"

THE DELIGHTS OF CHRISTMAS.
A NEW SONG BY R. P.
(Tune—"Since Love is my Plan.")
In the Poor Soldier.

When Christmas approaches each bosom is gay,
That festival banishes sorrow away,
While Richard he kisses both Susan and Dolly,
When tricking the house up with ivy and holly;
For never as yet it was counted a crime,

To be merry and cherry at that happy time.
                    For never as yet, &c.

Then comes turkey and chine, with the famous roast beef,
Of English provisions still reckon'd the chief;
Roger whispers the cook-maid his wishes to crown,
O Dolly! pray give me a bit of the brown;
For never as yet it was counted a crime,
To be merry and cherry at that happy time.
                    For never as yet, &c.

The luscious plum-pudding does smoking appear,
And the charming mince pye is not far in the rear,
Then each licks his chops to behold such a sight,
But to taste it affords him superior delight;
For never as yet it was counted a crime,
To be merry and cherry at that happy time.
                    For never as yet, &c.

Now the humming October goes merrily round,
And each with good humour is happily crown'd,
The song and the dance, and the mirth-giving jest,
Alike without harm by each one is expressed;
For never as yet it was counted a crime,
To be merry and cherry at that happy time.
                    For never as yet, &c.

Twelfth Day next approaches, to give you delight,
And the sugar'd rich cake is display'd to the sight,
Then sloven and slut and the king and the queen,
Alike must be present to add to the scene;
For never as yet it was counted a crime,
To be merry and cherry at that happy time.
                    For never as yet, &c.

May each be found thus as the year circles round,
With mirth and good humour each Christmas be crown'd,
And may all who have plenty of riches in store
With their bountiful blessings make happy the poor;
For never as yet it was counted a crime,

To be merry and cherry at that happy time.
                    For never as yet, &c.[81]

CHARLES LAMB ON CHRISTMAS.

In his essay on "Recollections of Christ's Hospital," Charles Lamb thus refers to the Christmas festivities of his schoolboy days:—

"Let me have leave to remember the festivities at Christmas, when the richest of us would club our stock to have a gaudy day, sitting round the fire, replenished to the height with logs, and the pennyless, and he that could contribute nothing, partook in all the mirth, and in some of the substantialities of the feasting; the carol sung by night at that time of the year, which, when a young boy, I have so often lain awake to hear from seven (the hour of going to bed) till ten when it was sung by the older boys and monitors, and have listened to it, in their rude chaunting, till I have been transported in fancy to the fields of Bethlehem, and the song which was sung at that season, by angels' voices to the shepherds."

In a sonnet sent to Coleridge, in 1797, Lamb says:—

> "It were unwisely done, should we refuse
> To cheer our path, as featly as we may—
> Our lonely path to cheer, as travellers use,
> With merry song, quaint tale, or roundelay.
> And we will sometimes talk past troubles o'er,
> Of mercies shown, and all our sickness heal'd,
> And in His judgments God remembering love:
> And we will learn to praise God evermore,
> For those 'glad tidings of great joy,' reveal'd
> By that sooth messenger, sent from above."

THE CHRISTMAS PLUM-PUDDING.
(*From an old print.*)

Writing to Southey, in 1798, Lamb tells the poet that Christmas is a "glorious theme"; and addressing his "dear old friend and absentee," Mr. Manning, at Canton, on December 25, 1815, Lamb says:—"This is Christmas Day, 1815, with us; what it may be with you I don't know, the 12th of June next year perhaps; and if it should be the consecrated season with you, I don't see how you can keep it. You have no turkeys; you would not desecrate the festival by offering up a withered Chinese bantam, instead of the savoury grand Norfolcian holocaust, that smokes all around my nostrils at this moment from a thousand firesides. Then what puddings have you? Where will you get holly to stick in your churches, or churches to stick your dried tea-leaves (that must be the substitute) in? Come out of Babylon, O my friend."

ITALIAN MINSTRELS IN LONDON, AT CHRISTMAS, 1825.
(*From a sketch of that period.*)

"Ranged in a row, with guitars slung
Before them thus, they played and sung:
Their instruments and choral voice
Bid each glad guest still more rejoice;
And each guest wish'd again to hear
Their wild guitars and voices clear."[82]

THE CHRISTMAS GAMES

at the beginning of the nineteenth century include the old Christmas game of *Forfeits*, for every breach of the rules of which the players have to deposit some little article as a forfeit, to be redeemed by some sportive penalty, imposed by the "Crier of the Forfeits" (usually a bonnie lassie). The "crying of the forfeits" and paying of the penalties creates much merriment, particularly when a bashful youth is sentenced to "kiss through the fire-tongs" some beautiful romp of a girl, who delights playing him tricks while the room rings with laughter.

Some of the old pastimes, however, have fallen into disuse, as, for instance, the once popular game of *Hot Cockles, Hunt the*

Slipper, and "the vulgar game of *Post and Pair*"; but *Cards* are still popular, and Snapdragon continues such Christmas merriment as is set forth in the following verses:—

SNAP DRAGON.

"Here he comes with flaming bowl,
Don't he mean to take his toll,
Snip! Snap! Dragon!
Take care you don't take too much,
Be not greedy in your clutch,
Snip! Snap! Dragon!

With his blue and lapping tongue
Many of you will be stung,
Snip! Snap! Dragon!
For he snaps at all that comes
Snatching at his feast of plums,
Snip! Snap! Dragon!

But old Christmas makes him come,
Though he looks so fee! fa! fum!
Snip! Snap! Dragon!
Don't 'ee fear him, be but bold—

Out he goes, his flames are cold,
Snip! Snap! Dragon!"

"Don't 'ee fear him, be but bold," accords with the advice of a writer in "Pantalogia," in 1813, who says that when the brandy in the bowl is set on fire, and raisins thrown into it, those who are unused to the sport are afraid to take out, but the raisins may be safely snatched by a quick motion and put blazing into the mouth, which being closed, the fire is at once extinguished. The game requires both courage and rapidity of action, and a good deal of merriment is caused by the unsuccessful efforts of competitors for the raisins in the flaming bowl.

BLINDMAN'S BUFF,

A favourite game of Christmastide, is thus described by Thomas Miller, in his "Sports and Pastimes of Merry England":—

"The very youngest of our brothers and sisters can join in this old English game: and it is selfish to select only such sports as they cannot become sharers of. Its ancient name is 'hoodman-blind'; and when hoods were worn by both men and women—centuries before hats and caps were so common as they are now—the hood was reversed, placed hind-before, and was, no doubt, a much surer way of blinding the player than that now adopted—for we have seen Charley try to catch his pretty cousin Caroline, by chasing her behind chairs and into all sorts of corners, to our strong conviction that he was not half so well blinded as he ought to have been. Some said he could see through the black silk handkerchief; others that it ought to have been tied clean over his nose, for that when he looked down he could see her feet, wherever she moved; and Charley had often been heard to say that she had the prettiest foot and ankle he had ever seen. But there he goes, head over heels across a chair, tearing off Caroline's gown skirt in his fall, as he clutches it in the hope of saving himself. Now, that is what I call retributive justice; for she threw down the chair for him to stumble over, and, if he has grazed his knees, she suffers under a torn dress, and must retire until one of the maids darn up the rent. But now the mirth and glee grow 'fast and furious,' for hoodman blind has imprisoned three or four of the youngest boys in a corner, and can place his hand on whichever he likes. Into what a small compass they have forced themselves! But the one behind has the wall at his back, and, taking advantage of so good a purchase, he sends his three laughing companions sprawling on the floor, and is himself caught through their having fallen, as his shoulder is the first that is grasped by Blindman-buff—so that he must now submit to be hooded."

BLINDMAN'S BUFF.
(*In the last century.*)

THE CHRISTMAS DANCE.

"Again the ball-room is wide open thrown,
        The oak beams festooned with the garlands gay;
The red dais where the fiddlers sit alone,
        Where, flushed with pride, the good old tunes they play.
Strike, fiddlers, strike! we're ready for the set;
        The young folks' feet are eager for the dance;
We'll trip Sir Roger and the minuet,
        And revel in the latest games from France."[83]

"Man should be called a dancing animal," said *Old Florentine*; and Burton, in his "Anatomy of Melancholy," says, "Young lasses are never better pleased than when, upon a holiday, after *even-song*, they may meet their sweethearts and dance." And dancing is just as popular at Christmas in the present day, as it was in that mediæval age when (according to William of Malmesbury) the priest Rathbertus, being disturbed at his Christmas mass by young men and women dancing outside the church, prayed God and St. Magnus that they might continue to dance for a whole year without cessation—a prayer which the old chronicler gravely assures us was answered.

THE CHRISTMAS DANCE.

CHRISTMAS EVE IN THE OLDEN TIME.

And well our Christian sires of old
Loved when the year its course had roll'd,
And brought blithe Christmas back again,
With all his hospitable train.
Domestic and religious rite
Gave honour to the holy night:

On Christmas Eve the bells were rung;
On Christmas Eve the mass was sung:
That only night in all the year,
Saw the stoled priest the chalice rear.
The damsel donn'd her kirtle sheen;

321

The hall was dress'd with holly green;
Forth to the wood did merry-men go,
To gather in the mistletoe.
Then open'd wide the Baron's hall
To vassal, tenant, serf, and all;
Power laid his rod of rule aside,
And Ceremony doffed his pride.
The heir, with roses in his shoes,
That night might village partner choose.
The lord, underogating, share
The vulgar game of "post and pair."

All hail'd, with uncontroll'd delight,
And general voice, the happy night
That to the cottage, as the crown,
Brought tidings of salvation down!

The fire, with well-dried logs supplied,
Went roaring up the chimney wide;
The huge hall-table's oaken face,
Scrubb'd till it shone, the day to grace
Bore then upon its massive board
No mark to part the squire and lord.

Then was brought in the lusty brawn
By old blue-coated serving man;
Then the grim boar's-head frowned on high,
Crested with bays and rosemary.
Well can the green-garbed ranger tell
How, when, and where the monster fell;
What dogs before his death he tore,
And all the baiting of the boar.
The wassail round in good brown bowls,
Garnish'd with ribbons, blithely trowls.
There the huge sirloin reek'd; hard by
Plum-porridge stood, and Christmas-pye;
Nor fail'd old Scotland to produce,
At such high tide, her savoury goose.
Then came the merry masquers in,
And carols roar'd with blithesome din

If unmelodious was the song,
It was a hearty note, and strong.
Who lists may in their mumming see
Traces of ancient mystery;
White shirts supplied the masquerade,
And smutted cheeks the visors made;
But oh! what masquers, richly dight,
Can boast of bosoms half so light!
England was merry England when
Old Christmas brought his sports again.
'Twas Christmas broached the mightiest ale,
'Twas Christmas told the merriest tale;
A Christmas gambol oft could cheer
The poor man's heart through half the year.

SIR WALTER SCOTT, 1808.

Lyson's "Magna Britannia" (1813) states the following as an

OLD ENGLISH CUSTOM.

"At Cumnor the parishioners, who paid vicarial tithes, claimed a custom of being entertained at the vicarage on the afternoon of Christmas Day, with four bushels of malt brewed into ale and beer, two bushels of wheat made into bread, and half a hundred weight of cheese. The remainder was given to the poor the next morning after divine service."

Mason ("Statistical Account of Ireland," 1814) records the following

IRISH CHRISTMAS CUSTOMS:—

"At Culdaff, previous to Christmas, it is customary with the labouring classes to raffle for mutton, when a sufficient number can subscribe to defray the cost of a sheep. During the Christmas holidays they amuse themselves with a game of kamman, which consists in impelling a wooden ball with a crooked stick to a given point, while an adversary endeavours to drive it in a contrary direction."

A writer in "Time's Telescope" (1822) states that in Yorkshire at eight o'clock on Christmas Eve the bells greet "Old Father Christmas" with a merry peal, the children parade the streets with drums, trumpets, bells, or perhaps, in their absence, with the poker and shovel, taken from their humble cottage fire; the yule candle is lighted, and—

"High on the cheerful fire Is blazing seen th' enormous Christmas brand."

Supper is served, of which one dish, from the lordly mansion to the humblest shed, is invariably furmety; yule cake, one of which is always made for each individual in the family, and other more substantial viands are also added.

Some Social Festivities

of Christmastide are sketched by a contributor to the *New Monthly Magazine*, December 1, 1825, who says:—

"On the north side of the church at M. are a great many holly-trees. It is from these that our dining and bed-rooms are furnished with boughs. Families take it by turns to entertain their friends. They meet early; the beef and pudding are noble; the mince-pies— peculiar; the nuts half play-things and half-eatables; the oranges as cold and acid as they ought to be, furnishing us with a superfluity which we can afford to laugh at; the cakes indestructible; the wassail bowls generous, old English, huge, demanding ladles, threatening overflow as they come in, solid with roasted apples when set down. Towards bed-time you hear of elder-wine, and not seldom of punch. At the manorhouse it is pretty much the same as elsewhere. Girls, although they be ladies, are kissed under the mistletoe. If any family among us happen to have hit upon an exquisite brewing, they send some of it round about, the squire's house included; and he does the same by the rest. Riddles, hot-cockles, forfeits, music, dances sudden and not to be suppressed, prevail among great and small; and from two o'clock in the day to midnight, M. looks like a deserted place out of doors, but is full of life and merriment within. Playing at knights and ladies last year, a jade of a charming creature must needs send me out for a piece of ice to put in her wine. It was evening and a hard frost. I shall never forget the cold, cutting, dreary, dead look of every thing out of doors, with a wind through the wiry trees, and the snow on the ground, contrasted with the sudden return to warmth, light, and joviality.

"I remember we had a discussion that time as to what was the great point and crowning glory of Christmas. Many were for mince-pie; some for the beef and plum-pudding; more for the wassail-bowl; a maiden lady timidly said the mistletoe; but we agreed at last, that although all these were prodigious, and some of them exclusively belonging to the season, the *fire* was the great indispensable. Upon which we all turned our faces towards it, and began warming our already scorched hands. A great blazing fire, too big, is the visible heart and soul of Christmas. You may do without beef and plum-pudding; even the absence of mince-pie may be tolerated; there must be a bowl, poetically speaking, but it need not be absolutely wassail. The bowl may give place to the bottle. But a huge, heaped-up, *over* heaped-up, all-attracting fire, with a semicircle of faces about it, is not to be denied us. It is the *lar* and genius of the meeting; the proof positive of the season; the representative of all our warm emotions and bright thoughts; the glorious eye of the room; the inciter to mirth, yet the retainer of order; the amalgamater of the age and sex; the universal relish. Tastes may differ even on a mince-pie; but who gainsays a fire? The absence of other luxuries still leaves you in possession of that; but

> 'Who can hold a fire in his hand
> With thinking on the frostiest twelfth-cake?'

"Let me have a dinner of some sort, no matter what, and then give me my fire, and my friends, the humblest glass of wine, and a few penn'orths of chestnuts, and I will still make out my Christmas. What! Have we not Burgundy in our blood? Have we not joke, laughter, repartee, bright eyes, comedies of other people, and comedies of our own; songs, memories, hopes? [An organ strikes up in the street at this word, as if to answer me in the affirmative. Right thou old spirit of harmony, wandering about in that ark of thine, and touching the public ear with sweetness and an abstraction! Let the multitude bustle on, but not unarrested by thee and by others, and not unreminded of the happiness of renewing a wise childhood. As to our old friends the chestnuts, if anybody wants an excuse to his dignity for roasting them, let him take the authority of Milton. 'Who now,' says he lamenting the loss of his friend Deodati,—'who now will help to soothe my cares for me, and make the long night seem short with his conversation; while the roasting pear hisses tenderly on the fire, and the nuts burst away with a noise,—

> 'And out of doors a washing storm o'erwhelms
> Nature pitch-dark, and rides the thundering elms?'"

CHRISTMAS IN THE HIGHLANDS.

From Grant's "Popular Superstitions of the Highlands" Hone gathered the following account:—

"As soon as the brightening glow of the eastern sky warns the anxious house-maid of the approach of Christmas Day, she rises full of anxiety at the prospect of her morning labours. The meal, which was steeped in the *sowans-bowie* a fortnight ago, to make the *Prechdachdan sour*, or *sour scones*, is the first object of her attention. The gridiron is put on the fire, and the sour scones are soon followed by hard cakes, soft cakes, buttered cakes, brandered bannocks, and pannich perm. The baking being once over, the sowans pot succeeds the gridiron, full of new sowans, which are to be given to the family, agreeably to custom, this day in their beds. The sowans are boiled into the consistence of molasses, when the *Lagan-le-vrich*, or yeast bread, to distinguish it from boiled sowans, is ready. It is then poured into as many bickers as there are individuals to partake of it, and presently served to the whole, old and young. It would suit well the pen of a Burns, or the pencil of a Hogarth, to paint the scene which follows. The ambrosial food is despatched in aspiring draughts by the family, who soon give evident proofs of the enlivening effects of the *Lagan-le-vrich*. As soon as each despatches his bicker, he jumps out of bed—the elder branches to examine the ominous signs of the day,[84] and the younger to enter on its amusements. Flocking to the swing, a favourite amusement on this occasion, the youngest of the family get the first '*shoulder*,' and the next oldest in regular succession. In order to add the more to the spirit of the exercise, it is a common practice with the person in the *swing*, and the person appointed to swing him, to enter into a very warm and humorous altercation. As the swinged person approaches the swinger, he exclaims, *Ei mi tu chal*, 'I'll eat your kail.' To this the swinger replies, with a violent shove, *Cha ni u mu chal*, 'You shan't eat my kail.' These threats and repulses are sometimes carried to such a height, as to break down or capsize the threatener, which generally puts an end to the quarrel.

"As the day advances, those minor amusements are terminated at the report of the gun, or the rattle of the ball clubs—the gun inviting the marksman to the '*Kiavamuchd*,' or prize-shooting, and the latter to '*Luchd-vouil*,' or the ball combatants—both the principal sports of the day. Tired at length of the active amusements of the field, they exchange them for the substantial entertainments of the table. Groaning under the '*sonsy haggis*,'[85] and many other savoury dainties, unseen for twelve months before, the relish communicated to the company, by the appearance of the festive board, is more easily conceived than described. The dinner once despatched, the flowing bowl succeeds, and the sparkling glass flies to and fro like a weaver's shuttle. As it continues its rounds, the spirits of the company become more jovial and happy. Animated by its cheering influence, even old decrepitude no longer feels his habitual pains—the fire of youth is in his eye, as he details to the company the exploits which distinguished him in the days of '*auld langsyne*;' while the young, with hearts inflamed with '*love and glory*,' long to mingle in the more lively scenes of mirth, to display their prowess and agility. Leaving the patriarchs to finish those professions of friendship for each other, in which they are so devoutly engaged, the younger part of the company will shape their course to the ball-room, or the card-table, as their individual inclinations suggest; and the remainder of the evening is spent with the greatest pleasure of which human nature is susceptible."

SWORD DANCING AT CHRISTMAS.

Hone's "Table Book" (vol. i.), 1827, contains a letter descriptive of the pitmen of Northumberland, which says:—

"The ancient custom of sword-dancing at Christmas is kept up in Northumberland exclusively by these people. They may be constantly seen at that festive season with their fiddler, bands of swordsmen, Tommy and Bessy, most grotesquely dressed, performing their annual routine of warlike evolutions."

And the present writer heard of similar festivities at Christmastide in the Madeley district of Shropshire, accompanied by grotesque imitations of the ancient hobby-horse.

CUMBERLAND.

"A. W. R.," writing to Hone's "Year Book," December 8, 1827, says:—

"Nowhere does the Christmas season produce more heart-inspiring mirth than among the inhabitants of Cumberland.

"With Christmas Eve commences a regular series of 'festivities and merry makings.' Night after night, if you want the farmer or his family, you must look for them anywhere but at home; and in the different houses that you pass at one, two, or three in the morning, should you happen to be out so late, you will find candles and fires still unextinguished. At Christmas, every farmer gives two 'feasts,' one called 't' ould foaks neet,' which is for those who are married, and the other 't' young foaks neet,' for those who are single. Suppose you and I, sir, take the liberty of attending one of these feasts unasked (which by the bye is considered no liberty at all in Cumberland) and see what is going on. Upon entering the room we behold several card parties, some at 'whist,' others at 'loo' (there called 'lant'), or any other game that may suit their fancy. You will be surprised on looking over the company to find that there is no distinction of persons. Masters and servants, rich and poor, humble and lofty, all mingle together without restraint—all cares are forgotten—and each one seems to glory in his own enjoyment and in that of his fellow-creatures. It is pleasant to find ourselves in such society, especially as it is rarely in one's life that such opportunities offer. Cast your eyes towards the sideboard, and there see that large bowl of punch, which the good wife is inviting her guests to partake of, with apples, oranges, biscuits, and other agreeable eatables in plenty. The hospitable master welcomes us with a smiling countenance and requests us to take seats and join one of the tables.

"In due time some one enters to tell the company that supper is waiting in the next room. Thither we adjourn, and find the raised and mince pies, all sorts of tarts, and all cold—except the welcomes and entreaties—with cream, ale, &c., in abundance; in the midst of all a large goose pie, which seems to say 'Come and cut again.'

"After supper the party return to the card room, sit there for two or three hours longer, and afterwards make the best of their way home, to take a good long nap, and prepare for the same scene the next night. At these 'feasts' intoxication is entirely out of the question—it never happens.

"Such are the innocent amusements of these people."

> "With gentle deeds and kindly thoughts,
> And loving words withal,
> Welcome the merry Christmas in
> And hear a brother's call."[86]

PROVISION FOR THE POOR ON CHRISTMAS DAY.

THE GIVING AWAY OF CHRISTMAS DOLES.

By the will of John Popple, dated the 12th of March, 1830, £4 yearly is to be paid unto the vicar, churchwardens, and overseers of the poor of the parish of Burnham, Buckinghamshire, to provide for the poor people who should be residing in the poorhouse, a dinner, with a proper quantity of good ale and likewise with tobacco and snuff on Christmas Day.[87]

This kindly provision of Mr. Popple for the poor shows that he wished to keep up the good old Christmas customs which are so much admired by the "old man" in Southey's "The Old Mansion" (a poem of this period). In recalling the good doings at the mansion "in my lady's time" the "old man" says:—

> "A woful day
> 'Twas for the poor when to her grave she went!
>
> * * * * *
>
> Were they sick?
> She had rare cordial waters, and for herbs
> She could have taught the doctors. Then at winter,
> When weekly she distributed the bread
> In the poor old porch, to see her and to hear
> The blessings on her! And I warrant them
> They were a blessing to her when her wealth
> Had been no comfort else. At Christmas, sir!
> It would have warmed your heart if you had seen
> Her Christmas kitchen; how the blazing fire
> Made her fine pewter shine, and holly boughs
> So cheerful red; and as for mistletoe,
> The finest bough that grew in the country round
> Was mark'd for madam. Then her old ale went
> So bountiful about! a Christmas cask,—
> And 'twas a noble one!—God help me, sir!
> But I shall never see such days again."

THE ROYAL CHRISTMASES

In the reigns of George IV. and William IV., though not kept with the grandeur of earlier reigns, were observed with much rejoicing and festivity, and the Royal Bounties to the poor of the metropolis and the country districts surrounding Windsor and the other Royal Palaces were dispensed with the customary generosity. In his "Sketch Book," Washington Irving, who was born in the reign of George III. (1783), and lived on through the reigns of George IV., and William IV., and the first two decades of the reign of Queen Victoria, gives delightful descriptions of the

FESTIVITIES OF THE NOBILITY AND GENTRY

of the period, recalling the times when the old halls of castles and manor houses resounded with the harp and the Christmas Carol and their ample boards groaned under the weight of hospitality. He had travelled a good deal on both sides of the Atlantic and he gives a picturesque account of an old English stage coach journey "on the day preceding Christmas." The coach was crowded with passengers. "It was also loaded with hampers of game, and baskets and boxes of delicacies; and hares hung dangling their long ears about the coachman's box, presents from distant friends for the impending feast. I had three fine rosy-cheeked schoolboys for my fellow-passengers inside, full of the buxom health and manly spirit which I have observed in the children of this country. They were returning home for the holidays in high glee, and promising themselves a world of enjoyment. It was delightful to hear the gigantic plans of the little rogues, and the impracticable feats they were to perform during their six weeks' emancipation from the abhorred thraldom of book, birch, and pedagogue."

Then follows Irving's graphic sketch of the English stage coachman, and the incidents of the journey, during which it seemed "as if everybody was in good looks and good spirits.

"Game, poultry, and other luxuries of the table, were in brisk circulation in the villages; the grocers,' butchers,' and fruiterers' shops were thronged with customers. The house-wives were stirring briskly about, putting their dwellings in order; and the glossy branches of holly, with their bright red berries, began to appear at the windows."

* * * * *

"In the evening we reached a village where I had determined to pass the night. As we drove into the great gateway of the inn, I saw on one side the light of a rousing kitchen fire beaming through a window. I entered, and admired, for the hundredth time, that picture of convenience, neatness, and broad, honest enjoyment, the kitchen of an English inn. It was of spacious dimensions, hung round with copper and tin vessels highly polished, and decorated here and there with a Christmas green... The scene completely realised poor Robin's [1684 humble idea of the comforts of mid-winter:

> 'Now trees their leafy hats do bare
> To reverence winter's silver hair;
> A handsome hostess, merry host,
> A pot of ale now and a toast,
> Tobacco and a good coal fire,
> Are things this season doth require.'"

Mr. Irving afterwards depicts, in his own graphic style, the Christmas festivities observed at an old-fashioned English hall, and tells how the generous squire pointed with pleasure to the indications of good cheer reeking from the chimneys of the comfortable farmhouses, and low thatched cottages. "I love," said he, "to see this day well kept by rich and poor; it is a great thing to have one day in the year, at least, when you are sure of being welcome wherever you go, and of having, as it were, the world all thrown open to you; and I am almost disposed to join with poor Robin, in his malediction on every churlish enemy to this honest festival:

> "'Those who at Christmas do repine,
> And would fain hence despatch him,
> May they with old Duke Humphry dine,
> Or else may Squire Ketch catch 'em.'

"The squire went on to lament the deplorable decay of the games and amusements which were once prevalent at this season among the lower orders, and countenanced by the higher; when the old halls of castles and manor-houses were thrown open at daylight; when the tables were covered with brawn, and beef, and humming ale; when the harp and the carol resounded all day long, and when rich and poor were alike welcome to enter and make merry. 'Our old games and local customs,' said he, 'had a great effect in making the peasant fond of his home, and the promotion of them by the gentry made him fond of his lord. They made the times merrier, and kinder and better; and I can truly say with one of our old poets:

> "'I like them well—the curious preciseness
> And all-pretended gravity of those
> That seek to banish hence these harmless sports,
> Have thrust away much ancient honesty.'"

THE CHRISTMASES OF QUEEN VICTORIA

have been kept with much bountifulness, but after the gracious manner of a Christian Queen who cares more for the welfare of her beloved subjects than for ostentatious display. Her Majesty's Royal bounties to the poor of the metropolis and its environs, and also to others in the country districts surrounding the several Royal Palaces are well known, the ancient Christmas and New Year's gifts being dispensed with great generosity. The number of aged and afflicted persons usually relieved by the Lord High Almoner in sums of 5s. and 13s. exceeds an aggregate of 1,200. Then there is the distribution of the beef—a most interesting feature of the Royal Bounty—which takes place in the Riding School at Windsor Castle, under the superintendence of the several Court officials. The meat, divided into portions of from three pounds to seven pounds, and decorated with sprigs of holly, is arranged upon a table placed in the middle of the Riding School, and covered with white cloths from the Lord Steward's department of the palace. During the distribution the bells of St. John's Church ring a merry peal. There are usually many hundreds of recipients and the weight of the beef allotted amounts to many thousands of pounds. Coals and clothing and other creature comforts are liberally dispensed, according to the needs of the poor. In times of war and seasons of distress hospitable entertainments, Christmas-trees, &c., are also provided for the wives and children of soldiers and sailors on active service; and in many other ways the Royal Bounty is extended to the poor and needy at Christmastide.

THE CHRISTMAS AT WINDSOR CASTLE, IN 1841,

is thus referred to in the "Life of the Prince Consort" (by Theodore Martin):—

"When Christmas came round with its pleasant festivities and its shining Christmas-trees, it had within it a new source of delight for the Royal parents. 'To think,' says the Queen's 'Journal,' 'that we have two children now, and one who enjoys the sight already, is like a dream!' And in writing to his father the Prince expresses the same feeling. 'This,' he says, 'is the dear Christmas Eve, on which I have so often listened with impatience for your step, which was to usher us into the present-room. To-day I have two children of my own to give presents to, who, they know not why, are full of happy wonder at the German Christmas-tree and its radiant candles.'

"The coming year was danced into in good old English fashion. In the middle of the dance, as the clock finished striking twelve, a flourish of trumpets was blown, in accordance with a German custom. This, the Queen's 'Journal' records, 'had a fine solemn effect, and quite affected dear Albert, who turned pale, and had tears in his eyes, and pressed my hand very warmly. It touched me too, for I felt that he must think of his dear native country, which he has left for me.'"

CHRISTMAS AT OSBORNE.

Writing from Cowes, on Christmas Eve, in reference to the Christmas festivities at Osborne in the last decade of the nineteenth century, a correspondent says:—

"After transacting business the Queen drove out this afternoon, returning to Osborne just as the setting sun illumines with its rosy rays the Paladin Towers of her Majesty's marine residence. The Queen desires to live, as far as the cares of State permit, the life of a private lady. Her Majesty loves the seclusion of this lordly estate, and here at Christmas time she enjoys the society of her children and grandchildren, who meet together as less exalted families do at this merry season to reciprocate the same homely delights as those which are experienced throughout the land.

"This afternoon a pleasant little festivity has been celebrated at Osborne House, where her Majesty, with an ever-kindly interest in her servants and dependants, has for many years inaugurated Christmas in a similar way, the children of her tenantry and the old and infirm enjoying by the Royal bounty the first taste of Christmas fare. The Osborne estate now comprises 5,000 acres, and it includes the Prince Consort's model farm. The children of the labourers— who are housed in excellent cottages—attend the Whippingham National Schools, a pretty block of buildings, distant one mile from Osborne. About half the number of scholars live upon the Queen's estate, and, in accordance with annual custom, the mistresses of the schools, the Misses Thomas, accompanied by the staff of teachers, have conducted a little band of boys and girls—fifty-four in all—to the house, there to take tea and to receive the customary Christmas gifts. Until very recently the Queen herself presided at the distribution; but the Princess Beatrice has lately relieved her mother of the fatigue involved; for the ceremony is no mere formality, it is made the occasion of many a kindly word the remembrance of which far outlasts the gifts. All sorts of rumours are current on the estate for weeks before this Christmas Eve gathering as to the nature of the presents to be bestowed, for no one is supposed to know beforehand what they will be; but there was a pretty shrewd guess to-day that the boys would be given gloves, and the girls cloaks. In some cases the former had had scarves or cloth for suits, and the latter dresses or shawls. Whatever the Christmas presents may be, here they are, arranged upon tables in two long lines, in the servants' hall. To this holly-decorated apartment the expectant youngsters are brought, and their delighted gaze falls upon a huge Christmas-tree laden with beautiful toys. Everybody knows that the tree will be there, and moreover that its summit will be crowned with a splendid doll. Now, the ultimate ownership of this doll is a matter of much concern; it needs deliberation, as it is awarded to the best child, and the judges are the children themselves. The trophy is handed to the keeping of Miss Thomas, and on the next 1st of May the children select by their votes the most popular girl in the school to be elected May Queen. To her the gift goes, and no fairer way could be devised. The Princess Beatrice always makes a point of knowing to whom the prize has been awarded. Her Royal Highness is so constantly a visitor to the cottagers and to the school that she has many an inquiry to make of the little ones as they come forward to receive their gifts.

"The girls are called up first by the mistress, and Mr. Andrew Blake, the steward, introduces each child to the Princess Beatrice, to whom Mr. Blake hands the presents that her Royal Highness may bestow them upon the recipients with a word of good will, which makes the day memorable. Then the boys are summoned to participate in the distribution of good things, which, it should be explained, consist not only of seasonable and sensible clothing, but toys from the tree, presented by the Queen's grandchildren, who, with their parents, grace the ceremony with their presence and make the occasion one of family interest. The Ladies-in-Waiting also attend. Each boy and girl gets in addition a nicely-bound story-book and a large slice of plum pudding neatly packed in paper, and if any little one is sick at home its portion is carefully reserved. But the hospitality of the Queen is not limited to the children.

On alternate years the old men and women resident on the estate are given, under the same pleasant auspices, presents of blankets or clothing. To-day it was the turn of the men, and they received tweed for suits. The aged people have their pudding as well. For the farm labourers and boys, who are not bidden to this entertainment, there is a distribution of tickets, each representing a goodly joint of beef for the Christmas dinner. The festivity this afternoon was brought to a close by the children singing the National Anthem in the courtyard.

"The Queen is accustomed to spend Christmas Day very quietly, attending service at the Chapel at Osborne in the morning, and in the evening the Royal family meeting at dinner. There are Christmas trees for the children, and for the servants too, but the houshold reserves its principal festivity for the New Year—a day which is specially set aside for their entertainment."

THE CHRISTMAS FESTIVITIES AT SANDRINGHAM

are observed with generous hospitality by their Royal Highnesses the Prince and Princess of Wales, who take special interest in the enjoyment of their tenants, and also remember the poor. A time-honoured custom on Christmas Eve is the distribution of prime joints of meat to the labourers employed on the Royal estate, and to the poor of the five parishes of Sandringham, West Newton, Babingley, Dersingham, and Wolferton. From twelve to fifteen hundred pounds of meat are usually distributed, and such other gifts are made as the inclemency of the season and the necessities of the poor require. In Sandringham "Past and Present," 1888, Mrs. Herbert Jones says:—"Sandringham, which is the centre of a generous hospitality, has not only been in every way raised, benefited, and enriched since it passed into the royal hands, which may be said to have created it afresh, but rests under the happy glow shed over it by the preference of a princess

"'Whose peerless feature joinèd with her birth,
Approve her fit for none but for a king.'

Shakespeare's *Henry VI*."

In a letter to the press a lieutenant of Marines makes the following reference to a Christmas entertainment given by H.R.H. the Duke of Edinburgh, in 1886: "Last night a large party, consisting of many officers of the Fleet, including all the 'old ships' of the Duke, and three or four midshipmen from every ship in the Fleet, were invited to a Christmas-tree at S. Antonio Palace. In the course of the evening two lotteries were drawn, all the numbers being prizes, each guest consequently getting two. I have had an opportunity of seeing many of these, and they are all most beautiful and useful objects, ranging in value from five shillings to perhaps three or four pounds. I should think that at least half the prizes I have seen were worth over one pound."

OTHER SEASONABLE HOSPITALITY AND BENEVOLENCE.

The good example set by royalty is followed throughout the land. Friendly hospitalities are general at Christmastide, and in London and other large centres of population many thousands of poor people are provided with free breakfasts, dinners, teas, and suppers on Christmas Day, public halls and school-rooms being utilised for purposes of entertainment; children in hospitals are plentifully supplied with toys, and Christmas parties are also given to the poor at the private residences of benevolent people. As an illustrative instance of generous Christmas hospitality by a landowner we cite the following:—

CHRISTMAS DINNER TO FIVE THOUSAND POOR.

On Christmas Eve, 1887, Sir Watkin Williams Wynn, Bart., the largest landowner in the Principality of Wales, gave his annual Christmas gifts to the aged and deserving poor throughout the extensive mining districts of Ruabon, Rhosllanerchrugog, Cern, and Rhosymedre, Denbighshire, where much distress prevailed in consequence of the depression in trade. Several fine oxen were slain in Wynnstay Park, and the beef was distributed in pieces ranging from 4lb. to 7lb., according to the number of members in each family. A Christmas dinner was thus provided for upwards of

5,000 persons. In addition to this, Lady Williams Wynn provided thousands of yards of flannel and cloth for clothing, together with a large number of blankets, the aged men and women also receiving a shilling with the gift. The hon. baronet had also erected an elaborate spacious hospital to the memory of his uncle, the late Sir Watkin Williams Wynn, M.P., and presented it to the parish.

DISTRIBUTIONS OF CHRISTMAS FARE TO THE POOR

are liberally made from various centres in different parts of London, and thus many thousands of those who have fallen below the poverty line share in the festivities of Christmastide.

This illustration of Christian caterers dispensing creature comforts to the poor children may be taken as representative of many such Christmas scenes in the metropolis. For over forty years the St. Giles' Christian Mission, now under the superintendence of Mr. W. M. Wheatley, has been exercising a beneficial influence among the needy poor, and, it is stated, that at least 104,000 people have through this Mission been enabled to make a fresh start in life. Many other Church Missions are doing similar work. In addition to treats to poor children and aged people at Christmastide, there are also great distributions of Christmas fare:—Joints of roasting meat, plum-puddings, cakes, groceries, warm clothing, toys, &c., &c.

POOR CHILDREN'S TREAT IN MODERN TIMES.

At a recent distribution of a Christmas charity at Millbrook, Southampton, the Rev. A. C. Blunt stated that one of the recipients had nearly reached her 102nd year. She was born in Hampshire, and down to a very recent period had been able to do needlework.

In many cities and towns Christmas gifts are distributed on St. Thomas's Day, and as an example we cite the Brighton distribution in 1886, on which occasion the Brighton Police Court was filled by a congregation of some of the "oldest inhabitants." And there was a distribution from the magistrates poor-box of a Christmas gift of half a sovereign to 150 of the aged poor whose claims to the bounty had been inquired into by the police. Formerly 100 used to be cheered in this way, but the contributions to the box this year enabled a wider circle to share in the dole. There was a wonderful collection of old people, for the average age was over 83 years. The oldest was a venerable widow, who confessed to being 96 years old, the next was another lady of 94 years, and then came two old fellows who had each attained 93 years. Many of the recipients were too infirm to appear, but the oldest of them all, the lady of 96 came into court despite the sharpness of the wind and the frozen roads.

THE CHRISTMAS AT BELVOIR CASTLE,

kept with generous liberality by the Duke of Rutland, in 1883, may be cited as an example of Christmas customs continued by the head of a noble house:

"The usual Christmas gifts were given to the poor of Knipton, Woolsthorpe, and Redmile—nearly two hundred in number—consisting of calico, flannel dresses, stockings, and handkerchiefs, each person at the same time receiving a loaf of bread and a pint of ale. Twenty-one bales of goods, containing counterpanes, blankets, and sheets, were also sent to the clergy of as many different villages for distribution amongst the poor. The servants at the Castle and workmen of the establishment had their Christmas dinner, tea, and supper, the servants' hall having been beautifully decorated. At one end of the room was a coronet, with the letter 'R'; and at the opposite end three coronets, with the 'peacock in pride,' being the crest of the Rutland family. The following mottoes, in large letters, were conspicuous, 'Long live the Duke of Rutland,' 'Long live Lord and Lady John Manners and family,' and 'A Merry Christmas to you all.' These were enclosed in a neat border. From the top of the room were suspended long festoons of linked ribbons of red, white, blue, and orange. All present thoroughly enjoyed themselves, as it was the wish of his Grace they should do."

Similar hospitalities are dispensed by other noblemen and gentlemen in different parts of the country at Christmas.

The lordly hospitality of Lincolnshire is depicted in

"THE BARON'S YULE FEAST:

A Christmas Rhyme; by Thomas Cooper, the Chartist" (1846); which is inscribed to the Countess of Blessington, and in the advertisement the author offers "but one apology for the production of a metrical essay, composed chiefly of imperfect and immature pieces: The ambition to contribute towards the fund of Christmas entertainment." The scene of the Baron's Yule Feast is depicted in Torksey's Hall, Torksey being one of the first towns in Lincolnshire in the Saxon period. After some introductory verses the writer says:

> "It is the season when our sires
> Kept jocund holiday;
> And, now, around our charier fires,
> Old Yule shall have a lay:—
> A prison-bard is once more free;
> And, ere he yields his voice to thee,
> His song a merry-song shall be!
>
> Sir Wilfrid de Thorold freely holds
> What his stout sires held before—
> Broad lands for plough and fruitful folds,—
> Though by gold he sets no store;
> And he saith, from fen and woodland wolds
> From marish, heath, and moor,—
> To feast in his hall
> Both free and thrall,
> Shall come as they came of yore.

* * * * *

Now merrily ring the lady-bells
Of the nunnery by the Fosse:—
Say the hinds their silver music swells
'Like the blessed angels' syllables,
At His birth who bore the cross.'

And solemnly swells Saint Leonard's chime
And the great bell loud and deep:—
Say the gossips, 'Let's talk of the holy time
When the shepherds watched their sheep;
And the Babe was born for all souls' crime
In the weakness of flesh to weep.'—
But, anon, shrills the pipe of the merry mime
And their simple hearts upleap.

'God save your souls, good Christian folk!
God save your souls from sin!—
Blythe Yule is come—let us blythely joke!'—
Cry the mummers ere they begin.

Then, plough-boy Jack, in kirtle gay,—
Though shod with clouted shoon,—
Stands forth the wilful maid to play
Who ever saith to her lover, 'Nay'—
When he sues for a lover's boon.

While Hob the smith with sturdy arm
Circleth the feigned maid;
And, spite of Jack's assumed alarm,
Busseth his lips, like a lover warm,
And will not 'Nay' be said

Then loffe the gossips, as if wit
Were mingled with the joke:
Gentles,—they were with folly smit,—
Natheless, their memories acquit
Of crime—these simple folk!

No harmful thoughts their revels blight,—
Devoid of bitter hate and spite,
They hold their merriment;—
And, till the chimes tell noon at night,
Their joy shall be unspent!

Come haste ye to bold Thorold's hall,
And crowd his kitchen wide;
For there, he saith, both free and thrall
Shall sport this good Yule-tide."

In subsequent verses the writer depicts the bringing in of the yule log to the Baron's Hall,

"Where its brave old heart
A glow shall impart
To the heart of each guest at the festival.

* * * * *

They pile the Yule-log on the hearth,—
    Soak toasted crabs in ale;
And while they sip, their homely mirth
Is joyous as if all the earth
    For man were void of bale!

And why should fears for future years,
Mix jolly ale with thoughts of tears
    When in the horn 'tis poured?
And why should ghost of sorrow fright
The bold heart of an English knight
    When beef is on the board?

De Thorold's guests are wiser than
    The men of mopish lore;
For round they push the smiling can
    And slice the plattered store.

And round they thrust the ponderous cheese,
    And the loaves of wheat and rye;
None stinteth him for lack of ease—

For each a stintless welcome sees
    In the Baron's blythesome eye.

The Baron joineth the joyous feast—
    But not in pomp or pride;
He smileth on the humblest guest
So gladsomely—all feel that rest
    Of heart which doth abide
Where deeds of generousness attest
The welcome of the tongue professed
    Is not within belied."

* * * * *

In subsequent verses a stranger minstrel appears on the festive
scene, and tells his tale of love in song, acquitting himself

"So rare and gentle, that the hall
Rings with applause which one and all
Render who share the festival."

Some of the poets of this period have dealt playfully with
the festivities of Christmastide, as, for example, Laman Blanchard
(1845) in the following effusion:—

CHRISTMAS CHIT-CHAT.

IN A LARGE FAMILY CIRCLE.

"The day of all days we have seen
Is Christmas," said Sue to Eugene;
"More welcome in village and city
Than Mayday," said Andrew to Kitty.
"Why 'Mistletoe's' twenty times sweeter

Than 'May,'" said Matilda to Peter;
"And so you will find it, if I'm a
True prophet," said James to Jemima.
"I'll stay up to supper, no bed,"
Then lisped little Laura to Ned.
"The girls all good-natured and dressy,
And bright-cheeked," said Arthur to Jessie;
"Yes, hoping ere next year to marry,
The madcaps!" said Charlotte to Harry.
"So steaming, so savoury, so juicy,
The feast," said fat Charley to Lucy.
"Quadrilles and Charades might come on
Before dinner," said Martha to John.
"You'll find the roast beef when you're dizzy,
A settler," said Walter to Lizzy.
"Oh, horrid! one wing of a wren,
With a pea," said Belinda to Ben.
"Sublime!" said—displaying his leg—
George Frederick Augustus to Peg.
"At Christmas refinement is all fuss
And nonsense," said Fan to Adolphus.
"Would romps—or a tale of a fairy—
Best suit you," said Robert to Mary.
"At stories that work ghost and witch hard,
I tremble," said Rosa to Richard.
"A ghostly hair-standing dilemma
Needs 'bishop,'" said Alfred to Emma;
"What fun when with fear a stout crony
Turns pale," said Maria to Tony;
"And Hector, unable to rally,
Runs screaming," said Jacob to Sally.
"While you and I dance in the dark
The polka," said Ruth unto Mark:
"Each catching, according to fancy,
His neighbour," said wild Tom to Nancy;
"Till candles, to show what we can do,
Are brought in," said Ann to Orlando;
"And then we all laugh what is truly a
Heart's laugh," said William to Julia.
"Then sofas and chairs are put even,

And carpets," said Helen to Stephen;
"And so we all sit down again,
Supping twice," said sly Joseph to Jane.
"Now bring me my clogs and my spaniel,
And light me," said Dinah to Daniel.
"My dearest, you've emptied that chalice
Six times," said fond Edmund to Alice.
"We are going home tealess and coffeeless
Shabby!" said Soph to Theophilus;
"To meet again under the holly,
Et cetera," said Paul to fair Polly.
"Dear Uncle," has ordered his chariot;
All's over," said Matthew to Harriet.
"And pray now be all going to bedward,"
Said kind Aunt Rebecca to Edward!

CHRISTMAS EVE, 1849,

is the time of Robert Browning's beautiful poem of "Christmas Eve and Easter Day," in which the poet sings the song of man's immortality, proclaiming, as Easter Day breaks and Christ rises, that

"Mercy every way is infinite."

"Mercy every way is infinite."

And, in his beautiful poem of "In Memoriam," Lord Tennyson associates some of his finest verses with the ringing of

THE CHRISTMAS BELLS.

"Ring out, wild bells, to the wild sky,
    The flying cloud, the frosty light:
    The year is dying in the night;
Ring out, wild bells, and let him die.

Ring out the old, ring in the new,
    Ring, happy bells, across the snow:
    The year is going, let him go;
Ring out the false, ring in the true.

Ring out old shapes of foul disease;
    Ring out the narrowing lust of gold;
    Ring out the thousand wars of old,
Ring in the thousand years of peace.

Ring in the valiant man and free,
    The larger heart, the kindlier hand;
    Ring out the darkness of the land,
Ring in the Christ that is to be."

* * * * *

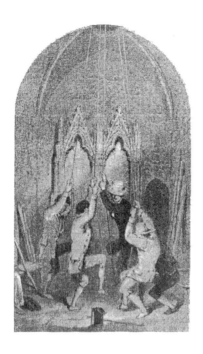

THE CHRISTMAS BELLS.

As the poet Longfellow stood on the lofty tower of Bruges Cathedral the belfry chimes set him musing, and of those chimes he says:

"Then most musical and solemn, bringing back the olden
    times,
With their strange, unearthly changes, rang the melancholy
    chimes,
Like the psalms from some old cloister, when the nuns sing
    in the choir;
And the great bell tolled among them, like the chanting of
    a friar.
Visions of the days departed, shadowy phantoms filled my
    brain:
They who live in history only seemed to walk the earth
    again."

were first circulated in England in 1846. That year not more than a thousand copies were printed, and that was considered a large sale. The numbers distributed annually soon increased to tens and hundreds of thousands, and now there are millions of them. Mr. J. C. Horsley, a member of the Royal Academy, designed this first card which was sent out in 1846. It represents a family party of three generations—grandfather and grandmother, father and mother, and little children—and all are supposed to be joining in the sentiment, "A Merry Christmas and a Happy New Year to you." The card was issued from the office of one of the periodicals of the time, *Felix Summerley's Home Treasury*. It was first lithographed, and then it was coloured by hand.

Christmas and New Year Cards became very popular in the decade 1870-1880. But then, however, simple cards alone did not suffice. Like many other things, they felt the influence of the latter-day *renaissance* of art, and by a sort of evolutionary process developed cards monochrome and coloured, "Christmas Bell" cards, palettes, scrolls, circular and oval panels, stars, fans, crescents, and other shaped novelties; embossed cards, the iridescent series, the rustic and frosted cards, the folding series, the jewel cards, the crayons, and private cards on which the sender's name and sentiments are printed in gold, silver, or colours; hand-painted cards with landscapes, seascapes, and floral decorations; paintings on porcelain; satin cards, fringed silk, plush, Broché, and other artistically made-up novelties; "art-gem" panels; elaborate booklets, and other elegant souvenirs of the festive season. Many of the Christmas booklets are beautifully illustrated editions of popular poems and carols.

"Quartette" cards, "Snap" cards, and other cards of games for the diversion of social gatherings are also extensively used at Christmastide.

Rustic Christmas Masque.

In compliance with a wish expressed by the Lady Londesborough, a Masque, entitled, "Recollections of Old Christmas," was performed at Grimston at Christmas, 1850, the following prologue being contributed by Barry Cornwall:—

"When winter nights grow long,
    And winds without blow cold,
We sit in a ring round the warm wood-fire,
    And listen to stories old!
And we try to look grave (as maids should be),
When the men bring in boughs of the laurel tree.
    O the laurel, the evergreen tree!
    The poets have laurels—and why not we?

How pleasant when night falls down,
    And hides the wintry sun,
To see them come in to the blazing fire,
    And know that their work is done;
Whilst many bring in, with a laugh or rhyme,
Green branches of holly for Christmas time!
    O the holly, the bright green holly!
    It tells (like a tongue) that the times are jolly!

Sometimes—(in *our* grave house
    Observe this happeneth not;)

But at times, the evergreen laurel boughs,
    And the holly are all forgot!
And then! what then? Why the men laugh low,
And hang up a branch of—the misletoe!
        Oh, brave is the laurel! and brave is the holly!
        But the misletoe banisheth melancholy!
Ah, nobody knows, nor ever *shall* know,
What is done under the misletoe!"

A printed copy of the Masque, which bears date, "Tuesday, XXIV December, MDCCCL.," is preserved in the British Museum.

"CHARACTERS

(Which speak)"Old Father Christmas	Hon. Mr. Thelluson
Young Grimston	Hon. Mr. Denison
Baron of Beef	Hon. Miss Thelluson
Plum-Pudding	Hon. Miss Denison
Mince-Pie	Hon. Miss Selina Denison
Wassail-Bowl	Hon. Miss Isabella Denison

"CHARACTERS

(Which do not speak, or say as little as possible—
all that they are requested to do)

Ursa Minor	Hon. Miss Ursula Denison
Baby Cake	Hon. Henry Charles Denison."

UNDER THE HOLLY BOUGH.

Ye who have scorn'd each other
Or injured friend or brother,
    In this fast fading year;
Ye who, by word or deed,

Have made a kind heart bleed,
    Come gather here.
Let sinn'd against and sinning,
Forget their strife's beginning;
Be links no longer broken,
Be sweet forgiveness spoken,
    Under the holly bough.

Ye who have lov'd each other,
Sister and friend and brother,
    In this fast fading year:
Mother, and sire, and child,
Young man and maiden mild,
    Come gather here;
As memory shall ponder
    Each past unbroken vow.
Old loves and younger wooing,
Are sweet in the renewing,
    Under the holly bough.

Ye who have nourished sadness,
Estranged from hope and gladness,
    In this fast fading year.
Ye with o'er-burdened mind
Made aliens from your kind,
    Come gather here.
Let not the useless sorrow
Pursue you night and morrow,
    If e'er you hoped—hope now—
Take heart: uncloud your faces,
And join in our embraces
    Under the holly bough.

Charles Mackay, LL.D.

The author of this beautiful poem (Dr. Charles Mackay) was born at Perth in 1814, and died on Christmas Eve, 1889, at his residence, Longridge Road, Earl's Court, Brompton.

GHOST STORIES.

Everybody knows that Christmas is the time for ghost stories, and that Charles Dickens and other writers have supplied us with tales of the true blood-curdling type. Thomas Hood's "Haunted House," S. T. Coleridge's "Ancient Mariner," and some other weird works of poetry have also been found serviceable in producing that strange chill of the blood, that creeping kind of feeling all over you, which is one of the enjoyments of Christmastide. Coleridge (says the late Mr. George Dawson)[88] "holds the first place amongst English poets in this objective teaching of the vague, the mystic, the dreamy, and the imaginative. I defy any man of imagination or sensibility to have 'The Ancient Mariner' read to him, by the flickering firelight on Christmas night, by a master mind possessed by the mystic spirit of the poem, and not find himself taken away from the good regions of 'ability to account for,' and taken into some far-off dreamland, and made even to start at his own footfall, and almost to shudder at his own shadow. You shall sit round the fire at Christmas time, good men and true every one of you; you shall come there armed with your patent philosophy; that creak you have heard, it is only the door—the list is not carefully put round the door, and it is the wintry wind that whistles through the crevices. Ghosts and spectres belong to the olden times; science has waved its wand and laid them all. We have no superstition about us; we walk enlightened nineteenth-century men; it is quite beneath us to be superstitious. By and bye, one begins to tell tales of ghosts and spirits; and another begins, and it goes all round; and there comes over you a curious feeling—a very unphilosophical feeling, in fact, because the pulsations of air from the tongue of the storyteller ought not to bring over you that peculiar feeling. You have only heard words, tales—confessedly by the storyteller himself only tales, such as may figure in the next monthly magazine for pure entertainment and amusement. But why do you feel so, then? If you say that these things are mere hallucinations, vague air-beating or tale-telling, why, good philosopher, do you feel so curious, so all-overish, as it were? Again, you are a man without the least terror in you, as brave and bold a man as ever stepped: living man cannot frighten you, and verily the dead rise not with you. But you are brought, towards midnight, to the stile over which is gained a view of the village churchyard, where sleep the dead in quietness. Your manhood begins just to ooze away a little; you are caught occasionally whistling to keep your courage up; you do not expect to see a ghost, but you are ready to see one, or to make one." At such a moment, think of the scene depicted by Coleridge:—

> "'Twas night, calm night, the moon was high;
> The dead men stood together.
>
> All stood together on the deck,
>   For a charnel-dungeon fitter:
> All fixed on me their stony eyes,
>   That in the moon did glitter.
>
> The pang, the curse, with which they died,
>   Had never passed away:
> I could not draw my eyes from theirs,
>   Nor turn them up to pray."

With this weird tale in his mind in the mystic stillness of midnight would an imaginative man be likely to deny the reality of the spirit world? The chances are that he would be spellbound; or, if he had breath enough, would cry out—

> "Angels and ministers of grace, defend us!"

"In the year 1421, the widow of Ralph Cranbourne, of Dipmore End, in the parish of Sandhurst, Berks, was one midnight alarmed by a noise in her bedchamber, and, looking up, she saw at her bedfoot the appearance of a skeleton (which she verily believed was her husband) nodding and talking to her upon its fingers, or finger bones, after the manner of a dumb person. Whereupon she was so terrified, that after striving to scream aloud, which she could not, for her tongue clave to her mouth, she fell backward as in a swoon; yet not so insensible withal but she could see that at this the figure became greatly agitated and distressed, and would have clasped her, but upon her appearance of loathing it desisted, only moving its jaw upward and downward, as if it would cry for help but could not for want of its parts of speech. At length, she growing more and more faint, and likely to die of fear, the spectre suddenly, as if at a thought, began to swing round its hand, which was loose at the wrist, with a brisk motion, and the finger bones being long and hard, and striking sharply against each other, made a loud noise like to the springing of a watchman's rattle. At which alarm, the neighbours running in, stoutly armed, as against thieves or murderers, the spectre suddenly departed."[89]

"His shoes they were coffins, his dim eye reveal'd
    The gleam of a grave-lamp with vapours oppress'd;
And a dark crimson necklace of blood-drops congeal'd
    Reflected each bone that jagg'd out of his breast."[90]

Welcome to Christmas.

By Mary Howitt.

He comes—the brave old Christmas!
    His sturdy steps I hear;
We will give him a hearty welcome,
    For he comes but once a year!

And of all our old acquaintance
    'Tis he we like the best;
There's a jolly old way about him—
    There's a warm heart in his breast.

He is not too proud to enter
    Your house though it be mean;

Yet is company fit for a courtier,
    And is welcomed by the Queen!

He can tell you a hundred stories
    Of the Old World's whims and ways,
And how they merrily wish'd him joy
    In our fathers' courting days.

He laughs with the heartiest laughter
    That does one good to hear;
'Tis a pity so brave an old fellow
    Should come but once a year!

But once, then, let us be ready,
    With all that he can desire—
With plenty of holly and ivy,
    And a huge log for the fire;

With plenty of noble actions,
    And plenty of warm good-will;
With our hearts as full of kindness
    As the board we mean to fill.

With plenty of store in the larder,
    And plenty of wine in the bin;
And plenty of mirth for the kitchen;
    Then open and let him in!

Oh, he is a fine old fellow—
    His heart's in the truest place;
You may know that at once by the children,
    Who glory to see his face.

For he never forgets the children,
    They all are dear to him;
You'll see that with wonderful presents
    His pockets are cramm'd to the brim.

Nor will he forget the servants,
    Whether you've many or one;

Nor the poor old man at the corner;
    Nor the widow who lives alone.

He is rich as a Jew, is Old Christmas,
    I wish he would make me his heir;
But he has plenty to do with his money,
    And he is not given to spare.

Not he—bless the good old fellow!
    He hates to hoard his pelf;
He wishes to make all people
    As gay as he is himself.

So he goes to the parish unions—
    North, south, and west and east—
And there he gives the paupers,
    At his own expense a feast.

He gives the old men tobacco,
    And the women a cup of tea;
And he takes the pauper children,
    And dances them on his knee.

I wish you could see those paupers
    Sit down to his noble cheer,
You would wish, like them, and no wonder,
    That he stay'd the livelong year.

Yes, he is the best old fellow
    That ever on earth you met;
And he gave us a boon when first he came
    Which we can never forget.

So we will give him a welcome
    Shall gladden his old heart's core!
And let us in good and gracious deeds
    Resemble him more and more!

December 21, 1850.

Writing on this subject, in the *Antiquary*, March, 1895, Mr. Harry Hems, of Exeter, introduces the reduced copy of an illustration which appears on the following page, and which he states was published in the *Illustrated London News*, January 11, 1851.

The picture (says Mr. Hems) "presents, as will be seen, a frosty, moonlight night, with a brilliantly-lit old farmhouse in the background. In the fore are leafless fruit-trees, and three men firing guns at them, whilst the jovial farmer and another man drink success to the year's crop from glasses evidently filled from a jug of cider, which the latter also holds a-high. A crowd of peasants— men, women and children—are gathered around, and the following description is appended:—

"'Amongst the scenes of jocund hospitality in this holiday season, that are handed down to us, is one which not only presents an enlivening picture, but offers proof of the superstition that still prevails in the Western counties. On Twelfth-even, in Devonshire, it is customary for the farmer to leave his warm fireside, accompanied by a band of rustics, with guns, blunderbusses, &c., presenting an appearance which at other times would be somewhat alarming. Thus armed, the band proceeds to an adjoining orchard, where is selected one of the most fruitful and aged of the apple-trees, grouping round which they stand and offer up their invocations in the following quaint doggerel rhyme:—

"'Here's to thee,
Old apple-tree!
Whence thou mayst bud,
And whence thou mayst blow,
And whence thou mayst blow,
And whence thou mayst bear
Apples enow:
Hats full,
Caps full,
Bushels, bushels, sacks full,
And my pockets full too!
Huzza! huzza!'

WASSAILING THE APPLE-TREES IN DEVONSHIRE.

The cider-jug is then passed round, and, with many a hearty shout, the party fire off their guns, charged with powder only, amidst the branches, sometimes frightening the owl from its midnight haunt. With confident hopes they return to the farmhouse, and are refused admittance, in spite of all weather, till some lucky wight guesses aright the peculiar roast the maidens are preparing for their comfort. This done, all enter, and soon right merrily the jovial glass goes round, that man who gained admittance receiving the honour of King for the evening, and till a late hour he reigns, amidst laughter, fun, and jollity. The origin of this custom is not known, but it is supposed to be one of great antiquity.

"'The illustration is from a sketch by Mr. Colebrooke, Stockdale.'"

We may add that, in the seventeenth century, a similar custom seems to have been observed in some places on Christmas Eve, for in Herrick's *Hesperides* the wassailing of fruit trees is among the Christmas Eve ceremonies:—

> "Wassail the trees, that they may beare
> You many a plum, and many a peare;
> For more or less fruits they will bring,
> As you do give them wassailing."

Writing from Exeter, in 1852, a correspondent says "the custom of welcoming this season of holy joy with 'psalms and hymns and spiritual songs' lingers in the cathedral city of Exeter; where, during Christmas Eve, the parish choirs perambulate the streets singing anthems, with instrumental accompaniments. The singing is protracted through the night, when the celebration often assumes a more secular character than is strictly in accordance with the festival. A more sacred commemoration is, however, at hand.

"At a quarter-past seven o'clock on Christmas morning the assemblage of persons in the nave of Exeter Cathedral is usually very numerous: there are the remnants of the previous vigil, with unwashed faces and sleepy eyes; but a large number are early risers, who have left their beds for better purposes than a revel. There is a great muster of the choir, and the fine Old Hundredth Psalm is sung from the gallery to a full organ, whose billows of sound roll through the vaulted edifice. The scene is strikingly picturesque: all is dim and shadowy; the red light from the flaring candles falling upon upturned faces, and here and there falling upon a piece of grave sculpture, whilst the grey light of day begins to stream through the antique windows, adding to the solemnity of the scene. As the last verse of the psalm peals forth, the crowd begins to move, and the spacious cathedral is soon left to the more devout few who remain to attend the morning service in the Lady-chapel."

A WELSH CHRISTMAS.

From the "Christmas Chronicles of Llanfairpwllycrochon," by R. P. Hampton Roberts, in *Notes and Queries*, December 21, 1878, we quote the following:

"Now Thomas Thomas, and Mary Jones, and all their neighbours, had great veneration for Christmas, and enjoyed much pleasure in looking forward to the annual recurrence of the feast. Not that they looked upon it as a feast in any ecclesiastical sense, for Llanfairpwllycrochon was decidedly Calvinistically Methodist, and rejected all such things as mere popish superstition.

"The Christmas goose was a great institution at Llanfairpwllycrochon. The annual goose club had no existence there, it is true, but the annual goose had nevertheless. Thomas Thomas, after his memorable visit to London, came home imbued with one English idea which startled the villagers more than anything had done since the famous bonfire on the outlying hill when the heir came of age, and it was a long time before they recovered from their surprise. It was nothing less than a proposition to substitute beef for the Christmas dinner instead of a goose. Here was a sad falling off from the ways of Llanfairpwllycrochon! And Thomas Thomas was a man who persisted in an idea once it entered his mind—an event of rare occurrence, it is true, and consequently all the more stubborn whenever it did occur. Thomas Thomas had, however, sufficient respect for the opinion of his neighbours to make him compromise matters by providing for himself alone a small beefsteak as an adjunct to the time-honoured goose.

"Another Christmas institution at Llanfairpwllycrochon was the universal pudding, mixed as is wont by every member of the family. Then there was the bun-loaf, or *barabrith*, one of the grand institutions of Llanfairpwllycrochon. Many were the pains taken over this huge loaf—made large enough to last a week or fortnight, according to the appetites of the juvenile partakers—and the combined "Christmas-boxes" of the grocer and baker went to make up the appetising whole, with much more in addition.

"Christmas Eve was a day of exceeding joy at Llanfairpwllycrochon. The manufacture of paper ornaments and 'kissing bushes,' radiant with oranges, apples, paper roses, and such like fanciful additions as might suit the taste or means of the house-holder, occupied most of the day. And then they had to be put up, and the house in its Christmas decorations looked more resplendent than the imagination of the most advanced villager—at present at school, and of the mature age of five and a half years, the rising hope of the schoolmaster, and a Lord Chancellor in embryo in fine—could have pictured. As a reward for the day's toil came the night's sweet task of making *cyflath*, *i.e.*, toffee. Thomas Thomas, and those who spoke the Saxon tongue among the villagers, called it 'taffy.' Once had Thomas Thomas been corrected in his pronunciation, but the hardy Saxon who ventured on the bold proceeding was silenced when he heard that he was not to think he was going to persuade a reasonable man into mutilating the English tongue. 'Taffy it iss, and taffy I says,' and there was an end of the matter. Without taffy the inhabitants of Llanfairpwllycrochon, it was firmly believed by the vicar, would not have known the difference between Christmas and another time, and it is not therefore matter for surprise that they should so tenaciously cling to its annual making. At midnight, when the syrupy stuff was sufficiently boiled, it would be poured into a pan and put into the open air to cool. Here was an opportunity for the beaux of the village which could not be missed. They would steal, if possible, the whole, pan and all, and entail a second making on the unfortunate victims of their practical joke.

"Sometimes the Christmas Eve proceedings would be varied by holding a large evening party, continued all night, the principal amusement of which would be the boiling of toffee, one arm taking, when another was tired, the large wooden spoon, and turning the boiling mass of sugar and treacle, this process being continued for many hours, until nothing would be left to partake of but a black, burnt sort of crisp, sugary cinder. Sometimes the long boiling would only result in a soft mass, disagreeable to the taste and awkward to the hand, the combined efforts of each member of the party failing to secure consistency or strength in the mixed ingredients.

"And then there were the carols at midnight, and many more were the Christmas customs at Llanfairpwllycrochon."

EFFECTS OF THE SEASON.

"These Christmas decorations are *so* jolly!"
She cried, zeal shining in her orbs of blue.
"*Don't* you like laurel gleaming under holly?"
He answered, "*I* love mistletoe over *yen!*"—*Punch.*

"ST. GEORGE" IN COMBAT WITH "ST. PETER."

YORKSHIRE SWORD-ACTORS.

Under this title, Mr. T. M. Fallow, M.A., F.S.A., writing in the *Antiquary*, May, 1895, gives an account of rustic performances which were witnessed at Christmastide in the neighbourhood of Leeds about fifteen years earlier, and he illustrates the subject with a series of pictures from photographs taken at the time, which are here reproduced. The play depicted is that of the "Seven Champions of Christendom," and in the picture on the preceding page "St. George" is shown engaged in combat with "St. Peter," while "St. Andrew" and "St. Denys" are each kneeling on one knee, a sign of their having been vanquished.

"It may be well to point out," says Mr. Fallow, "that in the West Riding, or at any rate in the neighbourhood of Leeds, the sword-actors were quite distinct from the 'mummers.' They generally numbered nine or ten lads, who, disguised by false beards as men, were dressed in costume as appropriate to the occasion as their knowledge and finances would permit, and who acted, with more or less skill, a short play, which, as a rule, was either the 'Peace Egg' or the 'Seven Champions of Christendom.' The following illustration shows two of the 'champions,' as photographed at the time stated:—

"ST. PETER."   "ST. DENYS."

"There was a little indefiniteness," says Mr. Fallow, "as to the characters represented in the play, but usually they were the King of Egypt, his daughter, a fool or jester, St. George, St. Andrew, St. Patrick, St. David, St. Denys, St. James, and a St. Thewhs, who represented a Northern nation—Russia, or sometimes Denmark—and whose exact identity seems obscure. The seven champions occasionally included St. Peter of Rome, as in the group whose photograph is given. St. George engaged in mortal combat with each champion in succession, fighting for the hand of the King of Egypt's daughter. When at length each of the six was slain, St. George, having vanquished them all, won the fair lady, amid the applause of the bystanders. Then, at the conclusion, after a general clashing and crossing of swords, the fool or jester stepped forward, and wound up the performance with an appeal for pecuniary recognition."

OTHER CHRISTMAS PERFORMANCES.

In a Christmas article, published in 1869, Dr. Rimbault mentions the performance of "St. George and the Dragon" in the

365

extreme western and northern parts of the country. The following five characters are given: Father Christmas, Turkish Knight, King of Egypt, St. George, Doctor. Other writers mention similar plays, with variations of characters, as seen in the rural parts of Northamptonshire, Warwickshire, and Staffordshire, and the present writer has himself seen such plays at Madeley, in Shropshire.

S. Arnott, of Turnham Green, writing in *Notes and Queries*, December 21, 1878, says: "When I was living at Hollington, near Hastings, in the year 1869, the village boys were in the habit of visiting the houses of the gentry at Christmas time to perform a play, which had been handed down by tradition." The description of the play which then followed shows that it was another variation of the well-known Christmas play, and included the "Turkish Knight," the "Bold Slasher," and other familiar characters.

A Scotch First Footing.

Writing on "Mid-winter Customs in the North," Mr. Edward Garrett says "it is not easy to write of 'Christmas customs in the North,' because many of them, even though connected with the Christmas festival, do not take place till January 6th, that being Christmas Day, Old Style, while most of them are associated with the New Year, either Old or New Style, one of the most striking celebrations coming off on January 11th, regarded as 'New Year's Eve.'

"Christmas itself has never been a national Scottish festival since the Reformation. On its purely festive side, it has become somewhat of a 'fashion' of late years, but its ancient customs have only lingered on in those districts where Episcopacy has taken deep root. Such a district is 'Buchan'—a track of country in the north-east of Aberdeenshire—a place which cannot be better described than in the words of one of its own gifted sons, Dr. Walter Smith:—

> "'A treeless land, where beeves are good,
>   And men have quaint, old-fashioned ways,
> And every burn has ballad lore,
>   And every hamlet has its song,
> And on its surf-beat, rocky shore
>   The eerie legend lingers long.

Old customs live there, unaware
   That they are garments cast away,
And what of light is lingering there
   Is lingering light of yesterday.'"

A SCOTCH FIRST FOOTING.

YULETIDE CUSTOMS IN SHETLAND.

The inherent Scandinavianism of the Shetlander, which leads him to repudiate the appellation of Scotchman, and to cherish in secret the old customs and superstitions of his ancestors, asserts itself yearly in the high jinks with which he continues to honour the old holy days of Yule. Until within the last two or three years, he pertinaciously adhered to the old style in his observance of these festivities. On Christmas Eve, New Year's Eve, and Uphelya—the twenty-fourth day after Yule, and that on which the holy or holidays are supposed to be "up"—the youths of Lerwick, attired in fantastic dresses, go "guising" about the town in bands, visiting their friends and acquaintances and reproducing in miniature the carnival of more southern climes. On one or other of these occasions a torchlight procession forms part of the revelry. Formerly blazing tar barrels were dragged about the town, and afterwards, with the first break of morning, dashed over the Knab into the sea. But this ancient and dangerous custom has very properly been discontinued. The dresses of the guisers are often of the most expensive and fanciful description. Highlanders, Spanish cavaliers, negro minstrels, soldiers in the peaked caps, kerseymere breeches, and scarlet coats turned up with buff, of the reign of George II., Robin Hoods, and Maid Marians were found in the motley throng. Some, with a boldness worthy of Aristophanes himself, caricature the dress, the walk, or some other eccentricity of leading personages in the town; others—for the spirit of "the Happy Land" has reached these hyperborean regions—make pleasant game of well-known political characters. Each band of guisers has its fiddler, who walks before it, playing "Scalloway Lasses," or "The Foula Reel," or "The Nippin' Grund," or some other archaic tune. Thus conducted, and blowing a horn to give notice of their approach, the maskers enter the doors of all houses which they find open, dance a measure with the inmates, partake of and offer refreshment, and then depart to repeat the same courtesies elsewhere. At daylight the horn of the Most Worthy Grand Guiser, a mysterious personage, whose personality and functions are enveloped in the deepest concealment, is heard summoning all the bands to end their revels, and when, in the cold grey dawn of the winter morning, the worthy citizens of Lerwick awake to pursue their wonted avocations, not a trace remains of the saturnalia of the night before.—Sheriff Rampini, in *Good Words*.

Now, passing from the islands to the sea itself, it is pleasant to note that in recent years Christian hearts have carried

CHRISTMAS CHEER TO THE NORTH SEA FISHERMEN.

Through the "Mission to Deep Sea Fishermen" twelve thousand brave and hardy fishermen have been cheered at Christmastide, for to their fleets the Mission's vessels now take medical and surgical aid, books and magazines, woollen garments and tobacco, which, as adjuncts to higher religious aid, are turning the once wild and desperate ocean roughs into clean-living sailors and good husbands and fathers—therefore are these days on the North Sea better far than those that are gone. Thousands of these brave men turn at Christmas to the M.D.S.F. flag as to the one bright link which binds them to friendly hearts ashore, assuring them that in England's Christmas festivities they and their like have a real part, and are no longer forgotten.

Some facts recorded by the Rev. John Sinclair[91] illustrate the dangers of the wild winter sea, and also set forth some

They were related to Mr. Sinclair by Mr. Traill, chief of the clan, with whom he stayed on the occasion of his visit to the island of Pappa Westra. The first of the two incidents was as follows:—"One Christmas Day," says Mr. Traill, "during a heavy gale, I wrapped my cloak about me, and started off with my telescope to walk upon the cliffs. Coming to the other side of the island, on which the surf was beating violently, I observed a vessel a few miles off fire a signal of distress. I hastened to the nearest point, and with the help of my glass perceived that she was Dutch built, and that, having lost her rudder, she was quite unmanageable. She fired several guns at short intervals, and my people came in large numbers to give assistance. But the surf was so fearful that nothing could be done. No boat could have lived a moment in such a sea. We were all utterly helpless. As the vessel drifted towards us, I could see the whole tragedy as distinctly as if it had been acted on the stage. Immediately below me were a number of my fellow-creatures, now alive and in health, and in a few moments they would all be mangled corpses. I could make out the expression of their features, and see in what manner each was preparing for inevitable death. But whether they climbed up into the shrouds, or held by ropes on deck while the sea was washing over the bulwarks, their fate was the same. The first wave lifted the vessel so high that I almost thought it would have placed her upon the land. She fell back, keel upwards. The next wave struck her with such terrific force against the cliffs that she was shivered at once into a thousand pieces; hardly two planks held together. It seemed as if she had been made of glass. Not a soul escaped. One or two bodies, with a few planks and casks, were all that ever reached the shore." Well might Mr. Traill add, "I was haunted for months by the remembrance of that heartrending sight."

The other story related by Mr. Traill shows that a Christmas party may be detained indefinitely in one of these remote islands, should the weather prove unfavourable. At Christmastide, a former Laird of Westra "collected a numerous party from all the neighbouring islands to celebrate the christening of his eldest son." His hospitalities cost him dear. A storm arose; his guests could not get away; instead of enjoying their society for a few days, he was obliged to entertain them at a ruinous expense for many weeks. His larder, his cellar, and his barns, were by degrees exhausted. His farm stock had all been slaughtered, except the old bull, which he was reserving as a last resource, when at length the wind abated, and a calm delivered him from this ruinous situation.

Thus it appears that in these remote islands of Scotland Christmas is not forgotten. But a writer in a well-known Scotch journal says the surest sign of the general joy is "Christmas in the Workhouse":—

"Christmas was gay in the old squire's hall,
    Gay at the village inn,
Cheery and loud by the farmer's fire,
    Happy the manse within;
But the surest signs of the general joy,
    And that all the world was happy—very,
Were the sounds that proved at the workhouse door
    That even 'the paupers' were merry."

A REMARKABLE CHRISTMAS GATHERING.

The Greenwich Hospital for Sick Seamen of all Nations presented on Christmas Day, 1880, a remarkable gathering of national representatives. There were 179 sailors, representing 31 nationalities, belonging to ships of 19 distinct nations. They were summed up thus:—England, 77; Wales, 3; Scotland, 9; Ireland, 11; Norway, 10; Sweden, 9; Finland, 6; United States, 5; Denmark, 5; British India, 4; France, 3; Germany, 3; Nova Scotia, 3; Russia, 2; Austria, 2; Italy, 2; Cape de Verd Islands, 2; Chili, 2; Jamaica, 2; Barbadoes, 2; St. Thomas, 2; Spain, 1; Portugal, 1; Canada, 1; New Brunswick, 1; Transvaal, 1; Gold Coast, 1; Brazil, 1; St. Kitts, 1; Mauritius, 1; Society Islands, 1. The mercantile marines represented were no bad index to the proportion of the carrying trade of the world each nation undertakes:—England, 96 vessels; Ireland, 3; Scotland, 16; Wales, 4; Norway, 7; Sweden, 5; United States, 6;

Denmark, 2; France, 2; Germany, 3; Nova Scotia, 7; Russia, 2; Netherlands, 4; Channel Islands, 2; New Brunswick, 2; Italy, 1; Zanzibar, 1; Spain, 1.

The early morning brought warm Christmas wishes to the patients. Each found by his bedside a packet addressed to him by name. Some good lady had taken the enormous pains to work a pretty, and, at the same time, stout and serviceable wallet, with the inscription, "My letters," embroidered thereupon, and to accompany this little gift, in every case, with a short and seasonable letter of Christmas wishes, using other languages than English, to suit the convenience of every recipient. The initials under which these offerings came were "N. C. H." Other gifts, Christmas cards and Christmas reading, in the shape of magazines and illustrated papers were gladly welcomed.

The decorations of the corridors and rooms had given occupation to the sick sailors for several days, and sentiments of loyalty to the Queen and the Royal Family were abundantly displayed, together with portraits of members of the Royal Family which had been drawn from fancy.

The officers and nurses had dedicated to them some specimens of real sailor poetry, combining the names of the staff. With grim humour, the "operation room" bore above it "Nil desperandum"; and the decorated walls of the hospital told the onlookers that "small vessels should keep in shore," that "windmills are not turned by a pair of bellows," that "good things are not found in heaps," that "hasty people fish in empty ponds," that "plenty, like want, ruins many," &c.

The dinner at one o'clock was a great success. All who could get out of bed made it a point of honour to be present. But for adverse winds keeping ships from entering the Thames, the guests would have been more numerous. But, as it was, the patients under the roof numbered 179. There were, of course, difficulties of language; but no "Jack" ever ploughed the sea who does not understand a Christmas dinner; and, besides, the hospital in its nurses and staff possesses the means of conversing in seventeen different languages.

The scene was a thoroughly Christmas one; and many other festive scenes, almost as interesting, were seen in all parts of England. Whether recorded or unrecorded, who does not rejoice in such efforts to promote "goodwill amongst men," and long for the time—

"When peace shall over all the earth
    Its ancient splendours fling,
And the whole world send back the song,
    Which now the angels sing."
    Which now the angels sing."

CHRISTMAS CRACKERS.

One of the popular institutions inseparable from the festivities of Christmastide has long been the "cracker." The satisfaction which young people especially experience in pulling the opposite ends of a gelatine and paper cylinder is of the keenest, accompanied as the operation is by a mixed anticipation—half fearful as to the explosion that is to follow, and wholly delightful with regard to the bonbon or motto which will thus be brought to light. Much amusement is afforded to the lads and lassies by the fortune-telling verses which some of the crackers contain. But the cracker of our early days was something far different from what it is now. The sharp "crack" with which the article exploded, and from which it took its name, was then its principal, and, in some cases, its only feature; and the exclamation, "I know I shall scream," which John Leech, in one of his sketches, puts into the mouth of two pretty girls engaged in cracker-pulling, indicated about the all of delight which that occupation afforded. Since then, however, the cracker has undergone a gradual development. Becoming by degrees a receptacle for bon-bons, rhymed mottoes, little paper caps and aprons, and similar toys, it has passed on to another and higher stage, and is even made a vehicle for high art illustrations. Considerable artistic talent has been introduced in the adornment of these novelties. For instance, the "Silhouette" crackers are illustrated with black figures, comprising portraits of well-known characters in the political, military, and social world, exquisitely executed, while appropriate designs have been adapted to other varieties, respectively designated "Cameos," "Bric-a-brac," "Musical Toys," &c.; and it is quite evident that the education of the young in matters of good taste is not overlooked in the provision of opportunities for merriment.

Hang up the baby's stocking ! Be
sure you don't forget ! The dear
little dimpled darling, she never
saw Christmas yet ! But I've
told her all about it, and she opened
her big blue eyes ; and I'm sure
she understood it—she looked so
funny and wise. *₊* Dear, what
a tiny stocking ! It doesn't take
much to hold such little pink toes
as baby's away from the frost and
cold. But then, for the baby's
Christmas, it will never do at all.
Why ! Santa wouldn't be looking for anything half so
small. *₊* I know what
will do for the baby. I've
thought of the very best
plan. I'll borrow a
stocking of Grandma's,
the longest that ever
I can. And you'll
hang it by mine,
dear mother, right
here in the corner,
so ! And leave a
letter to Santa, and
fasten it on to the
toe. *₊* Write—this
is the baby's stocking,
that hangs in the corner
here. You never have
seen her, Santa, for
she only came this
year. But she's
just the blessed'st
baby. And now
before you go,
just cram her
stocking with
goodies, from
the top clean
down to
t h e
toe !

FATALLY BURNT IN CHRISTMAS COSTUMES.

The Christmastide of 1885-6 was marred by two fatal accidents which again illustrate the danger of dressing for entertainments in highly-inflammable materials. In the first case a London lady, on Boxing Night, was entertaining some friends, and appeared herself in the costume of *Winter*. She was dressed in a white robe of thin fabric, and stood under a canopy from which fell pieces of cotton wool to represent snowflakes, and in their descent one of them caught light at the candelabra, and fell at deceased's feet. In trying to put it out with her foot her dress caught fire, and she was immediately enveloped in flames. So inflammable was the material that, although prompt assistance was rendered, she was so severely burnt as to become unconscious. A medical man was sent for, and everything possible was done for her; but she sank gradually, and died from exhaustion. The second of these tragical incidents plunged a Paris family in deep sorrow. The parents, who lived in a beautiful detached house in the Rue de la Bienfaisance, had arranged that their children and some youthful cousins were to play before a party of friends on New Year's Night on the stage of a little theatre which had just been added to their house. The play was to represent the decrepit old year going out and the new one coming in. The eldest daughter, a charming girl of fourteen, was to be the good genius of 1886, and to be dressed in a loose transparent robe. On the appointed evening, after the company had assembled, she donned her stage costume and ran into her mother's bedroom to see how it became her. While looking at herself in a mirror on the toilette table her loose sleeve came in contact with the flame of a candle and blazed up. She screamed for help and tried to roll herself in the bed clothes; but the bed, being covered with a lace coverlet and curtained with muslin was also set on fire, and soon the whole room was ablaze. By the time help arrived the girl's clothes were all burning into the flesh; but such was her vitality that, in spite of the dreadful state in which every inch of her body was, she survived the accident many hours.

Similar disasters occurred at Christmas festivities in 1889, at Detroit, and in 1891, at Wortley, Leeds. In the former several little children were fatally burnt, and in the latter fifteen children were set on fire, eleven of them fatally.

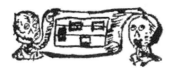

CHRISTMAS LITERATURE

is too large a subject to enter upon at length, for a bulky volume would scarcely suffice to describe the numerous Christmas annuals, illustrated Christmas numbers, newspaper supplements and variety papers which have become popular at Christmastide since the first appearance of Dickens's "Christmas Stories." The development of the Christmas trade in this light literature has been marvellous, and it is increasing year by year. And the same may be said of the charming gift-books which are published annually just before Christmas.

CHRISTMAS LETTER MISSIONS.

Through the various letter missions that have been established thousands of Christmas letters and illustrated missives, bright with anecdote, are despatched annually to the inmates of convalescent homes and hospitals, and are heartily welcomed by the recipients, for every one likes to be remembered on Christmas Day.

THE POST-OFFICE OFFICIALS AND POSTMEN

have, however, been very heavily weighted with these new Christmas customs. They have inflicted upon postmen and letter-sorters an amount of extra labour that is almost incredible. The postal-parcel work is also very heavy at the festive season.

THE RAILWAYS AT CHRISTMAS.

"Home for the holidays, here we go;
Bless me, the train is exceedingly slow!

Pray, Mr. Engineer, get up your steam,
And let us be off, with a puff and a scream!
We have two long hours to travel, you say;
Come, Mr. Engineer, gallop away!"[92]

This familiar verse recalls the eagerness of the schoolboy to be home for the Christmas holidays. And adults are no less eager to join their friends at the festive season; many travel long journeys in order to do so. Hence the great pressure of work on railway employés, and the congested state of the traffic at Christmastide. Two or three days before Christmas Day the newspapers publish what are called "railway arrangements," detailing the privileges granted by this and that company, and presenting the holiday traveller with a sort of appetising programme; and any one who will spend an hour at any of the great termini of the metropolis at this period can see the remarkable extent to which the public avail themselves of the facilities offered. The growth of railway travelling at Christmastide has, indeed, been marvellous in recent years, and it becomes greater every year. The crowded state of the railway stations, and the trains that roll out of them heavily laden with men, women, and children, wedged together by parcels bursting with good cheer, show most unmistakably that we have not forgotten the traditions of Christmas as a time of happy gatherings in the family circles of Old England.

79   Huish's "Life of George the Third."
80   *Gentleman's Magazine*, 1790.
81   Copied from an undated leaflet inserted in the British Museum copy of Brand's "Antiquities," by the late Mr Joseph Hazlewood.
82   Hone's "Every-day Book," 1826.
83   Herbert H. Adams.
84   "A black Christmas makes a fat kirk-yard." A windy Christmas and a calm Candlemas are signs of a good year.
85   The "savoury haggis" (from *hag* to chop) is a dish commonly made in a sheep's maw, of its lungs, heart, and liver, mixed with suet, onions, salt, and pepper; or of oatmeal mixed with the latter, without any animal food.
86   E. Lawrence.
87   "Old English Customs and Charities," 1842.
88   "Biographical Lectures."
89   "History of Berks," vol. xxv.
90   "Grim, King of the Ghosts."
91   "Old Times and Distant Places," 1875.
92   Eliza Cook.

But, as there is also much Christmas-keeping in other parts of
the world, we pass now to—

CHAPTER XII.

MODERN CHRISTMASES ABROAD.

CHRISTMAS-KEEPING IN THE ARCTIC REGIONS, 1850-1.

"The bluejackets are generally better hands than the red-coats at improvising a jollification—Jack, at any rate, does not take his pleasures sadly. The gallant bands that have from time to time gone forth to a bloodless campaign in the icy north, have always managed to keep their Christmas right joyously. Certainly they could not complain of uncongenial skies or unseasonable temperatures; while, so far as snow and ice are necessary to thorough enjoyment, the supply in the Arctic regions is on a scale sufficient to satisfy the most ardent admirer of an old-fashioned Christmas. The frozen-in Investigators under McClure kept their first Arctic Christmas soberly, cheerfully, and in good fellowship, round tables groaning with good cheer, in the shape of Sandwich Island beef, musk veal from the Prince of Wales's Strait, mince-meat from England, splendid preserves from the Green Isle, and dainty dishes from Scotland. Every one talked of home, and speculated respecting the doings of dear ones there; and healths were drunk, not omitting those of their fellow-labourers sauntering somewhere in the regions about, but how near or how far away none could tell. When the festival came round again, the *Investigator* and *Enterprise* were alone in their glory, and they were separated by miles of frozen sea; but they had solved the great problem.[93] On board the *Investigator*, frost-bound in the Bay of Mercy, things went as merry as the proverbial marriage-bell. After divine service, everybody took a constitutional on the ice until dinner-time; then the officers sat down to a meal of which the *pièce de résistance* was a haunch of Banks' Island reindeer, weighing twenty pounds, with fat two inches thick, and a most delicious flavour; while the crew were regaling upon venison and other good things, double allowance of grog included; and dinner discussed, dancing, singing, and skylarking filled up the holiday hours till bedtime; the fun being kept up with unflagging humour, and with such propriety withal as to make their leader wish the anxious folks at home could have witnessed the scene created amidst so many gloomy influences, by the crew of a ship after two years' sojourn in those ice-bound regions upon their own resources. Another Christmas found the brave fellows still confined in their snowy prison; but their table boasted plum-pudding rich enough for Arctic appetites, Banks' Land venison, Mercy Bay hare-soup, ptarmigan pasties, and musk-ox beef—hung-beef, surely, seeing it had been dangling in the rigging above two years. The poets among the men wrote songs making light of the hardships they had endured; the painters exhibited pictures of past perils; comic actors were not wanting; and the whole company, casting all anxiety to the winds, enjoyed themselves to the utmost."[94]

In the spring of 1870, before the breaking out of the Franco-German war, Germany sent out two ships, the *Germania* and the *Hansa*, with the hope of reaching the North Pole. As is usually the case in Arctic expeditions, little could be done during the first season, and the ships were obliged to take up their winter-quarters off the east coast of Greenland. They had already been separated, so that the crew of one vessel, had no idea of the condition of the other. An officer upon the *Germania* gives the following interesting account of their Christmas festivities in the Arctic regions:—

"To the men who have already lived many weary months among the icebergs, Christmas signifies, in addition to its other associations, that the half of their long night—with its fearful storms, its enforced cessation of all energy, its discomfort and sadness—has passed, and that the sun will soon again shed its life and warmth-giving beams on the long-deserted North. From this time the grim twilight, during which noon has been hardly distinguishable from the other hours, grows daily lighter, until at length all hearts are gladdened, and a cheerful activity is once again called forth by the first glimpse of the sun. Christmas, the midnight of the Arctic explorer, thus marks a period in his life which he has good cause to consider a joyful one.

"For days before the festival, an unusual activity was observable all over the ship; and as soon as the severe storm which raged from December 16th to the 21st had abated, parties were organised, under our botanist, Dr. Pansch, to certain points of Sabine Island, near to which we were anchored, where, in a strangely sheltered nook, several varieties of a native Greenland evergreen plant, *Andromeda tetragona*, were to be found. A great quantity of this plant was conveyed on board, to be converted into a Christmas-tree. Under the orders of Dr. Pansch, the Andromeda was wound round small pieces of wood, several of which were attached, like fir-twigs, to a large bough; and when these boughs were fastened to a pole, they formed a very respectable fir-tree.

"After dinner on Christmas Day, the cabin was cleared for the completion of the preparations; and on our recall at six o'clock, we found that all had assumed an unwontedly festive appearance. The walls were decorated with the signal-flags and our national eagle; and the large cabin table, somewhat enlarged to make room to seat seventeen men, was covered with a clean white cloth, which had been reserved for the occasion. On the table stood the 'fir' tree, shining in the splendour of many little wax-lights, and ornaments with all sorts of little treasures, some of which, such as the gilded walnuts, had already seen a Christmas in Germany; below the tree was a small present for each of us, provided long beforehand, in readiness for the day, by loving friends and relatives at home. There was a packet too for each of the crew, containing some little joking gift, prepared by the mirth-loving Dr. Pansch, and a useful present also; while the officers were each and all remembered.

"When the lights burned down, and the resinous Andromeda was beginning to take fire, the tree was put aside, and a feast began, at which full justice was done to the costly Sicilian wine with which a friend had generously supplied us before we left home. We had a dish of roast seal! Some cakes were made by the cook, and the steward produced his best stores. For the evening, the division between the fore and aft cabins was removed, and there was free intercourse between officers and men; many a toast was drunk to the memory of friends at home, and at midnight a polar ball was improvised by a dance on the ice. The boatswain, the best musician of the party, seated himself with his hand-organ between the antlers of a reindeer which lay near the ship, and the men danced two and two on their novel flooring of hard ice!

"Such was our experience of a Christmas in the north polar circle; but the uncertainties of Arctic voyaging are great, and the two ships of our expedition made trial of the widely different fates which await the travellers in those frozen regions: and while we on the *Germania* were singularly fortunate in escaping accidents and in keeping our crew, in spite of some hardships, in sound health and good spirits, the *Hansa* was crushed by the ice, and her crew, after facing unheard-of dangers, and passing two hundred days on a block of ice, were barely rescued to return home."

Yet even to the crew of the ill-fated *Hansa* Christmas brought some festivities. The tremendous gale which had raged for many days ceased just before the day, and the heavy fall of snow with which it terminated, and which had almost buried the black huts that the shipwrecked men had constructed for themselves upon the drifting icebergs from the *débris* of the wreck, had produced a considerable rise in the temperature, and there was every indication that a season of calm might now be anticipated.

The log-book of the *Hansa* thus describes the celebration of the festival:—"The tree was erected in the afternoon, while the greater part of the crew took a walk; and the lonely hut shone with wonderful brightness amid the snow. Christmas upon a Greenland iceberg! The tree was artistically put together of firwood and mat-weed, and Dr. Laube had saved a twist of wax-taper for the illumination. Chains of coloured paper and newly-baked cakes were not wanting, and the men had made a knapsack and a revolver case as a present for the captain. We opened the leaden chests of presents from Professor Hochstetter and the Geological Society, and were much amused by their contents. Each man had a glass of port wine; and we then turned over the old newspapers which we found in the chests, and drew lots for the presents, which consisted of small musical instruments such as fifes, jew's-harps, trumpets, &c., with draughts and other games, puppets, crackers, &c. In the evening we feasted on chocolate and gingerbread."

"We observed the day very quietly," writes Dr. Laube in his diary. "If this Christmas be the last we are to see, it was at least a cheerful one; but should a happy return home be decreed for us, the next will, we trust, be far brighter. May God so grant!"

CHRISTMAS IN THE CRIMEA.

The Christmas of 1854 was a dismal one for the soldiers in the Crimea, witnessing and enduring what Lord John Russell spoke of as "the horrible and heartrending scenes of that Crimean winter."

"Thanks to General Muddle," says a journal of the period, "the Crimean Christmas of 1854 was anything but what it ought to and might have been; and the knowledge that plenty of good things had been provided by thoughtful hearts at home, but which were anywhere but where they were wanted, did not add to the merriment of our poor overworked, underfed army; and although some desperate efforts were made to be jolly on dreary outpost and in uncomfortable trenches, they only resulted in miserable failure. The following Christmas was doubly enjoyable by comparison. The stubborn fortress (Sebastopol) had fallen at last to its more stubborn assailants; habit had deprived frost and snow of their terrors, and every hut ran over with hams, preserves, vegetables, and mysterious tins, till it resembled a grocer's store. The valleys of Miscomia, too, were rich in mistletoe, to be had for the trouble of gathering; but few cared to undergo that trouble for the sake of what only reminded them of unattainable sweets, and made them sigh for the girls they had left behind them."

In 1855, Messrs. Macmillan & Co. published a poem by H. R. F., entitled "Christmas Dawn, 1854," in which the writer pictures the festivities marred by war:—

"A happy Christmas!
Happy! to whom? Perchance to infancy,
And innocent childhood, while the germ of sin,
Yet undeveloped, leaves a virgin soil
For joy, and Death and Sorrow are but names.
But who, that bears a mind matured to thought,
A heart to feel, shall look abroad this day
And speak of happiness? The church is deckt
With festive garlands, and the sunbeams glance
From glossy evergreens; the mistletoe

Pearl-studded, and the holly's lustrous bough
Gleaming with coral fruitage; but we muse
Of laurel blent with cypress. Gaze we down
Yon crowded aisle? the mourner's dusky weeds
Sadden the eye; and they who wear them not
Have mourning in their hearts, or lavish tears
Of sympathy on griefs too deeply lodged
For man's weak ministry.
　　　A happy Christmas!
Ah me! how many hearths are desolate!
How many a vacant seat awaits in vain
The loved one who returns not! Shall we drain
The cheerful cup—a health to absent friends?
Whom do we pledge? the living or the dead?"

Thus did the poet, "sick at heart," explore "the realm of
sorrow"; and then again he mused:

"In humbler mood to hail the auspicious day,
Shine forth rejoicing in thy strength, O sun,
Shine through the dubious mists and tearful show'rs
That darken Hope's clear azure! Christ is born,
The life of those who wake, and those who sleep—
The Day-spring from on high hath looked on us;
And we, who linger militant on earth,
Are one in Him, with those, the loved and lost,
Whose early graves keep the red field they won
Upon a stranger shore. Ah! not in vain
Went up from many a wild Crimean ridge
The soldier's pray'r, responsive to the vows
Breathed far away in many an English home.
Not vain the awakened charities, that gush
Through countless channels—Christian brotherhoods
Of mercy; and that glorious sister-band
Who sow by Death's chill waters!—Not in vain,
My country! ever loved, but dearest now
In this thine hour of sorrow, hast thou learnt
To bow to Him who chastens. We must weep—
We may rejoice in weeping"

CHRISTMAS IN ABYSSINIA.

Wherever Englishmen are on the 25th of December, there is Christmas. Whether it be in the icy regions of the Arctic zone, or in the sweltering heat of tropical sunshine, the coming round of the great feast brings with it to every Englishman a hearty desire to celebrate it duly. And if this cannot be done in exactly home-fashion, the festival is kept as happily as circumstances will allow. In this spirit did our soldiers keep Christmas in Abyssinia, in 1867, with the thermometer at seventy-five in the shade, and even here the edibles included at least one traditional dish—a joint of roast beef. There was also an abundance of spur-fowls, guinea-fowls, venison, mutton, &c., and the place in which the festive board was spread was decorated with branches of fir and such other substitutes for holly and mistletoe as could be found.

CHRISTMAS-KEEPING IN INDIA

at different periods shows the same determination of our British soldiers to honour the Christmas festival.

In 1857, the saviours of our Indian Empire very nearly lost their Christmas. The army was encamped at Intha, within sight of Nepaul, waiting for the rain to clear off and the tents to dry, ere it moved on to drive the Sepoys into the Raptee. The skies cleared on Christmas morning, and Lord Clyde was for marching at once, but relented in time to save the men's puddings from being spoiled—not only relented, but himself gave a Christmas banquet, at which the favoured guests sat down to well-served tables laden with barons of beef, turkeys, mutton, game, fish, fowls, plum-puddings, mince-pies, &c. To allay the thirst such substantial fare created, appeared beakers of pale ale from Burton and Glasgow; porter from London and Dublin; champagne, moselle, sherry, and old port, 'rather bothered by travelling twenty miles a day on a camel back.' Following the chief's example, each regiment had a glorious spread, and throughout the wide expanse of tents sounds of rejoicing were heard, for the soldiers kept Christmas right merrily.

Similarly,

did their best to observe the Christmas festival in good old English style, even during the sieges of Ladysmith, Kimberley, and Mafeking, when provisions were to be had only at famine prices. The ingenious Tommy Atkins, in distant lands, has often found sylvan substitutes for mistletoe and holly, and native viands to take the place of plum-puddings and mince-pies, but it is not so easy to find substitutes for the social circles in old England, and when the time comes round for the Christmas dance Tommy's thoughts "Return again to the girl I've left behind me."

Moreover, it sometimes falls to the lot of soldiers and war correspondents to spend their Christmas in most outlandish places. Mr. Archibald Forbes has left on record (in the *English Illustrated Magazine*, 1885) an interesting account of his own

CHRISTMASTIDE IN THE KHYBER PASS.

In his graphic style the intrepid war correspondent describes the "ride long and hard" which Kinloch and he had through the Khyber to Jelalabad plain to fulfil "the tryst they had made to spend Christmas Day with the cheery comrades of Sir Sam Browne's headquarter staff." They had an adventurous journey together from the Dakka camp to Jumrood, where Forbes left Kinloch with Maude's division.

Further on, Mr. Forbes says: "I am not prepared to be definite, after five years, as to the number of plum-puddings forming that little hillock on the top of my dâk-gharry between Jhelum and Peshawur, on the apex of which sat the faithful John amidst a whirl of dust. At Peshawur the heap of Christmas gifts were loaded into the panniers of a camel, and the ship of the desert started on its measured solemn tramp up through the defiles of the Khyber." Then Mr. Forbes tells us how he joined Kinloch again at General Maude's headquarters at Jumrood. Kinloch "had not forgotten his tryst, but meanwhile there were military duties to be done." After the discharge of these "military duties," which included a night march to surprise a barbarous clan called Zukkur-Kehls, Forbes and Kinloch joined General Tytler's column on its return march to Dakka, because at Dakka they would be nearer to their friends of Sir Sam Browne's headquarters. "Tytler determined to make his exit from the Zukkur-Kahl Valley by a previously unexplored pass, toward which the force moved for its night's bivouac. About the entrance to the glen there was a fine forest of ilex and holly, large, sturdy, spreading trees, whence dangled long sprays of mistletoe; the mistletoe bough was here indeed, and Christmas was close, but where the fair ones whom, under other circumstances, the amorous youth of our column would have so enthusiastically led under that spray which accords so sweet a license? The young ones prattled of those impossible joys; but the seniors, less frivolous, were concerned by the increasing narrowness of the gorge, and by the dropping fire that hung on our skirts as we entered it. However, there was but one casualty—a poor fellow of the 17th Regiment had his thigh smashed by a bullet—and we spent the night under the ilex trees without further molestation... It was Christmas Eve when we sat chatting with young Beatson in his lonely post by the Chardai streamlet; but a few hours of morning riding would carry us to Jellalabad whither Sir Sam Browne's camp had been advanced, and we were easy on the score of being true to tryst. As in the cold grey dawn we resumed our journey, leaving the young officer who had been our host to concern himself with the watchfulness of his picquets and the vigilance of his patrols, there was a sound of unintentional mockery in the conventional wish of a 'Merry Christmas' to the gallant lad, and there was a wistfulness in his answering smile... The road to the encampment, the white canvas of whose tents showed through the intervening hills, was traversed at a hand gallop; and presently Kinloch and myself found ourselves in the street of the headquarter camp, shaking hands with friends and comrades, and trying to reply to a medley of disjointed questions. The bugles were sounding for the Christmas Day Church Parade as we finished a hurried breakfast. Out there on the plain the British troops of the division were standing in hollow square, the officers grouped in the centre... The headquarter street we found swept and garnished, the flagstaff bedecked with holly, and a regimental band playing 'Home, Sweet Home.' Dear old Sir Sam Browne did not believe in luxury when on campaign, but now for the first time I saw him at least comfortable... The mess anteroom was the camp street outside the dining tent; and at the fashionable late hour of eight we 'went in' to dinner, to the strains of the *Roast Beef of Old England*. It was a right jovial feast, and the most cordial good-fellowship prevailed. He would have been a cynical epicurean who would have criticised the appointments; the banquet itself was above all cavil. Rummaging among some old papers the other day, I found the *menu*, which deserves to be quoted: 'Soup—Julienne. Fish—Whitebait (from the Cabul River). Entrées—Cotelettes aux Champignons, Poulets à la Mayonaise. Joints—Ham and fowls, roast beef, roast saddle of mutton, boiled brisket of beef, boiled leg of mutton and caper sauce. Curry—chicken. Sweets—Lemon jelly, blancmange, apricot tart, plum-pudding. Grilled sardines, cheese fritters, cheese, dessert.' Truth compels the avowal that there was no table-linen, nor was the board resplendent with plate or gay with flowers. Table crockery was deficient, or to be more accurate, there was none. All the dishes were of metal, and the soup was eaten, or rather drunk, out of mugs and iron teacups. But it tasted none the worse on this account, and let it be recorded that there *were* champagne glasses, while between every two guests a portly magnum reared its golden head. Except 'The Queen,' of course, there were but two toasts after the feast— one was 'Absent Friends,' drunk in a wistful silence, and the other, the caterer's health, greeted with vociferous enthusiasm. A few fields off the wood had been collecting all day for the Christmas camp-fire of the 10th Hussars, and by ten o'clock the blaze of it was mounting high into the murky gloom. A right merry and social gathering it was round the bright glow of this Yule log in a far-off land. The flames danced on the wide circle of bearded faces, on the tangled fleeces of the postheens, on the gold braid of the forage caps, on the sombre hoods of beshliks... The songs ranged from gay to grave; the former mood in the ascendency. But occasionally there was sung a ditty, the associations with which brought it about that there came something strangely like a tear into the voice of the singer, and that a yearning wistfulness fell upon the faces of the listeners. The bronzed troopers in the background shaded with their hands the fire-flash from their eyes; and as the familiar homely strain ceased that recalled home and love and trailed at the heart strings till the breast felt to heave and the tears to rise, there would be a little pause of eloquent silence which told how thoughts had gone astraying half across the globe to the loved ones in dear old England, and were loath to come back again to the rum and the camp fire in Jellalabad plain. Ah, how many stood or sat around that camp fire that were never to see old England more? The snow had not melted on the Sufed Koh when half a squadron of the troopers were drowned in the treacherous Cabul river. No brighter soul or sweeter singer round that fire than Monty Slade; but the life went out of Monty Slade with his face to the foe and his wet sword grasped in a soldier-grip; and he lies under the palm trees by the wells of El Teb."

CHRISTMAS IN CANADA.

In Canada the severe and long-continued frosts convert a good deal of land and water into fields of ice, and skating is a very popular amusement of Christmastide. Sleighing is also very fashionable, and the large tracts of country covered with snow afford ample scope for the pastime. The jingle of the sleigh bells is heard in all the principal thoroughfares which at the season of the great winter festival present quite an animated appearance. The ears of the sleigh drivers are usually covered either by the cap or with a comforter, which in very cold weather is also wrapped over the mouth and nose.

"Christmas Day," says an English Colonist, "is spent quietly in our own houses. New Year's Day is the day of general rejoicing, when every one either visits or receives their friends: and so, thinking of the merry times we have had in Old England, and comparing them with the quietness of to-day, we feel more like strangers in a strange land than ever before.

"As a special treat, we are to have a real English Christmas dinner to-day, and our housekeeper has made a wonderful plum-pudding. The turkey is already steaming upon the table, and we soon fall to work upon him. He is well cooked, but there seems to be something wrong with his legs, which are so tough and sinewy that we come to the conclusion that he must have been training for a walking match. The rest of the dinner passes off very well, with the exception of the plum-pudding, which has to be brought to the table in a basin, as it firmly refuses to bind.

"After dinner we retire to the sitting-room, and sit round the stove talking, while those of us addicted to the fragrant weed have a quiet smoke. Thus passes Christmas afternoon.

"Tea-time soon comes round, and after we have refreshed ourselves, we resolve to end the day by paying a visit to a neighbour who possesses an American organ, and Christmas evening closes in to the music of those sweet old carols which that evening are heard over the whole world wherever an English colony is to be found."

CHRISTMAS IN AUSTRALIA.

Christmas festivities in Australia are carried on in what we should call "summer weather." There is no lack of good cheer and good living, but cold and snow are at this season unknown, and skating and snowballing, as a consequence, are sports unheard of at Christmastide by the youth in the Antipodes. Large parties and excursions are often arranged for spending a short time in the parks and fields, and Christmas picnics partake much of the character of English "gipsy-parties." The inhabitants being chiefly English, many of the ceremonies customary in English homes are observed, and the changes that are made are enforced for the most part by the difference in climate, and by the altered circumstances under which the various festivities are arranged.

In "A Summer Christmas," Douglas B. W. Sladen thus describes the Australian festivities:—

"The Christmas dinner was at two,
And all that wealth or pains could do
Was done to make it a success;
And marks of female tastefulness,
And traces of a lady's care,
Were noticeable everywhere.
The port was old, the champagne dry,
And every kind of luxury
Which Melbourne could supply was there.
They had the staple Christmas fare,
Roast beef and turkey (this was wild),
Mince-pies, plum-pudding, rich and mild,
One for the ladies, one designed
For Mr. Forte's severer mind,
Were on the board, yet in a way
It did not seem like Christmas day

With no gigantic beech yule-logs
Blazing between the brass fire-dogs,
And with 100° in the shade
On the thermometer displayed.
Nor were there Christmas offerings
Of tasteful inexpensive things,
Like those which one in England sends
At Christmas to his kin and friends,
Though the Professor with him took
A present of a recent book
For Lil and Madge and Mrs. Forte,
And though a card of some new sort
Had been arranged by Lil to face
At breakfast everybody's place.
When dinner ended nearly all
Stole off to lounges in the hall.

* * * * *

All save the two old folks and Lil,
Who made their hearts expand and thrill
By playing snatches, slow and clear,
Of carols they'd been used to hear
Of carols they'd been used to hear
Some half a century ago
At High Wick Manor, when the two
Were bashful maidens: they talked on,
Of England and what they had done
On byegone Christmas nights at home,
Of friends beyond the Northern foam,
And friends beyond that other sea,
Yet further—whither ceaselessly
Travellers follow the old track,
But whence no messenger comes back."

CHRISTMAS IN NEW ZEALAND.

In 1887, we received a letter from Mr. W. M. Stanton, of
Nelson, New Zealand, giving the following interesting account of
the colonists' observance of Christmas:—

"And now, as to Christmas, I wish I could express all I feel on this peculiarly English season of 'peace and goodwill.' I remember the picturesque snow (seen here only on the distant blue mountain tops), the icy stalactites pendant from the leafless branches, the twitter of the robin redbreast, the holly, and the mistletoe, decorated homes, redolent with the effects of the festive cooking, and the warm blazing firelight, the meeting of families and of friends, the waits, the grand old peals from the belfries; but, alas, here these childhood associations are dispelled, half broken, and we acclimatised denizens adapt our festivities to other modes—not that we forget the Christmas season, but enjoy it differently, as I will briefly tell you, as you ask, 'how we spend Christmas in New Zealand.' First, our ladies decorate the churches for the Christmas services, not with the evergreens of old exclusively; they do indeed affect the holly, ivy, and (New Zealand) mistletoe, but they make up with umbrageous and rich ferns, lachipoden, lauristinas, Portugal laurels, and our own beautiful evergreen, Ngaio, and with all the midsummer flowers at command; then the clerk, the storeman, the merchant, and the mechanic indulge in 'trips,' or day excursions, in small steamboats, to the neighbouring bays surrounding small townships, and villages on the coast. Others again, take the train for a day's outing and play quoits, rounders, lawn tennis, and the like; the sportsman, perhaps, preferring his gun and his dog; families, again, are picnic-mad, for your colonist can rival the Cockney any day for making his holiday in the country. It may be to 'the rocks' he goes to watch his youngsters paddling in the rolling tide, or to the toil of clambering up the 'dim mountain,' which seems to suit their hardy lungs better than the shade of the 'fern glen,' and a journey of eighteen miles to the Maori Pa is as nothing. The Union Company's fine coasting steamships run passengers at half fares at this season, and the result is an interchange of visits between the dwellers in Nelson, Wellington, Marlboro', and Wanjani, amongst whom there is much rivalry and more friendship. Then there is the Christmas regatta, the performance of the 'Messiah' by the musical societies, and the inevitable evening dances, and thus the New Zealand Christmas is spent.

"I am reminded, by my young clerk, that the mail is about closing, and that this letter must also close, if it is to go to-day, and thus I must omit the mention of the new year's festivities, which properly belong to our numerous Scottish fellow settlers who in their own country ignore Christmas as a popish superstition; they are, however, now becoming anglicised ('Englified' they call it) in their habits, and similarly the Midland county men of England enter into their Caledonian custom, from the harmless orgies of 'Hagmenae' to the frantic capers of 'Gillie Cullum,' to the skirl of the panting piper."

CHRISTMAS AT THE SANDWICH ISLANDS.

In "A Voyage in the *Sunbeam*," Lady Brassey gives an interesting account of the keeping of Christmas, 1876, on the Sandwich Islands. We quote the following extracts:—

"Twenty minutes' hard riding brought us to the door of the 'Volcano House,' from which issued the comforting light of a large wood fire, reaching half way up the chimney.

"Everything at this inn is most comfortable, though the style is rough and ready. The interior is just now decorated for Christmas, with wreaths, and evergreens, and ferns, and branches of white plumes, not unlike *reva-reva*, made from the path of the silver grass.

"The grandeur of the view in the direction of the volcano increased as the evening wore on. The fiery cloud above the present crater grew in size and depth of colour; the extinct crater glowed red in thirty or forty different places; and clouds of white vapour issued from every crack and crevice in the ground, adding to the sulphurous smell with which the atmosphere was laden. Our room faced the volcano: there were no blinds, and I drew back the curtains and lay watching the splendid scene until I fell asleep.

"*Sunday, December 24th (Christmas Eve)*—I was up at four o'clock to gaze once more on the wondrous spectacle that lay before me. The molten lava still glowed in many places, the red cloud over the fiery lake was bright as ever, and steam was slowly ascending in every direction over hill and valley, till, as the sun rose, it became difficult to distinguish clearly the sulphurous vapours from the morning mists. We walked down to the Sulphur Banks, about a quarter of a mile from the 'Volcano House,' and burnt our gloves and boots in our endeavours to procure crystals, the beauty of which generally disappeared after a very short exposure to the air. We succeeded, however, in finding a few good specimens, and, by wrapping them at once in paper and cotton-wool and putting them into a bottle, hope to bring them home uninjured.

"*Monday, December 25th (Christmas Day)*—Turning in last night was the work of a very few minutes, and this morning I awoke perfectly refreshed and ready to appreciate anew the wonders of the prospect that met my eyes. The pillar of fire was still distinctly visible, when I looked out from my window, though it was not so bright as when I had last seen it, but even as I looked it began to fade and gradually disappeared. At the same moment a river of glowing lava issued from the side of the bank we had climbed with so much difficulty yesterday, and slowly but surely overflowed the ground we had walked over. You may imagine the feelings with which we gazed upon this startling phenomenon, which had it occurred a few hours earlier, might have caused the destruction of the whole party.

* * * * *

"It would, I think, be difficult to imagine a more interesting and exciting mode of spending Christmas Eve than yesterday has taught us, or a stranger situation in which to exchange our Christmas greetings than beneath the grass roof of an inn on the edge of a volcano in the remote Sandwich Islands.

* * * * *

"The ride down to Hilo was as dull and monotonous as our upward journey had been. At last we reached the pier, where we found the usual little crowd waiting to see us off. The girls who had followed us when we first landed came forward shyly when they thought they were unobserved, and again encircled me with *leis* of gay and fragrant flowers. The custom of decorating themselves with wreaths on every possible occasion is in my eyes a charming one, and I like the inhabitants of Polynesia for their love of flowers.

"The whole town was *en fête* to-day. Natives were riding about in pairs, in the cleanest of bright cotton dresses and the freshest of *leis* and garlands. Our own men from the yacht contributed not a little to the gaiety of the scene. They were all on shore, and the greater part of them were galloping about on horseback, tumbling off, scrambling on again, laughing, flirting, joking, and enjoying themselves generally after a fashion peculiar to English sailors. As far as we know the only evil result of all this merriment was that the doctor received a good many applications for diachylon plaster in the course of the evening, to repair various 'abrasions of the cuticle,' as he expressed it.

"I think at least half the population of Hilo had been on board the yacht in the course of the day, as a Christmas treat. At last we took a boat and went off too, accompanied by Mr. Lyman. The appearance of the 'Sunbeam' from the shore was very gay, and as we approached it became more festive still. All her masts were tipped with sugar-canes in bloom. Her stern was adorned with flowers, and in the arms of the figurehead was a large bouquet. She was surrounded with boats, the occupants of which cheered us heartily as we rode alongside. The whole deck was festooned with tropical plants and flowers, and the decorations of the cabins were even more beautiful and elaborate. I believe all hands had been hard at work ever since we left to produce this wonderful effect, and every garden in Hilo had furnished a contribution to please and surprise us on our return.

"The choir from Hilo came out in boats in the evening, sang all sorts of songs, sacred and secular, and cheered everybody till they were hoarse. After this, having had a cold dinner, in order to save trouble, and having duly drunk the health of our friends at home, we all adjourned to the saloon, to assist in the distribution of some Christmas presents—a ceremony which afforded great delight to the children, and which was equally pleasing to the elder people and to the crew, if one may judge from their behaviour on the occasion.

"Then we sat on deck, gazing at the cloud of fire over Kilauea, and wondering if the appearance of the crater could ever be grander than it was last night, when we were standing on its brim.

"So ended Christmas Day, 1876, at Hilo, in Hawaii. God grant that there may be many more as pleasant for us in the future!"

CHRISTMAS ON BOARD THE "SUNBEAM," 1879.

"The wind is chill,
But let it whistle as it will
We'll keep our Christmas merry still."

In "Sunshine and Storm in the East, or Cruises to Cyprus and Constantinople," Lady Brassey gives an interesting account of the celebration of Christmas on board the *Sunbeam*, between Malta and Marseilles, December 25, 1879:—"We had service early and then spent a long busy morning in arranging all the presents for the children, servants, and crew, and in decorating the cabin. We could not manage any holly, but we had carefully preserved one bough of mistletoe from Artaki Bay, and had brought on board at Malta baskets full of flowers, so that all the pictures, lamps, and even walls, were wreathed with festoons of bougainvillæa, ivy, and other creeping plants; while in every available corner were placed, vases, bowls, and soup-plates, containing flowers. If not exactly 'gay with holly-berries,' so dear to English hearts from their association with yule-tide at home, the general appearance of the cabins was highly satisfactory. In the meantime they had been busy in the kitchen and pantry departments, preparing all sorts of good things for dinner, and pretty things for dessert, in order that the crew and servants might enjoy a more sumptuous repast than usual. A Christmas tree, a snow man, or an ice cave, for the distribution of presents, was not within the limit of our resources; but we decorated our tables and sideboards with bright shawls and scarves, and wreathed and divided the surface of each with garlands of flowers, placing in every division a pretty Christmas card, bearing the name of the recipient of the present, which was hidden away among the flowers beneath... For the men there was plenty of tobacco, besides books and useful things; for the children toys; and for ourselves, slippers and little remembrances of various kinds, some sent from home to meet us, others recent purchases. The distribution over, one or two speeches were made, and mutual congratulations and good wishes were exchanged. Then the crew and servants retired to enjoy the, to them, all-important event of the day—dinner and dessert. After our own late dinner, we thought of those near and dear to us at home, and drank to the health of 'absent friends.'"

A MISSIONARY'S CHRISTMAS IN CHINA.

In a letter from Tsing Cheu Fu Chefoo, December 24, 1887, the Rev. A. G. Jones, Baptist missionary, says:—

"Mr. Dawson asks how Englishmen spend Christmas in China. Well, it depends. Some spend it at the ports dog-racing and eating pudding—having a night of it. The missionaries generally take no notice of it. In our mission we hold one of the semi-annual dedication-of-children services on Christmas. We think it a very appropriate day for the recognition of the sacredness of the gift of trust of children. The idea is a Chinese one, originating with one of our Christians, and we adopted it as the day for the custom. Tomorrow will be Christmas Day, and I have come out twenty miles this evening to hold a service of that kind with the semi-annual communion as it happens. It will be a cold, cheerless room in a clay-built cabin down in the corner of a bare valley in a trap and basalt district with sparse vegetation and a bare aspect. A cold spot with a handful of Christians, bearing their testimony alone out on the margin of our field of work. I hope to see 40 or 50 patients up to sundown, and then have worship with them at night. That will be my Christmas. This evening—in the city—all the children and our wives are having a Christmas tree in the theological lecture-room, and on Tuesday next I guess we'll have our dinner. John Bull, Paddy, Sandy, and Taffy all seem to agree in *that* feature. My Sunday will only be a sample of others. So it goes—working away. Now I must say goodbye. Many thanks and many good wishes."

A VISIT TO CHRISTMAS ISLAND.

Letters were received in December, 1887, from H.M.S. *Egeria*, Commander Pelham Aldrich, containing particulars of a visit she had recently made to Christmas Island, which she was ordered to explore for scientific purposes. Christmas Island is situated in the Indian Ocean, in latitude 11° south, longitude 105° 30' east; it is 1,100 feet above the sea, is twelve miles long and eight miles broad. The officers and men told off for exploring purposes found that the whole place was composed of coral and rock; notwithstanding this, however, it is covered almost completely with trees and shrubs, the trees, which are of large dimensions, seeming to grow literally out of the rock itself, earth surfaces being conspicuous by their absence. It is uninhabited by human beings, nor could any traces of animals be discovered, but seabirds swarm over every part of the island, and about four hundred wood pigeons were shot by the explorers while they remained there. No fruits or vegetable matter fit for consumption could, however, be found, nor the existence of any supply of fresh water, and the belief is that the vegetation of the island is dependent for nourishment on the dews and the heavy rains that fall.

CHRISTMAS IN AMERICA.

Writing just before the Christmas festival of 1855, Mr. Howard Paul says the general manner of celebrating Christmas Day is much the same wherever professors of the Christian faith are found; and the United States, as the great Transatlantic offshoot of Saxon principles, would be the first to conserve the traditional ceremonies handed down from time immemorial by our canonical progenitors of the East. But every nation has its idiocratic notions, minute and otherwise, and it is not strange that the Americans, as a creative people, have peculiar and varied ways of their own in keeping this, the most remarkable day in the calendar. Now and then they add a supplemental form to the accepted code—characteristic of the mutable and progressive spirit of the people—though there still exists the Church service, the conventional carol, the evergreen decorations, the plum-puddings, the pantomime, and a score of other "demonstrations" that never can legitimately be forgotten.

Society generally seems to apportion the day thus: Church in the morning, dinner in the afternoon, and amusements in the evening. The Christmas dinners concentrate the scattered members of families, who meet together to break bread in social harmony, and exchange those home sentiments that cement the happiness of kindred. To-day the prodigal once more returns to the paternal roof; the spendthrift forsakes his boon companions; the convivialist deserts the wine-cup. The beautiful genius of domestic love has triumphed, and who can foresee the blessed results?

Parties, balls, and fêtes, with their endless routine of gaieties, are looked forward to, as pleasures are, the wide world over; and all classes, from highest to lowest, have their modes of enjoyment marked out. Preparation follows preparation in festal succession. Sorrow hides her Gorgon head, care may betake itself to any dreary recesses, for Christmas must be a gala!

There is generally snow on the ground at this time; if Nature is amiable, there is sure to be; and a Christmas sleigh-ride is one of those American delights that defy rivalry. There is no withstanding the merry chime of the bells and a fleet passage over the snow-skirted roads. Town and country look as if they had arisen in the morning in robes of unsullied white. Every housetop is spangled with the bright element; soft flakes are coquetting in the atmosphere, and a pure mantle has been spread on all sides, that fairly invites one to disport upon its gleaming surface.

We abide quietly within our pleasant home on either the eve or night of Christmas. How the sleighs glide by in rapid glee, the music of the bells and the songs of the excursionists falling on our ears in very wildness. We strive in vain to content ourselves. We glance at the cheerful fire, and hearken to the genial voices around us. We philosophise, and struggle against the tokens of merriment without; but the restraint is torture. We, too, must join the revellers, and have a sleigh-ride. Girls, get on your fur; wrap yourselves up warmly in the old bear-skin; hunt up the old guitar; the sleigh is at the door, the moon is beaming. The bells tinkle and away we go!

An old English legend was transplanted many years ago on the shores of America, that took root and flourished with wonderful luxuriance, considering it was not indigenous to the country. Probably it was taken over to New York by one of the primitive Knickerbockers, or it might have clung to some of the drowsy burgomasters who had forsaken the pictorial tiles of dear old Amsterdam about the time of Peter de Laar, or Il Bombaccia, as the Italians call him, got into disgrace in Rome. However this may be, certain it is that Santa Claus, or St. Nicholas, the kind Patron-saint of the Juveniles, makes his annual appearance on Christmas Eve, for the purpose of dispensing gifts to all good children. This festive elf is supposed to be a queer little creature that descends the chimney, viewlessly, in the deep hours of night, laden with gifts and presents, which he bestows with no sparing hand, reserving to himself a supernatural discrimination that he seems to exercise with every satisfaction. Before going to bed the children hang their newest stockings near the chimney, or pin them to the curtains of the bed. Midnight finds a world of hosiery waiting for favours; and the only wonder is that a single Santa Claus can get around among them all. The story goes that he never misses one, provided it belongs to a deserving youngster, and morning is sure to bring no reproach that the Christmas Wizard has not nobly performed his wondrous duties. We need scarcely enlighten the reader as to who the real Santa Claus is. Every indulgent parent contributes to the pleasing deception, though the juveniles are strong in their faith of their generous holiday patron. The following favourite lines graphically describe a visit of St. Nicholas, and, being in great vogue with the young people of America, are fondly reproduced from year to year:—

"'Twas the night before Christmas, when all through the house,

> Not a creature was stirring, not even a mouse;
> The stockings were hung by the chimney with care,
> In the hope that St. Nicholas soon would be there.
> The children were nestled all snug in their beds,
> While visions of sugar plums danced through their heads;
> And mamma in her 'kerchief, and I in my cap,
> Had just settled our brains for a long winter's nap,
> When out on the lawn there arose such a clatter,
> I sprang from my bed to see what was the matter.
> The way to the window, I flew like a flash,
> Tore open the shutters, and threw up the sash;
> The moon on the breast of the new-fallen snow
> Gave the lustre of mid-day to objects below.
> When what to my wondering eyes should appear
> But a miniature sleigh and eight tiny reindeer;
> With a little old driver, so lively and quick,
> I knew in a moment it must be St. Nick.
> More rapid than eagles his coursers they came,
> And he whistled, and shouted, and called them by name—
> Now Dasher! now Dancer! Now Prancer! now Vixen!
> On Comet! on Cupid! on Donder and Blixen!
> To the top of the porch, to the top of the wall!
> Now dash away! dash away! dash away all!'
> As the leaves that before the wild hurricane fly,
> When they meet with an obstacle, mount to the sky;
> So up to the house-top the coursers they flew,
> With the sleigh full of toys, and St. Nicholas too.
> And then in a twinkling I heard on the roof,

The prancing and pawing of each little hoof;
As I drew in my head and was turning around,
Down the chimney St. Nicholas came with a bound.
He was dressed all in furs from his head to his foot
And his clothes were all tarnished with ashes and soot.
A bundle of toys he had flung on his back,
And he looked like a pedlar just opening his pack.
His eyes, how they twinkled! his dimples, how merry!
His cheeks were like roses, his nose like a cherry;
His droll little mouth was drawn up like a bow,
And the beard of his chin was as white as the snow.
The stump of a pipe he held tight in his teeth,
And the smoke it encircled his head like a wreath.
He had a broad face and a little round belly
That shook when he laughed, like a bowl full of jelly.
He was chubby and plump—a right jolly old elf;
And I laughed when I saw him, in spite of myself.
A wink of his eye and a twist of his head
Soon gave me to know I had nothing to dread.
He spoke not a word, but went straight to his work,
And filled all the stockings—then turned with a jerk,
And laying his finger aside of his nose,
And giving a nod, up the chimney he rose;
He sprang to his sleigh, to his team gave a whistle,
And away they all flew like the down of a thistle.
But I heard him exclaim, ere he drove out of sight,
'Happy Christmas to all, and to all a good night!'"

A curious feature of an American Christmas is the egg-nogg and free lunch, distributed at all the hotels and cafés. A week at least before the 25th fanciful signs are suspended over the fountains of the bars (the hotel-keepers are quite classic in their ideas) announcing superb lunch and egg-noggs on Christmas Day. This invitation is sure to meet with a large response from the amateur epicures about town, who, ever on the *qui vive* for a banquet gratis, flock to the festive standard, since it has never been found a difficult matter to give things away, from the time old Heliogabalus gastronomed in Phœnicia up to the present hour. A splendid hall in one of the principal hotels, at this moment, occurs to us. A table, the length of the apartment, is spread and furnished with twenty made dishes peculiar to the Christmas *cuisine*. There are *chorodens* and *fricassees*, *ragoûts* and *calipee*, of rapturous delicacy. Each dish is labelled, and attended by a black servant, who serves its contents on very small white gilt-edged plates. At the head of the table a vast bowl, ornamented with indescribable Chinese figures, contains the egg-nogg—a palatable compound of milk, eggs, brandy, and spices, nankeenish in colour, with froth enough on its surface to generate any number of Venuses, if the old Peloponnesian anecdote is worth remembering at all. Over the egg-nogg mine host usually officiates, all smiles and benignity, pouring the rich draught with miraculous dexterity into cut-glass goblets, and passing it to the surrounding guests with profuse hand. On this occasion the long range of fancy drinks are forgotten. Sherry-cobblers, mint-juleps, gin-slings, and punches, are set aside in order that the sway of the Christmas draught may be supreme. Free lunches are extremely common in the United States, what are called "eleven o'clock snacks" especially; but the accompaniment of egg-nogg belongs unequivocally to the death of the year.

The presentation of "boxes" and souvenirs is the same in America as in England, the token of remembrance having an inseparable alliance with the same period. Everybody expects to give and receive. A month before the event the fancy stores are crowded all day long with old and young in search of suitable *souvenirs*, and every object is purchased, from costliest gems to the tawdriest *babiole* that may get into the market. If the weather should be fine, the principal streets are thronged with ladies shopping in sleighs; and hither and thither sleds shoot by, laden with parcels of painted toys, instruments of mock music and septuagenarian dread, from a penny trumpet to a sheepskin drum.

Christmas seems to be a popular period among the young folk for being mated, and a surprising number approach the altar this morning. Whether it is that orange-flowers and bridal gifts are admirably adapted to the time, or that a longer lease of happiness is ensured from the joyous character of the occasion, we are not sufficiently learned in hymeneal lore to announce. The Christmas week, however, is a merry one for the honeymoon, as little is thought of but mirth and gaiety until the dawning New Year soberly suggests that we should put aside our masquerade manners.

In drawing-room amusements society has a wealth of pleasing indoor pastimes. We remember the sententious Question *réunions*, the hilarious Surprise parties, Fairy-bowl, and Hunt-the-slipper. We can never forget the vagabond Calathumpians, who employ in their bands everything inharmonious, from a fire-shovel to a stewpan, causing more din than the demons down under the sea ever dreamed of.

What, then, between the sleigh-rides, the bell-melodies, old Santa Claus and his fictions, the egg-nogg and lunches, the weddings and the willingness to be entertained, the Americans find no difficulty in enjoying Christmas Day. Old forms and new notions come in for a share of observances; and the young country, in a glow of good humour, with one voice exclaims, "Le bon temps vienara!"

President Harrison as "Santa Claus."

Writing from New York on December 22, 1891, a correspondent says: "President Harrison was seen by your correspondent at the White House yesterday, and was asked what he thought about Christmas and its religious and social influences. The President expressed himself willing to offer his opinions, and said: 'Christmas is the most sacred religious festival of the year, and should be an occasion of general rejoicing throughout the land, from the humblest citizen to the highest official, who, for the time being, should forget or put behind him his cares and annoyances, and participate in the spirit of seasonable festivity. We intend to make it a happy day at the White House—all the members of my family, representing four generations, will gather around the big table in the State dining-room to have an old-fashioned Christmas dinner. Besides Mrs. Harrison, there will be her father, Dr. Scott, Mr. and Mrs. M'Kee and their children, Mrs. Dimmick and Lieutenant and Mrs. Parker. I am an ardent believer in the duty we owe to ourselves as Christians to make merry for children at Christmas time, and we shall have an old-fashioned Christmas tree for the grandchildren upstairs; and I shall be their Santa Claus myself. If my influence goes for aught in this busy world let me hope that my example may be followed in every family in the land.'

"Christmas is made as much of in this country as it is in England, if not more. The plum-pudding is not universal, but the Christmas tree is in almost every home. Even in the tenement districts of the East side, inhabited by the labouring and poorer classes, these vernal emblems of the anniversary are quite as much in demand as in other quarters, and if they and the gifts hung upon them are less elaborate than their West side congeners, the household enthusiasm which welcomes them is quite as marked. As in London, the streets are flooded with Christmas numbers of the periodicals, which, it may be remarked, are this year more elaborate in design and execution than ever. The use of Christmas cards has also obtained surprising proportions. A marked feature of this year's Christmas is the variety and elegance of offerings after the Paris fashion, which are of a purely ornamental and but slight utilitarian character. There are bonbonnières in a variety of forms, some of them very magnificent and expensive; while the Christmas cards range in prices from a cent to ten dollars each. These bonbonnières, decked with expensive ribbon or hand-painted with designs of the season, attain prices as high as forty dollars each, and are in great favour among the wealthy classes. Flowers are also much used, and, just now, are exceedingly costly.

"While the usual religious ceremonies of the day are generally observed here, the mass of the community are inclined to treat the occasion as a festive rather than a solemn occasion, and upon festivity the whole population at the present time seems bent."

"Merry Christmas" with the Negroes.

A journalist who has been amongst the negroes in the Southern States of America thus describes their Christmas festivities:—

"Christmas in the South of the United States is a time-honoured holiday season, as ancient as the settlement of the Cavalier colonies themselves. We may imagine it to have been imported from 'merrie England' by the large-hearted Papist, Lord Baltimore, into Maryland, and by that chivalric group of Virginian colonists, of whom the central historical figure is the famous Captain John Smith, of Pocahontas memory. Perhaps Christmas was even the more heartily celebrated among these true Papist and Church of England settlers from the disgust which they felt at the stern contempt in which the Natal Day was held by 'stiff-necked Puritans' of New England. At least, while in New England the pilgrims were wont to work with exceptional might on Christmas Day, to show their detestation of it, traditions are still extant of the jovial Southern merrymaking of the festival. Christmas, with many of the Old England customs imported to the new soil, derived new spirit and enjoyment from customs which had their origin in the Colonies themselves. Above all was it the gala season—the period to be looked forward to and revelled in—of the negroes. Slavery, with all its horrors and wickedness, had at least some genial features; and the latitude which the masters gave to the slaves at Christmas time, the freedom with which the blacks were wont to concentrate a year's enjoyment into the Christmas week, was one of these. In Washington, where until the war slavery existed in a mild and more civilised form, the negro celebrations of Christmas were the peculiar and amusing feature of the season. And many of these customs, which grew up amid slavery, have survived that institution. The Washington negroes, free, have pretty much the same zest for their time-honoured amusements which they had when under the dominion of the oligarchy. Christmas is still their great gala and occasion for merry-making, and the sable creatures thoroughly understand the art of having a good time, being superior, at least in this respect, to many a *blasé* Prince and Court noble distracted with *ennui*. Those who have seen the 'Minstrels' may derive some idea, though but a slight one, of the negro pastimes and peculiarities. They are, above all, a social, enthusiastic, whole-souled race; they have their own ideas of rank and social caste, and they have a humour which is homely, but thoroughly genial, and quite the monopoly of their race. They insist on the whole of Christmas week for a holiday. 'Missus' must manage how she can. To insist on chaining them down in the kitchen during that halcyon time would stir up blank rebellion. Dancing and music are their favourite Christmas recreations; they manage both with a will. In the city suburbs there are many modest little frame-houses inhabited by the blacks; now and then a homely inn kept by a dusky landlord. Here in Christmas time you will witness many jolly and infectiously pleasant scenes. There is a 'sound of revelry by night.' You are free to enter, and observe near by the countless gyrations of the negro cotillon, the intricate and deftly executed jig, the rude melody of banjos and 'cornstalk fiddles.' They are always proud to have 'de white folks ' for spectators and applauders, and will give you the best seat, and will outdo themselves in their anxiety to show off at their best before you. You will be astonished to observe the scrupulous neatness of the men, the gaudy and ostentatious habiliments of 'de ladies.' The negroes have an intense ambition to imitate the upper classes of white society. They will study the apparel of a well-dressed gentleman, and squander their money on 'swallow-tail' coats, high dickeys, white neckties, and the most elaborate arts of their dusky barbers. The women are even more imitative of their mistresses. Ribbons, laces, and silks adorn them, on festive occasions, of the most painfully vivid colours, and fashioned in all the extravagance of negro taste. Not less anxious are they to imitate the manners of aristocracy. The excessive chivalry and overwhelming politeness of the men towards the women is amazing. They make gallant speeches in which they insert as many of the longest and most learned words as they can master, picked up at random, and not always peculiarly adapted to the use made of them. Their excitement in the dance, and at the sound of music, grows as intense as does their furor in a Methodist revival meeting. They have, too, dances and music peculiar to themselves—jigs and country dances which seem to have no method, yet which are perfectly adapted to and rhythmic with the inspiring abrupt thud of the banjo and the bones. As they dance, they shout and sing, slap their hands and knees, and lose themselves in the enthusiasm of the moment. The negroes look forward to Christmas not less as the season for present-giving than that of frolicking and jollity. Early in the morning they hasten upstairs, and catch 'massa' and 'missus' and 'de chillun' with a respectful but eager 'Merry Christmas,' and are sure to get in return a new coat or pair of boots, a gingham dress, or ear-rings more showy than expensive. They have saved up, too, a pittance from their wages, to expend in a souvenir for 'Dinah' or 'Pompey,' the never-to-be-forgotten belle or sweetheart."

CHRISTMAS IN FRANCE.

The following account of Christmas in France, in 1823, is given by an English writer of the period:—

405

"The habits and customs of Parisians vary much from those of our own metropolis at all times, but at no time more than at this festive season. An Englishman in Paris, who had been for some time without referring to his almanac, would not know Christmas Day from another day by the appearance of the capital. It is indeed set down as a *jour de fête* in the calendar, but all the ordinary business life is transacted; the streets are as usual, crowded with waggons and coaches; the shops, with few exceptions, are open, although on other *fête* days the order for closing them is rigorously enforced, and if not attended to, a fine levied; and at the churches nothing extraordinary is going forward. All this is surprising in a Catholic country, which professes to pay much attention to the outward rites of religion.

"On *Christmas Eve*, indeed, there is some bustle for a midnight mass, to which immense numbers flock, as the priests, on this occasion, get up a showy spectacle which rivals the theatres. The altars are dressed with flowers, and the churches decorated profusely; but there is little in all this to please men who have been accustomed to the John Bull mode of spending the evening. The good English habit of meeting together to forgive offences and injuries, and to cement reconciliations, is here unknown. The French listen to the Church music, and to the singing of their choirs, which is generally excellent, but they know nothing of the origin of the day and of the duties which it imposes. The English residents in Paris, however, do not forget our mode of celebrating this day. Acts of charity from the rich to the needy, religious attendance at church, and a full observance of hospitable rites, are there witnessed. Paris furnishes all the requisites for a good pudding, and the turkeys are excellent, though the beef is not to be displayed as a prize production.

"On *Christmas Day* all the English cooks in Paris are in full business. The queen of cooks, however, is Harriet Dunn, of the Boulevard. As Sir Astley Cooper among the cutters of limbs, and d'Egville among the cutters of capers, so is Harriet Dunn among the professors of one of the most necessary, and in its results most gratifying professions in existence; her services are secured beforehand by special retainers; and happy is the peer who can point to his pudding, and declare that it is of the true Dunn composition. Her fame has even extended to the provinces. For some time previous to Christmas Day, she forwards puddings in cases to all parts of the country, ready cooked and fit for the table, after the necessary warming. All this is, of course, for the English. No prejudice can be stronger than that of the French against plum-pudding—a Frenchman will dress like an Englishman, swear like an Englishman, and get drunk like an Englishman; but if you would offend him for ever compel him to eat plum-pudding. A few of the leading restaurateurs, wishing to appear extraordinary, have *plomb-pooding* upon their cartes, but in no instance is it ever ordered by a Frenchman. Everybody has heard the story of St. Louis—Henri Qautre, or whoever else it might be—who, wishing to regale the English ambassador on Christmas Day with a plum-pudding, procured an excellent recipe for making one, which he gave to his cook, with strict injunctions that it should be prepared with due attention to all particulars. The weight of the ingredients, the size of the copper, the quantity of water, the duration of time, everything was attended to except one trifle—the king forgot the cloth, and the pudding was served up, like so much soup in immense tureens, to the surprise of the ambassador, who was, however, too well bred to express his astonishment. Louis XVIII., either to show his contempt of the prejudices of his countrymen, or to keep up a custom which suits his palate, has always an enormous pudding on Christmas Day, the remains of which, when it leaves the table, he requires to be eaten by the servants, *bon gré, mauvais gré*; but in this instance even the commands of sovereignty are disregarded, except by the numerous English in his service, consisting of several valets, grooms, coachmen, &c., besides a great number of ladies' maids in the service of the duchesses of Angouleme and Berri, who very frequently partake of the dainties of the king's table."

In his "Year Book, 1832," Hone says that at Rouen, after the *Te Deum*, in the nocturnal office or vigil of Christmas, the ecclesiastics celebrated the "office of the shepherds" in the following manner:—

"The image of the Virgin Mary was placed in a stable prepared behind the altar. A boy from above, before the choir, in the likeness of an angel, announced the nativity to certain canons or vicars, who entered as shepherds through the great door of the choir, clothed in tunicks and amesses. Many boys in the vaults of the church, like angels, then began the '*gloria in excelsis.*' The shepherds, hearing this, advanced to the stable, singing '*peace, goodwill*,' &c. As soon as they entered it, two priests in dalmaticks, as if women (quasi obstetrices) who were stationed at the stable, said, 'Whom seek ye?' The shepherds answered, according to the angelic annunciation, 'Our Saviour Christ.' The women then opening the curtain exhibited the boy, saying, 'The little one is here as the Prophet Isaiah said.' They then showed the mother, saying, 'Behold the Virgin,' &c. Upon these exhibitions they bowed and worshipped the boy, and saluted his mother. The office ended by their returning to the choir, and singing, Alleluia, &c."[95]

Christmas Day in Besieged Paris.

Christmas, Paris,
Sunday, Dec. 25, 1870, 98th day of the Siege.

"Never has a sadder Christmas dawned on any city. Cold, hunger, agony, grief, and despair sit enthroned at every habitation in Paris. It is the coldest day of the season and the fuel is very short; and the government has had to take hold of the fuel question, and the magnificent shade-trees that have for ages adorned the avenues of this city are all likely to go in the vain struggle to save France. So says the Official Journal of this morning. The sufferings of the past week exceed by far anything we have seen. There is scarcely any meat but horse-meat, and the government is now rationing. It carries out its work with impartiality. The omnibus-horse, the cab-horse, the work-horse, and the fancy-horse, all go alike in the mournful procession to the butchery shops—the magnificent blooded steed of the Rothschilds by the side of the old plug of the cabman. Fresh beef, mutton, pork are now out of the question. A little poultry yet remains at fabulous prices. In walking through the Rue St. Lazare I saw a middling-sized goose and chicken for sale in a shop-window, and I had the curiosity to step in and inquire the price (rash man that I was). The price of the goose was $25, and the chicken $7."[96]

Christmas in Paris in 1886.

The Paris correspondent of the *Daily Telegraph* writes:— "Although New Year's Day is the great French festival, the fashion of celebrating Christmas something after the English custom is gaining ground in Paris every year. Thus a good deal of mistletoe now makes its appearance on the boulevards and in the shop windows, and it is evident that the famous Druidical plant, which is shipped in such large quantities every year to England from Normandy and Brittany, is fast becoming popular among Parisians. Another custom, that of decorating Christmas trees in the English and German style, has become quite an annual solemnity here since the influx of Alsatians and Lorrainers, while it is considered *chic*, in many quarters, to eat approximate plum-pudding on the 25th of December. Unfortunately, the Parisian 'blom budding,' unless prepared by British hands, is generally a concoction of culinary atrocities, tasting, let us say, like saveloy soup and ginger-bread porridge. In a few instances the 'Angleesh blom budding' has been served at French tables in a soup tureen; and guests have been known to direct fearful and furtive glances towards it, just as an Englishman might regard with mingled feelings of surprise and suspicion a fricassee of frogs. But independently of foreign innovations, Parisians have their own way of celebrating Noël. To-night (Christmas Eve) for instance, there will be midnight masses in the principal churches, when appropriate canticles and Adam's popular 'Noël' will be sung. In many private houses the *boudin* will also be eaten after the midnight mass, the rich baptising it in champagne, and the *petit bourgeois*, who has not a wine cellar, in a cheap concoction of bottled stuff with a Bordeaux label but a strong Paris flavour. The feast of Noël is, however, more archaically, and at the same time more earnestly, celebrated in provincial France. In the south the head of the family kindles the yule-log, or *bûche-de-Noël*, which is supposed to continue burning until the arrival of spring. Paterfamilias also lights the *calen*, or Christmas lamp, which represents the Star of Bethlehem, and then all repair to the midnight mass in those picturesque groups which painters have delighted to commit to canvas. The inevitable *baraques*, or booths, which are allowed to remain on the great boulevards from Christmas Eve until the Feast of the Kings, on January 6, have made their appearance. They extend from the Place de la Madeleine to the Place de la République, and are also visible on some of the other boulevards of the metropolis. Their glittering contents are the same as usual, and, despite their want of novelty, crowds of people lounged along the boulevards this afternoon and inspected them with as much curiosity as if they formed part of a Russian fair which had been temporarily transported from Nijni Novgorod to Paris. What was more attractive, however, was the show of holly, mistletoe, fir-trees, camellias, tea-roses, and tulips in the famous flower-market outside the Madeleine. A large tent has been erected, which protects the sellers of winter flowers from the rain, and this gives the market a gayer and more brilliant appearance than usual. What strikes one more than anything else, however, is the number of French people whom one sees purchasing holly bushes and mistletoe, which they carry home in huge bundles, after the good old English fashion. Notwithstanding the dampness and gloom of the weather, which hovers between frost and rain, the general aspect of Paris to-day is one of cheerful and picturesque animation, and the laughing crowds with whom one jostles in the streets are thoroughly imbued with the festive character of the season.

CHRISTMAS IN NORMANDY.

In describing the old-custom-loving people of Lower Normandy, a writer on "Calvados," in 1884-5, thus refers to the season of Christmas and Twelfth-tide: "Now Christmas arrives, and young and old go up to greet the little child Jesus, lying on his bed of straw at the Virgin Mother's feet and smiling to all the world. Overhead the old cracked bell clangs exultant, answering to other bells faint and far on the midnight air; a hundred candles are burning and every church window shines through the darkness like the gates of that holy New Jerusalem 'whose light was as a stone most precious—a jasper-stone clear as crystal.' With Twelfth-tide this fair vision suffers a metamorphosis, blazoning out into the paganish saturnalia of bonfires, which in Calvados is transferred from St. John's Eve *le jour des Rois*. Red flames leap skyward, fed by dry pine fagots, and our erstwhile devout peasants, throwing moderation to the winds, join hands, dance, and leap for good luck through blinding smoke and embers, shouting their rude doggerel:

> "'Adieu les
> Rois Jusqu'a douze mois,
> Douze mois passes
> Les *bougelées*.'"

PROVENÇAL PLAYS AT CHRISTMASTIDE.

Heinrich Heine delighted in the infantile childishness of a Provençal Christmas. He never saw anything prettier in his life, he said, than a Noël procession on the coast of the Mediterranean. A beautiful young woman and an equally lovely child sat on a donkey, which an old fisherman in a flowing brown gown was supposed to be leading into Egypt. Young girls robed in white muslin were supposed to be angels, and hovered near the child and its mother to supply to him sweetmeats and other refreshments. At a respectful distance there was a procession of nuns and village children, and then a band of vocalists and instrumentalists. Flowers and streaming banners were unsparingly used. Bright sunshine played upon them, and the deep blue sea formed a background. The seafaring people who looked on, not knowing whether to venerate or laugh, did both. Falling upon their knees they went through a short devotional exercise, and then rose to join the procession and give themselves up to unrestricted mirth. In the chateaux of the South of France *crèches* are still exhibited, and *crèche* suppers given to the poorer neighbours, and to some of the rich, who are placed at a table "above the salt." There are also "Bethlehem Stable" puppet-shows, at which the Holy Family, their visitors, and four-footed associates are brought forward as *dramatis personæ*. St. Joseph, the wise men, and the shepherds are made to speak in *patois*. But the Virgin says what she has to say in classical French. In the refinement of her diction, her elevation above those with her is expressed. At Marseilles an annual fair of statuettes is held, the profits of which are spent in setting up Bethlehem *crèches* in the churches and other places. Each statuette represents a contemporaneous celebrity, and is contained in the hollow part of the wax bust of some saint. Gambetta, Thiers, Cavour, Queen Victoria, Grévy, the Pope, Paul Bert, Rouvier (who is a Marseillais), the late Czar and other celebrities have appeared among the *figurines* hidden within the saintly busts.

CHRISTMAS IN CORSICA.

"A Winter in Corsica," by "Two Ladies," published in 1868, contains an interesting account of the celebration of Christmas in that picturesque island of the Mediterranean which is known as the birthplace of Napoleon Bonaparte—"One day shortly before Christmas our hostess, or landlady, was very busy with an old body in the kitchen, who had come to make sundry cakes in preparation for that festive season. We were all called down to see what was going on, and our attention was particularly directed to the great oven which was heated on purpose to bake them. One kind of cake was made of chesnut flour, another of eggs and *broche* (a kind of curds made from goats' milk), but the principal sort was composed chiefly of almonds, extremely good and not unlike macaroons, but thicker and more substantial. For several days previously, everybody in the house had been busy blanching and pounding almonds; not only the two servants, but Rose and Clara, the young work-women who were so often staying in the house, and who, indeed, at one time seemed to form part of the establishment. The old cook herself, a stout and dumpy person, was worth looking at, as she stood surrounded by these young women, who did very little but watch her operations; and the whole formed quite an animated picture of a foreign *ménage*, which one rarely has the opportunity of seeing.

* * * * *

"Towards Christmas, considerable preparations began to be made in the shops for the coming season, but chiefly, perhaps, for

New Year's Day, which is kept throughout France as a grand *fête* day. Sweetmeats in great variety filled the windows, and especially what were called *pralines*—an almond comfit covered with rough sugar, and of a peculiar flavour. They are very good, and cost three francs per pound.

* * * * *

"It seemed strange writing to friends at home wishing them 'a happy Christmas,' when we seemed scarcely to have done with summer.

"There was certainly a good deal of novelty in our mode of passing Christmas-time in Ajaccio.

"We had expressed the wish to be present at midnight mass, in the cathedral, on Christmas Eve, and our kind hostess readily promised to take us, and also said we should have a *petit souper* with her on our return. She told us afterwards that she had spoken to the organist, and obtained permission for us to go into the organ-loft, where we should have a good view over the church, and not be inconvenienced by the crowd. Accordingly, a little before eleven o'clock, we all went downstairs, and, accompanied by madame, as well as by a gentleman and his daughter, friends of hers, proceeded to the cathedral.

"As there is no gas in Ajaccio, the church of course is lighted only with candles, and very dim and gloomy it looked, especially at first, and during a dull monotonous kind of chanting, which we were told were the offices to the Virgin.

"By and by, as midnight drew near, and the mass was about to commence, a great number of candles were lighted on the high altar and in the side chapels, and the scene became more brilliant and animated. We looked down upon a perfect sea of heads, the women all wearing the national handkerchiefs, many of these of bright colours, and making them conspicuous among the men, of whom there were also a very large number.

"At length the organ struck up, the higher priests entered, wearing their richest robes, followed by numerous attendants. Each bowed and knelt as he passed the altar, and took his allotted place, and then the service began. At one point, supposed to be the moment of our Saviour's birth, there was quite an uproar. The people clapped their hands, and stamped, and shouted, trumpets sounded, and the organ pealed forth its loudest tones.

"Then there was a very sweet hymn-tune played, and some beautiful voices sang Adeste Fideles, which was by far the most pleasing part of the service to our minds. Next came the reading of the Gospel, with much formality of kissing and bowing, and incensing; the book was moved from side to side and from place to place; then one priest on his knees held it up above his head, while another, sitting, read a short passage, and a third came forward to the front of the enclosed space near the altar, flinging the censer round and about. Then the little bell tinkled, and all that mass of heads bowed down lower, the Host was raised, the communion taken by the priests, and at one o'clock all was over.

"We gladly regained the fresh air, which, though rather cold, was much needed after the close atmosphere of the crowded cathedral. The moon was very bright, and we hastened home with appetites sharpened by our walk, for what proved to be a handsome dinner, rather than a *petit souper*.

* * * * *

"For ourselves, we did not forget the old home custom of Christmas decorations, and took some pains to dress our *salon* with evergreens, which we brought down from the hills the previous day. Although we had neither holly nor mistletoe, we found good substitutes for them in the elegant-leaved lentiscus, the tree heath and sweetly perfumed myrtle; while round the mirror and a picture of the Virgin on the opposite wall we twined garlands of the graceful sarsaparilla. The whole looked extremely pretty, and gave quite a festive appearance to the room.

"On Christmas Day we joined some English friends for a walk, about eleven o'clock. It was a charming morning, bright and hot, as we strolled along the shore to the orange-garden of Barbacaja, where we gathered oranges fresh from the trees.

"On returning home to dinner no plum-pudding or mince-pies awaited us certainly, but we had tolerably good beef, for a wonder, and lamb, *merles*, and new potatoes.

* * * * *

"Christmas Day in Corsica is observed by the people as a religious festival, but not as a social one; and there are no family gatherings as in England and Germany. This arises, no doubt, from that non-existence of true domestic life which must strike all English taking up a temporary residence in France.

"There was a succession of *fête* days throughout Christmas week, when the shops were shut and the people dressed in holiday attire. But the great day to which every one seems to look forward is the first of the year, *le Jour de l'An*. Presents are then made by everybody to everybody, and visits of congratulation, or merely of ceremony, received and expected. The gifts are sometimes costly and handsome, but generally they are trifling, merely valuable as works of remembrance, consisting chiefly of bonbons, boxes of crystallised fruits, and other confectionery."

CHRISTMAS IN CHIOS.

FROM AN IVORY, BYZANTINE. BRITISH MUSEUM

The preceding illustration of Eastern art belongs to the same period as many of the Christmas customs which have survived in Chios, and it carries our thoughts back to the time when Byzantium was the capital of the Greek Empire in the east. From

415

an interesting account by an English writer in the *Cornhill Magazine*, for December, 1886, who spent a Christmas amongst the Greeks of this once prosperous isle of Chios, it appears that, two days before Christmas, he took up his quarters at "the village of St. George, a good day's journey from the town, on the slopes of a backbone of mountains, which divides Chios from north to south." On the morning following the arrival at St. George, "echoes of home" were heard which caused the writer to exclaim: "Surely they don't have Christmas waits here." Outside the house stood a crowd of children singing songs and carrying baskets. From the window, the mistress of the house was seen standing amongst the children "talking hard, and putting handfuls of something into each basket out of a bag." "On descending," says the writer, "I inquired the cause of this early invasion, and learnt that it is customary on the day before Christmas for children to go round to the houses of the village early, before the celebration of the liturgy, and collect what is called 'the luck of Christ'—that is to say, walnuts, almonds, figs, raisins, and the like. Every housewife is careful to have a large stock of these things ready overnight, and if children come after her stock is exhausted she says, 'Christ has taken them and passed by.' The urchins, who are not always willing to accept this excuse, revile her with uncomplimentary remarks, and wish her cloven feet, and other disagreeable things."

The writer visited the chief inhabitants of St. George, and was regaled with "spoonfuls of jam, cups of coffee, and glasses of mastic liquer"; and, in a farmyard, "saw oxen with scarlet horns," it being the custom, on the day before Christmas, for "every man to kill his pig, and if he has cattle to anoint their horns with blood, thereby securing their health for the coming year.

"It is very interesting to see the birthplace of our own Christmas customs here in Greece, for it is an undoubted fact that all we see now in Greek islands has survived since Byzantine days. Turkish rule has in no way interfered with religious observances, and during four or five centuries of isolation from the civilised world the conservative spirit of the East has preserved intact for us customs as they were in the early days of Christianity; inasmuch as the Eastern Church was the first Christian Church, it was the parent of all Christian customs. Many of these customs were mere adaptations of the pagan to the Christian ceremonial—a necessary measure, doubtless, at a time when a new religion was forced on a deeply superstitious population. The saints of the Christian took the place of the gods of the "Iliad." Old customs attending religious observances have been peculiarly tenacious in these islands, and here it is that we must look for the pedigree of our own quaint Christian habits. We have seen the children of St. George collecting their Christmas-boxes, we have spoken of pig-killing, and we will now introduce ourselves to Chiote Christmas-trees, the *rhamnæ*, as they are called here, which take the form of an offering of fruits of the earth and flowers by tenants to their landlords.

"The form of these offerings is varied: one tenant we saw chose to make his in the shape of a tripod; others merely adorn poles, but all of them effect this decoration in a similar fashion, more gaudily than artistically. The pole is over a yard in height, and around it are bound wreaths of myrtle, olive, and orange leaves; to these are fixed any flowers that may be found, geraniums, anemones, and the like, and, by way of further decoration, oranges, lemons, and strips of gold and coloured paper are added.

"On Christmas morning the tenants of the numerous gardens of Chios proceed to the houses of their landlords, riding on mules and carrying a *rhamna* in front of them and a pair of fowls behind. As many as three hundred of these may be seen entering the capital of Chios on this day, and I was told the sight is very imposing. At St. George we had not so many of them, but sufficient for our purpose. On reaching his landlord's house the peasant sets up the trophy in the outer room, to be admired by all who come; the fowls he hands over to the housewife; and then he takes the large family jars or *amphoræ*, as they still call them, to the well, and draws the drinking water for his landlord's Christmas necessities.

"In the afternoon each landlord gives 'a table' to his tenants, a good substantial meal, at which many healths are drunk, compliments exchanged, and songs sung, and before returning home each man receives a present of money in return for his offerings. A Greek never gives a present without expecting an equivalent in return."

Another Christmas custom in Chios which reminded the writer of the English custom of carol-singing is thus described: "There are five parishes in the village of St. George, each supplied with a church, priests, acolytes, and candle-lighters, who answer to our vergers, and who are responsible for the lighting of the many lamps and candles which adorn an Eastern church. These good people assemble together on Christmas Day, after the liturgy is over, and form what is called 'a musical company'; one man is secured to play the lyre, another the harp, another the cymbals, and another leads the singing—if the monotonous chanting in which they indulge can be dignified by the title of singing. The candle-lighter, armed with a brass tray, is the recognised leader of this musical company, and all day long he conducts them from one house to another in the parish to play, sing, and collect alms. These musicians of St. George have far more consideration for the feelings of their fellow-creatures than English carol-singers, for the candle-lighter is always sent on ahead to inquire of the household they propose to visit if there is mourning in the house, or any other valid reason why the musicians should not play, in which case the candle-lighter merely presents his tray, receives his offering, and passes on. Never, if they can help it, will a family refuse admission to the musicians. They have not many amusements, poor things, and their Christmas entertainment pleases them vastly.

"The carols of these islands are exceedingly old-world and quaint. When permission is given the troupe advance towards the door, singing a sort of greeting as follows: 'Come now and open your gates to our party; we have one or two sweet words to sing to you.' The door is then opened by the master of the house; he greets them and begs them to come in, whilst the other members of the family place chairs at one end of the room, on which the musicians seat themselves. The first carol is a genuine Christmas one, a sort of religious recognition of the occasion, according to our notions fraught with a frivolity almost bordering on blasphemy; but then it must be remembered that these peasants have formed their own simple ideas of the life of Christ, the Virgin, and the saints, to which they have given utterance in their songs. A priest of St. George kindly supplied me with the words of some of their carols, and this is a translation of one of the prefatory songs with which the musical company commence:—

> "Christmas, Christmas! Christ is born;
> Saints rejoice and devils mourn.
> Christmas, Christmas! Christ was fed
> On sweet honey, milk, and bread,

Just as now our rulers eat
Bread and milk, and honey sweet.'

After this the company sing a series of songs addressed to
the various members of the family, to the father, to the mother,
to the daughters, to the sons; if there chances to be a betrothed
couple there, they are sure to be greeted with a special song; the
little children, too, are exhorted in song to be good and diligent at
school. Of these songs there are an infinite number, and many of
them give us curious glimpses into the life, not of to-day, but of
ages which have long since passed away.

"The following song is addressed to the master of the house,
and has doubtless been sung for centuries of Christmases since the
old Byzantine days when such things as are mentioned in the song
really existed in the houses. This is a word-for-word translation:—

"'We have come to our venerable master;
To his lofty house with marble halls.
His walls are decorated with mosaic;
With the lathe his doors are turned.
Angels and archangels are around his windows,
And in the midst of his house is spread a golden carpet
And from the ceiling the golden chandelier sheds light.
It lights the guests as they come and go.
It lights our venerable master.'

On the conclusion of their carols the musicians pause for rest,
the cymbal-player throws his cymbal on the floor, and the candle-
lighter does the same thing with his tray, and into these the master
of the house deposits his gifts to his parish church, and if they
are a newly-married couple they tie up presents of food for the
musicians in a handkerchief—figs, almonds, &c., which the cymbal-
player fastens round his neck or ties to his girdle.

"Before the musicians take their departure the housewife
hurries off to her cupboard and produces a tray with the inevitable
jam thereon. Coffee and mastic are served, and the compliments
of the season are exchanged. Whilst the candle-lighter is absent
looking for another house at which to sing, the musicians sing their

farewell, 'We wish health to your family, and health to yourself. We go to join the *pallicari*.'

"In villages where the singing of carols has fallen into disuse the inhabitants are content with the priestly blessing only. To distribute this the priest of each parish starts off on Christmas morning with the candle-lighter and his tray, and an acolyte to wave the censer; he blesses the shops, he sprinkles holy water over the commodities, and then he does the same by the houses; the smell of incense perfumes the air, and the candle-lighter rattles his tray ostentatiously to show what a lot of coppers he has got."

Christmas in a Greek Church.

"Swan's Journal of a Voyage up the Mediterranean, 1826," gives the following account of Christmas in a Greek Church:—

"Thursday, January 6th, this being Christmas Day with the Greek Catholics, their 'churches are adorned in the gayest manner. I entered one, in which a sort of raree-show had been set up, illumed with a multitude of candles: the subject of it was the birth of Christ, who was represented in the background by a little waxen figure wrapped up in embroidery, and reclining upon an embroidered cushion, which rested upon another of pink satin. This was supposed to be the manger where he was born. Behind the image two paper bulls' heads looked unutterable things. On the right was the Virgin Mary, and on the left one of the eastern Magi. Paper clouds, in which the paper heads of numberless cherubs appeared, enveloped the whole; while from a pasteboard cottage stalked a wooden monk, with dogs, and sheep, and camels, goats, lions, and lambs; here walked a maiden upon a stratum of sods and dried earth, and there a shepherd flourishing aloft his pastoral staff. The construction of these august figures was chiefly Dutch: they were intermixed with china images and miserable daubs on paper. In the centre a real fountain, in miniature, squirted forth water to the ineffable delight of crowds of prostrate worshippers."

Christmas in Rome.

Hone[97] states that after Christmas Day, during the remainder of December, there is a Presepio, or representation of the manger, in which our Saviour was laid, to be seen in many of the churches at Rome. That of the Ara Cœli is the best worth seeing, which church occupies the site of the temple of Jupiter, and is adorned with some of its beautiful pillars. On entering, we found daylight completely excluded from the church; and until we advanced, we did not perceive the artificial light, which

CALABRIAN SHEPHERDS PLAYING IN ROME AT CHRISTMAS.
(*From Hone's "Every-day Book*," 1826)

was so managed as to stream in fluctuating rays, from intervening silvery clouds, and shed a radiance over the lovely babe and bending mother, who, in the most graceful attitude, lightly holds up the drapery which half conceals her sleeping infant from the bystanders. He lies in richly embroidered swaddling clothes, and his person, as well as that of his virgin mother, is ornamented with diamonds and other precious stones; for which purpose, we are informed, the princesses and ladies of high rank lend their jewels. Groups of cattle grazing, peasantry engaged in different occupations, and other objects, enliven the picturesque scenery; every living creature in the group, with eyes directed towards the Presepio, falls prostrate in adoration. In the front of this theatrical representation a little girl, about six or eight years old, stood on a bench, preaching extempore, as it appeared, to the persons who filled the church, with all the gesticulation of a little actress, probably in commemoration of those words of the psalmist, quoted by our blessed Lord—"Out of the mouths of babes and sucklings Thou hast perfected praise." In this manner the Scriptures are *acted*; not "read, marked, and inwardly digested." The whole scene had, however, a striking effect, well calculated to work upon the minds of a people whose religion consists so largely in outward show. [From "A Narrative of Three Years in Italy."

As at the beginning, so in the latter part of the nineteenth century, the church celebrations of Christmas continue to be great Christmas attractions in the Eternal City.

From the description of one who was present at the Christmas celebration of 1883, we quote the following extracts:—

"On Christmas morning, at ten o'clock, when all the world was not only awake, but up and doing, mass was being said and sung in the principal churches, but the great string of visitors to the Imperial City bent their steps towards St. Peter's to witness the celebration of this the greatest feast in the greatest Christian Church.

"As the heavy leather curtain which hangs before the door fell behind one, this sacred building seemed indeed the world's cathedral; for here were various crowds from various nations, and men and women followers of all forms of faiths, and men and women of no faith at all. The great church was full of light and colour—of light that came in broad yellow beams through the great dome and the high eastern windows, making the candles on the side altars and the hundred ever-burning lamps around the St. Peter's shrine look dim and yellow in the fulness of its radiance; and of colour combined of friezes of burnished gold, and brilliant frescoes, and rich altar pieces, and bronze statues, and slabs of oriental alabaster, and blocks of red porphyry and lapis lazuli, and guilded vaulted ceiling, and walls of inlaid marbles.

"In the large choir chapel, containing the tomb of Clement IX., three successive High Masses were celebrated, the full choir of St. Peter's attending. In the handsomely carved old oak stalls sat bishops in purple and rich lace, canons in white, and minor canons in grey fur capes, priests and deacons, and a hundred acolytes wearing silver-buckled shoes and surplices. This chapel, with its life-size marble figures resting on the cornices, has two organs, and here the choicest music is frequently heard.

"Of course the choir chapel was much too small to hold the great crowd, which, therefore, overflowed into the aisles and nave of the vast church, where the music could be heard likewise. This crowd broke up into groups, each worthy of a study, and all combining to afford an effect at once strange and picturesque. There are groups of Americans, English, French, Germans, and Italians promenading round the church, talking in their respective native tongues, gesticulating, and now and then pausing to admire a picture or examine a statue. Acquaintances meet and greet; friends introduce mutual friends; compliments are exchanged, and appointments made. Meanwhile masses are being said at all the side altars, which are surrounded by knots of people who fall on their knees at the sound of a little bell, and say their prayers quite undisturbed by the general murmur going on around them.

"Presently there is a stir in the crowd surrounding the choir chapel; the organ is at its loudest, and then comes a long procession of vergers in purple and scarlet facings, and cross and torch bearers, and censer bearers, and acolytes and deacons and priests and canons and bishops, and a red-robed cardinal in vestments of cloth of gold wrought and figured with many a sacred sign, and, moreover, adorned with precious stones; and High Mass at St. Peter's, on Christmas Day, is at an end.

"During the day most of the shops and all the Government offices were open. Soldiers were drilled all day long in the Piazza Vittorio Emanuele, and were formally marched to their various barracks, headed by bands discoursing martial music; whilst the postmen delivered their freight of letters as on ordinary days of the week. In the afternoon most of those who were at St. Peter's in the morning assembled to hear Grand Vespers at the handsome and famous church of San Maria Maggiore, one of the oldest in Christendom, the Mosaics on the chancel arch dating from the fifth century. The church was illuminated with hundreds of candles and hung with scarlet drapery, the effect being very fine; the music such as can alone be heard in Rome. On the high altar was exhibited in a massive case of gold and crystal two staves said to have been taken from the manger in which Christ was laid, this being carried round the church at the conclusion of Vespers. Almost every English visitor in Rome was present."

CHRISTMAS AT MONTE CARLO.

"Every one has heard of the tiny principality of Monaco, with its six square miles of territory facing the Mediterranean, and lying below the wonderful Corniche-road, which has been for ages the great highway south of the Alps, connecting the South of France with Northern Italy. Of course many visitors come here to gamble, but an increasing number are attracted by the beauty of the scenery and the charm of the climate; and here some hundreds of Englishmen and Englishwomen spent their Christmas Day and ate the conventional plum-pudding. Christmas had been ushered in by a salvo of artillery and a High Mass at the cathedral at eleven on Christmas Eve, and holly and mistletoe (which seemed strangely out of place amongst the yellow roses and hedges of geraniums) were in many hands. As illustrating the mildness of the climate and the natural beauty of the district, the following flowers were in full bloom in the open air on Christmas Day: roses of every variety, geraniums, primulas, heliotropes, carnations, anemones, narcissus, sweetwilliams, stocks, cactus, and pinks; and to these may be added lemon trees and orange trees laden with their golden fruit. As evening wore on a strong gale burst upon the shore, and Christmas Day closed amongst waving foliage and clanging doors and clouds of dust, and the fierce thud of angry surf upon the sea-shore below.

J. S. B."
"January 2, 1890.

CHRISTMAS EVE FESTIVITIES IN GERMANY.

In "The German Christmas Eve," 1846, Madame Apolline Flohr recalls her "childish recollections" of the Christmas festivities in the "happy family" of which she was a member. They met amid the glare of a hundred lights, and according to an old-established custom, they soon joined in chaunting the simple hymn which begins:—

> "Now let us thank our God;
>> Uplift our hands and hearts:
> Eternal be His praise,
>> Who all good things imparts!"

After the singing (says the writer), I ventured for the first time, to approach the pile of Christmas gifts intended for my sisters, my brothers, and myself.

The Christmas tree, always the common property of the children of the house, bore gilded fruits of every species; and as we gazed with childish delight on these sparkling treasures our dear parents wiped away the tears they had plentifully shed, while our young voices were ringing out the sweet hymn, led by our friend, Herr Von Clappart, with such deep and solemn emotion.

Now, as the dear mother led each child to his or her own little table—for the gifts for each were laid out separately, and thus apportioned beforehand—all was joy and merriment.

A large table stood in the midst, surrounded by smaller ones, literally laden with pretty and ingenious toys, the gifts of friends and kindred. We liked the toys very much indeed. We were, however, too happy to endure quiet pleasure very long, and all prepared to assemble around the Christmas tree. After a delightful dance around the tree, and around our dear parents, our presents were again examined; for the variety of offerings made on these occasions would much exceed the belief of a stranger to our customs. Every article for children's clothing was here to be found, both for ornament and use; nor were books forgotten. It was then I received my first Bible and Prayer-book; and at the moment the precious gift was placed in my hand, I resolved to accompany my parents to church the following morning at five o'clock. (This early attendance at public worship on Christmas morning is a custom observed in Central Germany, and is called Christ-Kirche.)

The ceremony of withdrawing, in order to attire ourselves in some of our new dresses, having been performed, we re-entered the apartment, upon which the great folding-doors being thrown open, a second Christmas tree appeared, laden with hundreds of lights. This effect was produced by the tree being placed opposite some large looking-glasses, which reflected the lights and redoubled their brilliancy.

Here hung the gifts prepared by the hands of the children for their beloved parents.

My eldest sister, Charlotte, had knitted for her mother a beautiful evening cap, and a long purse for her father.

Emily presented each one of the family with a pair of mittens; and the little Adolphine made similar offerings of open-worked stockings, her first attempt.

Our parents were also surprised and delighted to receive some drawings, exceedingly well executed, by my brothers, accompanied by a letter of thanks from those dear boys, for the kind permission to take lessons which had been granted to them during the last half-year.

The great bell had called us together at five o'clock in the afternoon, to receive our Christmas gifts; and though at eleven our eyes and hearts were still wide awake, yet were we obliged to retire, and leave all these objects of delight behind us. All remembered that, at least, the elder branches of the family must rise betimes the next morning to attend the Christ-Kirche, and to hear a sermon on the birth of the Saviour of Mankind.

The great excitement of the previous evening, and the vision of delight that still hovered around my fancy, prevented my sleeping soundly; so that when the others were attempting to steal away the next morning to go to church, I was fully roused, and implored so earnestly to be taken with the rest of the family, that at length my prayer was granted; but on condition that I should keep perfectly still during the service.

Arrived at the church we found it brilliantly illuminated, and decorated with the boughs of the holly and other evergreens.

It is quite certain that a child of five years old could not understand the importance, beauty, and extreme fitness of the sublime service she so often witnessed in after life; yet I can recollect a peculiarly sweet, sacred, and mysterious feeling taking possession of me, as my infant mind received the one simple impression that this was the birthday of the Saviour I had been taught to love and pray to, since my infant lips could lisp a word.

Since early impressions are likely to be permanent, it is considered most important in my fatherland to surround, Christmas with all joyous and holy associations. A day of days, indeed, it is with us—a day never to be forgotten.

So far is this feeling carried, that it is no uncommon pastime, even at the beginning of the new year, to project plans and presents, happy surprises, and unlooked-for offerings, to be presented at the far-off time of Christmas festivity.

Another writer, at the latter end of the nineteenth century, gives the following account of the Christmas festivities at the German Court, from which it appears that the long-cherished Christmas customs are well preserved in the highest circle in Germany:—

CHRISTMAS AT THE GERMAN COURT.

In accordance with an old custom the Royal Family of Prussia celebrate Christmas in a private manner at the Emperor William's palace, where the "blue dining-hall" on the first floor is arranged as the Christmas room. Two long rows of tables are placed in this hall, and two smaller tables stand in the corners on either side of the pillared door leading to the ballroom. On these tables stand twelve of the finest and tallest fir-trees, reaching nearly to the ceiling, and covered with innumerable white wax candles placed in wire-holders, but without any other decoration.

In the afternoon of the 24th great packages are brought into this room containing the presents for the members of the Imperial household, and in the presence of the Emperor his Chamberlain distributes them on the tables under the trees. The monarch always takes an active part in this work, and, walking about briskly from one table to the other, helps to place the objects in the most advantageous positions, and fastens on them slips of white paper on which he himself has written the names of the recipients. The Empress is also present, occupied with arranging the presents for the ladies of her own household. The two separate tables still remain empty, until the Emperor and the Empress have left the room, as they are destined to hold the presents for their Majesties.

At four o'clock the entire Royal Family assemble in the large dining-hall of the Palace for their Christmas dinner. Besides all the Princes and Princesses without exception, the members of the Imperial household, the chiefs of the Emperor's military and civil Cabinets, and a number of adjutants are also present.

Shortly after the termination of the dinner the double doors leading to the blue hall are thrown wide open at a sign from the

Emperor, and the brilliant sight of the twelve great fir-trees bearing thousands of lighted tapers is disclosed to view. This is the great moment of the German Christmas Eve celebration. The Imperial couples then form in procession, and all proceed to the Christmas room. The Emperor and the Empress then personally lead the members of their households to the presents which are grouped in long rows on the tables, and which comprise hundreds of articles, both valuable and useful, objects of art, pictures, statuary, &c. Meanwhile, the two separate tables still remain hidden under white draperies. In other rooms all the officials and servants of the palace, down to the youngest stable-boy, are presented with their Christmas-boxes. At about nine o'clock the Imperial Family and their guests again return to the dining-room, where a plain supper is then served. According to old tradition, the menu always includes the following dishes: "Carp cooked in beer" (a Polish custom), and "Mohnpielen," an East Prussian dish, composed of poppy-seed, white bread, almonds and raisins, stewed in milk. After the supper all return once more to the Christmas room, where the second part of the celebration—the exchange of presents among the Royal Family—then comes off.

The Emperor's table stands on the right side of the ballroom door, and every object placed on it bears a paper with an inscription intimating by whom the present is given. The presents for the Empress on the other table are arranged in the same manner. Among the objects never missing at the Emperor's Christmas are some large Nuremberg ginger cakes, with the inscription "Weihnachten" and the year. About half-an-hour later tea is taken, and this terminates the Christmas Eve of the first family of the German Empire.

CHRISTMAS THROUGHOUT GERMANY,

it may be added, is similarly observed in the year 1900. From the Imperial palace to the poor man's cottage there is not a family in Germany that has not its Christmas tree and "Weihnachts Bescheerung"—Christmas distribution of presents. For the very poor districts of Berlin provision is made by the municipal authorities or charitable societies to give the children this form of amusement, which they look forward to throughout the year.

THE CHRISTMAS FESTIVITIES IN AUSTRIA

are similar to those in Germany, the prominent feature being the beautifully-adorned and splendidly-lighted Christmas-tree. At one of these celebrations, a few years ago, the numerous presents received by the young Princess Elizabeth included a speaking doll, fitted with a phonograph cylinder, which created no small astonishment. Among other things, the doll was able to recite a poem composed by the Archduchess Marie Valerie in honour of Christmas Eve.

The poor and destitute of Vienna are not forgotten, for, in addition to the Christmas-tree which is set up at the palace for them, a large number of charitable associations in the various districts of Vienna have also Christmas-trees laden with presents for the poor.

CHRISTMAS EVE IN ST. MARK'S, VENICE.

You go into the Duomo late on Christmas Eve, and find the time-stained alabasters and dark aisles lit up with five hundreds of wax candles over seven feet high. The massive silver lamps suspended across the choir have the inner lamps all ablaze, as is also the graceful Byzantine chandelier in the centre of the nave that glitters like a cluster of stars from dozens of tiny glass cups with wick and oil within. In the solemn and mysterious gloom you pass figures of men and women kneeling in devotion before the many shrines. Some are accompanied by well-behaved and discreet dogs, who sit patiently waiting till their owners' prayer shall be over; whilst others less well trained, run about from group to group to smell out their friends or growl at foes. You slowly work your way through the throng to the high altar. That unique reredos, brought from Constantinople in early times—the magnificent "Pala d'Ora," an enamelled work wrought on plates of gold and silver, and studded with precious stones—is unveiled, and the front of the altar has a rich frontispiece of the thirteenth century, which is of silver washed with gold, and embossed figures. Numbers of ponderous candles throw a glimmer over the treasures with which St. Mark's is so richly endowed, that are profusely displayed on the altar. Bishops, canons and priests in full dress are standing and kneeling, and the handsome and much-beloved Patriarch of Venice officiates, in dress of gorgeous scarlet and cream-coloured old lace, and heavy-brocaded cope, that is afterwards exchanged for one of ermine, and flashing rings and jewelled cross. There is no music, but a deep quiet pervades the dim golden domes overhead and the faintly-lighted transepts. Stray rays of light catch the smooth surface of the mosaics, which throw off sparkles of brightness and cast deeper shadows beyond the uncertain radiance. After the midnight mass is celebrated you pass out with the stream of people into the cold, frosty night, with only the bright stars to guide you through the silent alleys to your rooms, where you wish each other "A Merry Christmas!" and retire to sleep, and to dream of the old home in England.—*Queen.*

SASSOFERRATO (GIOVANNI BATTISTA SALVI) 1605-85

MUSEUM NAPLES

An English writer who spent a Christmas in Naples a few years ago, says:—

In the south Christmas is bright and gay, and in truth noisy. The *festa natalizie*, as it is called in Naples, is celebrated by fairs and bonfires and fireworks. In the Toledo, that famous street known to all the world, booths are erected beside the shops, flaming in colour, and filled with all sorts of tempting wares. Throughout Christmas Eve an immense crowd of men, women, and children throng this street, nearly a mile in length. The vendors shriek at the top of their voice, praising themselves and their goods, and then, with merry peals of laughter, exhibit with Neapolitan drollery all the arts of their trade. The crowd catch the contagious spirit of fun, and toss witticisms to and fro, until the welkin rings with shouts and laughter. A revolution in Paris could not create greater excitement, or greater noise, than the Christmas fair at Naples, the largest, and certainly the merriest, in the world. As night draws on the mirth grows uproarious; improvisations abound. Pulcinello attracts laughing crowds. The bagpipes strike with their ear-piercing sounds, and arise shrill above universal din. Fireworks are let off at every street corner, flaming torches carried in procession parade the streets; rockets rise in the air, coloured lamps are hung over doorways, and in the midst of the blaze of light the church bells announce the midnight Mass, and the crowd leave the fair and the streets, and on bended knee are worshipping.

CHRISTMAS IN SPAIN.

Spain in winter must be divided into Spain the frigid and Spain the semi-tropic; for while snow lies a foot deep at Christmas in the north, in the south the sun is shining brightly, and flowers of spring are peeping out, and a nosegay of heliotrope and open-air geraniums is the Christmas-holly and mistletoe of Andalusia. There is no chill in the air, there is no frost on the window-pane.

When Christmas Eve comes the two days' holiday commences. At twelve the labourers leave their work, repair home, and dress in their best. Then the shops are all ablaze with lights, ribbons and streamers, with tempting fare of sweets and sausages, with red and yellow serge to make warm petticoats; with cymbals, drums, and *zambombas*. The chief sweetmeats, peculiar to Christmas, and bought alike by rich and poor, are the various kinds of preserved fruits, incrusted with sugar, and the famous *turrni*. This last, which is of four kinds, and may be called in English phraseology, "almond rock," is brought to your door, and buy it you must. A coarse kind is sold to the poor at a cheap rate. Other comestibles, peculiar to Christmas, are almond soup, truffled turkey, roasted chestnuts, and nuts of every sort.

Before the *Noche-buena*, or Christmas Eve, however, one or two good deeds have been done by the civil and military authorities. On the twenty-third or twenty-fourth the custom is for the military governor to visit all the soldier prisoners, in company with their respective defensores, or advocates; and, *de officio*, there and then, he liberates all who are in gaol for light offences. This plan is also pursued in the civil prisons; and thus a beautiful custom is kept up in classic, romantic, Old-world Spain, and a ray of hope enters into and illuminates even the bitter darkness of a Spanish prisoners' den.

It is Christmas Eve. The poor man has his relations round him, over his humble *puchero* (stew): the rich man likewise. *Friends* have not come, "for it is not the custom." In Spain only blood relations eat and drink in the house as invited guests. Families meet as in England. Two per cent. of the soldiers get a fortnight's leave of absence and a free pass; and there is joy in peasant homes over peasant charcoal pans. The dusky shades of evening are stealing over olive grove and withering vineyard, and every house lights up its tiny oil lamp, and every image of the Virgin is illuminated with a taper. In Eija, near Cordova, an image or portrait of the Virgin and the Babe new-born, hangs in well-nigh every room in every house. And why? Because the beautiful belief is rooted in those simple minds, that, on Christmas Eve, ere the clock strikes twelve, the Virgin, bringing blessings in her train, visits every house where she can find an image or portrait of *her Son*. And many a girl kneels down in robes of white before her humble portrait of the Babe and prays; and hears a rustle in the room, and thinks, "the Virgin comes: she brings me my Christmas Eve blessing;" and turns, and lo! it is *her mother*, and the Virgin's blessing is the mother's kiss!

In Northern Andalusia you have the *zambomba*, a flower-pot perforated by a hollow reed, which, wetted and rubbed with the finger, gives out a hollow, scraping, monotonous sound. In Southern Andalusia the *panderita*, or tambourine, is the chief instrument. It is wreathed with gaudy ribbons, and decked with bells, and beaten, shaken, and tossed in the air with graceful abandon to the strains of the Christmas hymn:

> "This night is the good night,
> And therefore is no night of rest!"

Or, perhaps, the Church chant is sung, called "The child of God was born."

Then also men click the castanet in wine-shop and cottage; and in such old-world towns as Eija, where no railway has penetrated, a breast-plate of eccentrically strung bones—slung round the neck and played with sticks—is still seen and heard.

The turkeys have been slaughtered and are smoking on the fire. The night is drawing on and now the meal is over. Twelve o'clock strikes, and in one moment every bell from every belfry clangs out its summons. Poltroon were he who had gone to bed before twelve on *Noche-buena*. From every house the inmates hurry to the gaily-lit church and throng its aisles, a dark-robed crowd of worshippers. The organ peals out, the priests and choir chant at this midnight hour the Christmas hymn, and at last (in some out-of-the-way towns) the priests, in gaudiest robes, bring out from under the altar and expose aloft to the crowds, in swaddling-clothes of gold and white, the Babe new-born, and all fall down and cross themselves in mute adoration. This service is universal, and is called the "Misa del Gallo," or Cock-crow Mass, and even in Madrid it is customary to attend it. There are three masses also on Christmas Day, and the Church rule, strictly observed, is that if a man fail to attend this Midnight Mass he must, to save his religious character, attend all three on Christmas Day. In antique towns, like Eija, there are two days' early mass (called "Misa di Luz") anterior to the "Misa del Gallo," at 4 a.m., and in the raw morning the churches are thronged with rich and poor. In that strange, old-world town, also, the chief dame goes to the Midnight Mass, all her men-servants in procession before her, each playing a different instrument.

Christmas Eve is over. It is 1.30 a.m. on Christmas morning, and the crowds, orderly, devout, cheerful, are wending their way home. Then all is hushed; all have sought repose; there are no drunken riots; the dark streets are lit by the tiny oil lamps; the watchman's monotonous cry alone is heard, "Ave Maria purissima; las dos; y sereno."

The three masses at the churches on Christmas Day are all chanted to joyous music. Then the poor come in to pay their rent of turkeys, pigs, olives, or what not, to their landlord, and he gives them a Christmas-box: such as a piece of salt fish, or money, or what may be. Then, when you enter your house, you will find on your table, with the heading, "A Happy Christmas," a book of little leaflets, printed with verses. These are the petitions of the postman, scavenger, telegraph man, newsboy, &c., asking you for a Christmas-box. Poor fellows! they get little enough, and a couple of francs is well bestowed on them once a year. After mid-day breakfast or luncheon is over, rich and poor walk out and take the air, and a gaudy, pompous crowd they form as a rule. As regards presents at Christmas, the rule is, in primitive Spain, to send a present to the *Cura* (parish priest) and the doctor. Many Spaniards pay a fixed annual sum to their medical man, and he attends all the family, including servants. His salary is sent to him at Christmas, with the addition of a turkey, or a cake, or some fine sweetmeats.

On Christmas Eve the provincial hospitals present one of their most striking aspects to the visitor. It is a feast-day, and instead of the usual stew, the soup called *caldo*—and very weak stuff it is—or the stir-about and fried bread, the sick have their good sound meats, cooked in savoury and most approved fashion, their tumbler of wine, their extra cigar. Visitors, kindly Spanish ladies, come in, their hands laden with sweets and tobacco, &c., and the sight of the black silk dresses trailing over the lowly hospital couches is most human and pathetic. At last *night*—the veritable Christmas Eve comes. The chapels in these hospitals are generally on the ground floor, and frequently sunk some feet below it, but open to the hospital; so that the poor inmates who can leave their beds can hobble to the railing and look down into the chapel— one mass of dazzling lights, glitter, colour, and music: and thus, without the fatigue of descending the stairs, can join in the service. At half-past eleven at night the chapel is gaily lit up; carriage after carriage, mule-cart after mule-cart rattles up to the hospital door, discharging crowds of ladies and gentlemen in evening dress; thus the common people, chiefly the young, with their tambourines and zambombas, pour into the chapel from *Campo*, and alley, and street, and soon the chapel is filled; while above, sitting, hobbling, lying all round the rails, and gazing down upon the motley and noisy throng below, are the inmates of the hospital. The priest begins the Midnight Mass, and the organs take up the service, the whole of which, for one hour, is chanted. Meanwhile, the tambourines and other musical instruments are busy, and join in the strains of the organ; and the din, glitter, and excitement are most exhilarating. And thus the occupants of the Spanish provincial hospitals join in the festivities of Christmastide, as seen by one who has dwelt "*Among the Spanish People.*"

CHRISTMAS CUSTOMS IN NORWAY.

A writer who knows the manners and habits of the people of Norway, and their customs at Christmastide, says:—

At Christiania, and other Norwegian towns, there is, or used to be, a delicate Christmas custom of offering to a lady a brooch or a pair of earings in a truss of hay. The house-door of the person to be complimented is pushed open, and there is thrown into the house a truss of hay or straw, a sheaf of corn, or a bag of chaff. In some part of this "bottle of hay" envelope, there is a "needle" as a present to be hunted for. A friend of mine once received from her betrothed, according to the Christmas custom, an exceedingly large brown paper parcel, which, on being opened, revealed a second parcel with a loving motto on the cover. And so on, parcel within parcel, motto within motto, till the kernel of this paper husk—which was at length discovered to be a delicate piece of minute jewellery—was arrived at.

One of the prettiest of Christmas customs is the Norwegian practice of giving, on Christmas Day, a dinner to the birds. On Christmas morning every gable, gateway, or barn-door, is decorated with a sheaf of corn fixed on the top of a tall pole, wherefrom it is intended that the birds should make their Christmas dinner. Even the peasants contrive to have a handful set by for this purpose, and what the birds do not eat on Christmas Day, remains for them to finish at their leisure during the winter.

On New Year's Day in Norway, friends and acquaintances exchange calls and good wishes. In the corner of each reception-room is placed a little table, furnished all through the day with wine and cakes for the refreshment of the visitors; who talk, and compliment, and flirt, and sip wine, and nibble cake from house to house, with great perseverance.

Between Christmas and Twelfth Day mummers are in season. They are called "Julebukker," or Christmas goblins. They invariably appear after dark, and in masks and fancy dresses. A host may therefore have to entertain in the course of the season, a Punch, Mephistopheles, Charlemagne, Number, Nip, Gustavus, Oberon, and whole companies of other fanciful and historic characters; but, as their antics are performed in silence, they are not particularly cheerful company.

CHRISTMAS IN RUSSIA.

With Christmas Eve begins the festive season known in Russia as *Svyatki* or *Svyatuie Vechera* (Holy Evenings), which lasts till the Epiphany. The numerous sportive ceremonies which are associated with it resemble, in many respects, those with which we are familiar, but they are rendered specially interesting and valuable by the relics of the past which they have been the means of preserving—the fragments of ritual song which refer to the ancient paganism of the land, the time-honoured customs which originally belonged to the feasts with which the heathen Slavs greeted each year the return of the sun. On Christmas Eve commences the singing of the songs called *Kolyadki*, a word, generally supposed to be akin to *Kalendæ*, though reference is made in some of them to a mysterious being, apparently a solar goddess, named Kolyada. "Kolyada, Kolyada! Kolyada has come. We wandered about, we sought holy Kolyada in all the courtyards," commences one of these old songs, for many a year, no doubt, solemnly sung by the young people who used in olden times to escort from homestead to homestead a sledge in which sat a girl dressed in white, who represented the benignant goddess. Nowadays these songs have in many places fallen into disuse, or are kept up only by the children who go from house to house, to congratulate the inhabitants on the arrival of Christmas, and to wish them a prosperous New Year. In every home, says one of these archaic poems, are three inner chambers. In one is the bright moon, in another the red sun, in a third many stars. The bright moon—that is the master of the house; the red sun—that is the housewife; the many stars—they are the little children.

The Russian Church sternly sets its face against the old customs with which the Christmas season was associated, denouncing the "fiendish songs," and "devilish games," the "graceless talk," the "nocturnal gambols," and the various kinds of divination in which the faithful persisted in indulging. But, although repressed, they were not to be destroyed, and at various seasons of the year, but especially those of the summer and winter solstice, the "orthodox," in spite of their pastors, made merry with old heathenish sports, and, after listening to Christian psalms in church, went home and sang songs framed by their ancestors in honour of heathen divinities. Thus century after century went by, and the fortunes of Russia underwent great changes. But still in the villages were the old customs kept up, and when Christmas Day came round it was greeted by survivals of the ceremonies with which the ancient Slavs hailed the returning sun god, who caused the days to lengthen, and filled the minds of men with hopes of a new year rich in fruits and grain. One of the customs to which the Church most strongly objected was that of mumming. As in other lands, so in Russia it was customary for mummers to go about at Christmastide, visiting various homes in which the festivities of the season were being kept up, and there dancing, and performing all kinds of antics. Prominent parts were always played by human representatives of a goat and a bear. Some of the party would be disguised as "Lazaruses," that is, as the blind beggars who bear that name, and whose plaintive strains have resounded all over Russia from the earliest times to the present day. The rest disguised themselves as they best could, a certain number of them being generally supposed to play the part of thieves desirous to break in and steal. When, after a time, they were admitted into the room where the Christmas guests were assembled, the goat and the bear would dance a merry round together, the Lazaruses would sing their "dumps so dull and heavy," and the rest of the performers would exert themselves to produce exhilaration. Even among the upper classes it was long the custom at this time of year for the young people to dress up and visit their neighbours in disguise. Thus in Count Tolstoy's "Peace and War," a novel which aims at giving a true account of the Russia of the early part of the present century, there is a charming description of a visit of this kind paid by the younger members of one family to another. On a bright frosty night the sledges are suddenly ordered, and the young people dress up, and away they drive across the crackling snow to a country house six miles off, all the actors creating a great sensation, but especially the fair maiden Sonya, who proves irresistible when clad in her cousin's hussar uniform and adorned with an elegant moustache. Such mummers as these would lay aside their disguises with a light conscience, but the peasant was apt to feel a depressing qualm when the sports were over; and it is said that, even at the present day, there are rustics who do not venture to go to church, after having taken part in a mumming, until they have washed off their guilt by immersing themselves in the benumbing waters of an ice-hole.

Next to the mumming, what the Church most objected to was the divination always practised at Christmas festivals. With one of its forms a number of songs have been associated, termed *podblyudnuiya*, as connected with a *blyudo*, a dish or bowl. Into some vessel of this kind the young people drop tokens. A cloth is then thrown over it, and the various objects are drawn out, one after another, to the sound of songs, from the tenor of which the owners deduce omens relative to their future happiness. As bread and salt are also thrown into the bowl, the ceremony may be supposed to have originally partaken of the nature of a sacrifice. After these songs are over ought to come the game known as the "burial of the gold." The last ring remaining in the prophetic bowl is taken out by one of the girls, who keeps it concealed in her hand. The others sit in a circle, resting their hands on their knees. She walks slowly round, while the first four lines are sung in chorus of the song beginning, "See here, gold I bury, I bury." Then she slips the ring into one of their hands, from which it is rapidly passed on to another, the song being continued the while. When it comes to an end the "gold burier" must try to guess in whose hand the ring is concealed. This game is a poetical form of our "hunt the slipper." Like many other Slavonic customs it is by some archæologists traced home to Greece. By certain mythologists the "gold" is supposed to be an emblem of the sun, long hidden by envious wintry clouds, but at this time of year beginning to prolong the hours of daylight. To the sun really refer, in all probability, the bonfires with which Christmastide, as well as the New Year and Midsummer is greeted in Russia. In the Ukraine the sweepings from a cottage are carefully preserved from Christmas Day to New Year's Day, and are then burnt in a garden at sunrise. Among some of the Slavs, such as the Servians, Croatians, and Dalmatians, a *badnyak*, or piece of wood answering to the northern Yule-log, is solemnly burnt on Christmas Eve. But the significance originally attached to these practices has long been forgotten. Thus the grave attempts of olden times to search the secrets of futurity have degenerated into the sportive guesses of young people, who half believe that they may learn from omens at Christmas time what manner of marriages are in store for them. Divinings of this kind are known to all lands, and bear a strong family likeness; but it is, of course, only in a cold country that a spinster can find an opportunity of sitting beside a hole cut in the surface of a frozen river, listening to prophetic sounds proceeding from beneath the ice, and possibly seeing the image of the husband who she is to marry within the year trembling in the freezing water. Throughout the whole period of the *Svyatki*, the idea of marriage probably keeps possession of the minds of many Russian maidens, and on the eve of the Epiphany, the feast with which those Christmas holidays come to an end, it is still said to be the custom for the village girls to go out into the open air and to beseech the "stars, stars, dear little stars," to be so benignant as to

"Send forth through the christened world
Arrangers of weddings."

W. R. S. RALSTON, in *Notes and Queries*,
Dec. 21, 1878.

CHRISTMAS-KEEPING IN AFRICA.

"A certain young man about town" (says *Chambers's Journal*, December 25, 1869), "once forsook the sweet shady side of Pall Mall for the sake of smoking his cigar in savage Africa; but when Christmas came, he was seized with a desire to spend it in Christian company, and this is how he did spend it: 'We English once possessed the Senegal; and there, every Christmas Eve, the Feast of Lanterns used to be held. The native women picked up the words and airs of the carols; the custom had descended to the

Gambia, and even to the Casemanche, where it is still preserved. A few minutes after I had ridden up, sounds of music were heard, and a crowd of blacks came to the door, carrying the model of a ship made of paper, and illuminated within; and hollowed pumpkins also lighted up for the occasion. Then they sang some of our dear old Christmas carols, and among others, one which I had heard years ago on Christmas Eve at Oxford:

> Nowel, Nowel, the angels did say,
> To certain poor shepherds in fields as they lay—
> In fields as they lay keeping their sheep,
> One cold winter's night, which was so deep.
> > Nowel, Nowel, Nowel, Nowel,
> > Born is the King of Israel.

You can imagine with what feelings I listened to those simple words, sung by negresses who knew not a phrase of English besides. You can imagine what recollections they called up, as I sat under an African sky, the palm-trees rustling above my head, and the crocodiles moaning in the river beyond. I thought of the snow lying thick upon the ground; of the keen, clear, frosty air. I thought of the ruddy fire which would be blazing in a room I knew; and of those young faces which would be beaming still more brightly by its side; I thought of—oh, of a hundred things, which I can laugh at now, because I am in England, but which, in Africa, made me more wretched than I can well express.'

"Next day, sadness and sentiment gave way, for a while at least, to more prosaical feelings. When Mr. Reade sat down to his Christmas dinner, he must have wished, with Macbeth, 'May good digestion wait on appetite,' as he contemplated the fare awaiting discussion, and to which a boar's head grinned a welcome. Snails from France, oysters torn from trees, gazelle cutlets, stewed iguana, smoked elephant, fried locusts, manati-breasts, hippopotamus steaks, boiled alligator, roasted crocodile eggs, monkeys on toast, land crabs and Africa soles, carp, and mullet—detestable in themselves, but triumphant proof of the skill of the cook—furnished forth the festival-table, in company with potatoes, plantains, pine-apples, oranges, papaws, bananas, and various fruits rejoicing in extraordinary shapes, long native names, and very nasty flavours; and last, but not least, palm-cabbage stewed in white sauce, 'the ambrosia of the gods,' and a bottle of good Bordeaux at every's man's elbow. When evening came, Mr. Reade and a special friend sought the river: 'The rosy wine had rouged our yellow cheeks, and we lay back on the cushions, and watched the setting sun with languid, half-closed eyes. Four men, who might have served as models to Appelles, bent slowly to their stroke, and murmured forth a sweet and plaintive song. Their oars, obedient to their voice, rippled the still water, and dropped from their blades pearls, which the sun made rubies with its rays. Two beautiful girls, who sat before us in the bow, raised their rounded arms and tinkled their bracelets in the air. Then, gliding into the water, they brought us flowers from beneath the dark bushes, and kissed the hands which took them, with wet and laughing lips. Like a dark curtain, the warm night fell upon us; strange cries roused from the forest; beasts of the waters plunged around us, and my honest friend's hand pressed mine. And Christmas Day was over. We might seek long for a stranger contrast to an Englishman's Christmas at home, although—to adapt some seasonable lines—

Where'er An English heart exists to do and dare, Where, amid Afric's sands, the lion roars, Where endless winter chains the silent shores, Where smiles the sea round coral islets bright, Where Brahma's temple's sleep in glowing light—In every spot where England's sons may roam, Dear Christmas-tide still speaks to them of Home!

93   The discovery of the North-West Passage for navigation from the Atlantic Ocean to the Pacific, by the northern coasts of the American continent; first successfully traversed by Sir R. McClure in 1850-1.

94   *Chambers's Journal*, December 25, 1869.

95   Fosbroke's "British Monachism."

96 "Reminiscences of the Siege and Commune of Paris," by Ex-Minister E. B. Washburne.
97 "Year Book."

* * * * *

PRESENTATION AT THE TEMPLE BY P. W. MOODY
MODERN STAINED GLASS IN BISHOPGATE CHURCH

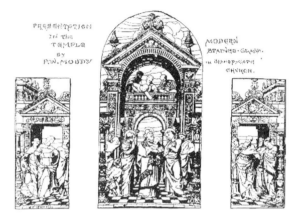

SIMEON RECEIVED THE CHILD JESUS INTO HIS ARMS, AND BLESSED GOD

Luke 11 25-32

CHAPTER XIII.

CONCLUDING CAROL SERVICE OF THE NINETEENTH CENTURY.

Now, returning from the celebrations of Christmas in distant parts of the world, we conclude our historic account of the great Christian festival by recording the pleasure with which we attended the

CONCLUDING CAROL SERVICE OF THE NINETEENTH CENTURY

at a fine old English cathedral—the recently restored and beautiful cathedral at Lichfield, whose triple spires are seen and well known by travellers on the Trent valley portion of the London and North Western main line of railway which links London with the North.

LICHFIELD CATHEDRAL.
(By permission of Mr. A. C. Lomax's Successors Lichfield)

Christmas carols have been sung at Lichfield from long before the time of "the mighty Offa," King of the Mercians, in whose days and by whose influence Lichfield became for a time an archiepiscopal see, being elevated to that dignity by Pope Adrian, in 785. And, in the seventeenth century, the Deanery of Lichfield was conferred upon the Rev. Griffin Higgs, the writer of the events connected with the exhibition of "The Christmas Prince" at St. John's College, Oxford, in 1607, whose authentic account of these interesting historical events will be found in an earlier chapter of this work.

The Christmas carols at Lichfield Cathedral, sung by the full choir at the special evening service on St. Stephen's Day (December 26th), have, for many years, attracted large and appreciative congregations, and the last of these celebrations in the nineteenth century (on December 26, 1900) was well sustained by the singers and attended by many hundreds of citizens and visitors. Eight Christmas Carols and an anthem were sung, the concluding Carol being "The First Nowell"; and the organist (Mr. J. B. Lott, Mus. Bac., Oxon) played the Pastoral Symphony from Sullivan's "Light of the World," Mendelssohn's March ("Cornelius"), the Pastoral Symphony from Handel's "Messiah," and other exquisite voluntaries. From the anthem, E. H. Sears's beautiful verses beginning

> "It came upon the midnight clear,
> That glorious song of old,"

set to Stainer's music and well sung, we quote the concluding predictive stanza:

> "For lo, the days are hast'ning on,
>   By prophet-bards foretold,
> When with the ever-circling years
>   Comes round the age of gold;
> When peace shall over all the earth
>   Its ancient splendours fling,
> And the whole world give back the song
>   Which now the angels sing."

BIBLIOBAZAAR

The essential book market!

Did you know that you can get any of our titles in large print?

Did you know that we have an ever-growing collection of books in many languages?

Order online:
www.bibliobazaar.com

Find all of your favorite classic books!

Stay up to date with the latest government reports!

At BiblioBazaar, we aim to make knowledge more accessible by making thousands of titles available to you- *quickly and affordably*.

Contact us:
BiblioBazaar
PO Box 21206
Charleston, SC 29413

1015340

Printed in Great Britain by
Amazon.co.uk, Ltd.,
Marston Gate.